SPECIAL REPORT

ON

SAVINGS BANKS,

MADE BY

EMERSON W. KEYES,

DEPUTY SUPERINTENDENT OF THE BANK DEPARTMENT,

AND

TRANSMITTED TO THE LEGISLATURE BY THE SUPERINTENDENT,
PURSUANT TO JOINT RESOLUTION OF THE SENATE
AND ASSEMBLY.

ALBANY:
VAN BENTHUYSEN & SONS' STEAM PRINTING HOUSE.
1868.

State of New York.

No. 7.

IN SENATE,

January 8, 1868.

REPORT

CONCERNING SAVINGS BANKS.

STATE OF NEW YORK:
BANK DEPARTMENT,
ALBANY, *Jan.* 8, 1868.

To the Legislature:

I have the honor to transmit herewith to the Legislature, a Report concerning Savings Banks, made pursuant to a resolution of the Legislature, at the last session.

GEORGE W. SCHUYLER,
Superintendent.

REPORT.

Bank Department,
Albany, *January* 5, 1867.

To the Honorable the Legislature of the State of New York:

At the last session of the Legislature, the following resolution was adopted:

Whereas, The large and rapidly increasing sums on deposit in the savings banks of this State render it an object of special importance, that these investments should be properly secured, and the control and management of the institutions holding this trust should be carefully guarded by clear, consistent and uniform provisions of law; and whereas, the report of the Superintendent of the Banking Department, relative to savings banks, discloses many defects and many conflicting and incongruous provisions in existing laws relating to these institutions; therefore,

Resolved (if the Assembly concur), That the Superintendent of the Banking Department be, and he is hereby authorized and directed to revise and consolidate the laws relating to savings banks and institutions for savings in this State, with such amendments thereto as he may deem important, and report the same in the form of one complete and general act, together with such facts and suggestions in relation thereto, as he may find it desirable and expedient to communicate to the Legislature at the commencement of its annual session in 1868. And for the purpose of enabling him more thoroughly and intelligently to perform the duty hereby imposed, he is further authorized and empowered, and it shall be his duty to make himself, or cause to be made by his deputy, an examination of such and so many of the savings banks and institutions for savings in this State, as he shall find it necessary or expedient to visit and examine, and he shall possess all the authority in relation to such examination of savings banks and institutions for savings, as is now conferred upon him in regard to banks of issue and deposit, by chapter two hundred and forty-two of the Laws of eighteen hundred and fifty-four. The expenses of such examination shall be audited by the Superintendent, and paid from and charged to the savings bank expense account, and shall be assessed upon the savings banks and institutions for savings in this State, and collected in the same manner as is now provided by law for other expenses of these institutions.

In pursuance of the requirement and authority of the said resolution, I directed the deputy superintendent to visit all the savings banks in this State, organized and doing business on the first day of January, 1867, and to obtain from them such facts concerning their condition and workings, as, when reported to the Legislature, would enable your honorable body to take intelligent action in providing by law for a more consistent, uniform and stringent administration of this important trust.

The report of the deputy superintendent upon the execution of the duty assigned to him, is herewith submitted, as the best exposition of the theory, practices, law and needs of savings banks, that I could present in obedience to the requirements of the Legislature.

The insufficiency of the law, or laws, in their present form, to afford all the information essential to a perfect knowledge of the workings of savings banks, is clearly revealed in this report; as well as their conflict, inconsistency, incongruity, too prevalent laxity, and general want of uniformity.

The magnitude of this great and ever increasing interest, whether considered as a provident means for the benefit of the working classes, as a power in our social economy through the stimulus which it gives to production, and through the public order and public virtue which it promotes, or as centers of accumulated capital, supplying the means to carry forward public improvements and works of private enterprise, is set forth in the text and accompanying exhibits with clearness and force.

It is not to be presumed that the conclusions reached by the deputy superintendent, upon the various questions discussed by him, will be uniformly concurred in, either by the managers of savings institutions, by the general public, or perhaps by your honorable body; but I believe their leading features will meet with general and cordial approval.

The superior opportunities for observation which he has enjoyed, the thoroughness with which these have been improved, and the research, study and care which he has devoted to the subject, impart great value to his opinions, and entitle them to mature and careful consideration. For myself I find pleasure in giving them my cordial approval and indorsement.

The practical action of the Legislature will be upon the act herewith submitted as a part of the accompanying report. Believing that it will serve to render uniform and equal the restraints of law upon these institutions, and will work salutary and needed reforms in their administrations, I trust it may receive your early and favorable action.

It is a source of especial gratification, in view of the embarrassments to which these institutions have been exposed, to note the wonderful prosperity and the substantial character of their development.

If any justification, other than the exceeding importance of the subject considered, is required for the unusual length of the deputy superintendent's report, it will be found in the objects and purposes for which the report is made, as set forth in the resolution directing it.

It is evident that much of the crude and incongruous legislation of the past, concerning savings banks, has proceeded from vague, indistinct and general ideas of their nature and requirements; founded upon partial views, slight examination, and hastily formed conclusions. No full exposition of their theory, operations and results in this State has ever before been made, and hence no basis furnished from which intelligent and consistent legislation could be expected.

It was very desirable, if only as a part of the history of our social and material progress and development, that such an exposition should be prepared; and its preparation was especially demanded at this time, when it is proposed to embody the experience and results of the past, into a general provision of law, that shall ensure in the future a broader and more harmonious development of this important interest.

I submit the report and accompanying enhibits as the best compliance I could make with the resolution of the Legislature, and in the hope that it will receive at your hands the careful attention to which the subject of it is entitled, and that your final action, in the enactment of a general law for savings banks, may mark the beginning of a new and still more prosperous era in the history of these institutions in our State.

Respectfully submitted,

G. W. SCHUYLER, *Sup't.*

BANK DEPARTMENT,
ALBANY, *December* 20, 1867.

HON. G. W. SCHUYLER, *Superintendent :*

SIR—In compliance with instructions under your appointment, I have visited every savings bank in this State, organized and doing buiness January 1st, 1867. Savings banks organized since that date could have no experiences that would be of value for the purpose contemplated by my appointment, and were not, therefore, embraced in the list of my visitations.

The Corning Savings Bank, organized in 1860, and reporting regularly to the department for the purpose of preserving its charter from forfeiture, is not practically open for business, and the deposits, July 1, being only $215.14, there could be no facts connected with its management that would repay visitation. It was therefore omitted.

The Elmira Savings Bank holds an anomolous position, the character of which will be more fully set forth in a subsequent part of this report. I visited the last chief officer of the institution, and called also to see the assignee, but did not find him. The information sought has been obtained since, however, through correspondence, and will be found in its proper place.

The whole number of savings banks that reported to the department, January 1, 1867, was eighty-six, of which I have visited eighty-five, the greater number of them twice, and a large number several times, making in all one hundred and sixty-seven visitations, extending from the remote extremity of Long Island on the east, to Chautauqua county on the west.

I wish to bear testimony to the uniform courtesy, cordiality indeed, with which I have been received by the trustees and officers of these institutions, and to the readiness with which they have placed at my disposal everything that would facilitate the purpose of my visit.

Very many of them, especially in the larger cities of the State have expressed great interest in the object proposed to be accomplished, regarding it as highly important in itself, and as having the effect, through a full report, and subsequent discussion by the Legislature, to direct public attention to the present and increasing magnitude of the savings banks interest in our State. It is with great pleasure that I thus publicly acknowledge my obligation to the many gentlemen who have in this manner cheered and encouraged me in the discharge of a very laborious and responsible duty.

The ultimate object of the examination—the results of which are embodied in this report—is expressed in the resolution of the Legislature authorizing and directing the same, and is, the submission to the Legislature, about to convene, for its consideration and approval, of a general law, clear, consistent and uniform in its provisions, for the organization of savings banks, and the administration of their affairs.

The preparation of such a law on your part, and its intelligent consideration on part of the Legislature, requires certain precedent knowledge.

1*st.* Concerning the objects and purposes of savings banks, as these stand revealed in the theory of their primary institution and in the history of their practical development.

2*d.* Concerning their character and condition at the present time—their embodied results—both in detail, as independent individual corporations, and in the aggregate as a system, having a beneficent purpose in common, and in common, affected by the weakness, errors or misfortunes of any member.

3*d.* Concerning the business management, operations, methods, plans, schemes, devices the interior processes in short, by which these external and revealed conditions, these embodied results are wrought out.

4*th.* Concerning the external influences of our political system, our social organization, our material resources and the means of their development, of our industrial problem, embracing the condition of the working classes, of our financial system and the competitions of financial institutions, to promote or retard the prosperity of savings banks.

5*th.* Concerning the laws under which our savings banks have been instituted, and under which they have expanded to their present proportions, in order that the extent to which these have contributed to the favorable or adverse conditions disclosed, may be duly noted and considered.

It would be alike presumptuous and false in me, to assume that I have brought, as the result of my labors, a fund of information so elaborate and exhaustive as I have sketched in the foregoing outline, I can only say that such has been my ideal; in that direction I have labored in the collection and compilation of facts, in observing operations, in making inquiries, in receiving suggestions, in discussing questions of theory and questions of practice, and in the reflection, reading and study with which my mind has been busily engaged since I received your instructions.

As is common, in the pursuit of knowledge, I am conscious *now*, of having surveyed only the surface of this field of inquiry; of being only better prepared to execute such commission than when I began; of simply knowing better than I did then, what *ought* to be known, and the direction in which, and the methods by which that knowledge should be sought; all which is neither flattering to my pride, nor available for the purposes of this report, and I speak of it only in self-extenuation, to give assurance that the imperfectness of this exposition of the workings and wants of our savings bank system, which will be marked and manifest as questions from time to time arise, for which answer will be sought in vain in this report, is as apparent to my consciousness, as it can be to that of any to whom it shall be disclosed. But I am not permitted to indulge the "luxury of woe" in the form of self-deprecation, unalloyed with the gratifying conviction, that some excuse for short-comings may be found in the nature of the subject to be investigated; in the limited extent to which, previously, labors in the same direction have been prosecuted in the broad extent of territory to be traversed; in the disadvantages of single, unaided effort in making examinations as the basis of tabular statements and final conclusions; not to mention the limited time allotted for the completion of the work, and the divided occupation of that time with other necessary official duties.

Keeping steadily in view the ultimate object of this investigation, as set forth in the resolution directing it, and my ideal of the precedent conditions to its perfect realization, I have not been content to enact the *rôle* of an "original discoverer" exclusively, but have availed myself of all the sources of information that I could command. I have consulted reports of savings banks in previous years, and have made analyses and comparisons illustrative of their workings or exemplifying principles or practices under discussion. I have examined with care the reports of committees of the Legislature charged with the performance of specific or general duties in relation to these institutions, and the report of examiners appointed by one of your predecessors, and have made free with the results of their labors. I have studied the reports and laws relating to these institutions in other States, and their history in Great Britain and Ireland, for a broader and more practical knowledge of their capabilities, and of the conditions under which they attain the highest and most assured success. I have read legal opinions upon their nature and powers, and the limitations of legislative authority over their affairs; I have examined whole volumes of their by-laws, and pages of newspaper correspondence and controversy concerning their theory and practices; I have ransacked the volumes of laws from 1819 to 1867 for charters, amendments and general laws, which I have read, examined and compared, until the sight of a volume of the Session Laws has much the same effect upon me as upon the traditional "rogue" in the couplet, though I hope not for the same reason!

I have even consulted the columns of newspaper advertisements for information concerning the workings of these institutions not elsewhere disclosed; and finally, I have made my own observations in the course of an extended but hasty visitation, have gathered some facts that seemed to me important and that had never been gathered before, have solicited suggestions from all quarters and got them from a good many; and the substance of all, after passing through the crucible of my own mind, is herewith presented in this report, and reduced to practical form in the act hereto appended for your consideration, and for submission, with such modifications or amendments as you choose to suggest, to the Legislature for its final action.

I am conscious that such a treatment of the subject will make this report more elaborate and voluminous than was contemplated by the Legislature, or perhaps by yourself, in giving effect to their resolution; but I find in my own mind ample justification for this, in the importance of the subject itself, in the character and magnitude of the interests involved in it already, and their daily increasing magnitude and importance, and in the fact of the prevalent ignorance upon the subject over the greater portion of our State.

Theory and Results of Savings Banks.

Following for the present, the line of discussion indicated concerning the information desirable as a basis for intelligent legislation upon this subject, I propose, before presenting the more detailed results of my examination and study, to consider the nature and objects of savings banks, as revealed in the theory of their institution and in the conditions of their present practical development. The remaining topics can hardly be discussed in the order of their statement, but will be considered in their logical relation to various questions of interest which the nature of the subject will force upon our attention.

Savings banks, both in Europe and America, had their origin in efforts to ameliorate the condition of the poor. Their plans and purposes partook largely of the character of a charity. Thus the first of these institutions, of which we have any reliable account, originated in 1798 in a voluntary offer on part of wealthy and benevolent gentlemen in a district of England, to receive from the working people in their neighborhood sums as small as two pence, and to repay the amount at Christmas, or in the winter season, with the addition of one-third, as a bounty for economy.*

These institutions continued mere voluntary organizations until 1817, when they were first recognized by parliament through an act for their incorporation. They did not even then change their essential character as charitable enterprises, for the interest allowed by the government on deposits, exceeded that received from ordinary investments in the funds.

A tract written by John Bowles, and published in London in 1817, entitled "Reasons for the Establishment of Provident Institutions called Savings Banks," etc., deals with the question as a means of alleviating the misfortunes of poverty; and so prominently is this view of the case presented, that the pamphlet is found in our State Library bound in a volume entitled "The Poor!"

In this country these institutions had the same charitable inception. The first appears to have been a voluntary association in Philadelphia, organized in 1816, under the name of the Philadelphia Saving Fund Society, and was incorporated by act of the Legislature in February, 1819.

In March of the same year, the first savings bank was incorporated in this State, under the title of The Bank for Savings in the City of New York, which still continues one of the safest and most prosperous institutions in the country.

As throwing light upon the character in which the enterprise was viewed, I quote from the preamble, as follows:

"Whereas, the society for the prevention of pauperism in the city of New York, have petitioned the Legislature for an act of incroporation, for the laudable purpose of encouraging in the community habits of industry and economy, by receiving and

* For this, and most of the facts connected with savings banks in Great Britain, I am indebted to a work on the History of Savings Banks, by William Lewins.

vesting in government securities," &c., &c., "such small sums of money as may be saved from the earnings of tradesmen, mechanics, laborers, minors, servants and others, thereby affording the two-fold advantage of security and interest; and the Legislature considering it their duty to cherish all laudable attempts to *ameliorate the condition of the poor* and laboring class of the community; Therefore, Be it enacted, &c."

It will thus be seen that these institutions had their origin exclusively in a desire to ameliorate the condition of the poor, and hence, the popular idea of savings banks is, that they are a part of the charitable machinery of society, like asylums and homes for the indigent, whereby the poor, the weak and the defenceless, are provided and cared for; and that as such, these enterprises are to be cherished and promoted.

Whatever in the purposes of the founders of savings banks, and in the early character of these institutions may have justified this conception of them, in their results as a practical *fact* to-day, they have outgrown their early distinctive character as charitable institutions, and take their place proudly in the front rank among the great powers of the social state.

And this, without losing the provident and beneficent features which characterized their humble origin. Still to them may go the humblest toiler with her hardly earned, carefully saved pence; still to them the strong man, who would drive away the temptations to vicious indulgence by putting safely aside the means by which that indulgence may be procured.

Justice to the 500,000 depositors in the savings banks of this State, demands that the institutions which *do not support them*, but which they so munificently endow, should be clearly distinguished from those of a charitable or eleemosynary character.

The latter maintain or aid, at the public expense, those whose claims are urged in the name of humanity alone, whom misfortune has bereft of the power of protecting themselves.

But savings banks are in no respect a charge upon the State, nor upon society in any of its municipal or corporate forms of embodiment. The only beneficiary aid they receive, is the gratuitous service of the gentlemen composing the boards of trustees, which is less than that often given by interested partisans to promote the success of the party to which they are allied. Is *politics* then *a charity!*

The moneys deposited in savings banks are the fruits of toil, the evidences of power, of industry, of thrift, of independence. The depositors are not objects of charity, but sturdy contributors to the accumulations to which we so proudly point as evidence of our national growth and prosperity. They are the producers of wealth through labor effectively applied; they consume so much as they require, and the surplus they put aside as an accumulating fund for future investment,—in more extended business, in a home secure from landlord's caprice or rapacity, or for the day when sickness or misfortune shall compel recourse to the surplus earnings of more prosperous years. They ask for no *charity*, they receive none.

I would not disguise nor undervalue the *effect* of these institutions upon the welfare and prosperity of the depositors. If they had no other significance than this, they would be proud monuments of the success of a noble idea, and worthy of the fostering care of the State.

But like most enterprises having their inception in the natural wants of society at a given time, they have far outgrown in significance, usefulness and power, the comparatively narrow scope and purpose of their original design, and that, without any sacrifice of that purpose to new and grander objects of attainment.

They have become an important feature of our political economy. Not only are they a magnificent fact of $140,000,000 of accumulations, but they are promoters of social order, a stimulus to productive industry, creditors of the government, reservoirs of capital flowing out into myriad channels of public and private enterprise. They are no more charities than the corporate organizations, fostered by legislation, by which capitalists gridiron the country (and city) with railroads, girdle it with telegraph wires, or fill the valleys with the hum of machinery, are charities. Nor yet so much, for these have granted to them special rights and privileges, which the public and individuals must surrender, and which are demanded out of consideration for the greater good which the public and individuals are presumed to derive from the promotion of these enterprises.

But savings banks, though equally a public good, ask no favors from the public in return; they acquire no right of way, no easements, no water power, no monopoly. They are by virtue of their being, under the laws of the State, an incentive, an encouragement to honest labor to do its best, that it may reap its own just rewards.

They suggest the *opportunity*; the *destiny* is wrought out through toil, in patience and in hope thus inspired.

They appeal less than almost any organization of corresponding benefit to humanity, to man's cupidity and avarice. Their motives are addressed to his better nature. He who saves his earnings by depositing them in a savings bank, has almost invariably a worthy object in view. He saves not for greed, but for future need.

The desire to acquire is an instinctive principle wisely implanted in the human breast, and nothing stimulates its exercise so actively as *acquisition*. The experience of almost every one will confirm this proposition. The history of savings banks, if written, would be full of illustrations of this truth.

While a man has nothing, he is reckless, improvident; but the moment he has consecrated a portion of his earnings, however small, to a fixed and worthy purpose, invested them in permanent and remunerative form, the desire to increase the amount takes full possession of him. To this end he practices self-denial, diligently employs otherwise unoccupied hours, and abandons habits of prodigality or self-indulgence. In the course of my visitations I have heard many a story illustrative of the power of this principle, long dormant, aroused and made active through the instrumentality of savings banks. It is of course impossible to estimate how much has thus been saved to individuals, and to the world through this agency. We can but generalize—but the generalization, crude as it may be, contains the germ of a most valuable, economic truth, which legislators and statesmen may well turn aside to ponder.

The interest society has in the promotion of habits of industry, sobriety and thrift among its individual members, for their own advantage, would of itself justify and demand the most careful guardianship of all the means and institutions having this object in view. The whole case might be submitted and rest upon this proposition.

But to my view the most hopeful as well as the most cheering aspect of this question, is that derived from a consideration of the benefits conferred, through the agency of savings banks, upon society itself.

Contrast the productive value to society of the man who *saves* with that of a man who has no such ambition. The former has a motive that impels him to lose no time, indeed to make overtime. He is therefore a more effective producer, for the stiumlus of this impelling motive. He adds more to the aggregate of material that is to be distributed among the sons and daughters of earth. Here, too, is the germ of a principle in political economy that should engage the profound consideration of wise statesmanship. What would be the effect if this incentive to industry could be made universally operative among mechanics and laborers? Who has not been the victim of disappointment in the fulfillment of some promised labor, and been met with the plea of the master that the workman upon whom he depended had been indulging in his periodical spree, and been off work for a few days, or perchance weeks, as the case might be? Your disappointment, perhaps loss, would have been prevented, had that workman acquired a habit of self-denial through the desire to add to his small accumulations in the savings bank. And not only is your loss or inconvenience to be borne as best it may, but the work must now be done by him from time which he might otherwise devote to productiveness in another direction, or by another who would else be otherwise employed. The world then, as well as you and he, is the worse for his indulgence.

This is not the place for a disquisition upon the evils of intemperance and the respective merits of prohibition and regulation of the sale of intoxicating liquors, but upon one point all classes are agreed, and upon that we may safely take our stand, and that is that all moral influences that serve to restrain excessive indulgence in drink are proper, and may with propriety be encouraged. And among the moral forces operating as such restraint, I believe there is none more effective and salutary than the desire of saving, awakened and stimulated through the agency of savings institutions. It is no answer to this to say that intemperance prevails in spite of savings banks, and that with a savings bank on one corner and a saloon on the other, the latter will seem to do the more prosperous business. That is only assertion, and lacks confirmation. But if it were even so, the true test could be applied, only by closing up the savings bank to see by how much the business of the saloon would be increased by the experiment. It is enough that we know that some will yield to the mild restraints of a desire to save, once thoroughly awakened, and if it be but one in a thousand thus rescued from idleness, vice and crime, and made a worthy, industrious member of society, the experiment that costs nothing is well worth repeating if for that result alone.

And there are milder forms of dissipation, or at least of extravagance, that interrupt the course of business, and create a distaste for steady industry, the excess of which would find a measure of restraint in a prevalent desire to accumulate, incited and stimulated by the opportunities for investment which savings banks afford. Some recreation, an occasional unbending of the energies of mind and body from the strain of too severe and constant application, is demanded by the laws of our being, and its indulgence in *rational* forms serves by the better conditions which it promotes to render more effective the productive powers of the individual. That such festivities may be increased rather than diminished, is the aspiration of all who have at heart the welfare of the working classes.

But there are forms of recreation common to our people, that are not relaxation; that exhaust rather than invigorate, that demoralize rather than elevate and improve, and that are expensive in the outlay of both time and money, to a degree far exceeding any compensating advantage or enjoyment derived from them.

The parade through the country of an excursion company, so common a few years ago, was more exhausting to those engaged in it than would have been steady labor at home. The expense, in money alone, of one of those excursions of say fifty members, would serve to take a hundred families an average of thirty miles into the country, for two or three days, thus furnishing real rest and needed change to this larger number, to say nothing of the healthful moral influence of families taking their rest and enjoyment together, promoting that home and family feeling which is among the strongest ties that bind society together.

The significance of the foregoing illustration to the subject under discussion is this: that there are so many days abstracted from the productive forces of labor, with no compensating advantage to any one in the form of rest, rational enjoyment, or otherwise; and any conservative influence that shall tend to diminish the aggregate of such losses, is entitled to co-operation and encouragement. And this conservative influence is found in the institution of savings banks. It is safe to assume, that the depositors in these rarely indulge in such expensive and profitless entertainments. The little deposit in the savings bank is the talisman that charms many a man from indulgence in reckless folly. It is thus, as promoters of public virtue, as conservators of public wealth, as stimulators of public industry, that these institutions are to be regarded with favor and cherished with peculiar care.

Again, they serve to promote public order, through the interest in its preservation, which the possession of property always inspires. The depositor has something at stake in society—something sacred, which the disruption of social order would imperil. They were not the depositors in savings banks that went surging through the streets of New York in 1863, threatening, burning, destroying and murdering.

The savings bank depositor is, therefore, a better citizen, neighbor, friend, for the restraint upon him imposed by the possession of property. His earnings are not only *deposited*, but they are *invested* on his behalf—in the bonds of the nation, the State, the city, the county, the town—or on the mortgage of stores on Broadway or the residence on Fifth avenue ; and how jealous is he now of the honor and financial integrity of those communities whose creditor he is.

Forty-nine million dollars of the bonds of the United States Government are held by the savings banks of this State. In the maintenance of the faith that is to redeem these bonds at maturity, five hundred thousand men and women are interested, and woe to the political aspirations of that man, and burial without hope of resurrection, for that party, whose watchword shall be to break faith with these creditors. Suppose some ambitious legislator had proposed, at the hight of the success of our free banking system, to destroy the security of the circulating notes which constitute its best and most popular feature. We may well believe that he and his project together would have been buried forever under the wave of righteous indignation which he would have aroused. But the public interest of our citizens in the Government securities, exceeds by $6,000,000 that ever held in the circulating notes of this State ! What, then, may we anticipate will be the reply of the people to the Butlers, the Stephenses and the Pendletons, who propose to practically destroy securities in which they have invested $49,000,000 of their hard-earned wages !

When statesmen look with dismay upon the proportions of our national debt, and find no solution for our financial problem but in practical repudiation, the stern, hard sense of the common people, the toilers in workshop and field, awakened by their imperiled interests, will *achieve* a solution through these timid and paltering statesmen, or *over* them through others, upon the basis of unswerving integrity to the spirit of the bond—a solution worthy of a great and free people. It is by influences like these that the depositor in our savings banks becomes a more thoughtful, intelligent and conservative citizen.

But this discussion discloses another feature of interest in connection with savings banks, quite distinct from the "charity" view of them with which we set out. One of the staple elements in all systems of political economy is capital—wealth aggregated. It builds railroads, it constructs and operates manufactories, it develops mines, it diffuses the products of industry, bringing to every man's door the commodities which he cannot produce, and taking from his hands the fruits of his labors and conveying them to others in exchange. In the hands of the State it constructs canals, carries on war, endows charities, supports free schools for the education of the people, erects public edifices, and aids in the development of material resources.

In the old systems of public economy, mankind were divided into two classes—the capitalist and the laborer—but through the agency of savings banks, in these later years, our political economy must be written anew, for behold, the laborers have become the capitalists in this new world! Thirty-one millions of the earnings of the *poor* are loaned to the *rich* on bond and mortgage in this State! Is any local improvement projected, the savings bank is the capitalist who advances the money to the corporation. How many public or corporate enterprises have been carried to successful completion through the agency of savings banks we may never know, but the names of the securities in which the moneys of savings banks are invested, will be a suggestive indication of the power of these institutions in promoting public improvements, or aiding in the discharge of public obligations. We have Water Company bonds in Syracuse, Auburn, Poughkeepsie, New York and Brooklyn; Sewerage bonds, Street Improvement bonds, Court House bonds in Brooklyn and New York; Riot Damage bonds, Harlem River Improvement, Central Park, Public Park, Prospect Park, Washington Park, Fire Indemnity, New Aqueduct (Croton), Gowanus canal, Union Free School, and many others of similar character. The name of local securities issued to aid, in some form, in the prosecution of the late war, is legion, but some of the most suggestive are such as Soldiers' Aid, Family Aid, Substitute Relief, and the like. Pages of this report could be filled with merely the names of securities as significant as the above, making an aggregate of $23,000,000 invested in local securities alone.

Nor should we lose sight of the character in which savings banks are thus revealed as a sort of a co-operative union of the industrial classes. Their savings aggregated as capital, minister to these public enterprises; but these public enterprises demand laborers for their prosecution, and thus return to labor in the form of wages what they have borrowed from it in the form of capital. The laborers get better wages for the facility with which, through savings banks, the requisite capital can be procured, which is equivalent to having their capital returned to them in full, with extra dividends, by instalments called wages, while, at the same time, they hold in their pass-book the original certificate which entitles them to have it *again* returned to them with ordinary dividends called interest! What other capitalist is able to make so safe, and at the same time so profitable an investment of his money? Other "unions" are formed as combinations of labor *against* capital, but here is a combination of labor *and* capital. The former seeks to control the price of labor by arbitrary dicta, the latter affects the price of labor favorably to the laborer through the operation of natural laws. The former has a fund which offers a premium to idleness, by contributing to the support of a laborer while on a strike; the fund of the latter incites to industry by flowing into the channels of enterprise which demand labor for their prosecution. I do not make these comparisons invidiously, but because the scope and power of savings banks, as organized to-day, can best be seen, when these are exhibited in their relation to other institutions of beneficent purpose, that accomplish the very objects for which they are organized less perfectly than these whose primary purpose is wholly different.

This discussion concerning the nature and purposes of savings banks, appears to me now to have reached this conclusion: that whatever they may have been in the eyes of their founders—looking as philanthropists—seeking only some simple means of ameliorating the condition of the poor by helping them to help themselves; the system in its present practical development, while successful beyond the wildest dreams of its projectors, in the direction in which they looked for success, has, without growing away from its original design, which it still holds as the germ of its organic life, expanded beyond the limited scope assigned to its early being, and become to-day a power in the State, an element in its public economy, an educator, a reformer, an instrument in the promotion of public order, an efficient ally of the government, a public benefactor; and in these relations it should command not only the sympathy which its primitive purpose would naturally enlist, but the broader comprehension, the more respectful consideration, the more carefully matured action which statesmanship gives to questions of the first magnitude in the affairs of State.

Condition and Workings of Savings Banks.

We are now prepared to discuss the more practical features of our subject, as disclosed in the condition and workings of savings banks in this State. As already indicated, I shall, in my exposition of this branch of the subject, avail myself not only of the facts derived from the examination in which I have been engaged, but of the reports of savings banks made to this department.

Before entering upon the work of visitation assigned to me, I prepared a series of blanks, in book form, containing inquiries designed to elicit both facts and opinions upon points which I deemed of importance. These inquiries were as follows:

Items of Fact and Opinion Relative to Savings Banks, Derived from an Examination of the
Made 1867.

FACTS.

I.

Organization.

1. Number of trustees authorized by charter:

Names of Trustees.

2. Number that are trustees in other savings institutions:

3. Number that are directors in any bank of circulation where deposits of this institution are kept:

4. Limitations of charter or of law, relative to who may be trustees:

5. Vacancies, how created:

6. Vacancies, how filled:

7. Officers of the board or institution elected from its members

8. Officers, clerks and other employees not members of the board:

9. Standing committees of the board, and how constituted and appointed:

10. Special committees of the board, on the day of 1867, and how appointed:

11. Committees, standing or special, not from the members of the board, and how appointed:

II.

Expenditures.

12. Committees of the board receiving compensation for their services, and rate:

13. Committees not of the board receiving compensation and rate:

14. Officers elected or appointed from the members of the board, receiving compensation for their services, and the rate per annum during the year 1866:

15. Officers, clerks, and other employees, receiving compensation for their services, and the rate per annum during the year 1866.

16. Members of the board to whom moneys have been paid under contracts for labor and material furnished to the institution within five years from 1st January, 1867:

17. Members of the board who have received commissions for service, or for favor from the institution, or from parties with whom the institution has had dealings:

Cash Transactions During the Year 1866.

Receipts.

Cash on hand 1st Jan., 1866, before the transactions of the day:

Deposited in bank	$	
Deposited in vault		$
From depositors		
From interest on mortgages		
From interest on stocks		
From interest on loans		

From interest on deposits in bank.............. $
From premium on gold........................
From mortgages paid, called in, or foreclosed......
From redemption of stocks..................
From repayment of loans.....................
From sales of real estate....................
From sales of stocks.......................
From rents..................................
From other sources enumerated below..........

$

Payments.

To depositors................................ $
Loans on bond and mortgage..................
Loans on stocks and other securities............
For purchase of stocks and bonds..............
(Par value thereof...........$)
For building or construction account...........
For repairs..................................
For furniture and fixtures.....................
For rent ....
For salaries ....
For suits at law..............................
For printing, advertising, stationery and blank books,
For fuel and lights............................
For taxes and assessments......................
For incidental expenses per petty cash...........
For other expenses enumerated below...........
Cash on hand 31st December, 1866, after the transactions of the day:
Deposited in bank.................. $
Deposited in vault.................

$

STATE OF NEW YORK, } ss:
COUNTY. }

of the

being duly sworn, doth depose and say that the foregoing statement of the receipts and payments on account of the

during the year 1866, is correct and true, according to the best of his knowledge, information and belief.

Sworn before me, this
day of 1867.

III.

Investments.

Assets of the on the day of 1867.

	Par value.	Cost.
Bonds and mortgages........................$		
U. S. bonds and treasury notes,........	$	
New York State bonds...............		
Bonds of other States		
Bonds of cities in this State		
Bonds of towns in this state...........		
Loans on stocks and other securities, available fund		
Other securities.............................		
Real estate		
Cash in bank		
Cash in vault		

STATE OF NEW YORK, } *ss:*
County.

being duly and severally sworn, each for himself saith, that he is
and that as such
he did on the day of 186 , personally examine the securities, notes, obligations and evidences of debt belonging to and constituting the assets of the
and that he counted the money in the vault of the said institution or bank, and that he compared the amount stated as being on deposit in bank on that day with the vouchers of the cashiers of the deposit banks, and that the foregoing statement of the assets of the as found upon such examination, is correct and true.

Sworn before me, this day of 186 .

20. Investments yielding no revenue:

21. Average amount kept on deposit in bank during the year 1866 .... $

At what rate of interest ?

22. Amount reserved for daily transactions... $

IV.

Conduct of Business.

23. Regular meetings of the Board :

24. Number constituting a quorum :

25. Average number attending the regular meetings during 1866 :

26. Penalty for non-attendance :

27. By what action or by whose final voice are loans upon bond and mortgage effected ?

28. Do. concerning purchases or sales of stocks and bonds :

29. Do. of temporary or call loans :

30. Do. deposits in banks :

31. Hours during which bank is open :

32. Regulations concerning the duties and conduct of officers and clerks :

33. Regulations to be observed by depositors :

34. Regulations concerning interest on deposits :

35. How long before interest on unclaimed deposits ceases :

36. Examination and comparison of books and vouchers and assets, for proof of accuracy and fidelity—by whom made, and how often :

37. Facts not enumerated :

Opinions.

38. What number of trustees is best for a thorough and efficient working organization ?

39. What provisions of law are desirable in defining or limiting the constituency of the board ?

40. Would efficiency of organization be promoted by removal of restriction that no person shall be a trustee in two or more institutions ; or otherwise ?

41. Does the provision that no trustee shall be at the same time a director in a bank of discount where the savings institution has deposits, impair the efficiency of organization ?

42. What acts or omissions of duty should be prescribed by law creating a vacancy, which the board should be authorized or directed to declare?

43. By whom should vacancies in office be filled?

44. Should offices be designated by law, or left to discretion of the board?

45. Should the offices of secretary, treasurer, cashier, teller, attorney, surveyor, etc., be held by members of the board or by others?

46. Should members of the board, acting in any possible capacity for the board, receive compensation for their services?

47. Should there be legislative prohibition against the practice of letting any contracts for labor or material for the institution to members of the board?

48. Should there be a statutory provision prohibiting members or officers of the board from receiving commissions from the institution, or from parties with whom the institution has dealings?

49. Should the Legislature prescribe the frequency of regular meetings, or is that better left to the discretion of the board?

50. Should quorum be prescribed by law, and what number or proportion of members should constitute quorum?

51. Is the law at present too rigid or too lax relative to the investments which may be made by savings banks?

52. If too rigid, in what respect should the power be extended?

53. If too lax, to what should investments be limited.

54. Would it not be well to limit by law the proportion of aggregate deposits to be invested in bond and mortgage?

55. Is it desirable to limit the proportion of investment in different classes of stocks?

56. Is it practicable to secure interest on the deposits made by savings banks in banks of discount?

57. Is the limit of twenty per cent of deposits greater or less than is desirable?

58. Is the limit of $100,000 that may be made in one bank too great or too small?

59. Would not call loans on United States or New York State stocks exclusively, with ten per cent margin from par value, or from market value when less than par, be as safe as a deposit in banks, and be as available and more profitable?

60. What limitations concerning dividends to depositors is it practicable to prescribe by law, and what should be left to the discretion of trustees?

61. What surplus in gross or proportional to deposits, is safe for the institution and just to the depositors?

62. What limit should the statute prescribe to the amount that may be received on deposit from one individual?

63. Does the law at present sufficiently protect the deposits of married women made in their own name, and do they sufficiently protect savings banks from suits at law regarding such deposits on complaint of husbands?

64. If not, what further provisions are necessary in this regard?

65. Is not uniformity in the powers and privileges conferred, and in the duties imposed on savings institutions, especially in the cities of New York and Brooklyn, important for the highest good of all?

66. Is the effect of multiplying these institutions salutary or otherwise?

67. Opinions on points not enumerated:

A few blanks, slightly different in form, were first used, but the foregoing embrace the line of inquiry substantially pursued in all cases.

The more important facts elicited are given, together with such opinions as have been suggested outside of the immediate line of inquiry.

The statistics of cash transactions, and of assets, are presented in full, for the following reasons:

The statement of cash transactions is especially valuable, as exhibiting phases of the operation of savings banks never before disclosed, and embracing some of the most important features in the management of these institutions. Among these are their expenses—ordinary, extraordinary and incidental. Various sources of revenue are brought to view, as from rents, premium on gold, and chance profits, as well as from the simple interest on investments at currency value. The course of business can likewise be noted, the stocks bought and sold, the amount loaned and returned on securities, the taxes paid, etc., etc.

The deductions from these facts, the lesson they teach, the moral they point, will be more fully disclosed in the progress of this report.

The statement of assets, is, in itself, less important, as a similar statement, with full schedules, is made by the savings banks in January and July of each year ; and for the same reason the liabilities which could be found by reference to previous reports are not here embraced. But two desirable results are secured by the statement of assets in the *form* herewith submitted, that are not reached in the regular reports.

1st. A classification of the assets, distinguishing the different kinds as Government, State, other State, city, county and town, so as to reveal at a glance the proportions of each held by any bank.

2d. In the form of verification to the possession of these assets by the bank.

The annual reports which include the statement of assets of each savings bank, are sworn to by the two principal officers of the institution from the best of their knowledge and belief. But such an affidavit is not incompatible with two conditions, either of which would render it worthless.

The officers may be dishonest and in collusion, or one dishonest and the other ignorant, and the report falsely made to hide the dishonesty of both or of the one, who may have abstracted the assets.

Or the chief officers may both be honest, but accept and swear from knowledge and belief, to a statement prepared by a subordinate who has access to the securities and charge of the books.

It is very easy to make the books call for a given amount of securities, and to make a statement to correspond with such amount.

But the practical question is, what is the *evidence* that the reported securities are in possession of the institution? It was to meet and answer this natural and pertinent inquiry, that I prepared the form of affidavit noted on page 24.

It was intended that this should be made by a committee of trustees after a personal examination of the assets. The presumption against collusion in such case is so strong as to amount to certainty. The idea of making an examination of the assets of each savings bank myself, was suggested to me, but abandoned for its impracticability. The manipulation in counting all the securities and the large deposits of cash on hand, in some of the banks, amounting in the aggregate to many millions of dollars, would of itself have been a labor of months. Two could do it in a fourth of the time, but under your authority as restricted by the resolution of the Legislature, I must do my work unaided. Thus satisfied at once of the impracticability of making an examination myself, I sought the best practical substitute in the affidavit of a committee of trustees who had made, or who should make, such an examination.

A popular and natural apprehension prevails, that through the negligence of trustees to carefully supervise the affairs of these institutions, abuses may creep into the management, and frauds, defalcations and abstractions of securities be effected and concealed for years, to be revealed at last, to the despairing gaze of thousands whose hopes are wrecked amid the ruins of fabrics they had so long regarded as impregnable, and where, in simple, trusting confidence, they had placed the little store that should give them a christian burial and save them from a pauper's grave.

The history of English savings banks, almost from the time of their institution until the present, is a series of illustrations of the naturalness of this apprehension, and of the fact that no character however high, no calling however sacred, no confidence however seemingly deserved, is a safe substitute for a careful, thorough and intelligent supervision by trustees, of the minutest details of their trust.

The most astounding frauds were perpetrated by officers of savings banks, often clergymen, and always men of the highest respectability, and enjoying the confidence of the community and of the trustees in a marked, often in an eminent degree. It was this overweening confidence, this perfect trust in the integrity of reputable men, that led to the terrible disasters that too often followed. In this blind confidence no thorough examination and comparison of the books was made, and the returns of the institutions to the government office, as prepared by the officer in charge, were sworn to by the trustees without suspicion or question. Here was every incitement to dishonesty; the temptation, the opportunity to embezzle, and to hide the fact, and the confidence which would be slow to suspect and would never investigate until suspicion should be aroused; here was a conjunction of conditions, of which the result might have been predicted, but concerning which history, rather than prophecy, brings to us the impressive lesson.

Within a period of thirteen years, defalcations occurred amounting to nearly $900,000; and these do not embrace the earlier and more disastrous cases of failure from this cause.

The wretchedness and despair that fell upon the hearts and desolated the homes of thousands, it were vain to attempt to portray. But it was truly said by Mr. Gladstone, "that the evil done is unfortunately not to be measured by the actual amount of money loss; there is an amount of evil such as figures can convey no idea of; and it is impossible that the public confidence in these institutions can be that which it ought to be, while these losses are liable to occur at all." To his honor, be it said, that to the remedying of such defects in the savings bank system of Great Britain, Mr. Gladstone immediately and vigorously addressed himself, and with great success, through a system to which I may find occasion to refer more fully hereafter.

Admonished by such examples as these, of the dangers that *might* be lurking in our system, the affidavit referred to was prepared as a test of the extent to which similar neglect in administration had involved the savings banks of our State in peril.

I hoped by means of it to establish two important facts. First, that the savings banks of our State, upon some given day within the present year, were in a sound and prosperous condition, as shown by a personal examination of their assets, by a committee of trustees, and not by an affidavit of officers upon "the best of their knowledge and belief." Second, that such examination was in the usual course of business, and not exceptional; which fact would remove all grounds of apprehension arising from the perils of neglectful supervision.

I know of nothing that could inspire greater confidence in these institutions, than the knowledge, generally diffused, that all their transactions are regularly and thoroughly supervised and examined by a committee of trustees, at least once or twice in each year.

And it is my pleasure to report that most of the savings banks in our State have such an examination of their condition, resources, and affairs generally, at least twice in each year, and some of them oftener, as quarterly or monthly. How prevalent is this custom, will be found more satisfactorily set forth in the answer to question 36, of facts and opinions, as transcribed in the returns under the last item of "Other Facts," in the appendix, A.

The assets reported in the tables herewith submitted, may therefore be relied upon as having been in possession of the institution on the day named.

In a few instances which will be noted, the affidavit is made, not by a committee of trustees, but by officers of the institution who have made the examination. While for the reasons and the purposes stated, it would be preferable to have had the affidavit of others than officers in charge, it was in some cases found impracticable to secure this within the limited time allowed for preparing the statement, owing to the absence of members of such committee, or other causes. But such cases are exceptional, not only to this report, but to the usages of these institutions themselves.

No just comparison can be instituted between the assets thus reported, and those given in the reports of January last, for the reason that they are not in all cases reduced to the same basis of value, the practice being different in different banks, of reporting par, market or cost value, and besides, they do not correspond in time, it not being a part of my purpose that they should.

An approximate comparison can be made, sufficient to establish the substantial correctness of each upon the basis of computation assumed, and at the times respectively reported.

Owing to the necessity of commencing the computation found in exhibit B, before my visitations were completed, by reason of the great labor involved, requiring ample time, they are all made from the data in the report of last January.

The prosperous condition of the savings banks in our State, in their aggregate as a system, is sufficiently apparent from their statements to the Bank Department from year to year. This prosperity is shown in the increase of deposits from $41,422,672, in 1858, to $131,769,074 in 1867; in the increase of aggregate surplus from 5½ per cent of the total assets in 1858, to 7 per cent of the same in 1867; in the character of their investments, not exceeding 10 per cent of which are objectionable, and these, not specifically, but as a class not desirable for savings banks; in the increase in the number of these institutions outside of cities, in which there was already a savings bank, from 14 in 1857, to 33 in 1867; and in the increased per cent of interest received, from less than 6 per cent on the gross assets of 1858, to 6½ per cent on the gross assets of 1866.

These conditions of prosperity are fortunately not specious but real, and are a most gratifying indication of the industry and frugality of our people, and of the fidelity and skill with which this important trust has been administered.

Faithful Administration.

As constituting an important feature of evidence concerning the substantial character of these institutions, and as further illustration of the prudent management which is so important an element in their prosperity, it is proper in this connection to notice one great fact that stands conspicuously forth in the history of savings banks in this State, that since their organization in 1819, but two have failed, and not one through fraud or embezzlement by their officers.

When we consider the magnitude of this trust, the immense sums which during the last fifty years have passed through the hands of these officers, amounting to a total of many hundreds of millions of dollars, it is the most remarkable financial record of which history bears witness that not a dollar of loss has been sustained through the dishonesty of those upon whom such vast responsibility has been imposed. Of the two failures referred to a more full account is given elsewhere.

Increase of Deposits.

An increasing aggregate of deposits in savings banks is a certain indication of the prosperity of the laboring classes. It betokens liberal wages and frugal habits. It is a presumptive indication of a prosperous condition of the institutions by which they are held, but it is not a *positive* indication. For however large the line of deposits—which constitute liabilities—they are indications of weakness rather than strength, unless there is an equal or greater amount of resources with which to pay them. No savings bank *reports* an amount of liabilities exceeding its resources, though in some few instances, where there is no margin, or but a very narrow one, by the inclusion among the resources of such items as "furniture," "fixtures" and "account books," the practical preponderance is clearly with the *liabilities!*

Surplus held by Savings Banks.

Real prosperity is a compound quality into the composition of which various elements enter, but of these *strength*, an assured equality of resources to liabilities, indicated by a reasonable surplus of the former, is the most important; any apparent prosperity that, upon investigation, proves to be destitute of this element, is fictitious. To provide for this element of assured strength, savings banks are authorized by law to accumulate a surplus of ten per cent of their deposits to meet any contingencies of business.

The aggregate surplus of all the savings banks on the 1st of January last was seven per cent of the aggregate assets—an increase as before shown, of one and a half per cent since 1858.

But an aggregate surplus is not a fair criterion of general soundness; for if this surplus were all held by half the savings banks, while the remainder had none, or had a balance of liabilities against them, the condition of these institutions might well excite apprehension. A reference to column 1, table B, in the appendix, will disclose the exact proportion of assets held as surplus by each savings bank on the 1st of January last.

Of these I have selected and arranged the following, whose surplus on that basis is less than two per cent. As some of these have recently been organized, I give the year of incorporation of each, in order to afford a just basis of comparison.

Name of Savings Banks.	Year chartered.	Total surplus.	Per cent of surplus.
Albany City	1850	------	----
Albany Exchange	1856	$668	1-2
Mechanics' and Farmers', Albany	1855	16,888	1 6-10
Mutual, Auburn	1862	3,653	1 1-2
Emigrant, Brooklyn	1863	644	6-10
German, Brooklyn	1866	869	6-10
Long Island, Brooklyn	1865	1,372	1
Emigrant, Buffalo	1848	309	2-10
Harlem, New York	1863	906	1-10
Market, New York	1863	11,774	1 9-10
North River, New York	1866	------	----
Sixpenny, New York	1853	8,064	1 8-10
Up-Town, New York	1866	------	----
Central, Troy	1857	------	----
Manufacturers', Troy	1857	------	----
Mutual, Troy	1857	------	----
State, Troy	1856	243	1-10
Central, Utica	1851	1,588	1
National, Utica	1865	1,126	4-10

Name of Savings Banks.	Year chartered.	Total surplus.	Per cent of surplus.
Chautauqua County	1866	6	2-100
Chenango County	1860	684	8-10
Cohoes	1851	------	----
Cortland	1866	------	----
Mechanics', Fishkill-on-Hudson	1866	499	1 3-10
Skaneateles	1866	1,031	1 9-10

The whole number thus reporting less than two per cent of surplus is twenty-five, of which number eight have none, nine have less than one per cent, and eight have one per cent or more. Eight of the whole number were organized some time during the year 1866, and more than half of them since 1860, and of course can not be expected to have a surplus to compare with institutions of longer standing. Several of those reporting no surplus, or but very little, have a large part of their resources in cash, hence of course are not liable to the contingency of depreciation. But this, and other aspects of the workings of our savings bank system, suggested by the foregoing statement, are reserved for discussion in connection with topics to which they are more intimately related.

The exhibit of surplus as a whole, however, reveals a degree of individual as well as of collective strength in these institutions, that is full of encouragement and promise.

The per cent or ratio of profits, can only be approximately estimated, for the reason that the gross profits during any year are derived from a varying amount of investment.

But an approximation sufficiently close for our purpose, can be obtained, by finding the ratio which the interest received during any year bears to the assets at the beginning of the year, and comparing this with the ratio of interest to assets in some subsequent year obtained in like manner. By such computation it appears that the rate of interest received has advanced a trifle over one-half per cent in eight years. There is, of course, a practical and economical limit to this ratio, beyond which it is neither possible nor expedient to go. As a rule, investments affording perfect security can not be made at a rate exceeding seven per cent, or legal interest, and it is difficult to make them in the large amounts required by savings banks, even at so favorable a rate. And besides, allowance must be made for that portion of assets awaiting investment, or held as a reserve to meet current payments, and deposited, at a rate of interest not commonly exceeding four per cent.

An average of six per cent is as high as should be anticipated under ordinary conditions, and the rate realized during 1866, $6\frac{4}{10}$ per cent as found at the foot of column 6, table B, in the appendix, is the result in a great measure of *extraordinary* financial conditions. The investment largely in Government securities, yielding $7\frac{3}{10}$ per cent or 6 per cent compounded, currency interest; or 6 per cent gold interest, equivalent to 8 per cent or more in currency, has served to raise the average rate beyond all common experience in the past, or reasonable expectation in the future, when coin shall again become the standard currency.

But as a passing condition, affecting the present prosperity of savings banks, it was entitled to consideration in this place.

The receipt of greater profits as interest, has enabled savings banks generally to declare larger dividends than before, until 6 per cent on all sums up to $5,000, is the prevailing rate. The policy of a uniform rate upon all sums is elsewhere considered. Whether so high a rate as six per cent will prove to be altogether an unmixed good, is a question involved in some doubt in my mind, in view of the difficulty which most, if not all our savings banks, will experience in adhering to this rate after a return to specie payments shall reduce 8 and 9 per cent investments to those of 6 per cent. But that period appears just now too remote and contingent to excite very lively *apprehensions* of disaster from its coming!

The increase of deposits has been spoken of as indicating a gratifying degree of prosperity among the working classes, and as evincing the growth of habits of industry and frugality which it is an important mission of savings banks to foster and promote.

Withdrawal of Deposits.

It will be seen from column 3, of table B, appendix, that in only fourteen savings banks did the withdrawals exceed the deposits in 1866. The aggregate increase of deposits during that year was $11,001,146.49.

While this, when found in connection with prudent and honest administration, has properly been considered among the evidences of the growing prosperity of these institutions, I desire to enforce the seeming paradox that a decrease in the amount of deposits, through an excess of withdrawals, may equally be an indication of prosperity, and afford a demonstration of the utility of savings banks, more conclusive and triumphant than that derived from an increase of such deposits.

We must bear constantly in mind that the utility of saving is in the future use to which that saving is applied. If our savings banks only encouraged hoarding for its own sake, the noblest feature that characterizes them would be destroyed. It is a noble purpose only that ennobles any deed. It is then the future *use* for which the sacrifice of saving is made, that invests it with a peculiar interest and charm. When the occasion for that use arrives, the little deposit is withdrawn, and its ultimate purpose is realized. That is the depositor's hour of triumph. It was that *purpose* that imparted strength and endurance to his arm in toil, and that fortified his determined self denial. If it was a pleasing sight to look upon him, in the fulfillment of his high resolve, turning away from the allurements of vicious companionship and indulgence, and putting aside week after week the little portion that by and by should serve the secret purpose of his heart, is it not more pleasing *now* to witness the full fruition of his hopes, as he withdraws his store and applies it to the purpose cherished so ardently and so long?

The occasion to use the amount so carefully and worthily saved, may come in a season of prosperity, when it will procure a home, set up a son in business, furnish a daughter's outfit, or educate both sons and daughters for usefulness in the world; or it may come with adversity, when employment is scarce and wages are low, when sickness disables and prostrates, increases the needs but checks the supplies; or when death closes the scene, and the last tribute of affection to one whom some hearts have loved, must be paid. Upon one of my visits, I was unable to see the secretary, by reason of his absence at the funeral of a depositor. She was a young woman who had no relatives in that part of the State, if anywhere indeed, and who supported herself by sewing. For several years she had been a regular depositor, in small sums, at the savings bank. A few days before her death, she sent for the secretary and told him that she had saved those earnings for the event then so near, and gave him directions to procure for her a lot in the cemetery for her grave, and requested him to defray the expenses of her funeral, and procure a plain tablet, to mark her final resting place, with what should remain of the little sum she had saved.

And who will say that the fulfillment of the cherished purpose of that friendless girl, sad and mournful as was the occasion of it, was not a prouder vindication of the usefulness of savings banks, than was the simple record of her deposits from time to time, reported among the evidences of the prosperity of that growing institution? The future historian of the savings banks of our State will rehearse many such a story, and point to *them* as the conclusive answer to any question of their success.

During the months of February, March and April last, the deposits of many savings banks in New York city were rapidly diminished. The occasion of it was an unusual movement in real estate. Hundreds, and perhaps thousands of depositors, withdrew their deposits to invest in a "lot up-town," on which they might build a house or shop that should yield them a better income than the savings bank could pay. Many of these became borrowers from the institution to which they had been lenders before, it being a wise and just policy with many of our savings banks to give a preference in loans upon bond and mortgage, to these who have built up the institution by their patronage.

A casual observer might have looked upon this reduction in the aggregate resources of those institutions as an unfortunate incident—as evidence of waning prosperity. But one who grasps the deep and real significance of savings banks, would see herein the *best effect* of their provident ministry, and rejoice in the evidence of the prosperity promoted by their agency, thus clearly and tangibly revealed.

The feature of any savings bank which first, last and always commands attention and awakens interest, which is regarded as embracing, in concentrated form, all the material evidence concerning the character of its management and the degree of public confidence to which it is entitled is,—its

Investments.

To this, in fact, all other questions relating to savings banks are subordinate, for upon this their very existence depends.

If these institutions are not *safe* they are *nothing*—for the purposes of their creation. And they are only *safe* as their investments are secure beyond any contingency less remote or less fatal than the disruption of the State itself.

I trust that the fullness of discussion of this branch of the general subject will stand justified by its importance.

Ten columns of table B in the appendix, are appropriated to expressing the proportion of the different classes of investments made by the savings banks of this State, as reported on the 1st of January last. For detailed information concerning the investments of each institution, reference is made to that table.

The following summary gives the amount and the per cent of each class of investments of all the savings banks, as reported for the first of January last, not expressed with perfect accuracy, the cents and remoter decimals being omitted :

	Amount.	Per cent.
1. Bonds and mortgages	$31,112,168	22
2. U. S. stocks and treasury notes	48,723,419	34 4-10
3. New York State stocks	8,760,935	6 2-10
4. City, county and town bonds	23,167,788	16 3-10
5. Bonds of other States	8,922,321	6 3-10
6. Other securities	947,423	7-10
7. Deposited in banks, Trust Co's, &c.	8,628,517	6 1-10
8. Kept in vault	3,193,943	2 2-10
9. Loaned on stock or other securities,	5,575,500	3 9-10
10. Otherwise invested	2,648,300	1 9-10
Total	$141,680,313	
Due depositors	131,769,074	
Surplus	$9,911,239	6.96

A difference will be noted between the aggregate of resources stated above, and as stated in the annual report which is thus explained. In the schedules accompanying the annual reports, the items of investment are given in par and market value, while the aggregates are carried into the summary at cost, and this summary is aggregated for the Department report.

But in making a calculation of the per cent of each class of investments, it was necessary, of course, to refer to the items, and these were taken at market value, the same at cost as stated in the aggregates of the report not being given.

The per cent of surplus, however, in table B is upon the aggregate as stated in the report.

The difference is not a material one, but serves to illustrate the imperfection in the form of reporting to this Department, elsewhere more fully considered.

As a general average, the above is a most flattering exhibit. The proportion of stocks of this State strikes one at first as being unduly small, but it must be remembered that the most of this class of securities were put in market many years ago, when they commanded a premium, as a basis for banking, that placed them beyond reach for ordinary investment. Of the late seven per cent bounty loan, savings banks availed themselves to a fair extent.

The fifth, sixth, ninth and tenth items are the ones whose contemplation gives least satisfaction, though the last, as it includes the real estate owned by these institutions, is not so bad as it might appear at first sight.

But these are averages only, while the extent to which any individual savings bank exceeds or falls below this average can be ascertained only by consulting the table above referred to.

We must not forget that while we are considering a system in its general results, it is a system composed of independent parts, each having a constitution and mode of operation peculiar to itself. If these constituted a harmonious whole, the deficiencies of one being compensated out of the abundance of another, an average condition of assured solvency and strength might suffice. But the errors and weakness of one are not thus counterbalanced by the prudence and strength of another. The integrity of each is impaired by its own indiscretions; its depositors, be they few or many, are put in peril by its weakness, and if the worst comes, all the independent yet related members of the system suffer through a prevailing want of confidence inspired by disaster, and are fortunate if they suffer in nothing more.

Our discussion proceeds, then, with this natural and pertinent inquiry, Is it possible to organize and conduct these institutions on a basis that shall render their safety at all times and under all circumstances *certain*—their failure IMPOSSIBLE ?

I believe it is, and I believe the general principles that have been recognized in the legislation of this State tend in that direction, and are the secret of the success that has marked the growth and progress of these institutions, that in fifty years have witnessed but two inconsiderable failures.

In what manner and in what direction those principles have been departed from in modern practice, will appear as we proceed with our inquiry.

In organizing the operations of a savings bank three conditions must be provided for :

1*st.* Perfect Security—the return to each depositor beyond all peradventure, of every dollar of his deposits.

2*d.* A fair profit in the way of dividends or interest accruing from his investment.

3*d.* Ability to return the deposits with accrued dividends at all ordinary times upon demand, without previous notice.

These conditions must be considered together; if either be left out of view our conclusions will be faulty, and our means insufficient for the purpose to be accomplished.

Perfect Security is of course the primary consideration; but this may be easily secured if depositors will forego any question of profits. Doubtless many would do this if it were demonstrated to their satisfaction that profits were incompatible with perfect safety.

But they have the assurance of long and reliable experience that perfect security and moderate profits may be combined.

And it is the active deposit, ever working ceaselessly, noiselessly, by day and by night, in sunshine and in storm, in time of plenty and in time of want, never hungry, never weary, never drowsy, never cold, never sick, never idle, that works steadily on asking for nothing, "but to be let alone," always earning, never spending, compounding itself, winding itself up, making no trouble, giving no anxiety; this active, persistent, tireless, faithful deposit, that goes forth lean and in a few brief years returns fat; this is what has charms for the humblest depositor, not less than for the owner of large possessions. To eliminate from our system the element of *profit*, is to strike at the root of the tree. But it is fruitless to discuss conditions foreign to our experience, and that form no part of any rational plan of operations. It is enough that so long as money can command perfectly safe investment at *not less* than two per cent per annum, so long there is a margin for *some* profit to depositors, in the prudent managment of savings banks; for we are not now concerned with the *amount* of profits, which are only to be *fair*, by bearing a reasonable ratio to the rate of interest on safe investments, to answer our demand.

Conceding then the perfect practicability, as well as the necessity, of combining safety and profit, we must meet and provide for the remaining condition of payment on demand; for, to make these institutions popular and successful, we must obstruct the way with the fewest possible conditions.

The depositor wishes to know, not only that he can have his

own again with interest, but that he can have it at his own option, in his own time, when his real or fancied needs are most urgent. You withhold from him one of the incentives to saving, if you require him to place his own beyond his reach, subject to your option concerning his withdrawal. You repel, when you should attract him, if you require him to spend two days to withdraw his deposit, when one would suffice. Everything, consistent with perfect security, must yield to the convenience of the depositor. The system, to be perfect, must be attractive, and among the attractive features, by no means the least considerable, is this guarantee to return to the depositor his money on demand.

We are prepared, therefore, to discuss this question of investments under the three-fold aspect of security, profit and repayment on call. The first two are so intimately allied that they cannot well be considered separately.

The investments, commonly and justly regarded as most safe and reliable under all emergencies, are what are denominated

Public Stocks.

These are the obligations in the form of stocks and bonds—terms used interchangeably—or interest-bearing notes, of a Government possessing the power to *tax* its people, or otherwise to command a revenue. Whilst there is no power less considerable than the Government itself that can coerce the payment of its obligations, this power of the Government to *coerce its people, through taxation*, to furnish means for the payment of debts contracted in their name, on their behalf, and in their interest, affords a far better guarantee than would be a right of action at law.

There are, of course, remote contingencies possible, that may defeat the redemption of the obligations of a sovereign State. It may perish by conquest, or be dissolved by internal strife, or it may incur obligations so largely disproportioned to the resources of its people that payment is impossible. Whatever significance these considerations may have in their relation to the effete monarchies of Europe, to the semi-civilized republics of Mexico and South America, or to the experimental State-craft of the late so-called Confederate States, they have none whatever in relation to the government of the United States, or of the State of New York. The debt of the United States, large as it is, beyond precedent in our history, if it be wisely funded in long term bonds, as it may be with judicious management, will prove to be altogether within the assured ability of the country to discharge within any rational period of payment. The same is true of the debt of this State, and indeed of any State in the Union whose debt was incurred for legitimate purposes not hostile to the general government. True, the bonds of some of the States were greatly jeopardized by the late war, but the restoration of peace, though not of course followed by immediate resumption, has resulted in efforts in that direction, such as give a strong assurance of ultimate payment with interest. The restoration of these States to political tranquility, their practical relations with the general government renewed, their paralyzèd industry invigorated by the institution of free labor, their exhaustless resources developed and applied to practical results, the infusion of new elements of enterprise and activity, when wrought into the reorganized structure of their society, as these must be in a few years, will witness an era of material prosperity transcending all past experience. Of the $9,000,000 of bonds of other States held by our savings banks, I apprehend there will be no material loss sustained beyond the deferred payment of interest.

Another feature that imparts to public stocks a marked value over other securities is their ready convertibility, under all ordinary circumstances, at the full value expressed upon their face. Of course there will be extraordinary occasions when even public stocks can not be thrown upon an open market except at a loss, but such occasions are exceptional to all ordinary rules, and must be specifically provided against. But even at such times the fluctuations of public stocks will be less than of others, and it is their steady, reliable character, promising no splendid return, but fulfilling the promise made, that makes them favorites for permanent investment.

Municipal Securities.

Another class of securities in which savings banks are authorized to invest, by chapter 257, Laws of 1853, and by some of the later charters, [see appendix] is the bonds of municipal corporations, as cities, villages, counties or towns, in this State. This authorization is not however uniform, as the general act referred to applies only to savings banks in the counties of New York and Kings, and the charters that embrace this general provision are comparatively few. Very many, however, do authorize investments in city bonds, and a less number in the bonds of both cities and counties of this State, besides a general law of 1863 and 1864, authorizes investments in county and city bonds. I can conceive of no good reason for making any discrimination between savings banks in regard to this class of investments. If safe, they are safe for all ; if unsafe, they are perilous to any. They should be open to all or closed to all, according as they abide the test which we are now applying to all securities, to determine their character as a safe and proper investment for savings banks. A thorough analysis of their character, for the purposes of such a test is now in order.

They are in a limited sense *public stocks;* they are also in a stricter sense corporate stocks, being issued by a municipal or political corporation, as a city, village county or town. For the purpose of denoting the distinction between these and government stocks, national or State, on the one hand, and the stocks or bonds of private corporations on the other, I shall, perhaps with more precision than strict propriety, characterize these as MUNICIPAL SECURITIES. They are more commonly spoken of as BONDS than as STOCKS, which latter designation is applied more generally to the bonded debt of the State or of the general government. In the summary of charters found in the appendix, I have for the convenience of uniformity called them generally "stocks," though in the statutes they are commonly termed bonds, while Government and State securities are called stocks. The distinction between stocks and bonds is really so marked and obvious, that I regard it as unfortunate that the terms should ever have become so confused as to be used interchangeably ; but taking terms and things as we find them, and not as we would have them, I shall hope to avoid confusion by following the nomenclature above indicated.

The first savings bank charter in this State, that of the Bank for Savings in the city of New York, authorized investments to be made only in United States or New York State stocks, but in the following year, 1820, an amendment was procured, authorizing investments upon the credit of the city of New York, by loaning its funds to that corporation. The nature of the security is of course the same, whether the loan be made directly to the city upon its obligation, expressed in some due and legal form, to repay, or be made by the purchase in open market of its obligations, legally made and duly exposed for sale.

The principle of municipal credit as a reliable security for savings bank investments, was thus early recognized. I do not need to trace the growth and extension of this principle, in its application to other cities than New York, to counties, and finally to towns. The curious in such matters will find it fully detailed in the various charters and amendments cited in the appendix, and in the general laws there given in full. But we do not propose to follow precedents that challenge us upon the ground of their high authority, their venerable antiquity, or their unbroken uniformity, but as they are commended to our favorable judgment by the voice of reason and the teachings of a salutary experience.

Our inquiry is only concerning the character of municipal securities as a safe and prudent investment for savings banks.

These municipalities not being, like the State, sovereign over all their domestic affairs, not possessing in themselves unlimited power to contract debt and to tax the people for its payment, they can act only under a delegated authority. They must be *empowered* by law to contract the debt acknowledged by their obligations in the form of bonds, and to levy the necessary taxes for its payment. Hence, the authority conferred upon savings banks, by either special or general laws, to invest in municipal securities is commonly restricted in terms to such securities as are authorized by law. The form in which this restriction is expressed is not the same in all charters, some requiring an authority to tax for the means of payment, as a condition precedent to investment; while others, and the greater number require only the authority of the Legislature to incur the debt, and what is equivalent, to issue the bonds. The latter is the form of the provision in the general law of 1853, before cited. If any doubt were removed or additional security given, by conferring the taxing power in terms, where it is of course clearly implied, it were well to have it inserted as a condition of the investment; but otherwise, there can be no occasion to incumber the statute with needless provisions.

Another precedent condition of safety in such investments is, that the total indebtedness of any municipality, as thus authorized, shall not exceed its assured ability to pay. Several considerations enter into the determination of this question.

The first, is of course the ratio of the debt to the population, and more especially to the value of the taxable property of the municipality issuing its bonds. It would clearly be very unsafe to invest in the debt of a city or town, though authorized by the

Legislature to be contracted, if there were no limit to the amount of debt thus authorized. The safety of investments in municipal securities is found, therefore, to depend very greatly upon the discreet exercise of its powers by the Legislature. But the same is true, as we have seen, with regard to the character of PUBLIC STOCKS, and great as is the debt of cities, counties and towns in this State, I believe no one regards it as beyond the ability of those municipalities to pay, or its full payment at maturity as in the least degree doubtful. Indeed, we know from experience, as well as from public discussions and public records, that this aggregate of municipal debt, in our State, is being paid by means of taxation with unexampled rapidity. The fact of so heavy a debt affords occasion for wise counsels and prudent action by the Legislature in the delegation of power to create *further* debt, but I believe that from no quarter comes the expression of a fear lest the burden be already greater than we can bear, if only wise counsels *do* prevail concerning the imposition of further and additional burdens.

It must not, however, be overlooked that municipal indebtedness is in the nature of a third mortgage, the debt of the Nation and of the State being as it were *prior liens* upon all the productive resources of the country. The whole burden which the country has to bear, and of which the municipality must bear its due proportion, must be gravely considered in determining the value of municipal securities as an investment.

But other considerations than the present value of taxable property, and the aggregate of population, may enter into our estimate of the ability of a municipal corporation to faithfully fulfill its obligations. Such are, its rate of increase in wealth and population, as shown in its past history, and as estimated from a knowledge of its undeveloped resources, and the attractions which these hold forth to capital and enterprise, to go in and make it more populous and more productive. These are the considerations which give a more marked importance and a readier sale to city bonds; those of New York being always quickly absorbed by capital seeking investments, for the reason that the future growth and resulting financial ability of that city are, in the convictions of men, so unlimited.

On the other hand, a strictly rural community, as an agricultural county, will not bear nearly the proportion of debt to its population and taxable property, that will a manufacturing, or mining, or commercial county, for the reason that the future growth of the former will be inconsiderable as compared with that of the latter, and in the creation of any corporate debt the *future* is to a greater or less extent *discounted.*

Again, the *purpose* of the debt will more or less affect our estimate of its value as a security. The owner of valuable lots in the city of New York will sell them, and advance money besides, to the purchaser who will erect dwellings or stores upon the property purchased. He invests his money in a *debt* amply secured by the increased value of the property which that money has helped to improve. Considered as a purely commercial transaction, independent of the sentiment of patriotism, the debt incurred for destructive purposes, as in war, or of unproductive investment, as in public buildings, is less promising as a security than if incurred for public improvements that enhance the value of property, or increase the productive resources of the community. True, the contracting of debt for *destructive* purposes *may be* the highest wisdom, as in the case of our own, where the object was to preserve the government upon which the value of *all* investments depends. But this is the force of a stern necessity, like that of a traveler waylayed by robbers, who cheerfully surrenders his purse, if he may thereby save his life:—he may have made a good investment *under the circumstances*, but he will hardly regard it on the whole as a splendid financial transaction, which it is desirable to repeat at frequent intervals.

Of course, considerations like these can never arise where there is a manifest and unquestioned ability to pay, regardless of the purpose for which the debt was incurred, but that they are pertinent to a full discussion of the conditions of safety in making investments, is apparent from a suggestion like this: Suppose all the bonds issued by the city of New York during the last fifty years, had been for *riot damages*, instead of being so largely for public improvements, like the Croton Water Works, or the Central Park, would they have been negotiated as easily, as advantageously, to the city, as they have been? or would they in such case have been as safe and reliable a security for holders, as the bonds of that city now are? The suggestion answers itself, and covers the whole ground of the present discussion.

In this view, the bonds of a town, to an amount within an ascertained and reasonable proportion of its taxable property, given in aid of a railroad that will, first, be additional taxable property within its borders, and secondly, by opening up easier communication with markets, enhance the value of real estate, tend to promote immigration, and the consequent construction of more houses, the cultivation of more acres, and generally the productive power, the debt paying ability of the people, are certainly a more secure investment than would be the bonds of the same town given for the same amount, for a purpose unconnected with such prospective development.

I would disclaim any purpose of furnishing an argument *pro* or *con* upon the ulterior question which has no place in this discussion, as to the policy or impolicy of conferring upon the people of towns authority to tax themselves for the benefit of private corporations, in anticipation of the public benefit to be derived from improvements thus aided. The whole scope of these reflections has reference only to the suggestion of the leading conditions of safety in municipal securities. If there is one thought that I would impress more earnestly than another in connection with this subject, it is, that only the wisdom and integrity of the people, expressed through their chosen representatives, can impart safety and value to any public securities, National, State or municipal.

There is a feature of municipal securities that we have not considered and that deserves a passing notice. There is no power in the people by whom, or in whose name, they are issued, to *repudiate* their obligations. The Legislature that authorized the debt to be contracted, and the levy of taxes to pay the same, may make its statute mandatory instead of permissive, and compel the enforcement of payment with all the power of the State. Even any defect in the law, or in the form of compliance with its provisions, may be, as they often have been, cured by subsequent legislation. Indeed, the Session Laws are full of statutes ratifying and confirming the action of towns and counties, in the creation of debts that had no shadow of legal validity until thus confirmed by the Legislature. Municipal securities are therefore free from the danger of repudiation, on the one hand, and of the subtleties of counsel who sometimes darken wisdom in dealing with the glorious uncertainties of law, on the other.

The admission of city and county bonds, as an investment for savings banks, is now quite general, and little question, I presume, is likely to arise in any quarter as to the propriety of continuing and extending the provision so as to embrace all savings banks. Concerning the further extension of the principle of municipal securities as an investment, so as to embrace village and town bonds, the question seems to me to be determined by precisely the same considerations as the other. If the authority to issue the securities is undoubted, if the prescribed forms of law have been complied with, if the amount of the debt authorized is, in view of all the circumstances to be considered, clearly within the limit of assured ability to pay, I can see no reason why the bonds of a town are not as secure an investment, as are the bonds of any city or county for their correspondingly larger proportion of debt.

The security of all municipal obligations rests, as we have seen and stated, finally, upon the same basis, the wisdom and integrity of the people expressed through their representatives in the Legislature. If we cannot confide in this security, it is because of our distrust in representative government itself, which with us is to distrust everything, and take away every incentive to accumulation.

Bonds and Mortgages

Are allowed as an investment by the charters of all savings banks, and, before public stocks became so abundant and so remunerative, were, because of their higher interest, a favorite form of investment. Their security as an investment, were taken under all the restrictions commonly imposed as to the proportionate value of the property to the amount loaned, and to the class of property, as improved, unincumbered, productive, &c., is as a rule, unquestioned. They are thus made a first lien upon property capable of producing an income.

In the abstract of charters, in the appendix, I have, for the sake of brevity, omitted the conditions, common to all charters, as to the kind of property upon which loans may be made, and also those which require the assignment of a policy of insurance, where any part of the estimated value is in the buildings, as the common instinct of prudence has, I believe, ever been sufficient to ensure such precautions, even when not specifically required. But, in a general act, I deem it best that it should contain the essence of all salutary provisions, and I have, accordingly, inserted there all the restrictive requirements that will ensure greater safety.

It will be observed, however, that there is no little diversity in the provisions concerning loans on bond and mortgage.

The first relates to the proportion of the amount loaned to the value of the property, most charters requiring the value to be twice the loan—a few, not more than three or four, authorizing loans of two-thirds the value. One-half the value may be regarded as the standard, and is as much as should be allowed. The restriction of some charters to a valuation, exclusive of buildings, seriously interferes with making desirable investments in this class of securities. The law seems to be defective, generally, however, in not providing for any authorized or competent appraisal of the value of the property.

As a convertible security, bonds and mortgages are not to be depended upon; their virtue is exhibited only in repose. For this reason it would be unwise to have too large a proportion of the deposits of savings banks invested in these, as they may be termed, *fixed securities.* While the average of investments in these securities, twenty-two per cent, does not appear to be too high, there are individual exceptions, as where the proportion is nearly seventy per cent. If this *is* too high a proportion to safely meet all the emergencies which savings banks may encounter, and to me it seems clear that it is, there is need that some limitation be expressed in the law; it is not safe to leave too much to the discretion of trustees, where, in any instance, that discretion has proved to be unwisely exercised.

My own judgment would be, that one-third of the amount of deposits is as large a portion as it is wise to have invested in securities so stable as bonds and mortgages, but deferring somewhat to the generally expressed opinion that the whole subject is better left to the discretion of Trustees, I provide in the act herewith submitted for 40 per cent of all the assets to be thus invested. This is nearly twice the average amount of this class of investments, and exceeds the proportion held by any of the savings banks, with nine exceptions.

Another point to be considered is the restriction upon the locality of lands on which loans shall be made. The provisions in this regard will be found to be various. Most restrict loans to lands located in this State, some to particular counties of this State, while a few are so broad in their provisions that loans may be made under them, upon real estate situated anywhere, from the Southern continent to our newly acquired territory at the North pole! I am clearly of opinion that loans should be restricted to lands lying in this State, where the laws relating to conveyances may be presumed to be well understood, and where disputed questions of law would be determined by judges elected by our own people, and questions of fact by a jury of our own citizens.

With regard to the question of further limitation, as to the county where the bank is located, or counties adjoining, something may be said upon both sides, but the weight of argument appears to me to be opposed to further territorial restriction than the boundaries of our own State. The opposing argument to this view entitled to most consideration, is the difficulty of securing reliable and disinterested testimony in localities remote from the institution, of the value of the lands on which the loan is to be effected. But the objection would be nearly as strong against any less limitation than the county itself. If trustees have *no* sense of responsibility, and are *disposed* to make loans regardless of the character of the security, they are perhaps as liable to do this upon lands within their own county as upon those more distant. If it be provided that in addition to any other testimony concerning the value of premises, the appraisal of the supervisor of the town shall be procured, or if in a remote city, of the mayor of the city, I think the ample security of such loans will be assured. Another question that has exercised my mind not a little in this connection, is to what extent, and under what circumstances, if any, the value of buildings should be excluded from the appraised value of premises.

It would seem that with the assignment of a policy of insurance for such amount, as would leave the balance secured by the land alone, amply protected, the safety of the investment would be assured. But there are some considerations bearing upon this question that can not be dismissed without examination. First, such security is practically an investment in a *risk*. The loan is not made upon the value of the real estate, but upon the solvency of an insurance company. It may be solvent—it may not. Failures of insurance companies, and failure to pay policies in consequence, are not unknown to our history. And besides, the claim may be contested upon any one of a thousand pretexts, valid or otherwise, and the expense of litigation incurred; or the defense to the claim may be sustained, and the loss of the claim be added to the expenses and costs of a suit. Are not these contingencies too many and too real to be lightly considered? They are such as have been suggested to me by managers of savings banks, and have impressed me with much force. But in answer, it will be said, that in our large cities, as in New York, where the chief value of premises is in the buildings, loans could never be effected unless these were duly considered in the appraisal. This is doubtless true—but would after all not be a conclusive answer to the objection stated, if it could be demonstrated, that such risks were as a rule, or to any considerable extent, unsafe. But is such a proposition demonstrable? The *rule* is, that policies of insurance *are paid;* failure to pay is the rare exception. All experience substantiates this, and we have a right to be guided in the future, by uniform experience in the past. The losses from such risks would then, under the general law of averages, be very few and comparatively small. Such losses might be borne without impairing the integrity of the institutions incurring them. The preservation of every savings bank from the possible loss of any possible amount, is an attainment at which in this discussion we have not aimed; we would do this if we could, but it is hardly possible to do this and do anything, except hoard the deposits without investment at all. We seek to protect the *depositors* against any possible loss. A savings bank may sustain, now and then, a trifling loss, whose worst result will be a slight diminution of its gross profits. The depositor need not suffer in mind, body or estate, from such few losses as would accrue from risks of the character we speak of. The surplus may be a little impaired by them; or if they occur in the earlier history of the institution, may retard its growth for a time, but on the whole, I can see in this form of investment no real danger threatening the integrity of the system, or putting in peril the sacred principle of *safety*, which is our guiding star.

Investments authorized by the charter of a savings bank would, of course, where there were no special conditions imposed, be legitimately effected upon the vote of a majority of a quorum of trustees. But investments in bond and mortgage are frequently guarded by restrictions like the following:

In some charters the loan must be approved by the unanimous vote of a quorum of trustees; in others by the affirmative vote of a certain number; in others by a vote of the majority of all the trustees present and absent; in others by the unanimous vote of all the trustees present; and in others by the affirmative vote of those present—not more than one, two or three dissenting—the number varying in different charters.

The form and connection in which these restrictive provisions are commonly introduced are singularly infelicitous, and have the strange effect of closing the door to injudicious investments in one direction, only to open it wide to an unlimited discretion in another!

That such is not the design of the law I fully believe, but that such *is* its practical effect will appear from the following citation, and from the fact that under the power thus conferred savings banks *do* invest in corporate and other securities, nowhere specifically authorized in terms. The following is an extract from the charter of one savings bank, and is substantially like that of many others :

" No money deposited in the said bank shall be invested, except in the securities of stocks mentioned in this section, in opposition to the vote of any three trustees ; but money may be loaned by it on unincumbered real estate worth at least double the amount to be secured thereby."

In the act herewith submitted, I have endeavored to surround with proper safeguards the effecting of loans upon bond and mortgage, without incorporating therewith incongruous provisions to render nugatory the salutary restrictions of the law concerning other investments.

Real Estate.

A characteristic feature in the charters of all savings banks in this State, is the limitation imposed upon their power to acquire and hold real property. The object of this limitation is obviously to avoid the dangers to which these institutions would be exposed, if the trustees were authorized to employ the large means at their command in the wild and hazardous speculations incident to "operations" in real estate. Great gains, fabulous profits, even if they could be assured, would, when realized, tend to the utter demoralization of these institutions. Their simple and beneficent character and purpose as a means to the encouragement of habits of industry and economy, would speedily be changed, and they become excited centers of worldliness, craft and greed. The standard of their success would no longer be solid investments, moderate profits, prompt payment and impregnable strength, but colossal operations, brilliant manifestoes, and magnificent dividends. No longer the resort of the industrious and frugal, their doors would be thronged by frenzied adventurers of every degree, eager to clutch the prized and promised *cent per cent.* But such success, so destructive of every principle that renders savings banks an object of solicitude and pride, could not be enduring. No axiom is more familiar in mathematics than this in finance, that great profits and great hazards keep company together. In a system of institutions conducted upon the scale above planned, some one, sooner or later, would be over-expanded, burst, and be buried forever amid the general ruin it had wrought. The design of securing for these institutions only such a moderate degree of prosperity as should perfectly serve the purpose of their creation, preserve them from great temptations, which dazzle only to blind and to destroy, or from being themselves a temptation to the avarice and greed of others, was wisely conceived, and by no provisions is that design more effectually promoted than by those which limit their acquisition of real property.

Besides the real estate which savings banks are authorized to acquire by foreclosure of mortgages, the enforcement of judgments, or to secure the payment of debts due to them, all of which are essential to save them from loss in their investments, they are further authorized to hold "such as may be requisite for their immediate accommodation for the convenient transaction of their business." The possession by a savings bank of a place of business which it can call its own, over which it has absolute and undisputed control, I regard as important for the following among other reasons :

It imparts an air of permanence and stability to its business, justifying greater confidence in its dealings.

It insures suitable and convenient apartments for the transaction of business, which are not always procurable on lease.

The furniture and fixtures are permanent, and not subject to impaired value by the wear and tear of removal from place to place, and their refitting to premises for which they were not originally constructed.

The expense of fitting up new rooms from time to time is saved.

The hazards to which their securities are exposed by frequent removal are avoided.

It gives to the institution the option of its associates, by no means an unimportant consideration in view of the nature of its business.

It affords an opportunity for greater security against robbery, by the construction of a suitable vault, and against fire, by a choice in location, or by the erection of a fire-proof building.

Desirable as is the possession of a banking house, several points should be well considered before such investment is resolved upon.

First, The institution should have been in operation so long, that a safe judgment may be formed concerning its permanent success, under all the emergencies to which it may be exposed.

Second. Its prosperity, whether great or only moderate in *degree* should be of a solid, enduring character ; not ephemeral, spasmodic, the result of transient causes, or unusual conditions that may speedily pass away.

Third. The ratio of interest received, to fair dividends declared for a series of years past, should be carefully estimated, to see whether the margin will justify so large a non-productive investment.

Fourth. Into the above estimate, the saving of rent and other expenses, incident to the occupation of leased premises will enter; also, *per contra*, the necessary current expenses of the institution, as affecting the margin of net profits for investments, upon which the expediency of building depends.

Fifth. The surplus of assets over liabilities must be duly considered, for it can hardly be deemed prudent, upon even the most favorable showing of net profits, to put in the fixed form of real estate, any considerable sum for which there is even a remote liability of demand.

To illustrate, I will suppose the case of a savings bank in one of our interior towns :

Its assets are, say		$300,000
Liabilities		288,000
Surplus		$12,000
Received for interest, average 6 per cent		$18,000
Paid depositors dividends, average 5 per cent	$12,000	
Current expenses	5,500	
		17,500
Net surplus account		$500
Banking house will cost, say		$15,000
Interest on that amount at 6 per cent		$900
Deduct rent of premises occupied, say		200
Institution debtor to annual difference of		$700
Equivalent to a principal sum of		$11,600

It will be seen that the above calculation does not include certain items, as taxes, insurance, etc., incident to the ownership of real estate, and which will at least partially offset the saving effected in rent.

It is easy from these data to determine upon the expediency of investing in a banking house. The assets, invested at an average rate of six per cent, yield a net profit to the institution after paying dividends and expenses, of $500. If they invest $15,000 in a banking house yielding no income, they diminish their annual receipts by the sum of $900, but save the expense of rent, $200, leaving a practical reduction of income equal to $700. But this leaves them $200 less than will be required to pay dividends and expenses. It will not do to trust to an increase of business to make good the deficiency, for the business *may not* increase, may indeed diminish, and in the management of savings banks, *nothing* must be left to *chance.* If the banking house is built under conditions like those assumed, the trustees must either reduce the rate of dividends or declare them from anticipated profits in the future. The former is an unpleasant alternative; the latter, not upon any consideration to be entertained for a moment. The only safe course, in such case, is to defer the erection of a banking house until the ratio of profits to expenses and dividends will leave a larger working margin for an unproductive investment.

In the above estimates we have left out of view the question of revenue to be derived from renting a portion of the premises not required by the institution for its own use.

Only, by a most liberal, not to say forced, construction of the statute above cited, can it be made to sanction the erection or purchase of a banking house, from which an income in the way of rents may be derived. But such practice is not uncommon. The Metropolitan Savings Bank, in New York city, has recently erected a banking house which it is estimated can be made to yield an income from rents, equal to eight per cent upon the cost, leaving them the use of a splendid and commodious banking room, and other apartments, upon the first floor, rent free. Safe and reliable investments for savings banks, at so profitable a rate, are rare indeed. If such an investment is contrary to law, the law should be amended, and made conformable to reason and the fitness of things. It is unreasonable that savings banks should be allowed to erect a banking house for their own accommodation, at a very considerable expense, but should be prohibited from adding another story to an inconsiderable additional expense, from which a moderate income upon the whole investment may be derived. No comparison can be instituted between a single specific investment like this, and a general indiscriminate power to purchase, hold and convey real estate, such as was characterized in our opening remarks upon this subject.

The statute in its present form leads to anomalies like this. A savings bank in one of the cities of our State, has a fine, commodious, well-appointed banking house, of ample dimensions upon the ground, and two stories in height. In answer to my inquiry concerning the use made of the second story, I was informed, that as the charter did not authorize the savings bank to derive an income from its banking house, the second floor of the building had been fitted up as a public hall, and was used *gratuitously* for that purpose!

It struck me that the *logic* of the *law*, rigorously applied, would reach a conclusion a *little earlier* than it had done in their experience, and would have stopped short, about where the second story began, and left them there in the full possession of the real estate "requisite for their immediate accommodation for the convenient transaction of business!"

It follows, of course, that where a banking house is to be constructed with a view to an income from any portion not required by the institution for its own use, the questions of expediency and safety in making such investment will be materially changed.

Thus, in the case above supposed, if by an expenditure of $15,000 a building can be erected which, besides furnishing proper accommodations for the bank, will produce an income of say $600, we have in this, and the saving of rent, a revenue from the investment equal to $800,—leaving $400 per annum as the net profit to favor of surplus account. Practically it adds $100 a year to their expenses for rent.

If for any reason, a savings bank prefers the exclusive occupancy of its premises, and is so strong as to be able to afford the indulgence, there is of course no objection to it; but they should have the right of choice between that, and an investment in that form, yielding an income.

A few charters limit the gross value of the real estate that may thus be held for "its accommodation," while the older charters limit the annual value of the estate so held, but couple the limitation with a proviso or condition, or explanation, or *something*, that I have spent much time in the vain effort to comprehend. If I may judge from the practice of the various institutions, under that form of provision, it means *nothing at all*, and that is very nearly what I have made of it!

It will be apparent upon suggestion, that no arbitrary sum can be fixed as the limit of investment in a banking house. But the general conditions of such investment, upon the basis given in previous pages, should be expressed in the law.

Under such limitations as to time and circumstances, as I have ind cated, I regard an investment of a reasonable proportion of the funds of a savings bank, in real estate for its own use, and for a moderate income, as every way expedient and desirable.

These then, PUBLIC STOCKS, BONDS OF MUNICIPAL CORPORATIONS, BONDS AND MORTGAGES, properly restricted as to the value of premises, as to proportions of assets invested in them, and REAL ESTATE, to the extent of a banking house for use and for income when desirable, are in my own mind, as they are in existing recognition of law, and as confirmed by a long and successful experience, the investments through which savings banks may be made secure und impregnable depositories of the savings of our people.

Among all the opinions that have been expressed by officers of savings banks, but one has proposed that this limitation be enlarged. Most of those that regard the present provisions of law in regard to investments as too rigid, are excluded from the operation of the general law of 1853, authorizing investment in bonds of cities, counties and towns in this State, and they only desire that the privilege of investment thus accorded should be extended to all savings banks alike. This desire is natural and just, and should be favorably considered, though many seem not to be aware that the acts of 1863 and 1864 do extend the power to invest in city and county bonds, uniformly to all savings banks in the State.

A few have favored a limitation that would exclude county and town bonds, but I can see no reason as before stated why these, when authorized by the Legislature, are not as safe as the bonds of cities that depend for their security upon the diseretion exercised by the same Sovereign Power.

But, as I have already shown, there is a provision in many charters under which they may, and under which some *do* invest in corporate securities, as railroad bonds. This provision was clearly never designed to give such authority, and should at once be effaced from the statutes relating to these institutions. I believe the discretion that has been exercised in regard to such investments has been as prudent as any discretion in that direction could be, but "that way is death" to the principle of perfect security upon which alone these institutions can long endure. The admission of such securities *at all* must be without discrimination by the statute, leaving the selection, of course, to the wisdom of trustees. But if we may depend upon their wisdom to select from a class of securities, some of which are good, some bad, some indifferent and some worthless, why then need any restriction be imposed at all? There is but one safe way, and that is to limit the discretion of trustees in making investments, to those securities which, as a class, rest upon the firm foundations of *public wealth* and *public faith*, or upon such real security as nothing less than an earthquake can jeopardize.

Strangely enough, one of the older charters does authorize investment in certain bank stocks—but the privilege has never been exercised.

Judged by this standard, we find in the condition of our savings banks the most gratifying evidences of security and strength. Eighty-four per cent of the investments of these institutions is in the securities whose superiority and value we have so fully considered. This is exclusive of investments in real estate, which are so commonly reported at merely nominal value, that they could not properly enter into a fair estimate of the true proportion they bear to other investments. I need only say, that my best observation enforces the conviction, that the real estate held by these institutions, either yields an income that makes it a profitable investment, or is held for the exclusive use of the institution, by those savings banks only whose surplus in other and convertible securities fully justifies their action.

Surplus as an Element of Safety.

In previous pages the surplus of savings banks has been considered as a sign of their prosperity. It is proper in this connection to consider this surplus as an indispensable element of strength and safety.

If a savings bank were subject to no contingencies in its business, if it were possible to protect every institution from any possible loss, no surplus would be required. But this we have shown and know to be impracticable. The profoundest wisdom, the most penetrating sagacity, the most consummate financial skill, is vain to place any one of these institutions upon a basis of absolute exemption from loss. These qualities, with strict integrity and conscientious care, may greatly diminish the chances of misfortune, but cannot eliminate them altogether. It must needs be that, sooner or later, slight or heavy losses will come. A bank of issue in which savings deposits are kept may fail, a claim for insurance may be successfully resisted, skillful burglars may get access to the cash, investments must sometimes be made at a premium that only return par on the day of redemption, or securities must sometimes be converted at a discount to meet unexpected emergencies. In these and many other ways which we need not enumerate, savings banks are exposed to perils which all cannot be so fortunate as to escape. We can only guard against needless exposure to these perils, and provide a means whereby the severity of the misfortune, when it comes, shall be greatly mitigated ; means that will enable the institution to sustain its losses without impairing its ability to meet in full the demands of every depositor. But this can only be done by the accumulation of a surplus of assets over all liabilities for the purpose of meeting such contingencies. In no other way can perfect security against loss be assured to the depositor. In this way it can be assured ; and yet, strangely enough, the provisions of the statutes in regard to this surplus, upon which the security of the depositor so greatly depends, are only permissive. If anything connected with the management of savings banks should be obligatory this should be. If in anything the discretion of trustees should be controlled by law, this, upon which so much depends, should surely be thus controlled.

No savings bank should be permitted to declare more than five per cent dividends, until it has accumulated a surplus of at least five per cent of its assets.

With regard to savings banks to be organized hereafter, such a provision is practicable, and would have the salutary effect of checking the mania for organizing these institutions in localities already sufficiently accommodated. To make such a requirement of savings banks already organized, might lead to consequences not only perilous to their own integrity, but embarrassing in kindred institutions. Concerning these, it will be better to leave them at liberty to declare such dividends as they can, from actual earnings, after paying necessary expenses, and putting aside one-half per cent per annum to account of surplus.

The amount of gross surplus which savings banks should be authorized to accumulate, presents a question upon which honest opinions may differ. The weight of opinion, so far as it has been expressed in answer to my inquiries, favors from fifteen to twenty per cent. With five per cent. as a minimum, I regard fifteen per cent. as a safe and sufficient maximum, and have so incorporated it in the general act submitted to your approval.

Payment of Depositors on Demand.

Having thus, by a carefully selected class of authorized investments, and by the accumulation of a reasonable surplus, provided beyond all contingency for the security of depositors, and for fair dividends from the profits of those investments, we are prepared now to consider how we may, without impairing that security, assure to them the repayment of th ir money with its accrued profits, on demand.

Obviously, this can only be done, by reserving from investment in a form available for use at any moment, a sufficient amount of cash funds to meet the calls of depositors. Such cash reserve has received in the charters of savings banks the designation of an "Available Fund," and by that name it will be known throughout this report.

The exact amount or proportion of the deposits in any savings bank which it may be necessary to keep thus available, it is impossible to determine. It will, of course, vary with times, seasons and circumstances. It will not be uniform with the same bank at different periods; it may not be the same with any two banks at the same time, and having each the same amount of deposits. As a rule, a new or nearly new institution, will require a larger available fund in proportion to its deposits than an old institution. And I would here suggest that this is one of the sources of peril arising from multiplying these institutions in the same locality. The new cannot attract deposits, unless they offer equal inducements in the way of dividends with the old. But the absence of surplus, and the necessity of keeping a larger available fund, compels a resort to dangerous expedients, in the way of declaring unearned dividends, or of making call loans upon doubtful securities.

But to return to the immediate topic of discussion, the amount or proportion to the deposits of this available fund, will best be determined by the practical experience of each institution.

And yet there must be some limit within which the discretion of trustees in this matter may properly be confined. If we cannot fix the least amount that will suffice for the purpose, because of the varying conditions to which it is to be applied, we certainly can determine what is the greatest amount that the common emergencies of savings banks will require. So surely as it cannot be necessary to hold *all*, nor even *half* of the deposits of any institution in available form for immediate use, so surely must there be some practicable limit, beyond which in this matter, it is not desirable to permit the trustees of these institutions to pass.

The central idea in the original institution of savings banks, as is evident from the declared purpose of their charters, and the powers conferred, and the duties imposed upon their corporators, was the *investment* of the deposits received by them, in unfailing secuiities. "Shall receive all sums of money that may be offered, &c., *for the purpose of being invested, etc.*," is the language of the *first* savings bank charter in this State.

Investment was made the first duty, the primary obligation; repayment was second, not only in the necessary order of events, but in the degree of obligation imposed; for this was required only under such regulations as the corporators themselves should prescribe. Of course such regulations could only be made with reference to a strict conformity to the mandatory provisions of the law concerning investment.

It was evidently conceived that in case there should not be on the whole a steady preponderance of deposits over the drafts, from which the latter could be met, the securities would at all times be convertible with sufficient readiness to meet the deficiency. Hence in this first charter there was no provision authorizing any available fund to be kept, nor even so much as the deposit in bank of temporary balances awaiting investment. The first provision authorizing deposits to be made in banks of issue was by amendment to this charter in 1830, and the term "available fund" first appears in the charter of the Buffalo Savings Bank in 1846.

That this central idea has not been lost sight of amid all the changes of the last half century is evident from the following:

"The object of the corporation hereby created shall be to receive on deposit such sums as may be offered therefor, and *investing* the same, etc.," "which deposits shall, as soon as practicable, *be invested* accordingly," is (with a singular disregard of the rules of grammar) the language of the *last* savings bank charter in this State.

But while this central idea of *investment* has been kept most prominently in view in all the statutes relating to savings banks, the idea of an available fund has of late years been steadily growing into prominence and favor, until it bids fair to be as distinguishing a feature of our savings bank system as is investment itself, and even now *more than half* the charters, original or amended, of these institutions, authorize an available fund of one-third of the deposits with the institution, "to be kept on deposit, on interest or otherwise, in such available form as the trustees may direct." (See provisions of charter, Appendix.)

Our practical concern is to know whether so large an uninvested fund can be necessary for the successful working of any savings bank or to enable it to meet any emergencies to which, in its legitimate business, it may be exposed. Fortunately we are not without some very convincing, if not conclusive, proofs on this question.

The largest and best conducted institutions have never reported nearly so large an available fund on hand. Their practice is to keep closely invested, and the experience they have had in passing through the financial vicissitudes of the last twenty or fifty years, enables them to judge with great accuracy as to what is necessary in this respect.

The general practice of savings banks is equally emphatic in its testimony as to the necessity for an available fund equal to one-third of the deposits. Leaving out the three, that though reporting, were practically closing on the first of January, 1867, and those which had commenced business during the previous year, and hence do not afford a just standard for estimate, and we find but fourteen whose available fund exceeded twenty-five per cent of their assets, and but twenty that exceeded twenty per cent, while more than half, and these including most of the largest and best institutions in the State, held not exceeding fifteen per cent of their assets as an available fund.

If more than half the savings banks, embracing some in all localities, cities, towns, vilages and farming districts, can do a safe and prosperous business, and meet promptly all the demands of their depositors, with an available fund varying from one and a half to fifteen per cent, as is the fact, is it not safe to assume that the remainder do not require a larger available fund than the maximum employed by the greater number?

Again the experiences to which savings banks have been subjected in passing through some of the more trying ordeals of our financial history, bring their testimony to aid in the solution of this question.

The year 1857 will best serve the purpose of illustration, for the reason that its bitter experiences still linger in the memory of men, and because we have no general report of the condition and workings of savings banks of an earlier date. Besides our gloomiest apprehensions for the future, fail to picture to the imagination aught more forbidding or disastrous, than fell upon us in that memorable year.

In that year the withdrawals exceeded the deposits by the total amount of $1,711.239, which was about four per cent of the total deposits at the beginning of the year. It thus appears that if the savings banks could have anticipated the full extent of the approaching crisis and its effect upon their business, they would have been fully prepared for it by putting aside four per cent of their deposits at the beginning of the year, together with the deposits made during the year. It is true, that as some of these deposits were made during the latter part of the year, after the panic had ceased these would have been unavailing as a part of the reserve to meet the unusual demands made during the crisis; but on the other h ınd, we have not considered the sums received by the savings banks for interest during the nine months of the year prior to the panic, and which, if the necessity could have been anticipated, might have been reserved to meet the exigency. From any point of view, therefore, four per cent of the deposits, together with the income from all sources, would have been ample to carry the savings banks of the State triumphantly through the crisis of 1857, and if through that, then certainly through any that is likely to sweep down upon us. I do not forget that while it is easy thus to demonstrate that an available fund of four per cent if distributed among savings banks according to their needs, would, together with the income of the year, have successfully carried them through the revulsion of '57, it by no means establishes the fact that such a reserve would have sufficed for each savings bank. This four per cent is the average drain upon the resources of all the institutions in the State. Some exceeded this average, while others of course fell short of it, and in some indeed the deposits even exceeded the withdrawals during that year. But such average is useful in revealing the aggregate or general result of the most unfavorable conditions, and accepting that as the minimum for which provision must be made, we have a basis upon which to estimate a maxium that will suffice for all emergencies.

Again, we have been considering, not the ordinary but the extraordinary necessities of savings banks, and the amount of available means required to meet the unusual demands at such periods. But it is not the part of wisdom to establish general laws, or to regulate usual practices upon the basis of exceptional conditions. The law should be adapted to the ordinary experience and needs of these institutions, with flexible provisions, applicable to unusual emergencies only.

The average business of our savings banks for the last six years, if it could have been anticipated, would have justified commencing business in 1862, without a dollar of reserve, depending upon deposits to pay depositors, and not only would they have sufficed, but have left a surplus, for investment, of $74,500,000 !

It is true this remarkable history could *not* be anticipated, and because it could not, some provision for possible reverses was necessary ; but if there is any virtue in the teachings of experience, we cannot fail to be instructed by these, that the provision for an available fund of one-third of the deposits of a savings bank, is founded upon a gross misconception of the requirements, either ordinary or extraordinary, of these institutions.

For the ordinary transactions of a savings bank firmly established and in a healthy condition, an available fund equal to ten per cent of the assets is ample provision, and many of our best institutions keep within this limit.

But causes may sometimes operate to check deposits and stimulate withdrawals, until an available fund of ten per cent will be exhausted.

An illustration of these has already been suggested in the experience of some savings banks last spring whose resources were much impaired by the withdrawal of deposits to answer the speculative movement in real estate.

But such conditions do not require to be provided for by a large available fund. Whenever deposits are withdrawn, because of the activity in any line of investments, there will be, in the nature of things, a favorable market for such securities as a savings bank should hold, and if all available resources are exhausted, then let securities be sold to meet the exigencies of the occasion. What are the securities for, if not to be converted when the depositor wants his money and the institution has invested to its last dollar?

But stagnation in business, the suspension of trade, the stopping of manufactories, by which causes, laborers in great numbers, are thrown out of employment, will affect the prosperity of savings banks, and greatly impair, if they do not exhaust, their available means provided for ordinary contingencies. Securities can not perhaps be sold at such times except at a loss; but what is the accumulated surplus for, but to meet just such occasions when they arise? There is a palpable inconsistency in making provision at the same time for a large surplus and for a large available fund. If a savings bank has the large available fund it has no occasion for a large surplus; or if it have the large surplus there is less occasion for a large available fund. In my own mind the preference is very decidedly in favor of the large surplus and a moderate available fund.

Banks not thoroughly established, must needs keep a larger amount of money subject to call than those whose general course of business, and the demands of the future upon whom, can, as a rule, be safely predicated from their past experience.

To meet the requirements of all, therefore, in their several conditions, and to remove all possibility of embarrassment to the free action of savings banks within the limits of assured safety, provision might be made for an available fund equal to twenty per cent of the deposits.

Most institutions would, as they now do, keep very far within this amount, and the Superintendent should be vested with power to interpose for the correction of any abuse in the exercise of the discretion conferred. Thus any savings bank that should obviously be controlled in the interest of a bank of discount desirous of securing the available fund as its deposit, whereby the dividends to depositors should be unreasonably diminished, or the accumulation of surplus be arrested, should be subject to the requirement of the Superintendent to change its policy, and invest a larger amount of its deposits in the securities authorized by law.

It is a significant fact that of the twenty-four savings banks that have more than fifteen per cent of assets deposited in bank, eleven are carried on by banks of discount, and of the remainder, two are converting their assets into cash for the purpose of closing, and three are but recently organized, and have hardly been able to make investments, hence are not proper subjects of comparison.

And of the rest, the least average deposit in bank, is kept by those not conducted by banks of discount.

Whatever available fund is provided and reserved, must obviously be kept in one of three ways: First, on hand in the vault or safe of the institution. Second, on deposit in bank, at not exceeding usually four per cent interest: or, Third, loaned on call on some kind of collateral security.

The proportion kept on hand in the institution is usually very small, as is proper that it should be, for the reason that in such form it is wholly unproductive, and besides, it is in that way exposed to hazards from robbery and fire, which most savings banks have only ordinary means to guard against. The largest amount on hand is kept by the Bowery Savings Bank, which, besides its ability to keep so large a sum unproductive, has vaults of capacity and strength hardly exceeded by any in the country. Of course all savings banks, according to their means, take reasonable precautions to protect their cash and securities from these casualties, but perfect security can be obtained only at an expense which few institutions can afford to incur.

Nor is it expedient to keep so large an amount as twenty per cent on deposit in banks of discount. So large a sum, yielding ordinarily not more than four per cent interest, would seriously affect the prosperity of the savings banks, and interfere with the payment of reasonable dividends. Besides, there are perils attending deposits in bank, as some savings banks have learned to their cost.

The act of April 15, 1853, applicable to the savings banks in New York and Kings counties, authorized deposits to be made in any bank of discount, to an amount equal to ten per cent of its capital, provided such sum should not exceed twenty per cent of all the deposits belonging to the savings bank. This provision was amended April 10, 1858, by restricting the total deposits of any savings bank in all banks of discount to twenty per cent of the deposits belonging to it, and the amount to be kept in any one bank, to $100,000.

This arbitrary sum, or any arbitrary limit, I regard as both impracticable and unreasonable. Under it, a savings bank with $5,000,000 of deposits, and keeping only $500,000 available, is required to have five different bank accounts, and if for any reason it is found expedient to keep available the whole amount authorized by law, ten bank accounts must be opened for the purpose. This is a small matter to be sure, if the requirement in its general application is essential to the safety of any savings bank. But we shall see that the reverse of this is true, and that danger, rather than security, is involved in this form of restriction.

The institution that must employ ten depositories for the safe keeping of its available means, has not the option of a judicious selection enjoyed by one that need employ but two or three or five. Among ten there can hardly fail to be one or more in which $100,000 is not a more hazardous deposit, than would be $200,000 or even $500,000 in some of the others.

But most significant is the unequal operation of such a provision in the safety it ensures. Under it in the case above supposed, the savings bank has exposed to the hazard of the failure of any one bank but two per cent of its deposits. Another institution, with deposits amounting to $500,000, may, under the provisions of this act have twenty per cent thus exposed. The operation of this provision can certainly require no further illustration to render apparent its absurdity.

A more rational provision would be to limit the deposits authorized to be made in banks of discount to some proportion of their capital. This was done in the act of 1853; but the ratio authorized may have been too small, as it would allow of but $100,000 of deposits to $1,000,000 of capital; and its value as a safeguard was destroyed by the concurrent authority to keep on deposit, in one bank, twenty per cent of all the deposits belonging to any savings bank, provided this did not exceed the ten per cent of capital of the deposit bank. A savings bank having $200,000 of deposits might thus deposit in a bank having $400,000 of capital, the whole of its available fund. There is then, under this provision, of course, a chance of losing it all, for the history of bank failures in this as well as in other States, will furnish not a few instances in which not one per cent of the capital was found to be in any available assets, and no greater amount has been realized from the liability of stockholders. As no savings bank can lose twenty per cent of its deposits without great danger, if not an absolute certainty of failure, it is clearly the dictate of prudence to guard them from the remotest possibility of such loss. This can be done by restricting the amount which they shall be authorized to keep in any one bank, to five per cent of their entire deposits. This is enough to have exposed to the possibility of loss from this source. Had the savings bank whose experience is elsewhere narrated, been thus restricted, it would not have so early encountered misfortune—or at least none nearly so severe, and though the ultimate result in that case may not prove altogether disastrous—*it might have been*, and its experience should serve as a warning to others of the direction in which danger lies, and as an admonition to the Legislature to the exercise of greater care in providing effectual safeguards for these institutions.

I would consider such a provision preferable to one confining deposits to any ratio of the capital of deposit banks, though for additional safety the two provisions might, if deemed advisable, be incorporated together.

Under such restrictions, the smaller savings banks would be prevented from hazardous exposure of their deposits upon the good faith, integrity or financial ability of any one bank, while the larger institutions would have greater freedom than now, without increased risk.

If any reason for the exercise of great caution concerning the deposits of savings banks in banks of discount, further than appears in the foregoing discussion, is required, it will be found in the fact that these banks have now to a very great extent passed from the supervision and control of State authority. By section four of the act of 1853, the assets of any insolvent bank, after the redemption of its circulating notes, were directed to be applied *first* to the payment of the deposits therein of any savings bank, thus making savings banks preferred creditors over all other depositors. This was a most wise and salutary provision, but of little practical utility now, while our banks for the most part derive their authority from and pass into liquidation under the provisions of the National banking law.

In this view, the banks and trust companies organized under, and subject to the control of the laws of our own State, are to be preferred as depositories for savings banks.

Call Loans.

But the business of a savings bank may be of such a character as to seem to require the retention of an available fund of full twenty per cent of the deposits belonging to it—as at a time when good investments are difficult to make—while to keep so large a proportion of its assets unproductive, or yielding not more than four per cent income, may seriously impair its ability to make fair and reasonable dividends to depositors.

This contingency is provided for in many of the later charters, and in the act of 1853, by authorizing the savings banks to which they relate, to loan their deposits upon the security of the stocks in which they are authorized to invest; though by one of those strange inconsistencies which characterize the whole course of legislation on this subject, the act of 1853 fails to enumerate U. S. stocks among those upon which loans may be made.

The state of the law upon this question of loans will, therefore, be found extremely mixed; some charters making no provision for them, others recognizing them to the same extent that investments are authorized, some limiting the margin to ten per cent, and others to twenty-five, some making the margin upon the basis of the par value, others of the market value of the stocks, others requiring no margin at all; whilst over all, are the general provisions referred to, applicable to all the savings banks in New York and Kings counties.

But the provision lately so common, that sweeps away all the barriers of prudence and safety by which we have been wont to regard these institutions as fortified, is that to which reference has already been made, which authorizes an available fund of not exceeding one-third of the whole amount of deposits, "which may be kept on deposit, on interest, or otherwise, in such available form as the trustees may direct." And as if that language were not broad enough or loose enough to allow of the exercise of an unlimited discretion in the use of this one-third, it is made in some charters to read: "May be kept on deposit, on interest or otherwise, *or* in such available form as the trustees may direct," which certainly ought to be liberal enough to satisfy the imagination of the most adventurous financier that ever dabbled in stocks.

It should be understood that there is a marked distinction between *loans* upon any given securities, and *investments* in those securities, and yet I have met officers of savings banks who have justified loans to an amount exceeding half of their deposits, made under authority of the above provision, upon the ground that all beyond the one-third thus authorized were secured by government stocks, in which, of course, they were authorized to *invest.* I need indulge in no extended argument to establish the fallacy of such a position.

But when the two provisions, of power to loan generally on stocks in which investments are authorized, and to keep one-third in such available form as the trustees shall direct, are found in the same charter, as is sometimes the case, we have a combination that would seem to be the extreme to which legislation could go in removing the safeguards that protect these institutions from possible abuses of discretion on the part of trustees. But no, for there is a step further, and that is to unite with these another provision to which also reference has been made, and that is, to require only a unanimous vote, or one nearly unanimous, in order to invest in any securities, from doubloons to shares in a flying ship! And at least three charters contain every one of these provisions.

Fortunately we may point to the condition of these institutions as affording internal and conclusive evidence that the great *indiscretion* of the Legislature has thus far been wisely overruled by the greater *discretion* of the trustees. But as the latter is an uncertain element, and may sooner or later be overcome, the duty of the Legislature in this matter is as apparent as though the perils from this lax state of the law were not merely possible, but were enforced by our daily experience and observation.

But our present business is to consider the theory and workings of that authority, now so commonly conferred, under which the available fund of a savings bank, generally one-third of the deposits in amount, may be kept in any form which the trustees may direct.

Under this authority we find loans are made on bank, insurance company, and steam and horse railroad stocks; steamship company, express and telegraph stock; railroad bonds and bonds of other private corporations. In the interior of the State we have, in Utica, manufacturing company and mortgage collaterals; in Rome, iron company obligations, mortgage assignments and, very largely, personal securities; in Syracuse, bank and salt company stocks; in Auburn, various manufacturing stocks, gas and water stocks, and personal securities; and in Rochester and Buffalo, bank stocks and other local securities.

The trustees of these institutions will say: "These are all good securities, they are at a premium in the market, or if less than par we take them at a corresponding margin, and in no case loan to exceed three-fourths of their par value, whatever may be the premium they will bring. They pay large dividends, and are in all respects safe and reliable."

To the extent of my observation, I accord to these gentlemen a careful, thoughtful and truly conscientious exercise of the discretion vested in them by the Legislature, and believe they have used the power conferred as prudently and sagaciously as any power so dangerous could be used. It is not the exercise of this discretion which I am now considering, but the discretion itself. Is it wise and safe to leave to any men, however prudent and trustworthy, a discretion so broad, so absolutely unlimited ?

If we may rely upon their judgment and integrity to select wisely from among miscellaneous securities, as collaterals for loans, why may we not with equal safety leave them to select from miscellaneous securities for investment ? But such a liberty would not be entertained for a moment. But if not safe as an investment, how are they safe as a collateral ? It may be said there is a responsible debtor behind the collateral. But the debtor is not safe without the collateral, the collateral is not safe without the personal liability of the debtor, wherein they can both be safe together? It is simply two chances between the creditor and danger, instead of but one. In short, if there is hazard in securities of this character as an investment, and hazard is personal liability as an investment, there is at least half the hazard where both are combined. But, as we have seen, we do not always have both combined, for under the discretion which this provision confers, we find personal securities alone, as a collateral for loans.

I know there are stocks and bonds of private corporations that are more marketable, command a higher premium, than any public stocks or municipal securities. But no public act can discriminate between these, and others of the same class less trustworthy, and the danger is that in the exercise of a general unlimited discretion, some of the latter may inadvertantly find favor.

But the chief danger to be apprehended from the admission of this class of securities is to be found in the unreliable nature of the best of them. The corporations that issue them have a limited capital, with a limited personal liability beyond that. Losses in business, frauds, embezzlements, over-issues, reckless and improvident management, have before now destroyed corporations that had the strongest hold upon the public confidence, and they may do it again. Of what corporation can it be predicted that no misfortune can visit it that shall render the security of its stock or bonds worthless ? Look upon the past for answer ! A fraudulent over-issue of stock may send its quotations from thirty or fifty premium, to near zero in a few hours. A Troy or Portland fire may drive an insurance company into insolvency. Reckless speculation by the officers may bring to grief the bank to which our confidence was anchored as to the rock of ages. A manufacturing company, rich, prosperous and powerful, meets with reverses,—prices fall with heavy stocks of goods on hand,—the demand for their products ceases, their paper at the bank is protested, and they and the bank go down in ruin together. Are not these every day occurrences? To what extent, then shall the deposits in our savings banks depend for their safety upon securities, either as investments or collaterals, subject to hazards like these? That is the practical question for the Legislature to meet and answer, in framing a law for the more efficient protection of these institutions.

But public stocks are liable to no such perils. They represent the wealth and resources, present and prospective, of the State, city or town that issues them. That wealth, in the aggregate will not diminish, it must increase; those resources will not be exhausted, but they will be developed. The houses are there, the stores and shops are there, the business interests that create wealth are there, the farms are there, and there they will remain. The owners may die or go away, others will come in their places who will cultivate the farms, run the machinery, transact the business and *pay taxes*.

A city, or county or town, cannot be embezzled or over issued. Frauds and mismanagement may add to their burdens, but cannot release them from their obligations, nor materially impair their ability to pay. In the orderly course of nature and of natural development, they must grow richer and more able as the country grows older and more populous. The poorest of these, therefore, is exposed to none of the hazards of final and irremediable loss, that wait upon the best securities of private corporations.

But I have frequently encountered this suggestion, that outside of the city of New York, or indeed in New York, but remote from its business center, government and State securities cannot, to any considerable extent, be obtained as collaterals for loans; hence the necessity for a vested discretion to receive as collaterals, other good and valuable securities. The first part of the proposition is doubtless true, but the last does not necessarily follow. The fallacy in the deduction consists in the assumption that a large available fund is necessary to meet the demands of business. Nor is it true, indeed, that these call loans are at all reliable as an available fund. The president of one savings bank told me that it was their practice not to call in these loans except as a last resort, and he had recently ordered the sale of some stocks to meet an unusual demand from depositors, in preference to calling in their loans. As it is only upon the ground of their availability that these loans can be justified at all, we see how fallacious is the argument in their support, in the light of such practices as the above.

Besides, there are hazards attending informalities in the assignment of the securities by which their sale after forfeiture may be vitiated, which render them less desirable than permanent investments. And again, they are subject to the fluctuations of the money market, which may when money is "easy," throw back upon the savings bank a large portion of its loans, and at just the time when investments in the best securities can only be made at a high premium.

But drawing no general conclusions from isolated cases, and conceiving that there may be occasions in the history of a savings bank when the available fund of twenty per cent, or some portion of it at least, must needs be kept in the form of call loans, and that the securities authorized for investment can not be obtained for collaterals, is it possible to provide any means for the admission of other securities as collaterals, without doing violence to the principle of safety which we must ever keep steadily in view?

We must bear in mind that our ultimate purpose is accomplished if we remove from each savings institution the possibility of failure. The chances of failure through the admission of this class of securities as collaterals is in this, that through the negligence or indifference of trustees acting under an authorized discretion, too many questionable securities may be received, or too many of one kind, which, though unquestionable when taken, may become worthless afterwards. The whole available fund secured by the stock of the New York Central railroad, though seemingly good, and really good as the market is to-day, still puts the whole amount upon the venture of the abiding value of that stock. It would evidently be much safer if the security were distributed among other stocks at proportionate rates of margin, even though some of them should not bear so high a character in the market, for the chances of the failure of *all* from the same operating causes, are diminished in a much greater ratio than the increase of the kinds of securities taken. It is the practical recognition of this principle by those institutions that deal most largely in loans upon these collaterals, that enables me to speak so confidently of their soundness and strength. But that vigilance and care may sometime be relaxed. It was in one instance that we have a record of, elsewhere given, (page 110) and the result was *failure.* Our aim is *never to repeat that experiment.*

How, then, shall we ensure continued care, prudence and integrity in the use of so large a discretion? *By making trustees responsible for its exercise.* This will operate beneficially in two ways. It will diminish the amount of such securities to the lowest practicable limit. Trustees will not "work for nothing and find themselves," and incur heavy liabilities besides, unless the conditions of their trust make it very clearly necessary and safe for them to do so. And it will stimulate the exercise of great caution in regard to the character of the securities received, and equal prudence and sagacity in distributing the loans so as to diminish to the utmost the chances of any considerable loss. If any further safeguards are deemed necessary, the statute might provide that not more than a given per cent of deposits should be loaned upon any one kind of security, or power might be vested in the superintendent to direct a proper distribution of the securities.

But with the total available fund limited to twenty per cent of the deposits, a portion of which would, of course, have to be in cash in hand or in bank, and the personal liability of trustees for any losses sustained upon loans secured by any other collaterals than those authorized for investment, I believe that perfect safety would be assured, and be made compatible with the payment of depositors on demand.

I will only remark further, what I will not stop to discuss, that personal securities and mortgage assignments should, however, be especially excluded from admission as collaterals for loans. Under no circumstances should they form any part of the assets of a savings bank.

PANICS.

While I believe that provisions such as I have suggested would carry any savings bank safely and triumphantly through any emergency, I have not as yet specifically considered the effect of a popular panic upon the integrity of these institutions.

These are wholly exceptional, and must be treated by exceptional methods.

The most effective remedy for panics is prevention. They are the offspring of a sense of insecurity, arising from ignorance of existing conditions. Every man distrusts his debtor because the failure, day after day, of those who were *supposed* to be abundantly solvent, renders impressive the fact that concerning the condition and circumstances of individuals, firms and corporations, nothing is absolutely *known*. Hence the sense of insecurity is universal, and the fear engendered by it is proportionate to the numbers affected, and the magnitude of the interests involved. These are all the people, and all their material possessions, prospects and hopes. It is no wonder that the fervor of frenzy is so passionate, so unreasoning, so wild.

But to this general condition of uncertainty, ignorance and doubt, savings banks might be and should be an exception. Depositors, through annual statements, through familiar expositions from time to time in the public journals of the day, and through official reports, should become thoroughly impressed with the conviction that their security rests upon the broad foundations of *public faith*, and that so long as there is a government left to fulfill its own obligations and enforce those which its sovereign power has authorized, their *savings bank can not fail*. They should know and understand that it rests upon a foundation wholly unlike that of any other financial institution;—that other banks may break, business men fail, and insurance companies go into liquidation, because their business is in its nature more or less hazardous, greater risks being taken that greater profits may be realized; but that so long as there remain people who must hire houses and stores, and work farms, so long as the government endures, their savings bank will rest secure and firm on its broad and deep foundations.

Knowing this, the feeling of insecurity, on which panic feeds, can not get possession of their souls, and no contagious fear will send them howling in wild chorus of demand for their deposits "*now*." And it is at such a time that the policy which I have advocated, of a general, close investment of assets in public securities, will prove its superiority. If the statements show a large investment in these *known* securities, this knowledge will impart confidence. But if there appears a large proportion of assets loaned on call, there arises the doubt, there is involved the uncertainty; "to whom loaned?" "upon what securities?" and the sense of insecurity is felt just in the ratio of these unknown quantities in the question. Or if there is a large deposit in bank; banks are failing—"what bank?" or "how soon may that in which my savings are kept go down with others?" All depositors will not of course reason thus, but many will, and all will be more or less affected by their *knowledge* of the condition of their savings bank; and besides, there is the contagion of confidence not less than the contagion of fear, and the intelligent will inspire the ignorant by their calmness and self-possession.

But suppose the worst to come at last, and frenzied depositors in throngs besiege the doors, clamorous for their due, and the available fund is exhausted, and securities must be sold at a ruinous sacrifice if payments are to be continued;—what then?

Obviously, to my mind, there is but one course to pursue consistently with both prudence and justice. The trustees are guardians of a sacred trust, and have no right to sacrifice that trust in obedience to a clamor founded on a senseless fear.

They owe to the depositors, besides money, calm and prudent counsels, wise and sagacious management of their interests, and if to respond to the demand stimulated wholly by fear and not at all by want, will be to sacrifice those interests, or the interests of any considerable number, they should not "long debate," but enforce the rule requiring notice, and refuse payment on demand while such payment can do no one any good, but must bring disappointment and perhaps ruin upon the greater number.

Such a policy did, in 1857, in one instance at least, go far to restore confidence and to allay the panic that threatened to convulse these institutions in one common ruin. It will always do this, and it is the part of wisdom as well as of duty to enforce the policy whenever the occasion arises for its use.

Certainly it does not require a very large available fund to meet this emergency in this way.

As a fitting conclusion to this discussion of the general theory of investments for savings banks, and as a flattering commentary upon the exhibit made by the savings banks of this State of the assets held by them as security for their depositors, I subjoin, by way of comparison, a statement of the kinds of securities authorized and held by the savings banks in other States of the Union:

New Hampshire.

Railroad stocks and bonds, western city bonds, manufacturing and bank stock, personal security loans, and local bonds.

Vermont.

Bond and mortgage, railroad and bank stock, town village and school district bonds, and personal securities. About twenty per cent of assets is invested in bank stock.

Massachusetts.

Bank stock, railroad bonds, loans on railroad stock, and personal security; public funds, county and town loans. Nearly one-sixth of aggregate securities are bank stocks.

Connecticut.

Bank stock, (large amounts, home and other State), railroad stocks and bonds, western city and county bonds, Brooklyn lots, Wisconsin lands and personal securities.

Rhode Island.

Chiefly bank stocks, corporation stocks, and personal securities.

New Jersey.

Real estate under foreclosure, (one bank has $29,268 so *invested*), railroad first mortgage bonds, and *discounted notes.*

Pennsylvania.

Discounted bills and notes, (of which $24,223.09 were under protest), judgments, and bank loans. The above constitute ninety-seven per cent of their investments.

From other States I have been unable to procure any reports showing the condition of their savings banks.

It will be understood that in all the above States some government and State securities are held by the savings banks. But those enumerated above constitute the *great bulk* of their investments.

With all the opportunity for improvement in our policy, we may look with pride and satisfaction upon the substantial character of the investments of our savings banks, not less than upon the grand aggregate which they have reached.

Increase of Savings Banks.

We must now consider the prosperity of our savings bank system, as indicated by the increase in the number of these institutions.

It may be assumed, generally, that wherever the opening of a savings bank will have the effect to attract as deposits, savings from labor, (that otherwise would be spent), in sufficient amount to pay the reasonable and legitimate expenses of conducting the business, besides fair dividends to depositors, after putting aside from the profits of each year a moderate amount as a surplus reserve for contingencies, that there, the organization of a savings bank would be an indication of the substantial growth and prosperity of the system.

It does not follow that every savings bank that is organized and *receives* a sufficient amount of deposits to pay expenses and dividends, and accumulate a surplus, is a desirable auxiliary to the system. Such do not fulfill all the conditions of the proposition. They must not merely *receive* deposits to be useful, but they must *attract* such as would otherwise fail to reach any savings depository.

If they only succeed in attracting depositors from institutions already established, and where they could enjoy every facility and advantage afforded by the new institution, or in attracting new depositors that but for them could, and naturally would, find their way to those already established, their existence does nothing to promote the prosperity of the system from any point of view in which the conditions of that prosperity may be considered. Two savings banks in the same block, each with $500,000 of deposits, certainly suggest no advantages over a single savings bank with $1,000,000 of deposits. The *disadvantages* which they suggest will be considered presently.

To be effective as an auxiliary to our savings bank system, any new institution must minister to those needs of the community which savings banks were instituted to supply. But where the supply is already afforded there are no *needs* to minister unto, and any further provision is redundance, waste. But waste is hurtful; it weakens, exhausts, destroys. This is as true in financial or political economy as in the animal economy. There is a natural waste that is salutary, essential; any excess is, more or less, according to its degree, exhausting and destructive. A savings bank cannot be conducted without waste, in the form of necessary expenses. These must be provided for in its organization. They are one of the most important elements to be considered. If they cannot be kept within a reasonable proportion of the anticipated or real earnings, the institution is not a success. The smaller the ratio they bear to those earnings, consistently with honest and capable management, the more there is left to divide to depositors, the more popular and attractive is the institution, the more extended its influence and power in the promotion of the objects for which it was created; or the more there is to put aside as a surplus for contingencies and hazards in business, the stronger and more secure it becomes, and thus attracts the attention of the thoughful and prudent to whom its condition becomes known, and thus extends the sphere of its usefulness.

Whatever disturbing element now comes in and destroys this nicely adjusted balance of conditions so favorable to prosperity and success, is certainly injurious, and not salutary in its operation and effects.

And such a disturbing element is another savings bank, established "around the corner," soliciting the deposits that might find, or that may have already found their way to the first institution. It is a source of weakness to the system in this, that it attracts the deposits that might be received in the older institution without additional expense, and the gross earnings of which therefore would be so much additional profit to the depositors, or augment by so much the surplus for their better security.

It is a source of weakness in this, that while attracting these deposits to itself, it imposes upon their earnings the burden of expenses which it is needless to incur, being elsewhere gratuitously provided, thus diminishing the profits to depositors, or leaving less to apply to the surplus for their more perfect security. In short, the expenses upon a given amount of deposits are in this way needlessly doubled, to the disadvantage of depositors and to the advantage only of the salaried officers of the new institution. Surely, in the multiplying of savings banks under conditions like these, we can find no sign of substantial growth and prosperity.

If it should occur to any one that principles so simple and obvious as the foregoing, suggesting themselves so naturally to any mind of average ability, require no elucidation or enforcement, and that the time and space here employed in their illustration, is needlessly expended, I would direct attention to the course and policy of legislation for the past few years, as the best evidence that these principles, at least in their practical bearing and application, have *not* been apprehended in that quarter, where we should look with confidence for a concentration of more than average ability, and where the measures affecting the prosperity and security of savings banks should be, more than elsewhere, carefully and intelligently considered.

In Albany there are now five savings banks, where two, properly conducted, would serve the public equally well.

In Auburn there are two, with full sets of officers looking into each others faces across the street, and with an aggregate of deposits of but a little over a million of dollars.

In Rochester there were two, both large and flourishing institutions, but either capable of transacting a very considerably increased amount of business without additional expense. But a charter was last winter granted to a new institution, that will be fortunate if, in two years, it can secure legitimate savings deposits equal in amount to the surplus assets of the other.

In Buffalo there were four, one of which, in eight years, had not reached $200,000 of deposits; but another was chartered last winter, upon what ground or pretext of public need I am unable to determine.

In Troy there are five chartered institutions, four of which are located within whistling distance of each other.

In Brooklyn there were ten; the last Legislature chartered three others, only one of which, however, has organized, but that one has located itself within easy call of three others.

In New York there were twenty-five, more than one to each ward in the city, but the number was augmented by three at the last session of the Legislature, and one of these is located within two blocks of another, chartered only the winter before, which takes from the savings of that neighborhood just twice the amount for expenses that is required, and diminishing by that excess their profits or their security.

And in Binghamton, a city of 10,000 inhabitants, the experiment of a savings bank at all, was initiated by the last Legislature, by reviving an old charter that had twice expired in the effort of the trustees to organize, and by granting a new charter to another corporation, in the hope, I suppose, that the vigor of the new might impart sufficient vitality to the old, at least to ensure the commencement of business, after a lapse of twelve years; a proceeding not without precedent of high authority, but perilous to the welfare of at least one of the parties concerned.

It is in no unkindness to the institution referred to that these criticisms are indulged. But in considering the relation of these institutions to the purpose of their organizations, and to the general prosperity of the system of which they are a part, we cannot forbear to note those conditions that retard or obstruct the highest form of their development, and among these is the wholly inconsiderate manner in which the Legislature has chartered them, without reference to the natural needs in any community which savings banks are instituted to supply.

At least these illustrations should serve to relieve the common place postulates with which this topic was introduced, from the charge of being needless and uncalled for.

I do not propose to descant upon the dangers to which such inconsiderate legislation exposes the system of savings banks security. These follow as evidently as the following propositions:

Union is strength.

Division is weakness.

Strength is security.

Weakness is insecurity, or according to its degree, *danger.*

The whole burden of our discussion has been from the beginning, and will be to the end, how to make these institutions *strong*, SECURE, IMPREGNABLE! If it can be done by multiplying them beyond the needs of a community for their personal convenience, then axioms and first principles are no more reliable than flights of fancy, and figures will lie faster and more egregiously than the letters of the alphabet.

But let us turn from these to more cheering and hopeful indications of the growth and prosperity of this provident power in our State. Within the last ten years there have been organized and are now in operation nineteen savings banks in localities where before there were no such institutions existing, against fourteen in existence the first of January, 1858, thus more than doubling the number of communities to whom these facilities have been extended, and the deposits in these, on the first of January last, aggregated the sum of $1,660,524.

Here is certainly an encouraging growth, for this estimate does not take in the sum that has been deposited and withdrawn, and which is as much to be considered in any legitimate estimate of the value of savings banks, as the sums left to be withdrawn at a future time; for these deposits have fulfilled their purpose as fully, indeed more fully than those remaining. They have been *earned*, and thus represent their share of the productive industry stimulated to exercise; they have been *saved*, and thus have aroused the provident habit which it is a part of the mission of savings banks to inspire; they have been *invested*, and have thus served the purpose of some public utility; they have received their *dividends*, thus rewarding industry and frugality; and they have been *with-*

drawn, and thus have fulfilled the ultimate purpose of their accumulation. The system that can produce results like these is certainly not wanting in the elements of substantial success.

And I have purposely left out of view in this calculation many institutions that have been organized in cities, particularly in New York and Brooklyn, where savings banks were already in operation, but which, by choosing some unoccupied field, have attracted depositors in large numbers, without inflicting injury upon other institutions, and which now rank among the leading institutions in the State. Such are some of the evidences of a healthy growth and expansion of the savings bank system in our State.

For the purpose of exhibiting the present condition of our savings bank system, in respect to the diffusion of its facilities among the people, and to the improvement of these facilities by the people, I have prepared the following table, arranged by counties, showing

1. The number of savings banks in each county at the present time, including those organized since 1st of January last.
2. The population.
3. The population of each savings bank.
4. The aggregate deposits 1st January, 1867.
5. The average amount of deposits for each individual of population.
6. The number of depositors or open accounts.
7. The average amount to each depositor.
8. The ratio of depositors to the population.

Steuben and Chemung counties are omitted, as for all practical purposes which we are considering, they have no savings bank.

COUNTIES.	1. No. of savings banks.	2. Population.	3. Population to each savings bank.	4. Aggregate of deposits in savings banks, Jan. 1, 1867.	5. Average of deposits for each individual of population, Jan. 1, 1867.	6. Number of depositors.	7. Average amount for each depositor.	8. Ratio of depositors to population.
*Albany	6	115,504	19,265	$3,781,515	$32 71	11,005	$343 00	1 in 10
†Broome	2	37,933	18,966	....	....	....	....	....
Cayuga	2	55,730	27,865	1,062,801	19 07	4,676	227 00	1 in 11
Chautauqua	1	58,528	58,528	25,430	0 43	118	215 00	1 in 580
Chenango	1	38,360	38,360	80,157	2 08	252	314 00	1 in 152
Columbia	1	44,905	44,905	297,070	6 61	1,483	200 00	1 in 30
Cortland	1	24,815	24,815	21,128	0 85	79	267 00	1 in 314
Dutchess	4	65,192	16,298	1,320,183	20 25	5,868	225 00	1 in 11
Erie	5	157,105	31,421	6,368,088	40 53	32,161	198 00	1 in 5
*Jefferson	2	66,448	33,224	104,964	1 57	682	154 00	1 in 97
*Kings	11	310,824	28,256	17,160,474	55 20	69,413	247 00	1 in 4
Madison	1	42,607	42,607	75,939	1 78	235	323 00	1 in 185
*Monroe	3	104,235	34,745	4,211,879	40 40	12,838	328 00	1 in 8
*New York	28	726,386	25,942	86,574,343	119 18	307,192	281 00	1 in 2⅓
Niagara	1	49,655	49,655	5,293	0 10	46	115 00	1 in 1097
Oneida	4	102,713	25,678	2,285,809	22 25	8,084	282 00	1 in 12
Onondaga	3	93,332	31,111	2,499,953	26 78	9,989	257 00	1 in 9
Orange	1	70,165	70,165	775,336	11 04	3,488	222 00	1 in 20
†Orleans	1	28,603	28,603	....	....	....	....	....
Oswego	1	76,200	76,200	292,967	3 84	1,519	192 00	1 in 50
Queens	2	57,997	28,998	162,559	2 80	1,287	126 00	1 in 44
Rensselaer	5	88,210	17,642	2,201,057	24 95	7,092	310 00	1 in 12
†Saratoga	1	49,892	49,892	....	....	....	....	....
Schenectady	1	20,888	20,888	352,317	16 86	1,169	301 00	1 in 16
Suffolk	2	42,869	21,434	356,671	16 64	1,966	181 00	1 in 21
Ulster	1	75,609	75,609	522,150	6 90	2,002	260 00	1 in 37
*Westchester	7	101,197	14,457	1,224,530	12 10	5,833	210 00	1 in 17

* Includes one or more organized since January 1st, 1867.
† Organized since January 1st, 1867.

It will be seen that the ratio of population to each savings bank varies from 14,457 in Westchester county, 76,200 in Oswego county.

The aggregate of deposits is, of course, necessarily more variable, and has no special comparative significance.

The average of deposits to each individual of population, shows a marked difference, being from ten cents in Niagara county, to $119.18 in New York.

The number of depositors, depending so much upon the aggregate population and its density, is not significant.

The average amount to each depositor exhibits a comparative uniformity, striking and suggestive, being from $115 in Niagara, to $343 in Albany; while the ratio of depositors to population exhibits the marked difference of from 1 in $2\frac{1}{3}$ in New York, to 1 in 1,097 in Niagara.

The latter county is, in all its aspects, so wholly exceptional, that but for the sake of embracing everything that *has* conditions, it might better be left out of the calculation altogether.

Chautauqua, Cortland and Madison are hardly to be judged by the common standard applied to other counties, for the reason that the one savings bank in each, only commenced business during the year from which the statement is made.

The most surprising fact of the table, is the ratio of depositors in New York. That it, by reason of its density of population and convenient access to savings banks, should show a much larger ratio than any other locality was to be expected, but a ratio of one in two and a third we certainly should not have anticipated. Nor is it true that one out of every two and a third of all the men, women and children in New York city is a depositor. Many persons living in adjacent counties, as Kings, Richmond and Westchester, and from New Jersey, deposit in the savings banks of the city. The accounts represent a large nnmber of depositors who have died or removed from the city, whose deposits have not been withdrawn by their representatives or by themselves. Many persons have accounts in different banks, or in the names of different persons though themselves the real depositors. In these ways the aggregate is made to represent a much larger proportion of depositors to the entire population of the city than the facts will warrant.

But after making all these allowances, the fact still remains that a very large proportion of the population of the city of New York are depositors in its savings banks. Just what that proportion may be it is impossible to ascertain, but it is enough to greatly enlarge our conceptions of the usefulness of these institutions.

The exhibit is altogether most hopeful and encouraging, showing, as it does, that 2,705,902 of our population have at least one savings bank within the county in which they reside, and that within twenty-seven counties of our State there is one savings bank for each 27,611 of the population.

But another disclosure is made by the exhibit, and that is less encouraging, and that should stimulate into active exercise the latent public spirit, which, from its manifestation in other departments, we have reason to believe is possessed by our people.

More than half the counties in our State have *no savings bank at all;* while several that have but one, ought to have two or more. There is but one county in the State (Hamilton) where a savings bank could not, and would not if judiciously located and in proper hands be adequately supported.

As evidence of this, let us look at a few facts: Westchester county with a population of 101,197, has seven savings banks, or one for each 14,457 of population. Of these, two (Portchester and New Rochelle) are recently organized, but are doing well, and though they may never attain the magnitude of others, they will do and are doing a vast amount of good in the accomplishment of the purposes for which savings banks are instituted.

The remaining five are located at Yonkers, Tarrytown, Sing Sing and Peekskill, on the line of the Hudson River railroad, having communication with the city of New York by several trains each day, which has the effect doubtless to withdraw depositors more or less to that city.

In Yonkers are two of the five; one recently organized is not embraced in our calculations; indeed the consideration of it at all belongs rather to that part of our discussion in which the needless multiplication of savings banks was treated as an element of weakness in our system.

The savings bank which helps to illustrate our argument is located in the town of Yonkers, having a population of 12,756. It has deposits amounting to $350,465 belonging to 1,855 depositors. It cannot draw largely from outside of its own population, for six miles below is the city of New York, across the river are the Palisades, and nine or ten miles above is

TARRYTOWN, in the town of Greenburg, having a population of

8,463, and having a flourishing savings bank, with $363,149 of deposits, from 1,339 depositors.

This savings bank, the "Westchester County," cannot attract depositors to any considerable extent from outside of the town in which it is located, except from the interior of the county, for the reason that Yonkers is below, and only four or five miles above is

Sing Sing, in the town of Ossining, with a population of 6,223, having a savings bank, with deposits amounting to $176,584, belonging to 722 depositors.

Here, too, the area from which depositors are drawn is limited to the town and remote region of the interior, as Tarrytown is just below, and some ten miles above, in the adjoining town of Cortlandt, is the.

Peekskill Savings Bank, with $282,620 of deposits, and 1,366 depositors out of a population of 9,343.

This savings bank, again, is limited in the area of its operations by a savings bank at Fishkill, in Dutchess county, some twelve or thirteen miles above.

These are practical illustrations of the successful organization and conduct of savings banks operating within a limited area and upon a limited population.

There are many villages and towns in our State where a similar exhibition of public spirit on part of citizens, in whom the public would have confidence in assuming the direction of such an enterprise, would be attended with similar gratifying results.

And the more strictly rural portions of our State bring their testimony to the readiness of the people to avail themselves of the benefits of savings banks when brought within their reach.

The Sag Harbor Savings Bank is located in a town of about 6,000 inhabitants, with a town adjoining of about 2,000, and the geographical situation and surroundings of these two towns is such that the savings bank can reach and effect nothing outside of them; yet it has over $100,000 of deposits from the rather sparsely settled area of these two towns.

Southold, a town of 6,000 inhabitants, has a flourishing savings bank with over $250,000 of deposits.

Glancing over our State, how many counties, in which there is no savings bank, have within themselves all the conditions of equal or greater success?

In Allegany it would seem that a savings bank might be sustained at one or other of the following points : Angelica, Belfast, Amity or Wellsville.

In Cattaraugus, at Ellicottville, Allegany or Olean.

In Chautauqua, besides the one at Fredonia, for which Dunkirk would have been the better location, one at Jamestown should be well supported.

In Chemung, at Elmira, with a population of 13,000, a savings bank ought to be sustained, the experience of the one now closing to the contrary notwithstanding.

In Clinton, at Plattsburgh, with a population of 7,000, and all the rest of the county to draw from, they ought to do as well as at Sag Harbor or Southold.

In Delaware at Delhi or Deposit.

In Essex, at Port Henry, in a town of nearly 4,000 inhabitants.

In Franklin, at Malone, with a population of 6,000.

In Fulton, at Johnstown or Gloversville, the latter employing a large number of operatives in manufacturing.

In Genesee, at Batavia.

In Greene, at Catskill.

In Herkimer, at Little Falls, in a town of 5,000 inhabitants, and the seat of very considerable manufactures.

In Lewis, at Lowville or Martinsburgh.

In Livingston, at Geneseo or Mount Morris.

In Madison, besides the one recently established at Oneida, Hamilton affords a good central point for another.

In Montgomery, at Amsterdam, Fonda, Fort Plain or Canajoharie. One has been chartered at Amsterdam, but has not been organized.

In Ontario, at Geneva or Canandaigua.

In Otsego, at Cooperstown. The Unadilla Bank for a long time served as a substitute for a savings bank, but its unfortunate termination is an apt illustration of the dangers that attend dealings with banks of discount.

In Putnam, at Carmel, drawing deposits from along the line of the Harlem railroad.

Richmond county has had a charter, but no organization has been effected under it.

In Rockland, at Clarkstown, Haverstraw or Orangetown.

In St. Lawrence, at Ogdensburgh, with a population of 11,000, or at Potsdam, with 6,000.

In Schoharie, at the Court House, Cobleskill, Richmondville or Middleburgh.

In Schuyler, at Havana or Watkins.

In Seneca, at Seneca Falls, a fine manufacturing village of 6,000 population in the town; or at Waterloo.

In Steuben, at Bath, Hornellsville or Corning. The savings bank at the latter place should be revived.

In Sullivan, at Monticello.

In Tioga, at Owego.

In Tompkins, at Ithaca.

In Warren, at Glen's Falls, a town of 7,000 inhabitants.

In Washington, at Fort Ann, Fort Edward or Whitehall.

In Wayne, at Lyons or Palmyra.

In Wyoming, at Perry, Warsaw or Attica; and

In Yates, at Penn Yan.

In some of the places I have indicated, it may not be practicable at present to establish a savings bank, but in very many of them it would, if the success that has waited on endeavor in other parts of the State affords any criterion by which to judge.

The eastern portion of the State has thus far done much more in the localities outside of cities, to extend and develop our savings bank system, than the western. I can not believe there is in the condition or character of the laboring classes of either section, anything to justify this difference.

Savings banks, in twenty-seven counties of the State, have opened up opportunities for the saving of surplus earnings to 2,705,902 inhabitants, and are now improved by 488,476 of that number, while the number that during the last fifty years have been blest in basket and store, as well as in wholesome moral influence, by the agency of these institutions, is many times greater than that appearing in the statistics for January 1, 1867. To estimate justly the benefits conferred by these institutions, we must not consider the good they are doing at any particular period of time, but the good they have done during all their career.

Take for example the bank for savings in the city of New York.

On the 1st of January, 1867, its power reached and effected 55,307 individuals—nay more than that, for a large number of these were heads of families, and the blessing of their provident care was felt and enjoyed by every member of their households.

But upon those remoter reachings of the power and influence of savings banks we can only generalize. We know only, that they must be vast, beyond our means to estimate, almost beyond our power to apprehend, even if we had the basis for computation; as we may count the stars, and measure their distances, and express the wonderful story of their journeyings in figures familiar to the eye, while the grandest apprehension of the intellect is utterly powerless to *realize* the vastness of the spaces traversed, thus condensed in statement within the limits of a line.

To return, therefore, to the known and real, we find that the 55,307 depositors in the Bank for Savings, on the 1st of January, 1867, are only what remain of 281,123 human souls that have, during a period of 47½ years, been blessed by its provident ministry.

Assuming a similar ratio for each savings bank for the period during which it has been in operation, we have the following result:

That the 488,501 depositors in the savings banks of this State, on the 1st January last, are what is left of more than 2,000,000 depositors that have at some time had dealings with these institutions.

It is to be regretted that we are left to calculations where accurate information ought to be accessible, but with the proverbial disregard of our people for statistics, no facts relating to anything but the present are called for, and I am indebted to the voluntary published statement of the Bank for Savings, for the basis of the foregoing calculations. I suppose, of course, the same information is to be found in the records of each savings bank, but it is not required of them in their reports, and the subject engaged my attention too late to call for the facts desired; an apt verification of my previous statement concerning the incompleteness of my labors.

But the computation is an approximation sufficiently close to give us some idea of the far-reaching influence of savings banks when extended over a series of years. If more than 2,000,000 people have been more or less directly benefited through their agency, during the fifty years that embrace the period of their infancy, what may we not hope for from the continuance of their operation, now that we have ninety-eight institutions and 488,500 depositors as a starting point, in place of the single savings bank with its 1,527 first year depositors, of forty-seven years ago.

Even with no increase in the number of these institutions, there opens before us for the next half century a grandeur of development and of power and influence for good, in this agency, almost overpowering in its magnitude. And when we reflect that neglect' indifference, or hasty and ill considered action on part of the State, in properly guarding and protecting this great interest, may turn all its vast enginery to the accomplishment of evil, how impressive is the thought of the responsibility resting upon those upon whose wisdom in counsel, and upon whose prudence in action, such momentous interests depend.

But we should not be, and we are not content with the present numerical distribution of savings banks in our State. We have seen that thirty-three counties, embracing a population of 1,125,-875 are destitute of the advantages which these institutions are designed to secure. What is there, we ask, in the condition, needs or circumstances of this 1,125,875, that should exempt them from the beneficent operations of this provident agency ?

That a large proportion of this population might have the advantages of savings banks rendered accessible to them, I have endeavored to render apparent. The increasing facilities for communication between remote points by the projection and completion of new lines of railroad, will, from year to year, render more and more practicable the institution of savings banks at convenient business centers thus opened, and made accessible to a previously sequestered population.

And even now there are many points where the same public spirit and regard for the best interests of labor, which we have noted as characterizing the institution of savings banks in other localities, would speedily result in the opening of these facilities where they are not now enjoyed.

In any community largely engaged in manufactures, not only would the relations of capital and labor be rendered more harmonious and confiding by the establishment of a savings bank, of which the proprietors of the manufacturing interests should be the managers, but they would, through the more systematic and effective labor thus promoted, and the better habits encouraged in their operatives, secure an advantage which would far more than repay the time and trouble consumed in managing its business and investments. And such an institution might be very inexpensively conducted, it need be opened but for one or two hours each day, or even on two or three days in the week, and the business of receiving and paying money might be done by some cashier, treasurer, secretary or accountant of the establishment, for a small compensation in addition to his regular salary ; and by dividing the labor of attendance among a dozen or fifteen trustees, one might always be present during the business hours of the institution, to encouage depositors by the interest thus manifested in their welfare, and to inspire them with confidence by the knowledge of his attentive supervision of the affairs of *their* savings bank.

I can imagine nothing that would serve better to establish cordial and friendly relations between employers and operatives than the institution by the former of savings banks for the benefit of the latter, in some such form as I have sketched; though, of course they should be equally free and accessible to all classes.

If the care and investment of the deposits should seem to render the acceptance of such a responsibility too onerous, provision could be made in the law whereby such an institution might be constituted a branch of some larger savings bank in the nearest city or town, with which arrangements might be made to receive the deposits of such branch in a gross sum, weekly or semi-monthly, and invest them, either at its own discretion or that of the trustees of the branch institution, as should be agreed, but only in the securities authorized by law, charging an agreed commission for the service, and rendering a strict account of the profits of such investments, from which the trustees of the smaller or branch institution could declare dividends to their depositors.

The details of such a plan need not be elaborated here, but it appears to me to be wholly practicable, and easily applied, and would serve to extend the benefits of savings banks to many localities, and to thousands of people where they are not now enjoyed.

But even by such means our savings bank system does not admit of indefinite expansion. In many parts of our State the business centers are widely scattered, and an average of two or three in a county where there is no city, would probably be the most that could be judiciously established, or successfully maintained.

This would still leave a very large portion of our people too remote from any savings bank to be practically benefited by them, for we cannot, within the next fifty or one hundred years, anticipate such an increase in the facilities for inter-communication that a railroad will pass through every town, still less have a station on every man's farm.

The question presented then is, whether any plan can be devised whereby this condition incident to the extended area and sparse settlement of our State can be overcome, and the benefits of savings bank investment be brought within the reach of all.

Savings Banks in Great Britain and Ireland.

In Great Britain and Ireland, this result has been effected in a manner so complete and satisfactory, that a brief reference to that system, may not be out of place here.

We have seen in previous pages, how unsatisfactory was the operation of the savings bank system in Great Britain and Ireland, especially in the want of protection it afforded to depositors, from loss through frauds of officers in charge, rendered possible by the negligence or indifference of trustees. Hardly less satisfactory was the practical working of the system, in respect to the convenience and readiness of access to savings banks secured to depositors, whereby the disposition to save, was thwarted and overcome by the impediments and restrictions thrown in the way of the people, in reaching a safe depository for their earnings.

These unfavorable conditions attracted the attention of philanthropists and statesmen, and the discussion and investigation of suitable and effective methods of reform in the system, agitated public and official circles for a number of years.

The happy suggestion of using the postal machinery of the realm for the purpose of receiving deposits for savings, at first crudely set forth, was taken up, committed to competent authorities to improve and render practical, and finally submitted to Parliament in the form of a bill authorizing such use.

A detailed history of the opposition in Parliament, and from influential sources outside of Parliament, to the proposed institution of postal savings banks, would be interesting, but is not necessary to my purpose, which is to present the final result as embodied in an effective system, and some facts illustrating its great success. Suffice it, that the courage and determination of the friends of reform triumph over the ridicule as well as the more dignified but not less bitter hostility of its foes, and in May, 1861, the Post office Savings Bank act received the royal assent. The preliminaries were completed, and the act given effect on the 16th of September following, by the opening of three hundred and one Money Order Post Offices as savings banks. The success attending the first experiment was so great, and the demand for an extension of facilities became so urgent, that more post offices were opened from time to time, until in March, 1866, the whole number of post office savings banks in the United Kingdom was 3,369, of which 2,469 were in England and Wales. The total amount deposited from 16th September, 1861, to 31st December,

1865, was £11,834,896, and withdrawn, £5,619,251; the number of depositors being 857,701. Whether we regard the increase in the aggregate of deposits, the number of depositors, the character of deposits as indicated by the reduced average amount to each, showing how the poorer classes were reached by this expansion of the system by diffusion of its facilities;—in every point of view, the results were most extraordinary and gratifying. For the ten years previous to 1861, the average annual increase of deposits in the old savings banks was at the rate of three and four-fifths per cent. During the year subsequent to the establishment of post office savings banks, the rate of increase was six and three-fourths per cent, or an improvement of nearly one hundred per cent.

The operation of the system may be briefly described. A person wishing to deposit not less than one shilling, can go to the nearest money order post office and leave his deposit, receiving a bank book, properly numbered, on which his name, address and occupation will be written. The amount of the deposit is entered on the book, attested by the signature of the post master, and stamped with the official stamp of the office. This is a sufficient voucher for the depositor, the Government being responsible for its safe transmission to the General Office.

The postmaster sends an account daily to the money order office in London, of each transaction, with the original signature of the depositors. It is there properly entered, and an acknowledgment is sent to each depositor. This is rather for the protection of the Government from frauds on part of its own officials, than as further security to the depositor, for whom the entry on the book is a competent voucher, still it is valuable as cumulative evidence; and if he does not receive such acknowledgment within ten days, he should make application for it, which he may do free of postage.

Subsequent deposits are made in the same way, and may be made at the same or at any other money order office in the kingdom, and so perfect is the system that one might make the whole round of the 3,369 post office savings banks in the kingdom, making deposits in each, and though he would add to the labor of the department, he would not confuse or embarrass its operations in the slightest degree.

Withdrawals are effected with equal readiness and ease. The depositor has only to call at any money order office, and ask for a blank form, which he fills up with the number of his deposit book, the place where deposited, the amount required, the place where he wants it paid, his name, address and occupation, and sends free of postage to the Postmaster General. The address is printed on the back of the form, so no misdirection, through ignorance or carelessness, can occur.

The draft or order is received, signature and other facts compared with those of the original deposit on file, the account examined, and if found correct, a warrant for the amount on the postmaster of the place designated in the order is drawn and forwarded to the depositor, and at the same time a duplicate copy of the warrant in the nature of an advice, is sent to the postmaster.

When the depositor presents his original warrant, the P. M. carefully compares the same with his advice, compares the signature to the receipt attached to the warrant with the original in the depositor's book, (which must always be presented), and if all is correct, he pays the money and makes an entry of the same in the withdrawal part of the depositor's book, signing and stamping it the same as in case of the deposit. To illustrate the working of the system as it would be if applied in this country: A person making his deposits in Portland, Maine, has occasion to visit San Francisco. At St. Louis, finding he will require money soon after his arrival at San Francisco, he goes to the post office, procures and fills out a form addressed to the Postmaster-General, directing payment to be made at San Francisco, and proceeds on his journey. Arriving at San Francisco, he receives, by due course of mail, the warrant on the postmaster of that city, from whom he receives his money.

I have necessarily omitted all but the barest outline of the working of the system. The deposits are all received by Government officials, and are invested in the funds. A uniform rate of interest of two and a half per cent is allowed on all sums not less than one pound, or some multiple thereof, but not exceeding £30 is received from any depositor in any one year.

Such, in brief, is the British saytem of savings banks, which has revolutionized the entire operations of making savings deposits, and has stimulated the latent thrift and provident spirit of the laboring classes to a degree far exceeding the anticipations of the most sanguine. But the measure, as its history reveals, met with stern and bitter opposition, and was carried through at last, only because *statesmen* turned aside from the petty interests of local legislation, or from the consideration of schemes of private emolument or gain, and concentrated their best energies, employed all their best powers to the elaboration and to the passage of an act of general public utility and beneficence.

Among those whose eminence and worth first gave character to this effort for reform, and upon whom their cause, triumphant, has since reflected higher and more merited honor, stands most prominent WILLIAM EWART GLADSTONE, then *Chancellor of the Exchequer*, who gave to the scheme all the weight of his great name, all the energies of his great mind, all the earnestness of his nature, and all the influence of his high official position.

May we not hope that some American Gladstone will arise in the councils of the Empire State, who by his force of character, his determined purpose, his intelligent apprehension of the principles of political science, his clear and intuitive apprehension of the adaptation of means to ends, his earnest convictions, and his warm, generous and active sympathies, shall identify his name as proudly with the development of the system of savings banks in our State?

It is impossible of course to render practicable such a system in our State.

The General government, and not the State, has the control of the post office system. Nor are the conditions in our country so favorable as in Great Britain for the development of such a system, for the United States, on the part of the General government. Our people are naturally jealous of the interference of government in affairs that may properly and safely be left to private enterprise. Guardianship, protection from abuse of power and privilege, they will except as the rightful prerogative of government; but not the substitution of official domination and monopoly, to the exclusion of private enterprise. Besides, we have not the limited area and compact population that renders possible the complete development of the English post office system.

Yet it appears to me that we may derive some ideas from the successful working of that system, of which we may make profitable use, in extending, and in perfecting the development of our own.

The National government has very properly recognized the claims of popular education, and of internal improvement, as promoters of national virtue, intelligence, wealth and power, by the grant of extensive areas of its public domain to the furtherance of these objects. If I have not failed entirely in my purpose, I have made it manifest that savings banks are at least a means whereby virtue and intelligence are promoted, and the productive energies of the people are stimulated to more active and efficient exercise, not less truly than are schools and railroads. The relative value of each, it is needless to discuss; we may admit if we will the leading superiority of the latter over the former, still if it has been made to appear that the influence of savings banks is in the same salutary direction of National virtue and National wealth, we have at least established their claim to recognition and aid from the General Government, wherever such aid may be beneficially exercised, to at least a degree corresponding with their conceded influence and power.

How can such aid be extended in such form as not to invest the General Government with a dangerous and offensive monopoly, leave the character and development of a system of savings institutions exclusively to the guardianship and control of State authority as now, and yet effect what the State is powerless to do, such an expansion of the facilities for reaching and depositing in savings banks, that the remote and secluded hamlet in the wilderness may have facilities for making such deposits, absolutely safe, and equal in convenience at least to those which it enjoys in communicating with friends by letter, or by which it receives intelligence from the outside world through magazines and newspapers?

May not a scheme somewhat like the following be elaborated and made practical? Let the General Government allow the *use* of the post-office for the receiving and free transmission of deposits to any savings bank in the country which the depositor may select, also, for the free transmission of orders or drafts upon any savings bank for moneys deposited, and the return of the same to the depositor.

Particular forms of bank books and blanks could be authorized and prepared by the General Government, or by savings banks, and furnished to every post office designated by the Government for that purpose. The experiment might begin here, as in England, upon as small a scale as should be thought desirable, and extended as the success attending it should warrant and demand.

On making a first deposit, the depositor should receive a book with the entry duly made and stamped by the postmaster, and should be entitled to a duplicate receipt from the savings bank as soon as the money should reach the institution.

Of course the Government should be responsible for the money deposited, until the same should reach the savings bank to which it should be addressed, and there after, of course, its responsibility should cease until its aid should be again invoked to return money to the depositor. If there should any objection arise upon the ground of danger from fraud at the savings bank through the officers refusing to acknowledge the receipt of moneys, this could be very easily overcome by the form of order or draft or acknowledgment, in which the transmission should be made, or by transmitting under enclosure to the Postmaster, in the town where the savings bank should be located, who would present the deposit in person and take an acknowledgment that should be an acquittance of the Government from further responsibility. The public interests promoted and served by the expansion of the savings bank system, would warrant the Government in doing this labor, and in assuming this responsibility through its own chosen officers without any return; but if this should be deemed inexpedient, a commission, sufficient to pay for the expense incurred through the extra tax upon the time of the Postmaster, might be charged and allowed by the savings bank, to be deducted from the dividend upon such deposits.

The details of such a scheme connot be elaborated here, nor is there any occasion that they should be. I only drop the crude suggestion by the way, in the hope that some one may find in it the germ of an idea which, with patient thought and care, may be wrought out in some practicable means for the diffusion of the benefits of savings banks to thousands who would otherwise ever remain strangers to all but their name.

Relations of Savings Banks to Banks of Discount.

The specific office of each of these two classes of institutions is clearly defined. They are so wholly distinct and unlike, that there is, or should be, no antagonism between them. For the same reason there should be no intimate connection between them.

It is the business of the bank of discount to make money for its stockholders, for those who have contributed to its capital, by the commissions, discounts, interest or whatever the gains may be called, which it receives for the accommodation afforded by it to the public. They are a public benefit as a great many other private enterprises are a public benefit. But they are still private enterprises, instituted by their projectors for their own advantage and emolument. Their capital and resources are largely invested in what is called business paper, that is, the notes of business men, having as their basis of security the products in various forms, and liable to various contingencies, in which they deal.

Of course such a business is more or less hazardous, especially when we reflect that the resources thus invested are not alone the capital which is paid in, and which, in the form of bank notes issued to the public, is payable on demand, but their deposits, which often greatly exceed the capital, and which are likewise payable on demand. In the ordinary course of business, therefore, every bank has outstanding liabilities payable on demand, which it has resources to meet, payable usually in from one to ninety days.

Such is the general character of the business, and though the salutary provisions of law for the enforcement of contracts and the prevailing commercial integrity of business men, and the course and laws of trade and commerce, enable those long practised in watching financial movements to steer clear of the more imminent dangers to which such business is necessarily exposed, still it is more or less hazardous, and can attract capital to it as an investment, only by the prospect of larger gains than hum-drum investments in bond and mortgage, or other securities at six and seven per cent will yield.

The bank of discount receives deposits, not primarily for the benefit of the depositor, though it is a fact that his convenience is promoted by the operation, but the bank uses them as a means to increase its own profits. In short, all the operations of a bank of discount, in issuing notes, receiving deposits, and discounting paper, are for the purpose of making money for the stockholders. The public so understand it, and expect to pay, and *do pay* accordingly, for the accommodation which they receive. The business is perfectly legitimate, honorable and important to the interests of the community, but that does not make savings banks of them, nor entitle them to be invested with savings bank powers.

Savings banks, on the contrary, are instituted, not for the promotion of the interests of their projectors, but for that of the depositors. SECURITY is their *first* consideration, *profit* for the depositors the second and subordinate.

The purpose of their institution will admit of no *hazards* ; they must be SAFE. Hence the profit to be realized from them can never exceed, can rarely equal the lawful rate of interest at which safe investments may be made, for into these same investments the deposits must be transformed, and the expenses of conducting the business will take something from the legitimate and moderate interest thus earned.

A savings bank, therefore, is not merely a bank that pays interest on deposits, but is an institution in the hands of disinterested persons, receiving deposits for the purpose of investment in those securities which experience has demonstrated to be the most reliable and safe. The profits of such an institution are the interest it receives, the occasional premium on securities sold, or the discount on securities purchased, rents from apartments in its banking house not required for its own use, and and a few other incidental sources. These, after deducting the necessary expenses of conducting the business, inure to the benefit of the depositor, in dividends, or in a reserve for surplus for his greater security, or both.

Such is the character of the business of a savings bank. Whenever it departs from this, and engages in discounting paper, or in buying or selling exchange, or doing any of the various kinds of business which banks of discount do, in so far it abandons its real character, and any tendency in this direction should be discountenanced and corrected. And so, too, banks of discount should be restrained from assuming the title or the character of savings banks, by the offer of interest upon individual deposits. The hazards of banks of discount, from the causes already noted of being liable to respond to their depositors on demend, from resources not yet due, are quite enough, without the weakening of their resources by the payment of interest upon these deposits which they hold by so precarious a tenure.

The only feature in common between a savings bank and a bank of discount is this: They *both receive deposits.* But from this common point, in all their theory, purpose and modes of operation they diverge. A law of our State prohibits any bank from holding itself out to the public as a savings bank. (See Appendix, page 347.)

The principle recognized in the prohibition is a salutary one and might with great propriety be extended further and prohibit banks of discount from accomplishing the same purpose without sign or notice, by allowing interest upon individual deposits. The only object of such practice is, of course, to attract deposits, but where there is no competition, deposits will come in the legitimate course of business without offering a bonus for them, and where there is competion, the result is that all advantage to either is effectually destroyed, by both or all engaging in a practice which all would be better off to abandon.

So, too, there is no good reason why private bankers should not be subjected to the same prohibition, for in some localities the practice of these in paying interest on deposits, is the most serious obstacle to success against which savings banks have to contend. The ignorant and unwary only know that a *bank* is a *bank*, and have no idea of the essential difference between a savings and any other bank. They fall into the office of the private banker, and are impressed with the advantage of a certificate of deposit bearing interest and transferable by indorsement, over a deposit book not thus transferable. They know the banker, and suppose him to be responsible ; they know the chief officer of the savings bank, and judge of the safety of the institution in the same way, from a knowledge of his personal responsibility. Supposing both, therefore, to be eqally responsible, he chooses between the respective form of deposit on the score of *convenience.* Not unfrequently, too, his ear is poisoned by the suggestion of the non-liability of the trustees of savings banks, and the greater safety, in consequence, of the deposit with the private banker, whose whole estate is a pledge to the depositor !

Such practices are a fraud upon the public, and a serious hindrance, oftentimes, to the progress of savings banks that have to compete with them. The distinction between savings banks and banks of discount, whether private or incorporated, in regard to their practices, should be as clearly defined by law as are their objects in the theory of the institution of each respectively. If the law should make that distinction to consist in withholding from the latter the right to pay interest on individual deposits under $5,000, the public would soon come to a realizing sense of the difference between them in this respect, and might in time learn the essential difference in the character of their security.

If the duty of the State to foster savings banks, by protecting them from this embarrassing competition, were not enough to justify such a prohibition, the duty it owes to the public at large, in protecting them from the perils to which they are exposed by these practices, is not only a *sufficient justification*, but, indeed, calls loudly for such action in the name of justice. The air has hardly yet ceased to vibrate with the wails of widows and orphans, who trusted their little inheritance to a bank that promised six and even seven per cent interest to depositors, and of course *failed* in the effort to make a profitable use of such deposits, except in hazardous speculations that proved ruinous to all concerned.

But whatever the State may do for the further protection of savings banks from such competition, and of the public from fraud and imposition, by amending the provisions of the act of 1858 in the manner indicated, its salutary purpose will to a great extent, be defeated under the new dispensation of banks not amenable to the authority of the State. I have before me the advertisement of a NATIONAL BANK in this State, proclaiming itself a SAVINGS BANK, and offering in that capacity six per cent interest upon deposits! What margin, I ask, is there for a safe and profitable employment of these deposits, in legitimate business, after paying the internal revenue tax upon them of one-half per cent? The Comptroller of the Currency has turned his attention to very many petty and inconsequential details in the administration of his pet banks. Would he not do well to turn to the weightier matters that affect the safe and successful operation of this gigantic monopoly?

But these are instances of the assumption of the function of savings banks by banks of discount upon their own responsibility and in their own name.

There is a danger of another sort, against which it may be important to provide, and that is, the taking possession, wholly or in part, of a duly incorporated savings bank by a bank of discount, and using it for its own special interest and advantage. There are three forms in which this appropriation may be made.

First. If a sufficient number of the trustees of a savings bank, to form a majority of a quorum, are at the same time directors in banks of discount, they may combine in the interest of their several institutions, and appropriate a larger proportion of deposits than is necessary or desirable to keep it in that form.

Second. Where trustees are indisposed to tax themselves with the labor of overseeing the operations of their trust, they may contract with the directors of a bank of discount to receive deposits, and generally to transact the business of the savings bank through their machinery, and thus the conduct, and to a great extent, the interests of the savings bank be made subordinate to the interests of the bank of discount.

Third. The trustee of a savings bank may be constituted chiefly or wholly from the directors of a bank of discount, and thus the institution become only a tender to the bank of discount.

The first of these provisions is guarded against in the cities of New York and Kings by prohibiting any trustee from being at the same time a director in a bank of discount where the savings bank deposits are kept.

The design of this provision is salutary, and meets with very general acceptance. It doubtless operates disadvantageously at times, in preventing an institution from securing the services of a competent financial adviser as a member of the board of trustees. But I believe the provision has wrought more of good than of evil in the administration of the affairs of savings banks in those two cities, and ought not to be abrogated unless some equally effective substitute can be found.

The question of extending the provision so as to apply to all savings banks in the State has engaged my attention not a little. In the towns and cities of the interior it would often be found difficult to secure the right class of men for trustees of a savings bank, without including some who were directors in a bank of discount. Whether the difficulty is an insuperable one may admit of doubt, but that it would often times prove extremely embarrassing is quite evident to my mind.

Besides, to get the full benefit of such a provision, it should have effect immediately, which would break up the existing organization of some institutions entirely, and perhaps in that way inflict greater evils than those from which we seek to escape.

The object being to prevent any bank, or combination of banks, from getting control of the deposits of the savings bank in their own interest, this might be effected by requiring a unanimous vote of a quorum of trustees to designate the banks in which the available deposits should be kept; or the proportion of trustees that may be directors in banks of discount might be limited. Then by limiting the proportion of deposits that might be kept in any one bank to five per cent, and the proportion in all banks to twenty per cent, and placing all under watchful supervision, to see that there is no violation or evasion of the law, and all opportunity to abuse of the power confided to trustees would, I believe, be effectually removed.

The delegation to a bank of discount of the powers and duties of the trustees of a savings bank, is a reprehensible practice.

Though the trustees have possession of the securities, and direct the investments, the relation between two institutions so diverse in their character and objects, is too intimate to be of mutual advantage, and, if either is to suffer from the connection, we may rest assured that it will not be the institution whose *business is to make money.* No bank is going to undertake the labor of conducting the working operations of a savings bank, unless there is something *to be made out of it.* The guarantee to pay expenses, means that they will employ some of their clerks, or a special clerk for the purpose, to receive and pay money and keep the accounts, and charge for the service—usually all the difference between the receipts and the dividends to depositors.

I am aware that better terms are sometimes made, as in the case of the Albany Savings Bank, which receives an addition to its surplus of $3,000 a year from the deposit bank that transacts its business; but the bank still makes a very handsome profit out of the operation, which the savings bank should realize and distribute as additional dividends to its depositors, or invest as further surplus for their greater security. In short, no such relation can exist between these institutions, without the strength or usefulness of the savings bank being impaired by the connection.

And, as a rule, the discount bank takes the business as a speculation, making the most it can from the investments and deposits, paying the smallest practicable dividends, and taking the difference for its trouble and expense. But as more can be made from discounts than from permanent investments at six or seven per cent, of course it is the policy of the discount bank to have a large portion of the savings deposits uninvested, for its own greater convenience and profit. In illustration of this tendency, note the large per cent of deposits in bank of the Albany Savings, the Schenectady and Chenango County, all of which are conducted by banks of discount under contract with the trustees. The latter, however, has, upon suggestion from the Department, changed its policy in this respect since the last annual report was made.

It is this tendency to expose the deposits of savings banks to the hazards of the successful management of a bank of discount, that renders this close intimacy of association between these institutions dangerous and improper.

I would not close my eyes to the fact that there are instances in which the business of savings banks is conducted by banks of discount, where this tendency is overcome by the wise and considerate control of trustees. Such are the Sing Sing, Fishkill, Rome, and perhaps others that do not occur to me now. These make a convenience of the bank of discount, and do not allow it to sacrifice the safety of their trust to its own pecuniary advantage. But even here is the danger ever lurking, that in the progress of events, through changes in the constituency of the boards of trustees, a more lax policy may sometime prevail, from which peril may impend and disaster befall.

The third form of appropriation of a savings bank by and in the interest of a bank of discount, has the same tendency and the same dangers as the last mentioned, besides, from its more intimate connection and identity of interest, added dangers peculiar to itself.

Exemplifications of this intimacy of relation, where the trustees of the savings bank are largely composed of the directors of a bank of discount that transacts the business of the institution, are found in the Albany City, Albany Exchange, Mechanics' and Farmers', of Albany; the Schenectady; and the Central, Manufacturer's, Mutual, and State, of Troy. Of these the Mechanics' and Farmers', of Albany, under the requirements of its charter, keeps its deposits quite closely invested. Of the remainder, all but one have much the larger portion of their deposits in bank, two have all in that form, and but one has any surplus worth mentioning.

Could the impolicy of this intimate connection between savings banks and banks of discount have stronger confirmation than is afforded by such disclosures?

But besides these, there are other dangers to which the prosperity, if not the security of savings banks thus controlled are exposed. If the discount bank finds upon its hands depreciated stocks, as New York State 5s, that will command but 93 to 95 in the market, they have to say the least, a strong *temptation* to sell the same at par to the trustees of the savings bank (themselves in that relation), at par. I do not *know* that this has ever been done, but if not, it has not been from lack of motive and opportunity. The exposure to such *chances* of mal-administration, is enough to mark the combination of rival interests in the same individuals under which it may be effected, with emphatic condemnation.

But the rival interests of savings banks and banks of discount assume at times, another form of development to the prejudice of the former.

The Manufacturers' Savings Bank of Troy, has exhibited a gradually diminishing line of deposits, from $129,569 in 1861, to $22,-714 in 1867. Presuming that this indicated a voluntary winding up of the affairs of the institution, this savings bank was marked "closing" in the last annual report from this Department. On inquiry, however, I find that the trustees have no intention of relinquishing their franchise, but true to their instincts as directors of the Manufacturers' National Bank, which all of them are, depositors are advised to make their deposits directly in the National Bank, and take a certificate bearing interest. In this way one of the half per cents of government tax is saved, that would have to be paid if the deposit was first made in the savings bank, and by the savings bank made in the National. If only this financial acuteness could be secured in the interest of the savings bank, it could not fail to be a most prosperous institution!

The depositors knowing no distinction between what should be the security of a savings bauk and the security of a deposit bank, which indeed in this, as in some other instances, is a distinction quite without a difference, and being assured, besides, that in this way they get the added security of the liability of the stockholders of the National Bank, are easily persuaded to make their deposit in the form proposed.

Other banks in that city do the same thing, but not to the same demoralizing extent. Can the impolicy of a relation that admits of such results as even a remote possibility, require further illustration or enforcement?

The system that permits such practices is wrong, because it destroys the essential and vital distinction between savings and other banks, which consists in the secure and reliable investments of the former, removed from all the hazards of business and misfortune that attend the latter.

It is wrong, in that it makes the prosperity of the savings bank subordinate to the prosperity of the bank of deposit.

It is wrong, in that it gives countenance and support to the error, too prevalent in the community, that savings and other banks are necessarily exposed to the same hazards, and that the commercial or financial crisis that destroys the integrity of the latter, must in the same degree impair the security of the former, whereby such crises *do* reach and affect, with frenzied apprehensions, the depositors in savings banks, to their own detriment and that of the institutions.

And, to state a paradox, *it is wrong* because *if it is right*, then the whole theory of savings banks, as a peculiar institution, is false and unfounded, for banks of discount can be made to serve every purpose equally well.

It is no answer to these objections to point to the high character of the deposit banks that thus direct the operations and control the destinies of savings banks. Other banks of standing equally high, and having the confidence of the community in full as great a degree, have come to grief within our recollection. There was nothing in their history, condition or circumstances, prior to their failure, that would not have justified their connection with the affairs of a savings bank as intimate and responsible as that enjoyed by any deposit bank to-day.

The boasted additional security derived from the personal liability of stockholders is purely visionary. Are A., B. and C. more responsible than the government of the United States, or of the State of New York, or even than the city, county or town of which their wealth is but an insignificant fraction? Their possessions in houses and lands may pass from their grasp, and creditors receive no benefit from them under their new proprietorship, but these possessions still pay taxes, and in this way maintain the credit of the State or municipality to which they belong.

And as a final consideration, if more can be needed, these banks of discount are now for the most part foreign coporations, over whose operations the State can exercise no control. They have possession of the books and records of the savings banks whose agents they are; they receive and disburse the deposits; they incur and pay expenses; and the State is powerless but by their grace and favor to exercise any scrutiny over their proceedings. I have in my intercourse received only courtesy from the officers of these institutions, but contrast the meagreness of the details which they report under the statement of Cash Transactions, with the fullness of the same from institutions that are free from these "entangling alliances," for confirmation of this view, that the more intimate the connection between savings banks and banks of discount, the further removed are the former from the protection, supervision and care of State authority.

That savings banks can be conducted with safety and success upon an absolutely free and independent basis, using banks of discount only in their legitimate sphere, as the public use them, as depositories for funds which they may require in the daily operations of business, is demonstrated by the sound and prosperous condition of these institutions in Newburgh, Poughkeepsie, Hudson, Oswego, Yonkers, Southold,, and other localities that might be named; not to mention those in Utica, Syracuse, Rochester and Buffalo, that still more perfectly exemplify this position. Most of these were organized prior to 1857, and successfully passed the ordeal of that trying year. If in these towns of limited population savings banks can be made strong, successful and prosperous, without leaning upon a bank of discount for support, surely in Albany, Schenectady and Troy they require no such adventitious aid. And not only *do* they survive and prosper, but, judged by any true and proper standard applicable to savings banks, they are *stronger* and *more successful* than any of the institutions which subsist under the *vulturous protection* of National banks!

German Savings Bank of Brooklyn.

In this connection, as a part of our passing history, throwing its light, or shadow rather, upon the condition and workings of our savings bank system, it may be well to introduce the experience of the German Savings Bank, of Brooklyn.

This institution was chartered in 1866, and commenced business on the 30th of June in that year. On the 1st of July, 1867, it

Reported assets	$252,799 90
Due depositors	250,723 03

Among the assets were $28,435.53 deposited in the Farmers' and Citizens' National Bank of Brooklyn, and $4,500 loaned upon the security of the stock of that bank. The failure of the Farmers' and Citizens' Bank, some time afterwards, led me to seek information as to the extent to which the savings bank would be affected or compromised thereby.

The following correspondence is therefore submitted as part of the history of savings banks, pertinent to our present inquiry:

Albany, 14*th October*, 1867.

George S. Bishop,
Cashier German Savings Bank, Williamsburgh:

By your July report you had $28,435.53 on deposit in Farmers' and Citizens' National Bank; also $4,500 loaned on stock of said bank as security. Will you please inform me what amount you had on deposit in that bank when it failed; also if you had any loans out on security of its stocks at that time; and whether the savings bank is likely to sustain any loss on either account of the failure of the bank? I want the information as a part of the history of the time to incorporate in my report. I understand the trustees of your bank have nobly come forward and put themselves in the breach; and I shall be very sorry to learn that they are likely to lose anything on account of their trust, or to learn of any embarrassment to your institution, which appeared to me to be so well conducted, and to be doing so prosperously. Your early reply will greatly oblige. Respectfully yours,

EMERSON W. KEYES,
Deputy Superintendent.

BROOKLYN, N. Y., *October 17th*, 1867.

Dear Sir—Yours of the 14th received, in reply to which I regret to have to inform you that the balance to the credit of this bank, remaining in the Farmers' and Citizens' National Bank when it closed, was nominally $36,451.87, of which $22,000 had been loaned on bond and mortgage, awaiting the call of the parties to whom the loans were made, leaving our available funds in the bank $14,451.87. The $4,500 call loan, which was also a portion of our available fund, remains the same as in July last. We are assured by the receiver that the assets of the Farmers' and Citizen's National Bank will probably be sufficient to repay every depositor in full.

The directors yet hope to regain possession of and close the affairs of their bank themselves, and return all deposits by installments as soon as possible. Should they not succeed, the receiver has expressed his intention of making a dividend in January next. Steps are also being taken to recover the $4,500 call loan, or to exchange the securities. Our trustees are men of responsibility, and express themselves willing to make up any deficiency that may occur. Any further information the Department may desire will be promptly furnished, and any suggestions you may wish to make will be thankfully received. Thanking you for the kindly feelings expressed in favor of our bank, and hoping that your efforts to establish these kindred institutions on the firm basis, that the sacredness of the trust demands may be successful,

I remain, very respectfully yours,
GEO. S. BISHOP, *Cashier.*

To EMERSON W. KEYES, Esq.,
Deputy Sup't Banking Dep't, Albany, N. Y.

It is to be hoped the institution will suffer only a temporary interruption of its prosperity from this connection with the misfortunes of its depository. The action of the trustees in offering to guarantee the depositors from loss is highly creditable, for as they were acting within the discretion authorized by their charter, they could not be made liable.

We can see how much worse it might have been, had they acted up to the full measure of their authorized discretion, and had a third of their deposits exposed to the hazards that attend the operations of banks of discount; or if the National Bank had been their agent conducting the business of the savings bank, having control of all its deposits; or suppose that a much larger proportion of their "available fund" had been in the form of call loans, secured by the stock of this "reliable and well-managed institution!" What a *mockery* is the term "available fund" applied to loans secured by stocks whose value depends upon the hazards of business, or upon the integrity of men with magnificent opportunities and grand temptations ever before them to betray the confidence reposed in them. Their liability to prove the most *unavailable* of any form of investment, is apparent from the experience of this institution.

On the other hand, had the discretion of the trustees been restricted in the manner I propose, and no more than five per cent of their deposits been in the keeping of the Farmers' and Citizens' Bank, the embarrassment to themselves and their customers would have been corespondingly diminished. Or had they been advised in advance, or their liability for losses incurred through the exercise of their discretion in the admission of such securities, they might have been more guarded in accepting anything so precarious as bank stock. Fortunately their own honor is in this instance an acceptable substitute for more stringent provisions of law.

But if from this transaction the legislative guardians of the sacred trust of $131,000,000, whose security is imperiled by the same conditions that became operative in the experience of the German Savings Bank, do not take to heart its salutary and impressive lesons, we may indulge in well-founded apprehensions lest some day our pride in the stability of our saving bank system be turned into shame and confusion over its untimely ruin.

Savings Banks that have Failed.

A further illustration of the practical workings of our system of savings banks, and of the points of weakness in legislative restriction or supervisory control, for which effective safeguards should be provided by law, may be found in the history of the two savings banks in our State that have failed.

That there are but two of these, I have already characterized as creditable to our history; but if it shall be found that either failure resulted from the exercise of legally authorized discretion by trustees without corresponding liability, and that equally liberal provisions still characterize the laws of savings banks, it will follow that the credit belongs to the wisdom and integrity of those who have administered the trust, and not to the sagacity of those who have framed the laws under which such misfortunes are possible,

Or if it shall be found that either was the result of practices forbidden by law, there will appear at least to have been some defect in the system or administration of supervisory functions, whereby such practices could be indulged without exposure and correction.

Fortunately, neither of these failures was so disastrous as to result in great misfortune to confiding depositors, or to involve other institutions in their calamity. The first of these was

THE KNICKERBOCKER SAVINGS INSTITUTION,

Located in the city of New York, and incorporated in 1851. It did business until 1854, when it failed, the primary cause of the failure being the suspension of the Knickerbocker Bank, a bank of discount, in which the deposits of the savings bank were kept.

There was due depositors at the time of failure, as nearly as can be ascertained, $472,671, on which there was paid in three dividends a total of 86⅓ per cent.

The assets at the time of failure consisted of

Bonds and mortgages	$324,091	
Deposit in Knickerbocker Bank	114,582	
Notes, mostly secured by Knickerbocker Bank stock as collateral,* say	33,000	
		$473,673
Interest was allowed by the court on the above deposit in bank		6,359
Total		$480,032

* I took from the books, by courtesy of the U. S. Trust Company, receiver, only the leading items of these, amounting to $29,519. The estimate above is nearly correct.

The amount realized from the assets was:

From mortgages	$275,748,	or 75 per cent.
From deposits in bank	113,939,	or 94 do
From notes, about	1,000,	or 3 do
Total	$390,667	

The savings bank was in fact little more than a *side issue* of the bank of discount, which, as we see, held nearly twenty-five per cent of its deposits, and whose friends, as owners of its stock had considerable more in the form of loans secured by pledge of the stock as collateral. The utter worthlessness of the collateral is apparent from the amount realized on the notes which it was given to secure, being in fact less than three per cent of their face.

It was this intimacy in the relations of the two institutions, well known to the depositors that precipitated the failure, for, accustomed to regard their interests as closely if not absolutely identified, the failure of the one caused a rush upon the other, which, in its embarrassed state, it could not long sustain, and its suspension inevitably soon followed. Had there not been this intimacy of relation, depositors would not have had their apprehensions excited by the failure of the bank of discount, and though embarrassment and loss to the savings bank could not have been averted, it might, out of an increasing business, and by judicious management of its assets, have recovered itself, or at least have converted its assets under more favorable auspices than at public sale, and thus have realized more for distribution to the depositors when closing became inevitable.

But without indulging in speculation as to what might have been, we learn from what did occur that dangers attend an unlimited discretion in trustees to invest in bonds and mortgages, and to keep so large an available fund as one-third of the entire deposits in such form as they may please to direct. More than 68 per cent of the deposits were invested in bonds and mortgages. which realized but 85 per cent of their face. And yet the unlimited discretion of trustees in regard to the proportion of such investment is, by some, earnestly contended for!

The operations of this savings bank were wholly within the limits authorized by their charter, which is no more liberal than the greater number of those in active operation to-day. Is not the duty of the Legislature in regard to this matter plain and imperative?

THE SIXPENNY SAVINGS BANK OF THE CITY OF ROCHESTER

Was incorporated in 1854 and failed in 1857. There was due depositors at the time of failure, about $69,000, on which there was paid by the receiver 95 per cent. Some forty of the depositors sued the trustees, and recovered in full, and about $1,000 was voluntarily paid by the trustees to others who refused to compromise or relinquish their claims.

The assets of the institution at the time of failure were:

Bonds and mortgages	$39,000
Notes and other claims, and bonds and mortgages assigned as collateral, about	30,000

The direct cause of the misfortune was the failure of the secretary and treasurer, who, in his business as broker or private banker, used the funds of the institution, giving to the trustees as security therefor collaterals that failed to realize their face when put upon the market. The bonds and mortgages held by the savings bank were very favorably negotiated, there being a loss upon them of only about $500 and, probably, some accrued interest.

The use of the deposits by the treasurer, in the manner stated, was a loan of the same to him, and was a violation of that provision of all charters of savings banks, which prohibits any trustee or officer from borrowing or in any manner using the deposits; and it was upon this ground that the trustees who consented to this use of the deposits, or who neglected to prevent it, were held liable to the depositors, and were compelled to make restitution.

These transactions occurred before the present system of oversight was established, and hence are not chargeable to any defect in the administration of the law, but to the absence of suitable provisions of law to secure a proper and efficient supervision. But it is pertinent to inquire whether the system of supervision through the Superintendent of the Banking Department, under the powers conferred upon him is, if efficiently administered, ample to prevent such palpable violations of the law. A very slight examination of his powers and duties under the law of 1857, will conclusively establish his powerlessness to prevent a repetition of the practices that resulted in the failure of the Sixpenny Savings Bank.

The law from which he derives his authority, prescribes what the trustees shall report, and gives to him no power or discretion to call for any other information. His right to visit and examine any savings bank under that act, must be predicated upon some neglect of the institution in regard to its report, or upon some *suspicion* of illegal or dangerous practices.

Applying these provisions to the case in hand, and there is no means by which he could have any knowledge of such practices, unless in respect to something else in the report, or by some rumor, his suspicions should be awakened, and be made the basis of an examination.

One of the most salutary, as well as one of the most important provisions, is that, common to all charters, prohibiting trustees from borrowing or using the deposits. But how is the Superintendent to know that the loan to A is to a trustee of the institution? The act of incorporation will not, perhaps, aid him, for A may not be a charter member, but may have been elected subsequently, to fill a vacancy. It is quite possible therefore for trustees, negligent of, or indifferent to their trust, to violate the law or to suffer it to be violated, in this most important particular, without attracting the attention of any supervisory authority.

A very simple provision would serve to correct this. Let the names of the trustees at a given time be reported to the Superintendent, who should record them in a book provided for that purpose. Whenever afterwards, any changes occur by the happening of vacancies or filling the same, let these also be reported and entered.

Then the name of every person to whom a loan is made should be reported, and as changes occur in these let them also be reported. The Superintendent would then have before him, at all times, the data from which to ascertain whether any loans were being made to trustees.

If it should be objected that this involves considerable labor, I answer, not so much as at first appears. The names once duly reported the changes would be infrequent. Even loans upon stock securities I should hope would be neither so abundant, nor so unstable, as to require any very considerable labor to transmit them to the Department.

But if it were very much more labor than it appears, its importance to any efficient or even tolerable supervision, would amply justify it. Here is one of the most essential safeguards for the security of savings banks, individually or as a system, in the form of a restriction upon the power of the trustees, and operating in direct opposition to their personal interests, rendered practically inoperative by the lack of any means whereby to expose and correct its violation! Can any mere clerical labor be too arduous, that will give effect to this most salutary and important provision? We have seen to what results this want of supervisory inspection has led in one instance, they might have been far more disastrous; we have no guaranty that in the future they may not be fearfully calamitous. We shall indeed be most fortunate if we may learn and practice wisdom, from an experience in which the element of misfortune mingles in so small a degree. To ensure this demands prompt and decisive action.

THE ELMIRA SAVINGS BANK.

In this connection it is proper to call attention to an irregularity in the voluntary closing of an institution, which, though having no unfortunate result in the particular instance cited, affords a precedent, than if commonly acted upon, might lead to serious consequences.

The Elmira Savings Bank was chartered in 1854.

When it first reported to this Department, in 1858, the amount due depositors was $1,742.

The deposits increased slowly up to 1863, when they amounted to $6,657. In 1864, they were $29,465; in 1865, $62,632; and in 1866, $69,476; with assets, $76,330.

During this year, the trustees resolved to close the institution, and pay off the depositors; and to this end *sold* the assets to Wm. T. Post, Esq.; that is, he agreed to take the assets and pay the depositors in full, with interest. He gave no bond for the execution of his contract. The assets consisted mostly of bonds and mortgages having some time to run.

Up to this time, however, he has fulfilled the terms of his contract, and his personal character and financial ability give satisfactory assurance that he will continue to do so.

Depositors receive the amount of their deposits, with six per cent interest, not compounded, and are paid on demand. There was due depositors September 1, 1867, $5,473.28, with assets in in the hands of the assignee sufficient to meet all claims.

The terms are, doubtless, satisfactory to depositors.

It does not appear, however, what was the special necessity for closing the bank, nor by what authority the assignment was made.

The dangerous tendencies of such a policy, if this transaction were to be accepted as a precedent for future action, are too apparent to require elucidation. If this transaction was lawful, what is to prevent the trustees of a savings bank with $500,000 or $1,000,000 of surplus, from selling the assets for a handsome bonus, and closing the institution by paying off the depositors at simple interest?

Obviously a method should be devised, whereby a trust that has become burdensome may be relinquished, by transferring it to competent authority, who should find for it other custodians, or close it in some prescribed and authorized manner for the exslusive benefit of the depositors.

Common Trust Saving Fund.

Among the means for ensuring the security of depositors against any possible casualties of business or of dishonesty, may be considered that proposed in your last annual report to the Legislature, of a Common Trust Savings Fund, to be created by contributions from each savings bank, in the ratio of its deposits or surplus, and held by the Superintendent, to be applied to the payment in full of the liabilities of any insolvent institution. The recommendation appeared to me to be eminently judicious and timely. Nor do I regard the objections that are urged against it, as having any considerable force, if it must be conceded that no safeguards of legislation and supervision can serve to render the insolvency of a savings bank impossible. Unless it is possible to put every savings bank beyond all contingency of failure, the State should do one of two things—either itself guarantee depositors from loss, or oblige these institutions to guarantee each other. Without a more direct interest in these institutions than it now has, or without some power in the appointment of officers, that should be responsible to it, the State cannot be expected to assume any such liability. We are then thrown back upon the other alternative of devising some means of making savings banks secure without any guarantees, through the careful provisions of the law concerning their investments and general management, and a system of supervision by which their condition may at all times be perfectly understood, and the requirements of the law concerning them rigidly enforced.

Having expended my energies upon the elaboration of devices to this end, and as I believe, with success, I have found it unnecessary to urge as an essential part of our system the Common Trust Savings Fund recommended in that report.

Deposits.

Among the subjects for consideration suggested by various provisions in different charters, is that relating to a limitation of the amount of deposits to be received by a savings bank from any one individual. Many charters, as will be seen, contain no limitation whatever, while in others it varies from $2,000 to $5,000, or even, in a few instances, $10,000. The act of 1853 limited the amount that should be received by any savings bank thereafter to be incorporated, in the counties of New York and Kings, to $1,000; but with the usual result in such cases, the general law being rendered uniformly inoperative by specific authority, in subsequent charters, to receive a larger amount.

The questions of policy involved in any limitation at all, through either specific prohibition of law or the wise and sulutary discretion of trustees, relate first, to the preservation of the original character and purpose of these institutions, as the resort exclusively of the poor, and secondly, to the greater security to the institution, resulting from holding only comparatively small deposits as against the larger sums, to meet the withdrawal of which would require the keeping of a much larger available fund.

So long as savings banks are made accessible to the poor with their small earnings, so long as these are made welcome and treated with courtesy and kindly consideration, savings banks do not lose their original and distinctive character as provident ministers to this deserving class. They may assume other characteristics not incompatible with their original purpose, when they receive the larger deposit of the more fortunate clerk, accountant or manager; but they no more lose their primitive character by so doing than when the remove from the little office where their small beginning was made to the marble or freestone banking house, with millions subject to their control.

Besides, who are the poor? We have them "always with us," but where shall the strict line be drawn between poverty and competence? One family will be poorer with $1,000 than another with $100, as where a widow is left with children to support and but $1,000 or even $5,000 from which to derive an income to aid her own efforts. She is certainly poorer than the mechanic, who can earn his three or four dollars a day, though he has in the savings bank but $100. Even a larger sum than $5,000 would not, in this country, indicate affluence; and if it were all that is left for the support of a deserving family, it might be a hardship to refuse to it the *security* of a savings bank deposit, at least until it could find more profitable investment elsewhere. I cannot think, therefore, that our savings banks are in any danger from this source of losing their distinctive character as beneficiary and provident institutions.

The suggestion of the relative insecurity to a savings bank from deposits in large sums, is entitled to consideration; but any danger from this direction might be averted by a limitation of the rate of dividends on sums above a certain limit, or by requiring them to be on deposit for a certain period, long enough to insure their profitable employment by the institution, before becoming entitled to dividends, or by an imperative requirement of notice before withdrawal, or by all of these combined. Under restrictions like these, savings banks would still afford a safe retreat for the little patrimony awaiting other investment, a purpose quite within the scope of their provident design, while they would hardly be attractive to the class of speculative adventurers, whose monopoly of these institutions we should indeed deprecate as baneful and destructive.

The idea of a limitation of the deposits of any one individual to a comparatively small amount, originated in England, and grew out of the anomolous fact that the interest allowed on these deposits was higher than the prevailing rate in government funds. Of course, under such conditions, some provision was indispensable to prevent a perversion of these institutions from their true purpose.

But with us the conditions are such as necessarily to keep the interest or dividends from savings banks uniformly below the legal rate authorized or received from other investments. So long as this condition characterizes our system, I think there is little danger to be apprehended from an accumulation of large deposits, and with such limitations as I have suggested, the whole question might safely be left to the discretion of trustees.

Whether any requirement that savings banks shall receive the smallest amount of deposits that may be offered, is necessary or desirable, is perhaps an open question. That much good has resulted from the voluntary assumption of this practice, I am fully persuaded, but much of the benefit has arisen from the cheerful and kindly spirit with which the action has been performed—a spirit far more likely to accompany voluntary than compulsory measures. If the suggestion is insufficient to incite to voluntary action, I should have little hope that any considerable good would result from such a requirement, made imperative.

Dividends.

The profits of savings banks are mainly derived from interest on investments. So are those of banks of issue, or stock banks. The profits of the latter, distributed to shareholders, are called dividends, while those of the former, distributed to depositors, are called interest.

I see no good reason for this distinction in the terms applied to essentially the same thing, produced in essentially the same way.

Interest has a special, legal and technical signification. It is always fixed and determinate in advance, either by law or by agreement of parties. Dividends are indeterminate until earned and declared, or *should be so*, and bare some ratio to profits; as, no profits, no dividend. All the characteristics of dividends attach to the distribution of profits to depositors; they have none of the characteristics of interest. I prefer and shall employ the term dividend, as being more significant, truthful and appropriate.

As upon almost every other subject of importance connected with savings banks, so in regard to this, it will be seen that the law is various.

The more common provision as will be found in the summary of charters in the appendix, is expressed with a great degree of uniformity in the following words:

"It shall be the duty of trustees to regulate the rate of interest (dividends) to be allowed to depositors, so that they shall receive, as nearly as may be, a ratable proportion of all the profits of the corporation, after deducting all necessary expenses."

A few charters authorize a rate of interest one per cent greater on deposits of $500 and under, than on those above that amount, others make such a classification of rates imperative.

Two authorize a classification of rates having regard to the time the principal sum has been on deposit, while a few leave the whole question to the discretion of trustees.

The act of 1853, to which reference has so frequently been made, and which applies to savings banks in New York and Kings counties only, in the sixth section provides, concerning all savings banks thereafter to be incorporated, "that the rate of interest on all deposits of $500 and under, shall be one per cent per annum greater than shall be allowed on any sum exceeding $500."

But the institutions incorporated since the passage of the act very generally disregard this requirement, either by authority of special provisions in their charters, inconsistent with the requirement, or because the inconvenience of submission has more terrors for them than the possible consequences of a violation of the law.

Others, and generally the older institutions in New York and Brooklyn, (the only part of Kings county in which there are any savings banks), make this classification in the rates of dividends paid, on their own motion, as a matter of policy, tending to the encouragement of the poor and humble, whose accumulations must be small, and to discourage large deposits, from those who are able to seek other investments, and for whose benefit savings banks were not instituted. These are uniformly quite emphatic in their expression of opinion that the provision is a salutary one, and should be enforced.

Nothing is clearer than that as a mandatory provision it should be uniform. If any institution is to be required to classify its rate of dividends upon the basis under consideration, then all should be. The real question is whether such a provision should be mandatory or only permissive, or whether, indeed, such a classification of rates should not be prohibited, and a uniformity of rate upon all sums be absolutely required.

Few I think would go to this length in the enforcement of uniformity, those favoring uniformity being content if the question should be left to the discretion of the trustees.

But the distinction between making such a provision mandatory, and leaving it permissive, is radical, and one concerning which, a very earnest sentiment is entertained and expressed on either side.

The grounds upon which such a provision is favored, have been stated above. To repeat, they are in brief:

1. To encourage small depositors whom savings banks were instituted exclusively to assist and benefit.

2. To discourage the accumulation of large deposits from those who are presumed to be competent to make their own investments.

The high regard which I entertain for the character and worth of those gentlemen who earnestly advocate the enforcement of this provision, their sincerity, their disinterestedness, the careful thought which I know they have given to the subject, and the experience in the practical workings of savings banks which they have enjoyed, all combine to entitle their opinions to a careful and candid consideration. In such a spirit, and with the sole purpose in view of arriving at a conclusion the nearest *right*, just, safe, and salutary, let us examine this question from their standpoint.

First, as to the encouragement of small depositors.

I think a fallacy has unconsciously wrought itself into this proposition. It seems to be assumed that the encouragement is found in the distinction between rates, and not in the rates themselves. Put in form, it would involve an absurdity like the following: "The savings bank that pays five per cent to depositors of $500, and but four per cent to depositors of larger amounts, thereby encourages the smaller depositors, more than the savings bank that pays six per cent to all depositors." Unquestionably this is not the form that it was intended the argument should take, but the facts before us and which must be made a part of the argument upon this question, compel the proposition to assume that form. What are the facts? That with a single exception the highest rate of dividends paid last year by any savings bank that had classified rates, was six per cent, while the savings banks that had a uniform rate for all depositors, generally paid six per cent. Thus, under either policy, the smaller depositors received six per cent. Wherein, then, were they the more "encouraged" by the one than by the other? Obviously, the policy of different rates possesses no peculiar features of encouragement to any class unless these be found in the selfish gratification of having received more than somebody else, which is our repudiated proposition over again. If, therefore, there is in reality no superior attraction to the small depositors in the policy of classified rates, as the facts of the case seem conclusively to establish, then the argument for a compulsory enforcement of such classification, upon this ground, is deprived of all force.

The argument to have weight, must be predicated upon conditions like these; out of an ascertained amount of profits to be divided, a uniform rate of but so much per cent to each depositor can be allowed, while with a classified rate, confining that per cent to depositors of over $500, one per cent more can be allowed to depositors of $500 or under. The argument is good, if these conditions exist, and not otherwise. The practical action of these institutions as detailed above, would seem to show that these conditions are, to say the least, unusual. I have, besides, an illustration directly in point, in the case of the South Brooklyn Savings Bank, which for sixteen years had, under a by-law, enforced classified rates of dividends, upon the basis which we are now considering. During the present year they have adopted the policy of uniform dividends, on the ground in the first place, that an arbitrary limitation of $500 was too easily evaded by the depositor, who would open different accounts in the same institution, in trust for wife, children or friends; and secondly, that the institution could as well pay six per cent on a , as five per cent on those of over $500, and six per cent on those of but $500 or less, and they exhibit this calculation in support of that view; the dividends credited to depositors for the year 1866, at five and six per cent, amounted to $84,522.99. It would have required but $4,769.14 more, to have made them uniformly six per cent.

It seems to me that this single instance sufficiently illustrates the impolicy of an enforced regulation of this kind. Here, such a law would compel the institution to withold from depositors what it had, and could afford to give, in order simply to note a class distinction between the *poor* labeled $500, and those of *affluence* labeled $501, or upwards! Nothing is thereby added to the gains of the poor, but something material is taken from the earnings of the others. And among the latter may be a widow, whose only support besides her own labors, is $1,000 in the savings bank. The ten dollars which her deposit has *earned*, and of which she is thus deprived, would go far to furnish her winter's coal or bread.

I by no means contend for an enforced uniformity; I would in this matter leave each institution free to act according to the conditions by which it shall find itself surrounded.

The second consideration of the undue encouragement given to depositors of large sums to make use of savings banks for other than their original purpose, I regard as being fully answered in the discussion of the limitation of the amount of deposits to be received from one individual. The savings bank cannot, as a rule, become attractive to depositors of independent means, so long as the ordinary dividends are less than the legal rate of interest. The insecurity attending deposits of considerable amounts, I would provide against by proper safeguards as there indicated, and having done that the more free for *all classes* the access is made to savings banks, the greater will be their prosperity, and the greater will be the benefits they confer upon those in whose special interest they were primarily instituted.

I have been furnished with the views upon this question, of an officer of one of the savings banks in the city of New York, to which I will give place, as having more value than the arguments of a mere observer like myself :

Argument, in opposition to the Law requiring that all sums on deposit in savings banks to one account of over five hundred dollars, shall be credited with interest at one per cent less than that paid on small deposits.

1. That the law is frequently rendered inoperative by the depositor opening duplicate accounts in his wife or children's names, or by opening fresh accounts in neighboring banks; some depositors thus have a number of accounts which could be kept more economically and safely in one, and with great saving of time to the depositor.

2. Other depositors not discovering this mode of evading the operation of the law, become dissatisfied and lose something of their previously strong desire to accumulate. The English banks recognizing this operation of the principle, directly reverse our policy, and average a scale of ascending interest, paying the largest percentage on the largest deposits.* It can scarcely be questioned that this plan operates favorably on the character of the depositor, stimulating his ambition and encouraging habits of prudence and self-denial.

3. Our citizens of foreign birth are usually very anxious to hold real estate, and while striving eagerly to accumulate a few thousand dollars for this purpose, do not as a rule understand modes of investments apart from the savings banks. They are embarrassed by this rule of descending interest for which they can detect no good reason.

4. That this limitation in tending to the multiplication of accounts not only increases the expenses of the bank, but encourages unnecessarily the increase of the number of savings banks, and thereby largely swells the aggregate of rents, salaries, and other expenses, without increasing the sums of deposits, the profits of which are to bear these expenses.

5. That the cost of keeping one account of five thousand dollars is no more than of keeping one of five dollars; hence no economical reason can exist for reduction of interest on the larger sums.

6. That no valid reason exists, either, for limitation of sums held by a person on deposit, or of interest to be paid thereon, as the interest must invariably be lower than the legal rate in order to allow a margin for expenses of the bank. All large sums will necessarily seek those modes of investment which pay the full

* This must refer to a practice of savings banks under the old system. In the Post Office Savings Banks the rate is uniform. E. W. K.

legal interest. Natural economical laws, therefore, afford all the limitations practically necessary.

7. That the law is especially unjust in affecting only New York and Brooklyn, and not other parts of the State; this injustice is more obvious when it is remembered that as money is more abundant in the cities than in the country, is easier earned and has less purchasing power, savings of over five hundred dollars become much more common in the former than in the latter.

8. That the law tends to drive capital from our city and State into New Jersey, where the policy of the savings banks in this particular, is more liberal than ours.

9. That the great advantage which savings banks confer upon the general public, in the accumulation and centralization of scattered funds that otherwise would be unavailable, as capital for the support of industry and promotion of enterprise, and that any policy which tends to divide, scatter, decentralize their accumulation, is of public injury.

10. That the whole idea of limitation is derived from the English system, which, while allowing an ascending scale of interest, puts a final limit to deposits because the rate of interest is larger than the legal rate, a bonus being allowed by government, and hence limitations are necessary, or else the banks would be employed by those for whom they were not designed.

But it by no means follows that the trustees of savings banks should be left to the exercise of an unlimited discretion in the matter of dividends. Whatever policy or practice in regard to dividends, as in regard to anything else, is calculated to impair the perfect security of depositors, or to operate injuriously to the system, or to work injustice to any individual or class of depositors, should be prohibited. Thus it seems to me the dictate of the commonest prudence, that no dividends should be declared in advance of ascertained profits.

It is customary for many savings banks to advertise that they will pay a given rate of interest. How do they know that they will be able to pay such a rate? They may have been able to pay that amount in previous years, and they *may* be able to pay it again, or they *may not*, Let them refer to their past record as an earnest of future probabilities, but give no pledges upon the contingency of future profits.

Doubtless, as a rule, the older institutions, with large surplus, might do this and not forfeit their pledge, but even these would do better to adhere to the principal of not *dividing* what they have not got. But it is commonly the newer institutions that make the greatest parade of promises, and of course, for the purpose of attracting deposits.

Even upon the organization of banks their trustees not unfrequently advertise that they will pay the highest rate of interest. Of course they will struggle to do this, but what are the probabilities that they can do this out of *fairly earned profits?*

Let them do their best, and when their profits are assured, declare their dividend.

Doubtless the impulse is strong with a new savings bank to hold out inducements equal to those of older institutions. But how *can* they do it with no resources? The older savings banks have a surplus, the profits on which enable them to make greater dividends to depositors than they could do otherwise. Take, for instance, the Bowery Savings Bank, the interest on its surplus, at seven per cent, is nearly one per cent on the whole amount due its depositors; and as there is always a large amount of deposits that are not entitled to dividends, it is doubtless fully one per cent on the deposits that are so entitled. If, therefore, the Bowery can only declare an average dividend of six per cent, one per cent of which is earned from a surplus that receives no dividend, how can the bank that organized, say on the first of May, and on the first of January has $200,000 deposits, declare dividends of six per cent, all of which must be on the profits of the $200,000? True, they do not have to declare dividends on the whole $200,000, but only on such portion of it as has been in the bank for not less than three or four months. But it is equally true that they have not profits from the whole $200,000. Some has been kept on hand for daily transactions, some in the bank at four per cent to meet immediate demands; and for the balance we cannot assume certainly a larger per cent of profit than is enjoyed by older institutions. With these disadvantages it does not seem possible that any savings bank can, during the first year, nor, indeed, during the first five years of its existence, pay dividends equal to older institutions, without, first, anticipating profits; or second, investing in doubtful securities at larger than average profits; or third, leaving no reserve for surplus. I anticipate an answer to these suggestions, that if new banks in the immediate neighborhood of old institutions do not declare as high dividends, they cannot secure the deposits. They cannot, of course, expect, by the mere fact of proximity, to withdraw depositors from the older institutions; and if they cannot, it is because no savings bank was needed for the accommodation of the public. If a community or neighborhood have no savings bank facilities sufficiently attractive to induce deposits, the offer of such facilities will stimulate deposits. If it has such already they do not require anything further.

The organization of new institutions should proceed wholly upon the theory of the wants of a community. These wants should be such as a moderate suggestion of profits at the first, will stimulate to action. All proper inducements should be employed to stimulate the habit of saving, but safety, with small profits, must be the leading idea of savings banks and especially in their early history. If this will not secure deposits, it is because the facilities of older organizations are more attractive, or because that community is not ripe for the experiment. But this aspect of our subject has been elsewhere fully discussed.

A sound principle of finance, allied to the last discussed, but far more vital, is that no dividend shall be paid or credited except out of profits actually earned. It might seem that a principle so obvious could require no enforcement from argument or from the law. But the fact that three savings banks did last year report dividends in excess of their profits from interest received, making no allowance for expenses, is conclusive that the obviousness of the principle has not prevented its being overlooked.

The State has not found it beneath its dignity to enforce this principle by salutary provisions of law concerning banks o issue, whose directors are prohibited from declaring dividends except from profits ; are not the depositors in savings banks entitled to equal consideration with those who have capital to invest in banking enterprizes ?

Such a prohibition concerning savings banks would not only be salutary in its restraint upon practices dangerous to their integrity, but would tend to check the disposition to establish new institutions in localties where savings bank facilities are already sufficiently provided. Indeed such a provision alone, rigidly enforced, would effectually remove all dangers that threaten our system from the reckless multiplication of these institutions.

There is considerable diversity in the practice of savings banks concerning dividends, in other respects than those named. All are supposed to declare dividends semi-annually, and most of them on the first of January and July, in each year, a few at other periods. I could wish there were perfect uniformity in respect to this time of declaring dividends, as otherwise it is impossible upon a given day, as the first of January, to give an exact statement of their liabilities.

Most institutions declare dividends only on moneys that have been on deposit for three months prior to the dividend; thus moneys deposited on the 1st of July and withdrawn on the 30th of December, would be entitled to no dividend; while a deposit made on the 1st of October, and remaining until the 1st of January, would be so entitled.

Dividends are estimated by these institutions only for full periods of three months, that is, a deposit made in August and remaining until January 1st, would be entitled to a dividend for only three months, the time from August to 1st of October, not being estimated. Some only declare dividends on sums deposited for full six months.

Other institutions allow deposits to become entitled to dividends from the first of the calendar month after the same are made, and to the first of the calendar month in which the same are withdrawn, while others allow the dividend to commence from the first of the month subsequent to the deposit, but declare it on none that have been withdrawn prior to the day for which the dividend is declared. The practical operation of these two methods would be, that under the first, a sum on deposit during any entire calendar month, would receive its proportionate rate of dividend for that time, while under the second, a sum to be entitled to a dividend from the first of the month subsequent to its being deposited, must remain on deposit until the next dividend is declared.

These are matters which the Legislature has heretofore left to the discretion of trustees, and I do not know that any interference, or control of this discretion, is desirable. Some of these practices seem liable to the charge of discriminating unjustly against short term deposits; but it is the long term deposits that earn the interest, and the security afforded is quite sufficient repayment for a deposit of only one or two months. Besides, it is a part of the policy to encourage not simply *deposits* of savings but their *accumulation*; and this can not be effected without some extra inducement to keep the deposit undisturbed.

I should be apprehensive, too, that to allow dividends on deposits for a month, when it is well known that for such period they can earn little or nothing for the institution, was undertaking more than could be done with due regard to safety, to say nothing of the injustice to depositors for a longer term, whose money alone really earns the interest that is thus divided.

Still, if the trustees are restricted to making dividends out of earnings, and required to reserve something for surplus, the danger from *over doing* will be substantially averted.

There is, however, a practice, now becoming quite common in the cities of New York and Brooklyn, which I regard as unsafe for the institution, and unjust to the larger portion of the depositors.

This is to offer at the beginning of each quarter, to allow dividends from the first of the month on the deposits made on or before the twentieth.

If the suggestion should be made that no savings bank will do this unless it can *afford* to do so, and that it is the best judge of what it can afford to do, I reply:

First. That we have evidence that under pressure savings banks *will do* that which they cannot afford to do, as where they pay more in dividends than they receive from interest; and,

Second. If a savings bank can *afford* to pay more than six per cent on a deposit for two months and ten days, then it can afford to pay more than six per cent on deposits that have remained for at least three months, and helped to earn the higher rate. It is unjust to the depositors for the longer time, that *their* earnings should be taken to enhance the profits of the short term depositors.

But aside from the injustice wrought by this practice, it is opposed to sound policy. Let us illustrate its atural effects.

Seeing the offer, A, on the 20th of April, withdraws from his usual balance of $7,000 or $10,000, in a bank of issue, $5,000, which he deposits in the savings bank. On the 1st of July he withdraws it, together with $75 dividend, earned in 72 days, while B, who deposited $5,000 on the 1st of April, gets no more. That is, A realizes on his investment at the rate of over seven and a half per cent per annum, while B, whose deposit has earned more for the institution than A's, realizes but six per cent. If the savings bank can thus *afford* to pay A seven and a half per cent, it is only because it *does afford* to deprive B of his just due.

But A is worldly wise, and withdraws his deposit to use in Wall street, or to loan on call, until the next quarter preceding dividend day shall offer him a further opportunity to make seven and a half per cent out of B's ea nings.

The deposits which are secured by this system of bonuses are of little value to the institutions that offer them; they are short lived, and cannot, in my opinion, as a rule, earn nearly as much as they receive.

The tendency of this practice must indeed be to destroy the real character and purpose of savings banks as incentives to industry and economy, and to convert them into financial drawing-rooms, where scheming men of the world, rapacious birds of prey, may repose for a time, while resting their opinions for some higher fight into the realms of stock fancy.

It is true that about the first of January and July, in each year, it is customary for savings banks to allow a few days of grace for depositors. Receipts, from various sources, fall due about this time, but do not come to hand until after the first of the month; and to lose a quarter's interest for one or two days of unavoidable delay, seems a hardship. I would provide for say five days' grace at such periods, and believe that this is the best that can be done consistently with justice to all, and safety to the institutions themselves.

Taxation of Deposits.

It seems natural in this connection to consider a question of some moment to these institutions as well as to the State.

Savings banks have, I conceive, been practically exempt from taxation in this State except upon their real estate. The depositors have been liable to taxation upon the amount of their deposits as personal property, but it is obvious that with no means for compelling a disclosure of such deposits, very little was likely to be realized from this source.

The United States Government has applied to these institutions the provisions of the internal revenue law, imposing a tax of one-half per cent per annum upon their deposits. The expenses for the year 1866, as detailed in the statement of their cash transactions, will be found to be very considerably augmented by this item.

I belive they have now secured a reduction of this tax, by having it applied only to sums exceeding $500 or $1,000. As these institutions frequently advertise to pay uniform rates of dividend on all sums up to $5,000, the question arises whether there is not in this policy a degree of injustice wrought toward the depositors of $500 or $1,000 and under. These receive their dividend only, while the former receive their dividend and the one-half per cent of tax imposed by the Government besides. It is, of course, for good reasons, and reasons urged by these institutions with such force as to prevail, that the Government exempted the smaller deposits from liability to taxation. Are not these deposits then entitled to the exclusive benefit of the exemption? In other words, ought not the tax that is paid upon the larger deposits to be assessed upon those deposits by reducing the dividends paid upon them by just the amount of the tax? This is quite a different question in principle from that previously discussed, concerning the propriety of uniform dividends. Or rather, it is a practical enforcement of the principle of uniformity there advocated. Under the policy now considered, the larger depositors, in effect, get the highest dividends. Uniformity would be promoted by paying them the same rate, including the Government tax.

The Legislature of 1866 incorporated into an Act for the taxation of the shares in State and National banks, a section which will be found in the appendix, providing for the taxation of savings banks upon their surplus. As this surplus belongs to depositors and is for their benefit, adding to their security and augmenting their profits or dividends, I see no good reason for subjecting this portion of their deposits to taxation, that would not apply with equal force to the whole amount of their deposits. At the last session of the Legislature this Act was so amended as to exempt so much of the surplus as should be invested in United States stocks, which is, in fact, an exemption of all, for but for a single institution reports a larger per cent of surplus than of U. S. stocks.

Confidently believing that the incentives to industry, economy and thrift afforded by savings banks are of more value to the State than it would derive from the exercise of its power to tax their deposits, I look with favor upon legislation in the direction of exemption from this burden. I would, however, be glad to see the power applied in the direction of preventing these institutions from becoming a too common resort for purposes of ordinary investment, by imposing a specific State tax of one per cent on all deposits exceeding $5,000. I do not propose this as a source of revenue, which it is not my province nor yours to consider, but as a means of imparting greater security to these institutions by discouraging the accumulation of too large deposits.

There is essential wisdom in exempting from taxation altogether genuine savings deposits, that is, such as are the result of the incentive afforded by savings banks to industry, prudence and thrift. If it could be demonstrated that the effect of taxing these would be to discourage their accumulation, the State would be greatly the loser by the adoption of such a policy, for not only would these accumulations be withdrawn from the reach of the tax gatherer, whereby taxation itself would be defeated, but the industrial force, stimulated into action by the incentive of saving thus destroyed would be lost.

But it is of course difficult, not to say impossible, to distinguish the deposits that are the result of the quickening influence of savings banks, from those which came by inheritance, or which are the surplus of comfortable, perhaps easily earned incomes. Probably the amount of the deposit is as fair an average test by which to distinguish these as could be applied. But the difficult question is to decide what is the amount that shall thus properly measure and determine the character of the deposit.

The measure applied for a similar determination but for a different purpose, by the act of 1853, and by some of the charters to which I have referred, is $500, and this is the measure, I believe, applied by the Government for the same purpose as the one we are now considering, to fix the limit of exemption from taxation. I regard this limit as quite too low. If it was just and fair in 1853, it must be very unfair now when for all the practical purposes of life, its purchasing power does not exceed one-half what it was then. To my mind $1,000 is the lowest limit at which the exemption of savings bank deposits should be placed, if we would avoid the dangers I have suggested, of discouraging their accumulation by imposing upon them too heavy burdens. It is for the interest of the State, as well as of the depositor, that these savings should be made, hence it can not, in the exercise of true wisdom, enter upon a policy that shall tend to their diminution. Indeed, I believe that the State would gain more through the promotion of the purposes for which savings banks are established, by exempting all below $5,000, than it would from the taxes received upon sums between $1,000 and $5,000.

For suppose the effect of instituting measures for the taxation of all sums over $2,000 should be to cause these very generally to be withdrawn, wherein then would the State be the gainer, at least after the first year? The possessor of $2,000 is generally a person of some shrewdness and sagacity, and he would know that in his hands it would most likely escape taxation, and might, at the same time, be so invested as to yield him an income equal to that which he received from the savings bank. Meantime the savings bank has lost a deposit, the profits on which went to reduce the average of expenses assessed upon the deposits, and to augment the surplus for the mutual security and advantage of all, so that the smaller depositors are affected in no inconsiderable degree by this policy, which, though it exempts them from its provisions, still reaches them through their interest in the institution whose prosperity is thus checked.

There is but one way in which these consequences could be prevented, and that is by such reforms in the laws relating to the assessment and collection of taxes as should leave no chance for the escape of that which should be made liable, so that when the deposit of $2,000 or $3,000 should be withdrawn from the savings bank the assessor should be able to follow it into the hands of its possessor, and prepare the way for the collector to impress it into the service of the State through the enginery of taxation. Then, finding that it is exposed to the same depletion in his own hands that it is in the savings bank, he will have no motive for withdrawing it from the savings bank.

Until, then, the State is prepared to revise its whole system of taxation in such manner as to equalize its burdens by imposing them alike upon all property that should help to bear them, sound policy dictates that the interests of our savings banks, and of the State itself, will be best promoted by leaving them free from any interference in this direction.

Of Trustees.

There can be no dissent from the opinion expressed by the worthy president of the Bowery Savings Bank, in the following words: "The success of this mighty expedient for awakening industry and securing its avails by economy, must always mainly depend upon the purity and unselfishness of the men who are chosen as its administrators."

In the earlier history of these institutions, when not more than one or two were chartered each year, and when the whole work of a Legislature could be comprised in a modest volume of not exceeding five hundred pages, it was possible to give some scrutiny to the character of those that should be named as guardians of this sacred trust; but when fourteen acts of incorporation of savings banks are passed at a single session, and the amendments to various charters and laws comprise fourteen more, and when the legislation of a session of one hundred and ten days, including fifteen Sundays and not less than twenty days of adjournment, fills two bulky volumes of more than twenty-five hundred pages, it is proper to inquire whether it is possible, under such conditions, to give that careful attention to the character of the corporators, or to the powers, privileges and duties of the corporation, or to the wants of the community for whose benefit the institution is proposed, which should be exercised where powers so important, involving trusts so sacred, and interests so momentous, are to be delegated.

We do not need to join in the popular clamor concerning the demoralization of modern legislation, to find conditions which fully account for the absence of that studied care, that calm deliberation, that jealous scrutiny which characterized the granting of charters in the earlier history of these organizations.

These conditions are found in the rapid development of our material interests, in the accumulation of capital seeking investment, in the ever increasing diversity of human employments, and the ever opening of new avenues for business and enterprise, and in the needs and desires for legislative recognition, protection, control or indulgence, to which these conditions give rise. And when to these are added, as incident thereto, the increasing demand, in a growing State, for special legislation affecting the rights, powers and interests of private and municipal corporations, which in the form of private and local bills, absorb the attention and energies of the representatives of the various constituencies from which these respectively emanate, resulting inevitably in combinations to forward the passage of bills regardless of any question of their merits, but solely for the support thereby secured for other measures that will be considered from the same interested stand-point, the "wonder grows" that serious disasters have not befallen our savings banks, since their inception is beset with so many perils.

How far it is possible to eliminate from existing conditions, those elements most unfavorable to careful and maturely considered legislation, is a question upon which the representatives of the people, in another than a legislative capacity, are now deliberating.*

Whatever success in this direction they may achieve, the people will be most grateful for; but they cannot, if they would, incorporate into the fundamental law, measures that will arrest the growth and development of the Empire State, in all that relates

*Constitutional Convention of 1867.

to its material prosperity; and it is in the necessities incident to this growth and expansion, that these unfavorable conditions are found.

That, in view of these conditions, in so far as they are inseparable from the natural growth and progress of our State, and in view of the increasing magnitude and importance of our savings bank interest, demanding more and more where it recieves less deliberation and care, in guiding and controlling its development, *some means* should be devised whereby it may be removed from the perils which now environ it, to my mind admits of no question, and is a proposition that can hardly give rise to discussion in any quarter. But the question as to what those means shall be, is one not so easily disposed of. Here the opinions of men may be influenced by their prejudices or by their interests. Here candid, unprejudiced and disinterested minds, intent and earnest in the pursuit of a wise and just solution of the question, will reach different conclusions. The question has been with me one of earnest, I may say, of anxious solicitude. I have bestowed upon it much careful thought, and I have reached conclusions, which I submit to you herewith, and if approved, through you to the Legislature for its sanction in the authoritative form of law.

I sought long and vainly for these means through the imposition of some form of restraint upon the action of the Legislature in granting charters for savings banks. My first draft of a general law required as a precedent condition to the incorporation of any savings bank, the submission through the Superintendent of the Banking Department, of an application, accompanied by a declaration setting forth the residence and occupation of the proposed corporators, and other material facts, with their personal acknowledgment, before a proper officer, of the facts set forth, and of their willingness to accept the responsibilities and discharge the duties of such trust. This was to be accompanied by a bill which should simply enact that the parties named in such declaration, were thereby constituted a body corporate under and pursuant to the provisions of the general law relating to savings banks. Such bill and accompanying declaration, together with the approval or disapproval of the Superintendent indorsed thereon, and his reasons, if stated to be referred to the appropriate committee, who should have no power concerning it except to report favorably or adversely upon the passage of the bill, without amendment, and if reporting favorably and the bill put on its passage, the same not to be the subject to any amendment. And no bill for the incorporation of any savings bank should be introduced in any other manner than as therein provided.

The object of such a provision was, first, that no bill for the incorporation of a savings bank should be considered without first having passed the scrutiny of an officer charged with the supervision of those institutions, and presumed to be well informed as to the propriety of establishing a savings bank at the place proposed in the declaration; and secondly, to ensure the exclusion from the act of incorporation, of any doubtful or unusual powers, by restricting it to a simple declaratory form of incorporation, referring to the unvarying provisions of the general law for the powers conferred and duties imposed. Of course, the general law would be subject to amendment by the usual course of legislation. I entertained an idea that the discretion of a *committee* of the Legislature in regard to the form in which, or the conditions under which they might report a bill could be controlled by law, the provisions of which would, from the necessity of the case, become a part of the rules of each house.

This scheme was very carefully elaborated, first in my own mind, and afterwards in the form of "AN ACT, &c.," as before stated.

Perhaps I *ought* to blush to confess it, though I know I *do not*, but one minute of study of the CONSTITUTION OF THE STATE OF NEW YORK, sections 10 and 13, of Article III, was worth more to *me* and to the "ACT" than the entire sum of my unaided cogitations for a whole week. I could only appropriate to myself the consoling reflection, that never having formed an integral part of the "embodied wisdom," I could not be *expected* to know what were all the individual or collective prerogatives appertaining to those respectable bodies.

Suffice it, that I there learned that each house could make its own rules, and that bills passed by one house could be amended by the other; whereupon my GRAND SCHEME dwindled into very insignificant proportions, if the term *proportion* may indeed be applied to *anything* of which *nothing* is left!

In short, the introduction of any act of incorporation could not in this way be prevented; and one introduced in the form prescribed, could, by a little plausible manipulation by way of amendment, be made to confer powers quite at variance with those of the general law.

There was left, therefore, no way in which the object sought could be attained, but by providing for the incorporation of savings banks without the intervention of the Legislature, except in the enactment of a general law authorizing such incorporation, prescribing the form of proceeding, and the powers, privileges and duties of the corporations thus formed, and designating some proper officer, invested with suitable discretionary powers, to supervise the proceeding and restrain abuses.

The result of my reflections in this direction will be found in the opening sections of the "act" herewith submitted.

It may be objected that those provisions do not prevent the Legislature from still passing special acts of incorporation for these institutions.

But the tendency to special legislation would certainly be greatly checked by such provisions. I apprehend that it is from no desire on the part of members of the Legislature to multiply statutes that so many are enacted; that they, one and all, would gladly be relieved from the consideration of so large a number; that they, as well as the public at large, deprecate the hasty and reckless passage of bills where so many are pressed upon their attention. But in regard to all bills to meet wants or exigencies, for which there are no general laws provided, they are bound to give them recognition, and if not more objectionable in purpose or form than the average, to give them even chances with others of being enacted into laws. No one who has not passed through the experience can appreciate the pressure to which legislators are subjected concerning bills, in which sometimes one, sometimes many of their direct constituents, or of their constituency in the State at large, are interested. They certainly do not court this annoyance—this besieging importunity by which they are urged to make a specialty of pushing forward a dozen different measures all at once! It would be an inexpressible relief if, concerning any class of bills urged upon their attention, they could say to their advocates, "There is a general law expressly adapted for the purpose you have in view. Go and organize under that, and do not encumber our files, occupy our time and engage our attention with matters with which we do not need to be concerned."

A case in point illustrating the effect of a general law in arresting special legislation is found in the General Free Banking Law of 1838. Prior to its passage the struggles for acts of incorporation for banks, that characterized the legislation of that period exceeded in intensity anything that we have witnessed in later years.

But the passage of the general law removed the struggles forever from the halls of legislation. Thereafter no bank was incorporated by act of the Legislature, though it was not until the adopting of the Constitution of 1846 that such legislation was prohibited.

Besides, it may be questioned whether, after the passage of a general law providing for the incorporation of savings banks, the Legislature would, under section 1 of article VIII of the Constitution, have power to incorporate them by special acts. But we need not discuss this view of a question which is not likely to become of practical importance.

As for the provisions of the act for the incorporation of savings banks, which I have prepared, I shall enter into no discussion of their merits, but content myself with an explanation of their objects and purposes in the proper place, and leave them to work their own way into favor or disfavor as they may.

Having thus, as I believe, provided effectual safeguards against the office of trustee being usurped by those whose deficiencies of character might render them unworthy or dangerous custodians of such a trust, I pass to consider one or two other points in connection with the general subject of trustees.

The first of these to which I shall refer relates to COMPENSATION FOR SERVICES.

A condensed summary of the opinions of the officers of savings banks will be found on page 181 of the Appendix; but these must, of course, be considered with that allowance which attaches to interested opinions.

There are three forms which the question assumes:

1st. The payment of trustees acting in the capacity of officers of the board, and devoting their time wholly or chiefly to the discharge of their duties.

2d. The payment of trustees for special services, as in acting upon committees whose duties require the employment of considerable time.

3d. The payment of trustees for ordinary services, as for attendance at regular meetings.

Concerning the first, the general principle may be considered to be settled so far as it can be by legislative recognition. A general law applicable to New York, Brooklyn and Buffalo, authorizes the payment of a salary to the president of any institution whose business does not prevent his regular and faithful attendance to the duties of his office.

The charters of the Troy and Poughkeepsie Savings Bank do the same; possibly some others, whose provisions in this respect escape my memory just now.

That of the Poughkeepsie Savings Bank restricts the payment to surplus earnings, but as these can always be controlled by the rate of dividends, it in effect places the whole discretion in the board of trustees.

There is no absolute standard fixed by the general law as to what constitutes "regular and faithful attendance to the duties of the office." Whether dropping into the institution each morning, on the way to *regular and faithful attendance to other business*, is a compliance with the letter or spirit of the law, I need not stop to discuss.

No means are provided, outside of the action of the board, whereby the question can be raised and passed upon by competent and disinterested authority.

It seems to me that it would be well in order to prevent any opportunity for abuse through favoritism or through indifference, to require at least something more than the vote of a bare majority of a quorum, to fix the rate of such compensation, and to provide that the question of compensation should never be construed as in the nature of a contract, but should always be subject to recision by a vote equal to that by which it may be established.

In regard to the compensation of other officers, as secretary, treasurer and the like, appointed from the members of the board, the charters as well as the practices are various. The older institutions are commonly extremely tenacious of their construction of the spirit and purpose of the law, and when they wish to make an officer of one of their own number, require him to resign as trustee before accepting the office. But the phraseology of the earlier charters is less open to a liberal construction than that of most later ones. In the first sixteen the provision is that "the trustees shall not directly or indirectly receive any pay or emolument for their services." In the seventeenth, and many subsequent, it is, that they "shall not *as such* receive any pay," etc., while a few of the latest put the whole question at rest by the emphatic language that "the trustees shall receive no pay for their services, *or otherwise*, from the corporation." Under the first form there are at least grave doubts as to the right of a trustee to hold a salaried office in the institution; under the second there is a little doubt in my mind that he may; while under the third there is no doubt at all that he cannot.

But we have chiefly to do with the question of policy involved in the second form of language, construed as authorizing trustees, holding permanent offices which take their entire time during business hours, to receive compensation. As whoever devotes his whole time to any duty is certainly entitled to compensation, the question rather resolves itself into whether it is sound policy to elect trustees to salaried offices. Here, as before stated, opinions differ. The grounds upon which such practice is opposed may be stated substantially as follows:

First. Savings banks being in a measure charitable institutions, they lose their distinctive character in this respect if those who conduct and manage them have any other than perfectly disinterested relations to their trust.

Second. If a trustee may be at the same time an officer, enjoying a comfortable salary, the purity of motive implied in the acceptance of an unpaid position of care and responsibility, which should be above possible question, is at once sullied with doubts and suspicions of selfish and interested designs.

Third. The confidence of depositors, and of the public at large, in these institutions, founded on the presumption of the disinterested character of their management, will be greatly impaired by the knowledge that this presumption is or may be wholly false.

I admire the firm and resolute adherence to this principle of strictly gratuitous service by trustees, which characterizes the management of many of the oldest and of the best of these institutions. Honor to the men who have so long and yet so faithfully discharged the responsible, oftentimes arduous, and always unrequited duties involved in the execution of their trust. Equal honor to those who have more lately accepted similar responsibilities from the same disinterested motives, and with the same determined purpose to follow the enterprise to a successful issue. These are the world's benefactors. Their names may not brighten the pages of history with the record of brilliant achievements in field or forum, but the unwritten story of many a life from which despair has been lifted through the agencies which these have instituted, and which, blessed and brightened in itself, has blessed and brightened other lives in its turn through an ever widening circle of influences, will one day bear testimony for them to the good they have unselfishly wrought, whereby the world has been made better for their having lived and labored in it.

But for all this there is another side to the question under discussion. The services rendered by these officers are unquestionably justly entitled to compensation. They are not expected to be gratuitously rendered. Within the limits of fair compensation therefore it is to the institution and to depositors a matter of indifference whether that service be rendered by a trustee or by another not connected with the management. The first objection seems to me to be thus disposed of. To make it valid the assumption must be so broad as to cover all possible service rendered to the institution, and demand that *all* be gratuitous. This would be charity. But this is of course wholly impracticable, and does not enter into the theories of any. The gratuitous service implied from the character of these institutions relates only to the duties performed by the trustees in their capacity as such, and does not cover the services requiring regular and constant attendance for their discharge. I do not see, therefore, how the character of these institutions is affected by the payment to one rather than to another, so long as it is conceded that payment to some one must be made.

The other objections are so nearly allied as antecedent and consequent, that the consideration of the former embraces that of the latter.

The acceptance of the position of trustee in a savings bank, in the hope thereby to secure an appointment to a salaried office seems to me to be based upon a contingency too remote to have any considerable weight as a controlling motive. Surely, all cannot be thus favored, and the chance of any one that he may be successful, solely upon the ground of his being trustee, is at best but as one to the whole number of trustees. And besides, the contingency is hardly a degree removed, if he may become a salaried officer upon resigning his position as trustee. So far as a suspicion of improper motive is concerned, it will attach as strongly to one who, being a trustee, resigns to accept the position of emolument, as to one who accepts such position without resigning. And yet the latter has been done in at least one instance within my knowledge, and without lessening public confidence in the personal worth of the officer, or in the character of the institution in which he labors for his just reward.

And further, to carry out this theory of placing the office of trustee upon a status superior to any possible suspicion of impurity or selfishness of motive in accepting the trust, the prohibition should extend further, and be made to embrace relatives or near friends, for the desire to aid one of these in obtaining a good situation, from motives of friendship or of personal interest, may be much stronger and far more selfish than such desire on behalf of one's self.

As a rule, the trustees of savings banks are men to whom the acceptance of any office that would confine them to a close application to its duties would be a great sacrifice ; the purity of *their* motives in accepting such trust would be far less open to suspicion if they should elect to the responsible offices in their gift, members of their own board, whose character and fitness they had learned from this association, rather than some relative or friend in the promotion of whose good fortunes they might have an interest, varying in intensity from natural affection to one hundred dollars, more or less !

In short, the confidence of the community in the management of these institutions will rest upon the known character of the persons composing the direction, and the conditions of security and success disclosed by their annual statements, rather than upon any adventitious circumstance of the election of a trustee, properly qualified for the place, to some office of emolument.

And this character and this success I would ensure, so far as it can be done by legislation, in the manner already so fully detailed in these pages.

There is an objection, however, to the holding of salaried office by a trustee that, if it could not be met and overcome, would be more serious than those already considered, if indeed it would not be conclusive against such practice.

That is, that such trustee has personal interests adverse to the interests of the institution whose guardian he is. His interest lies in the direction of small dividends or small reserve for surplus, if thereby his salary may be augmented. Even if intending to be impartial, it is scarcely possible for one so situated not to have his views and his action affected by considerations of self-interest.

But there is a remedy for this in prohibiting any trustee holding a salaried office, or an office to which there is any pay or emolument incidentally attached, from voting upon the question of such compensation. I would include in this prohibition the president as well as any subordinate officer; and in order that a proper circumspection should be exercised over the proceedings in such cases, I would require the minutes of all action of any board of trustees, concerning salaries or payments, for services of any kind, to trustees, with the yeas and nays upon the question, to be immediately transmitted to the Superintendent of the Bank Department for his information. Of course, where salary was once determined, there would be no occasion for transmitting further information until some action should be had effecting a change. With such restrictions, I believe the whole subject could with safety be left to the discretion of the trustees.

Though I have confined myself to a consideration of the objections stated or suggested to the practice, there are, to my mind, affirmative reasons to be found in the condition and circumstances of some institutions, why the discretion should be left with the trustees. But I need not dwell upon these, as I do not write to favor the policy of selecting officers from the board, but to oppose the restriction upon the right to do so, and for this, the removal of objections leaves the affirmative sustained.

The second branch of the inquiry, concerning the payment of trustees, as such, for extra or unusual services, involves much the same principles as the first, but are more difficult of application and tend more easily to degenerate into abuse. Of the importance of a rigid, thorough and frequent inspection of the affairs of these institutions by their trustees, I have elsewhere spoken. It is a duty appertaining to the proper management of the trust which they have accepted, and as such, cannot, under any law or charter of which I have any knowledge, be compensated. At least, such is my opinion, although the opinion as well as the practice of a few savings banks is against me on this question.

Upon the assumption that I am right in my view of the law, or if possibly wrong, in order to remove the question from all doubt, is it expedient in a general law to remove the real or supposed restriction upon the discretion of trustees, and to authorize payment for special and extra services? The objections to it are the same as those already considered, with additional ones derived from the greater liability to abuse and danger of payment for *constructive service*, and the increase of expenses beyond fair and reasonable limits.

It will also be urged that it is quite possible to secure this service gratuitously, and have it as effectively and thoroughly performed as if paid for.

If there were no practicable method by which the liability to abuse in the manner suggested could be averted, I should regard the question as concluded.

But it seems to me that this tendency may be effectually prevented.

In the first place I would allow no payment for such service until the institution had accumulated a surplus of not less than five per cent. This would incite to prudent management, in order to reach the required condition of security and ability. Nor then should it rest upon the declaration of the trustees that they had the requisite surplus, but upon an examination by and the certificate of the Superintendent.

Then any vote authorizing the payment of trustees for services rendered, should, before it became operative, be approved by the Superintendent of the Bank Department, who would, of course, be empowered to require such proofs of the service rendered or to be rendered, as would be to him satisfactory concerning the amount awarded. Upon the surplus becoming impaired so as to reduce it to an amount below five per cent, the power of payment should be suspended until the surplus should be again restored.

In this way, I think abuses might be prevented, unless the payment of trustees at all may be regarded as an abuse, which in the eyes of some I know it is.

But if a more thorough, general and frequent examination of all the affairs of these institutions, from the taking in of a dime from a newsboy to the investment of $100,000 in 5–20's, can be ensured by a fair and moderate compensation for the service, then are all the objections to it, when restricted in the manner indicated, to my mind, fully met and completely overthrown.

The last branch of our inquiry, relating to the payment of trustees for ordinary services, I shall dismiss very briefly. The only object of such a provision would be to stimulate to greater activity in the discharge of their duties those who from any cause may have grown indifferent or negligent. The facts, as presented in the answers to my inquiries, and in the reported conditions of these institutions, do not represent them as languishing from such cause. Of a very few is the average attendance at meetings less than a quorum, and I believe these would have their condition, in this respect, materially improved, if the forfeiture for continued absence from meetings were absolute and not discretionary.

While I can imagine no harm, but possible good, resulting from a provision granting a small payment in the way of bonus to such trustees as should attend every regular meeting during the year, this is the extent to which I would go in this direction, and I do not find any conditions earnestly demanding even this concession to indolence or indifference.

Borrowing Funds.

Our legislation, concerning savings banks, has been characterized by no measure more consistent, uniform or salutary than that which prohibits the trustees of these institutions from borrowing or in any manner using the funds deposited with them.

Amid all the change, innovation, diversity, incongruity, and, at times, absurdity of legislative caprice, this has most fortunately been adhered to as the one conservative feature that should redeem our system from contempt and preserve it from utter chaos. With salutary restrictions upon receiving pay for services, and with absolute prohibition against borrowing or using the funds deposited, the opportunities for financial "lame ducks" and impecunious adventurers have not been sufficiently alluring to lead them in any considerable numbers to seek to get the control of their institutions.

The provision is a wise recognition of that salutary principle in human affairs that the motive to appropriate, and the power to appropriate the property of others to one's own use, even with honest intent, should never be united in the same individual, or body. The motive, of course, exists independently of any possible restraint of law or otherwise, being found in the condition, circumstances and disposition of the trustee; and the power would proceed from and exist in the relations under which the trust is created, if it were not thus thrust aside by the stern command of the law.

I have elsewhere spoken of the incompleteness of this safeguard, by reason of there being no supervisory authority necessarily advised of any infractions of the law to which corrective measures might be at once applied. Though the authorized *power* is withheld, the unauthorized *opportunity*, with little risk of detection, still exists, and under such conditions the absolute security which we should be able to predicate of every savings bank in the State, is wanting.

I have found in two instances in my visitations, what I deemed violations of the spirit of this provision. I need hardly say that both these violations were under that mantle of the law, broader than charity, which authorizes an "available fund" "kept in such form as the trustees may direct." In one case, the loan was made to a trustee as *agent* of a manufacturing company. As what one does by an authorized agent he does by himself, the institution would hold that the company, and not the agent, was the borrower, and hence there was no infraction of the law.

I will not undertake to decide the question; I will only say the transaction, if not in itself a violation of the law, nor yet of the principle of safety which the law recognizes and is founded upon, at least seems to open a dangerous door to the employment of deception, misrepresentation and fraud, that should be speedily and effectually closed.

The other instance was of a loan to an individual; I have no doubt, from the inquiries I made, perfectly good, secured by the indorsement of one of the trustees. This was justified on the ground that the loan was not made to the trustee, hence no violation of the prohibition. Under the *available clause* above cited, they would be authorized to loan to the individual upon his own security, and the incident of having the name of the trustee as additional security, certainly could not make the transaction any *less* lawful. There is a resistless logic in the argument that I could not withstand; neither could I withstand the resistless force of the conclusions derived from it, that no loans should be made upon the security of any trustee, nor upon any personal securities, as notes, drafts, bills of exchange, etc., whatever. For if loans may be made, not to a trustee, but upon the *security* of a trustee, what is to prevent trustee A, who wants money, from getting neighbor B to borrow money from the savings bank upon the name or security of A, whom the money reaches in due course? I do not believe the transaction referred to is tainted with the slightest suspicion of such dealing; but that under such a construction of the law there is a broad highway opened to just such dangerous practices, to my mind admits of no question.

Whenever the time shall come that men, out of respect to the majesty of the law will obey its simple declarations, without reference to any penalty for its violation, or to any provisions for its enforcement, then we may dispense with any supervisory authority over the powers and duties of and restraints upon the trustees of savings banks; but until that good time comes, rigid scrutiny is the only real security.

Unclaimed Deposits.

The Legislature, in times past, has been more or less exercised concerning what are denominated "unclaimed deposits" in savings banks. As all deposits in the possession of any savings bank are unclaimed until called for, the term has no special or at least no appropriate significance. The right to make such claim on part of the depositor, or his representatives, never ceases, and under the agreement upon which the deposit is held, the institution must be prepared to respond to the demand when made.

The Legislature of 1862, by a committee of its members, examined the savings banks of the State for the purpose of ascertaining the amount of such unclaimed deposits for a series of years. Their report, which will be found in the Assembly documents of 1863, No. 201, disclosed a much smaller amount of these than had been anticipated; and I am informed by the officers of one institution, that quite a large proportion of the deposits reported by them as unclaimed have since been claimed and paid. While visiting the Seamen's Bank for Savings in the city of New York, they adjusted and paid a claim that had been left undisturbed for fourteen years. Such incidents are of frequent, if not of daily occurrence, and establish conclusively the fallacy of regarding a deposit as escheated, because for a series of years nothing has been added to nor taken from it. It is a very common occurrence for a parent, upon the birth an heir to his name and fortune, to make a deposit for him in a savings bank, with the intention of letting it remain undisturbed until the child becomes of age. These silent deposits are not dead, nor even dormant, though noiselessly they gather from the great depositories of the nation or the State, or from the busy marts of commerce, or the fields of toil, their tithes from the accumulations of industry, and hive them away, awaiting the sometime return of the master, who will require his own *with interest!*

The propositions that have been made at various times for the State to sequestrate these deposits, and hold them in trust for their proper owners, would seem to have been made without any accurate knowledge, either of their character or of the conditions under which they are held. It is as much a part of the contract between the institution and the depositor, that after a lapse of years, usually twenty, the gains to the institution from such deposit shall go to augment the dividends of other depositors, or to make their security more ample, as it is that until that time has elapsed, the deposit shall be duly and regularly accredited with its own earnings.

Besides the questions of sound policy and good faith involved in the proposition, I have before me the opinions respectively of an eminent jurist and an eminent advocate, that the exercise of any such power as that proposed, is contrary to the Constitution of the State, and could not be sustained.

Reports of Savings Banks.

In the last Annual Report upon Savings Banks, the defects of the law relating to supervision, and to the form of reports required from these institutions, were dwelt upon at considerable length. As it is proposed to have that report accompany this special report, for the better information of the Legislature, it is unnecessary that I should at any considerable length go over the ground there occupied.

I will only submit such independent considerations upon the subject, as have been forced upon my attention in the course of my investigations, and such further illustration of the defects there dwelt upon, as will expose them in stronger relief.

Concerning corporations employing their own capital in business enterprises, in which the only interest of the public relates to their financial stability, it is perhaps sufficient to require them, at stated periods, to report their actual condition. With the processes by which that condition was reached, the general public has little or no concern.

But concerning a sacred trust, held for the benefit of half a million of our people, it is the prerogative and the duty of the State, under whose authority the trust is vested, to demand, not only a statement from time to time of the condition of that trust, whereby its safety may be assured, but of the processes though which that condition was reached, in order that it may be seen if the trust has been wisely and prudently administered, in the exclusive interest of the benficiaries. In other words, the guardians, the administrators of such a trust, should be required to account, not only for what they have in hand or subject to their control on a given day, but for all that they have received, from whatever source, on account of their trust, and of the manner in which it has been expended or invested for the same account. Only in this way, indeed, can anything be known with certainty concerning the true *condition* of the trust; for summaries can easily be compiled that will present a very flattering statement of the mutual relations of liabilities and assets, that a little insight into the processes would reveal to be illusory, deceptive, *false.*

The reports from savings banks are liable to the double objection, that they neither exhibit results, reduced to any common standard by which comparisons can be instituted, or aggregates be truthfully repaired; nor processes, that is *operations* by which these reported conditions or results can be proved to be correct, by comparison with each other from year to year.

Thus, concerning the assets, some report them at cost, others at par value, and others at market value, which wholly deprives them of *all value* as affording any basis of comparison or aggregate. Some include in the liabilities the dividend due depositors on the day of the report, and others do not, from which it is impossible to know their true condition either absolutely or relatively.

It is but just to the trustees of these institutions to say, that these defects are in no way chargeable to them, for they commonly report what is required by law, and in the form required, and it is themselves that demand a reformation in the matter and form of these reports, as will be seen by reference to the opinions volunteered upon "points not enumerated."

The lesser faults may, perhaps, be corrected by changes in the form of the blank furnished, which I understand to be your purpose,* but no essential, radical improvement, that shall reveal the processes by which the reported results are reached can be effected, without a change in the law directing what shall be reported, or enlarging the discretion of the Superintendent as to what he may require.

Both are needful, for the law should be so full and explicit in its requirements, that there shall be no opportunity to escape a full exposition of affairs, by reason of negligence or indifference on part of the official supervisory head; and at the same time there should be ample authority to supplement the specific requirements of the law, by such other requirements as his experience and obser-

---

* Since writing the above I am advised of your conclusion, which I deem fully justified by the facts, that no material change can be made in the form of the blank without an amendment to the law.

vation shall suggest, as necessary for a more perfect revelation of the condition and working of these institutions.

These defects find a very elaborate illustration in table C of the appendix, which shows the difference between the gains reported and those estimated, upon the only basis afforded by the reports of savings banks to the department, and to me in their statement of cash transactions.

If the discrepancies between results or conditions reported, and those estimated upon the same basis, are so great where a material item, as expenses, omitted from the reports, is supplemented, as in table C, by the statement from cash transactions, we may expect to find still greater discrepancies, if our comparison be confined to the reports themselves for different years, from which this supplemented item is eliminated. And we shall find this to be the case, as appears from the comparisons which will presently follow. For the clearer understanding of the subjoined comparisons, a few suggestions must be premised.

The resources or assets of a savings bank, are augmented from one year to another, by the following items:

1. Cash received from depositors.
2. Interest or other profits from investments.

They are diminished by,

1. Payments to depositors.
2. Expenses.

If these sources of augmentation and diminution are fully reported each year, the resources of one year as compared with the one previous, will exactly correspond with the difference between the sum of the first two items above named and the last two.

Thus, for a hypothetical case, say—

Resources, 1st January, 1861		$500,000
Augmented by—		
Cash from depositors in 1861		700,000
Interest and profits on investments		40,000
		$1,240,000
Diminished by—		
Paid to depositors	$450,000	
Expenses	3,500	
		453,500
Resources 1st January, 1862		$786,500

If the expenses are not reported, our estimate will have to be made without including them, and the resources thus estimated will be $790,000. On comparing with the report which will state the resources as above at $786,500, we at once account for the difference between the estimated and reported resources, by charging this sum, $3,500, to expenses.

In every instance therefore, if the items of augmentation are fully reported, and the items of diminution also fully reported, except the expenses, the difference between the resources reported and the resources which we shall estimate, omitting the expenses, will be those expenses exactly. But if all the sources of augmentation and of diminution are *not* reported, and our estimate is made upon the supposition that the reported items *do* embrace all, we shall find unexplainable differences between the reported and estimated resources from year to year, to be generalized in our minds by referring them to these non-reported items, which to say the least, is a very unsatisfactory way of accounting for them, especially if these differences prove to be very great.

That this is precisely the case with the reports of savings banks, appears from the following comparative statements which I have selected at random from the reports of five different savings banks in New York city, for six years, beginning with 1st of January, 1861.

Taking the reported resources on that day, I add to these the reported items of augmentation, deposits and interest received, and subtract the reported item of diminution, the amount paid to depositors. The non-reported item of expenses should then appear in the margin as a difference between the resources called for by the calculation, and the resources reported. Of course, if all other sources of augmentation and diminution appear in the report, the difference between the resources from the calculation and from the report, will be just these expenses, no more, no less. Let us see, therefore, what is the value of the reports of savings banks, in revealing the operations through which their condition is reached.

Comparative Statement—I.

No.

Resources reported Jan. 1, 1861	$10,672,462 47	
Received from depositors during 1861	1,689,038 31	
Received for interest during 1861	571,970 37	
	$12,933,471 15	
Paid depositors	3,317,933 15	
Resources called for Jan. 1, 1862	$9,615,538 00	
Resources reported Jan. 1, 1862	$9,329,555 34	Being $285,982 66 less than called for.
Received from depositors during 1862	2,433,481 32	
Received for interest during 1862	528,850 90	
	$12,291,887 56	
Paid depositors during 1862	2,051,832 08	
Resources called for Jan. 1, 1863	$10,240,055 48	
Resources reported Jan. 1, 1863	$10,259,589 10	Being $19,533 62 more than called for.
Received from depositors during 1863	3,540,191 15	
Received for interest during 1863	576,377 71	
	$14,376,157 96	
Paid depositors during 1863	2,429,580 73	
Resources called for Jan. 1, 1864	$11,946,577 23	
Resources reported Jan. 1, 1864	$11,969,451 30	Being $22,874 07 more than called for.
Received from depositors during 1864	4,900,744 24	
Received for interest during 1864	726,271 75	
	$17,596 467 29	
Paid depositors during 1864	3,757,905 74	
Resources called for Jan. 1, 1865	$13,838,561 55	

Resources reported Jan. 1, 1865	$14,030,909 60	Being $192,348 05 more than called for.
Received from depositors during 1865	4,355,086 67	
Received for interest during 1865	800,584 04	
	$19,186,580 31	
Paid depositors during 1865	4,722,870 38	
Resources called for Jan. 1, 1866	$14,463,709 93	
Resources reported Jan. 1, 1866	$14,707,713 73	Being $244,003 80 more than called for.
Received from depositors during 1866	4,084,463 95	
Received for interest during 1866	877,782 68	
	$19,669,960 36	
Paid depositors during 1866	4,131,330 79	
Resources called for Jan. 1, 1867	$15,538,629 57	
Resources reported Jan. 1, 1867	$15,481,137 70	Being $57,491 87 more than called for.

No. 2.

Resources reported Jan. 1, 1861	$9,425,351 47	
Received from depositors during 1861	2,348,645 21	
Received for interest during 1861	494,121 48	
	$12,268,118 16	
Paid depositors during 1861	3,456,774 64	
Resources called for Jan. 1, 1862	$8,811,343 52	
Resources reported Jan. 1, 1862	$8,593,424 62	Being $217,918 90 less than called for.
Received from depositors during 1862	2,772,332 17	
Received for interest during 1862	492,894 96	
	$11,858,651 75	
Paid depositors during 1862	2,620,628 19	
Resources called for Jan. 1, 1863	$9,238,023 56	

Resources reported Jan. 1, 1863	$9,206,448 70	Being $31,574 86 less than called for.
Received from depositors during 1863	3,725,526 82	
Received for interest during 1863	598,983 88	
	$13,530,959 40	
Paid depositors during 1863	3,164,980 24	
Resources called for Jan. 1, 1864	$10,365,979 16	
Resources reported Jan. 1, 1864	$10,246,699 22	Being $119,279 94 less than called for.
Received from depositors during 1864	4,259,686 31	
Received for interest	679,886 31	
	$15,186,271 84	
Paid depositors during 1864	4,429,661 72	
Resources called for Jan. 1, 1865	$10,756,610 12	
Resources reported Jan. 1, 1865	$10,518,884 89	Being $237,725 23 less than called for.
Received from depositors during 1865	3,032,029 92	
Received for interest during 1865	627,430 83	
	$14,178,345 64	
Paid depositors during 1865	4,854,475 92	
Resources called for Jan. 1, 1866	$9,323,869 72	
Resources reported Jan. 1, 1866	$9,264,236 26	Being $59,633 46 less than called for.
Received from depositors during 1866	2,616,440 39	
Received for interest during 1866	622,375 03	
	$12,503,051 68	
Paid depositors during 1866	3,111,583 84	
Resources called for Jan. 1, 1867	$9,391,467 84	Being $119,585 03 less than called for.
Resources reported Jan. 1, 1867	$9,271,882 81	

No. 3.

Resources reported Jan. 1, 1861 ..	$2,149,231 22	
Received from depositors during 1861	723,477 46	
Received for interest during 1861,	129,012 71	
	$3,001,721 39	
Paid depositors during 1861	1,040,437 24	
Resources called for Jan. 1, 1862..	$1,961,284 15	
Resources reported Jan. 1, 1862..	$1,954,073 23	Being $7,210 92 less than called for.
Received from depositors during 1862	772,092 58	
Received for interest during 1862,	110,227 26	
	$2,836,393 07	
Paid depositors during 1862	865,615 88	
Resources called for Jan. 1, 1863..	$1,970,777 19	
Resources reported Jan. 1, 1863..	$1,968,992 32	Being $1,784 87 less than called for.
Received from depositors during 1863	1,027,046 08	
Received for interest during 1863,	112,437 70	
	$3,108,476 10	
Paid depositors during 1863	1,082,723 41	
Resources called for Jan. 1, 1864..	$2,025,752 69	
Resources reported Jan. 1, 1864..	$2,026,456 71	Being $704 02 more than called for.
Received from depositors during 1864	999,276 48	
Received for interest during 1864,	108,051 08	
	$3,133,784 27	
Paid depositors during 1864	1,244,714 50	
Resources called for Jan. 1, 1865..	$1,889,069 77	

Resources reported Jan. 1, 1865	$1,901,904 10	Being $12,834 33 more than called for.
Received from depositors during 1865	744,539 18	
Received for interest during 1865	109,548 14	
	$2,755,991 42	
Paid depositors during 1865	1,028,054 66	
Resources called for Jan. 1, 1866	$1,727,936 76	
Resources reported Jan. 1, 1866	$1,749,796 78	Being $21,860 02 more than called for.
Received from depositors during 1866	1,023,934 18	
Received for interest during 1866	115,253 08	
	$2,888,984 04	
Paid depositors during 1866	873,750 21	
Resources called for Jan. 1, 1867	$2,015,233 83	
Resources reported Jan. 1, 1867	$2,038,530 89	Being $23,297 06 more than called for.

No. 4.

Resources reported Jan. 1, 1861	$2,026,929 13	
Received from depositors during 1861	786,463 00	
Received for interest during 1861	108,565 62	
	$2,921,957 75	
Paid depositors during 1861	755,486 28	
Resources called for Jan. 1, 1862	$2,166,471 47	
Resources reported Jan. 1, 1862	$2,145,851 61	Being $20,619 86 less than called for.
Received from depositors during 1862	1,149,113 00	
Received for interest during 1862	146,935 73	
	$3,441,900 34	
Paid depositors during 1862	711,992 27	
Resources called for Jan. 1, 1863	$2,729 908 07	

Resources reported Jan. 1, 1863	$2,702,380 63	Being $27,527 44 less than called for.
Received from depositors during 1863	1,747,075 00	
Received for interest during 1863	240,019 34	
	$4,689,474 97	
Paid depositors during 1863	1,141,236 74	
Resources called for Jan. 1, 1864	$3,548,238 23	
Resources reported Jan. 1, 1864	$3,527,773 36	Being $20,464 87 less than called for.
Received from depositors during 1864	2,618,752 00	
Received for interest during 1864	291,158 54	
	$6,437,683 90	
Paid depositors during 1864	1,948,123 75	
Resources called for Jan. 1, 1865	$4,489,560 15	
Resources reported Jan. 1, 1865	$4,449,576 91	Being $39,983 24 less than called for.
Received from depositors during 1865	2,820,357 00	
Received for interest during 1865	304,447 38	
	$7,574,381 29	
Paid depositors during 1865	2,439,143 40	
Resources called for Jan. 1, 1866	$5,135,237 89	
Resources reported Jan. 1, 1866	$5,088,055 41	Being $47,182 48 less than called for.
Received from depositors during 1866	3,272,937 00	
Received for interest during 1866	392,862 39	
	$8,753,854 80	
Paid depositors during 1866	2,922,323 98	
Resources called for Jan. 1, 1867	$5,831,530 82	
Resources reported Jan. 1, 1867	$5,775,294 19	Being $56,236 63 less than called for.

No. 5.

Resources reported 1st Jan., 1861	$123,539 36	
Received from depositors during 1861	47.999 42	
Received for interest during 1861	6,663 27	
	$178,202 05	
Paid depositors during 1861	61,575 22	
Resources called for 1st Jan., 1862	$116,626 83	
		Being $728 83 less than called for.
Resources reported 1st Jan., 1862	$115,898 00	
Received from depositors during 1862	84,152 89	
Received for interest during 1862	11,463 95	
	$211,514 84	
Paid depositors during 1862	49,103 48	
Resources called for 1st Jan., 1863	$162,411 36	
		Being $3,324 36 less than called for.
Resources reported 1st Jan., 1863	$159,087 00	
Received from depositors during 1863	179,396 08	
Received for interest during 1863	18,862 85	
	$357,345 93	
Paid depositors during 1863	90,488 03	
Resources called for 1st Jan., 1864	$266,857 90	
		Being $3,573 38 less than called for.
Resources reported 1st Jan., 1864	$263,284 52	
Received from depositors during 1864	272,921 33	
Received for interest during 1864	18,046 63	
	$554,252 48	
Paid depositors during 1864	176,024 04	
Resources called for 1st Jan., 1865	$378,228 44	

Resources reported 1st Jan., 1865,	$381,818 40	Being $3,589 96 more than called for.
Received from depositors during 1865	283,445 02	
Received for interest during 1865,	43,207 32	
	$708,470 74	
Paid depositors during 1865	256,804 60	
Resources called for 1st Jan., 1866,	$451,666 14	
Resources reported 1st Jan., 1866,	$441,789 95	Being $9,876 19 less than called for.
Received from depositors during 1866	476,662 18	
Received for interest during 1866,	35,422 48	
	$953,874 61	
Paid depositors during 1866	295,074 75	
Resources called for 1st Jan., 1867,	$658,799 86	
Resources reported 1st Jan., 1867,	$650,449 55	Being $8,350 31 less than called for.

A remarkable feature of the foregoing exhibit is the extremes of difference between estimated and reported results of the same institution, and the diversity of these differences between the different institutions.

Two of them, Nos. 2 and 4, are uniformly less in reported than estimated resources, but these differences in No. 2 are extremely variable, being from the highest difference $237,725 to the lowest $31,574.

Nos. 1, 3 and 5 show differences sometimes in excess and sometimes short of the estimate, being in No. 1, from $285,982 less in one year, to $19,533 more in the next.

No. 3 presents less marked differences, showing, indeed, a rather gradual growth from $7,210 below the estimate, to $23,297 above the estimate.

These are only illustrations of what would appear concerning all savings banks, if similar comparisons were instituted between their several reports. There is, therefore, to be imputed to the institutions from whose reports these comparisons are made, no deficiencies or irregularities not liable to all, and for this reason I do not name them, but number them in an arbitrary order.

What is enforced by this exhibit, as by table C, is not that there *is* improper or dishonest management, whereby large sums are misappropriated or recklessly squandered, but that there *may be;* and the only way by which the public can be assured that there *is not*, is by requiring a report in detail of all sources of profit and of all sources of loss, so that not only may the true condition of each institution be known and verified, but the processes by which that condition was reached may stand clearly revealed.

If these discrepancies between results estimated upon a fair and natural basis, and results reported in gross, can be satisfactorily accounted for, as I assume they can be, they *should be* so accounted for. On the other hand, if my judgment is too charitable, and they *cannot* be explained without discredit to the management, then they should be exposed in all their deformity, that the abuses of the management may be corrected.

In short, among the reported conditions of savings banks, there should be no *unknown quantities*, concerning which any doubts or suspicions can possibly be harbored.

I present one more statement illustrating the inaccuracy of the present reports from savings banks, or rather, that their accuracy in the form in which they are made is not susceptible of *proof*, as it should be. This statement relates to the amount due depositors, which constitutes generally the grand total of liabilities which, with surplus, balances the resources. The amount due depositors on the first of January of any one year will be augmented during the year by exactly the amount of deposits received and the interest or dividends credited to the various accounts, and will be diminished by the payments made to depositors.

No other items enter into the calculation, and these are all reported. We shall look to these, therefore, confidently anticipating a *proof* of the reported amounts due depositors from year to year, in so far as *consistency* constitutes proof.

As a test, I have selected five other savings banks in the city of New York, and prepared a schedule showing the amount due depositors on the 1st of January, 1861, and the augmentations and diminutions in each year to 1867.

In one, the estimated and reported results correspond; while in the other four there are variances for which I am not always able to account.

Comparative Statement II.

No. 1.

Due depositor, Jan. 1, 1861	$10,294,995 08
Deposited during 1861	3,804,520 00
Interest credited to depositors in 1861	419,088 95
	$14,518,604 03
Withdrawn by depositors in 1861	5,345,570 35
Due depositors, Jan. 1, 1862	$9,173,033 68
Deposited during 1862	4,881,651 00
Interest credited to depositors in 1862	390,445 10
	$114,445,129 78
Withdrawn by depositors during 1862	4,202,635 35
Due depositors, Jan. 1, 1863	$10,242,494 43
Deposited during 1863	6,102,500 00
Interest credited to depositors in 1863	426,666 02
	$16,771,660 45
Withdrawn by depositors in 1863	4,592,472 94
Due depositors, Jan. 1, 1864	$12,179,187 51
Deposited during 1864	9,273,244 00
Interest credited to depositors in 1864	748,100 95
	$22,200,532 46
Withdrawn by depositors in 1864	7,695,104 91
Due depositors, Jan. 1, 1865	$14,505,427 55
Deposited during 1865	9,580,412 00
Interest credited to depositors in 1865	718,537 19
	$24,804,376 74
Withdrawn by depositors in 1865	9,614,630 00
Due depositors, Jan. 1, 1866	$15,189,746 74

Deposited during 1866	$8,027,670 00	
Interest credited to depositors in 1866	753,957 26	
	$23,971,374 00	
Withdrawn by depositors in 1866	8,372,604 59	
Due depositors, Jan. 1, 1867	$15,598,769 41	

No. 2.

Due depositors, Jan. 1, 1861	$1,086,547 95	
Deposited during 1861	398,484 56	
Interest credited to depositors in 1861	58,239 05	
	$1,543,271 56	
Withdrawn by depositors in 1861	420,823 95	
Should be due depositors, Jan. 1, 1862	$1,122,447 61	
Amount reported as due depositors, Jan. 1, 1862	$1,064,208 56	Difference $58,239 05 correspond'g with interest credited.
Deposited during 1862	454,678 30	
Interest credited to depositors in 1862	58,630 01	
	$1,577,516 87	
Withdrawn by depositors in 1862	333,425 30	
Should be due depositors, Jan. 1, 1863	$1,244,091 57	
Amount reported as due depositors, Jan. 1, 1863	$1,244,091 57	
Deposited during 1863	621,503 10	
Interest credited to depositors in 1863	68,114 96	
	$1,933,709 63	
Withdrawn by depositors in 1863	414,775 24	
Should be due depositors, Jan. 1, 1864	$1,518,934 39	

Amount reported as due depositors, Jan. 1, 1864	$1,518,934 39	
Deposited during 1864	773,588 54	
Interest credited to depositors in 1864	80,429 55	
	$2,372,952 48	
Withdrawn by depositors in 1864,	715,720 72	
Should be due depositors, Jan. 1, 1865	$1,657,231 76	
Amount reported as due depositors, Jan. 1, 1665	$1,576,793 21	Difference $80,438 55, correspond'g with interest cred. above, nearly.
Deposited during 1865	671,773 45	
Interest credited to depositors in 1865	79,168 19	
	$2,327,734 85	
Withdrawn by depositors in 1865,	808,745 34	
Should be due depositors, Jan. 1, 1866	$1,518,989 51	
Amount reported as due depositors, Jan. 1, 1866	$1,439,821 32	Difference $79,168 19, correspond'g with interest cred. above.
Deposited during 1866	824,033 55	
Interest credited to depositors in 1866	75,172 75	
	$2,339,027 62	
Withdrawn by depositors in 1866,	685,318 68	
Should be due depositors, Jan. 1, 1867	$1,653,708 94	
Amount reported as due depositors, Jan. 1, 1867	$1,578,536 19	Difference $75,172 75, correspond'g with interest cred. above.

No. 3

Due depositors, Jan. 1, 1861	$176,322 24	
Deposited during 1861	100,413 71	
Interest credited to depositors in 1861	8,575 59	
	$285,311 54	
Withdrawn by depositors in 1861,	117,860 76	
Should be due depositors Jan. 1, 1862	$167,450 78	
Amount reported as due depositors, Jan. 1, 1862	$167,451 18	Difference $0 40
Deposited during 1862	131,327 93	
Interest credited to depositors in 1862	8,387 08	
	$307,166 19	
Withdrawn by depositors in 1862,	103,679 89	
Should be due depositors, Jan. 1, 1863	$203,486 30	
Amount reported as due depositors, Jan. 1, 1863	$198,235 44	Difference $5,250 86
Deposited during 1863	226,255 66	
Interest credited to depositors in 1863	9,652 66	
	$434,143 76	
Withdrawn by depositors in 1863,	165,957 47	
Should be due depositors, Jan. 1, 1864	$268,186 29	
Amount reported as due depositors, Jan. 1, 1864	$258,543 66	Difference $9,642 63,
Deposited during 1864	303,013 73	correspond'g with interest
Interest credited to depositors in 1864	12,429 88	cred. above, nearly.
	$573,987 27	

Withdrawn by depositors in 1864,	$275,731 59	
Should be due depositors, Jan. 1, 1865	$298,255 68	
Amount reported as due depositors, Jan. 1, 1865	$298,694 33	Difference $438 65
Deposited during 1865	260,529 01	
Interest credited to depositors in 1865	14,766 06	
	$573,989 40	
Withdrawn by depositors in 1865,	275,365 49	
Should be due depositors, Jan. 1, 1866	$298,623 91	
Amount reported as due depositors Jan. 1, 1866	$299,123 91	Difference $500 00
Deposited during 1866	439,496 01	
Interest credited to depositors in 1866	14,629 73	
	$753,249 65	
Withdrawn by depositors in 1866,	300,042 13	
Should be due depositors, Jan. 1, 1867	$453,207 52	
Amount reported as due depositors Jan. 1, 1867	438,577 81	Difference $14,629 71, correspond'g with interest cred. above, less 2 cents.

No. 4.

Due depositors, Jan. 1, 1861	$255,244 38
Deposited during 1861	267,263 16
Interest credited to depositors in 1861	13,327 28
	$534,834 82
Withdrawn by depositors in 1861	201,502 76
Should be due depositors, Jan. 1, 1862	$333,332 06

Amount reported as due depositors, Jan. 1, 1862	$320,006 78	Difference $13,325 28, correspond'g nearly with interest cred.
Deposited during 1862	445,649 42	
Interest credited to depositors in 1862	17,616 80	
	$783,273 00	
Withdrawn by depositors in 1862	220,115 19	
Should be due depositors, Jan. 1, 1863	$563,157 81	
Amount reported as due Jan. 1, 1863	$545,541 01	Difference $17,616 80, correspond'g with interest cred. above.
Deposited during 1863	816,299 64	
Interest credited to depositors in 1863	29,885 26	
	$1,391,725 91	
Withdrawn by depositors in 1863	411,523 06	
Should be due depositors, Jan. 1, 1864	$980,202 85	
Amount reported as due depositors, Jan. 1, 1864	$950,317 29	Difference $29,885 56, correspond'g with interest cred. above.
Deposited during 1864	1,206,686 58	
Interest credited to depositors in 1864	48,724 02	
	$2,205,727 89	
Withdrawn by depositors in 1864	894,035 00	
Should be due depositors, Jan. 1, 1865	$1,311,692 89	
Amount reported as due depositors, Jan. 1, 1865	$1,262,968 87	Difference $48,724 02, correspond'g with interest cred. above.
Deposited during 1865	1,464,677 98	
Interest credited to depositors in 1865	63,100 62	
	$2,790,747 47	

Withdrawn by depositors in 1865	$1,183,386 67	
Should be due depositors, Jan. 1, 1866	$1,607,360 80	
Amount reported as due depositors, Jan. 1, 1866	$1,544,260 18	Difference $63,100 62, correspond'g with interest credited.
Deposited during 1866	1,949,380 49	
Interest credited to depositors in 1866	82,003 33	
	$3,575,644 00	
Withdrawn by depositors in 1866	1,167,269 10	
Should be due depositors, Jan. 1, 1867	$2,408,374 90	
Amount reported as due depositors, Jan. 1, 1867	$2,482,151 61	Difference $73,776 71

No. 5.

Due depositors, Jan. 1, 1861	$27,767 11	
Deposited during 1861	66,415 62	
Interest credited to depositors in 1861	1,360 94	
	$95,543 67	
Withdrawn by depositors in 1861	39,017 13	
Should be due depositors, Jan. 1, 1862	$56,526 54	
Amount reported as due depositors, Jan. 1, 1862	$55,166 00	Difference $1,360 54, correspond'g nearly with interest cred.
Deposited during 1862	278,313 12	
Interest credited to depositors in 1862	4,318 50	
	$337,797 62	
Withdrawn by depositors in 1862	82,327 59	
Should be due depositors, Jan. 1, 1863	$255,470 03	

Amount reported as due depositors, Jan 1, 1863	$251,229 35	Difference $4,240 68
Deposited during 1863	813,851 43	
Interest credited to depositors in 1863	14,698 39	
	$1,079,779 17	
Withdrawn by depositors, Jan 1, 1863	314,558 33	
Should be due depositors, Jan. 1, 1864	$765,220 84	
Amount reported as due depositors, Jan. 1, 1864	$750,522 45	Difference $14,698 39, correspond'g with interest credited.
Deposited during 1864	1,275,590 86	
Interest credited to depositors in 1864	41,420 44	
	$2,067,533 75	
Withdrawn by depositors in 1864	831,589 43	
Should be due depositors, Jan. 1, 1865	$1,235,944 32	
Amount reported as due depositors, Jan. 1, 1865	$1,194,523 88	Difference $41,420 44, correspond'g with interest credited.
Deposited during 1865	1,691,095 46	
Interest credited to depositors in 1865	63,022 99	
	$2,948,642 33	
Withdrawn by depositors in 1865	1,147,225 86	
Should be due depositors, Jan. 1, 1866	$1,801,416 47	
Amount reported as due depositors, Jan. 1, 1866	$1,739,349 71	Difference $62,066 76
Deposited during 1866	3,143,269 52	
Interest credited to depositors in 1866	93,453 40	
	$4,976,072 63	

Withdrawn by depositors in 1866	$1,693,031 70	
Should be due depositors, Jan. 1, 1867	$3,283,040 93	
Amount reported as due depositors, Jan. 1, 1867	$3,189,587 53	Difference, $93,453 40

The foregoing are extracts from computations concerning twenty different savings banks in the city of New York, furnished me by a gentleman residing in that city, who was himself once a trustee in a savings bank. Besides tables in full from which the above extracts are taken, there are many others prepared by him, showing the rate per cent of interest received and of dividends paid, and the difference between the rate reported as received, and what the assets, yielding a fair rate, should produce, and many other interesting calculations, all illustrating the point now under consideration, of the inadequacy of the present reports to give any true idea of the interior workings of these institutions. The computations are made from the reports of savings banks to this Department for the last seven years. I am unable to reproduce more than the above extracts, which have been carefully verified; but, for the purpose of illustrating the subject in hand, the foregoing will suffice equally as well as a greater number.

In making any change in the form of reports to be required of savings banks, reference must of course be had solely to what is essential to be known concerning their condition and workings. That we need to know both, I have elsewhere endeavored to make apparent. If we know at any given time the real condition of a savings bank, and are thereafter kept regularly informed of its workings, we have the data for knowing at all times its true condition, for this condition must be the result of its operations. But while its workings should be frequently reported, the results in the form of a statement of its condition should be occasionally reported, both as means of verifying the accuracy of the reported operations, and as a convenience, the making of such summary being more easily and economically effected by the clerical force of the several institutions, than by the clerical force of the supervisory department. There would then be left only the comparisons and verifications to make, with the preparation of the whole for the information of the Legislature.

To meet these wants, according to my idea, each savings bank should report every month its entire operations, embracing:

Receipts and payments of cash, and on what account;

Changes in investments since the last statement;

Profits and losses from sales or purchases of securities at a premium or below par, from foreclosure of mortgages or sales of real estate, or from any other sources; and,

Any other items or facts which should affect in any manner the financial condition of the institution.

Then, once a year, instead of semi-annually as now, report in full its resources and liabilities, though in an improved form, and such other facts as would exhibit the effect or influence of these institutions in promoting the objects which they were designed to secure.

In one respect I regard the present requirements concerning the reports of these institutions as alike onerous and needless; that is in regard to the full schedule, semi-annually, of the bonds and mortgages.

Of course the labor involved in its preparation is not to be considered for a moment, if any valuable purpose is to be served by it. But I can conceive of none.

A far better result may be attained, with far less labor, through the system above recommended, by reporting once, in detail, every bond and mortgage, and thereafter the changes only.

I need hardly say that the resources should be reported upon some uniform basis of value, or they are useless for comparison. At present there is a lack of uniformity, which accounts for some of the anomalies that we have been considering.

Indeed, to understand fully the condition of any institution, we need to have four facts reported concerning its investments. First, the par value; second, their cost; third, their market value, and fourth, the rate of interest they yield.

We want the par value, because that is the ultimate standard to which, in financial matters, all securities are reduced, or by which they are compared, and concerning which the rate of interest is expressed. Besides yielding income at a defined rate on par value, savings banks, as a rule, look to the ultimate redemption of their securities at par value, so that in this we have a measure of prospective ability, which it is important to consider.

The cost is material, as affording a basis of comparison between the interest at par value and the interest on the aggregate sum invested, from which the real profits or gains on investments must be estimated. It is an essential element in determining the real prosperity of a savings bank. Without it we can know little of the prudence and success of the management, and can have no detailed statement of what is done with the money of depositors.

The market value will enable us to judge of the ability of the institution to meet current demands upon its resources, with or without sacrifice or loss, and is essential to reveal its actual condition of solvency upon a given day.

The rate of interest is our only test of the working prosperity of a savings bank, a means of forecasting its future, and of comparing the value of different classes of securities.

With any one of these items omitted, we fail to obtain full information concerning the condition, workings and prospects of a savings bank.

In making the comparison, however, between resources and liabilities, we must, of course, choose between the three forms of expression, cost, par value and market value.

Cost is perhaps the more common, and is not without its advantage in revealing certain conditions of prosperity, or the reverse, that would not otherwise be disclosed.

Market value has its advocates upon the ground that the true condition of a savings bank, upon a given day, can be determined or known in no other way than by a statement of what its assets would bring in the market on that day.

But in view of the nature and objects of savings banks, and of their permanence, which gives them relations to the future not less intimate and important than to the present, I am persuaded that *par* is the best form in which the value of their securities can be expressed.

It would be less fluctuating than market value, and would give a better idea of the ability of the institution to meet not only the emergencies of the day, but of the future, which it is quite as certain to meet.

No savings bank expects to be called upon to meet all its liabilities, or to convert all its assets at once. Every savings bank looks forward to continuing business and answering demands for an indefinite period. The securities which to-day it may report at a market value of 107, ten or twelve years from now will be *paid* at 100, and this is therefore what they are *worth* to the institution as an *investment*, yielding an income for *savings bank* purposes.

True, they *may sell* them and realize *more*; but then the transaction will appear as an increase in their assets, and it is time enough for them to appear in that form when they have been so converted, and have realized the premium at which they are quoted. Until this is done, so long as they remain with the institution, yielding only the rate of interest named for them on the basis of their par value, they are for the common and ordinary purposes of savings banks worth to them but par. We may be glad to know from the schedule, that the institution, by reason of the premium which its securities bear, is able to meet any unusual demand upon its resources without loss, but for the purposes of a comparison which will show the general ability and stability of the institution, not only on a given day, but from year to year, a basis less fluctuating than market value should be assumed.

Besides, if all the securities are to be reported at their market value, what will become of the bonds and mortgages which we know can never, as a rule, bring their face in market? The same may be said of most interior city and county bonds; and yet, as an investment yielding revenue regularly to the savings bank, they are worth par, and properly so reported.

Cost would be a more stable form than market value, in which to report the assets, but would fail to reveal at once those relations to liabilities from which the solvency of the institution could be known.

Perhaps the statement could be made to combine the two forms of expression, par and market value, by giving a detailed list of the securities at par, and their aggregate premium in the market as a separate item for information only, and not as a part of the basis of comparison.

SUPERVISION.

The course of the discussion in the preceding pages has assumed a more direct and responsible supervision of savings banks than is provided for under the present law. The necessity for this must be apparent, or I have written in vain. The Superintendent should have power, and it should be his duty to visit and examine these institutions from time to time, for the purpose of verifying the reported statements of their condition and workings. Such visitation should always be made without previous notice, and should not, as now, be based upon the presumption of improprieties in the management, but should be a regular proceeding in the interest of these institutions, as well as of their depositors, verifying to them and to the public at large, by certificate of the Superintendent, the solvency and security of each savings bank so examined and found worthy of confidence.

With such examinations, and such changes in the form and matter of reports as I have recommended, and more consistent and guarded provisions of law relative to investments, I believe our savings banks would be placed upon a basis of security absolutely impregnable.

The one great purpose for which savings banks are instituted, and which entitles them to the fostering care and guardianship of the State, demands for their successful development, harmony of action among the individual members of the system.

Beneficent in their designs towards the humble and the industrious poor, their results reach far beyond this measure of their intent, and minister acceptably to the promotion of great National and State necessities, and to municipal and private enterprises.

Purposes like these are best promoted through the suppression of all jealousies, and the extinguishment of all possible rivalries. Special powers and privileges conferring upon some, seeming advantages not enjoyed by others, are opposed to sound policy, and tend to defeat that harmonious and symmetrical development and growth of this system of provident institutions, which is so essential to their highest prosperity, and to any well founded assurance of their stability and success.

Let it never be said of this noble system in our State, that purposes so beneficent and worthy, motives so pure and disinterested, results so grand and inspiring, as wait upon its ministry, were marred and defaced by petty strifes, jealousies and contentions among the brotherhood to whom its administration was confided.

Conclusion.

I have now brought to a close the labor commenced under your direction and authority, on the 25th of April last. Of its incompleteness, judged by any standard such as I would now apply to such a work, I have already spoken. I only know, that whatever reception the results of my labors may meet with elsewhere, *you* will be generous in your judgment, knowing the sincerity of purpose by which I have been animated.

My report has grown upon my hands, far beyond my original purpose or expectation. But in the limited time left to me for condensation, I could not make it more brief, and yet fulfill my design of presenting a full resumē of the theory and workings of this vast and growing interest. So far as I know, it is the first attempt of the kind in our State to give a thorough exposition of the nature, objects and present condition of these institutions. That the work had not fallen to better hands is a source of regret which I share in common with an appreciative public. If it shall serve to stimulate worthier efforts in the same direction, it will have accomplished some good.

Concerning the treatment of the subject, if I have not always preserved the staid gravity becoming a State paper, something may, perhaps, be pardoned to the intimacy of our personal and official relations, by which I may at times have been betrayed into a familiarity inspired by the sense that I was addressing not only my superior officer, but an indulgent friend, who would patiently bear with "my many infirmities."

In conclusion, I cannot forbear again to express my grateful acknowledgments to the gentlemen, one and all, connected with savings banks, who have so cheerfully responded to my demands upon them for information, very often, as I have good reason to know, involving a very considerable amount of labor.

To the clerks in the Department, I am indebted for very material aid rendered in the preparation of the tables and exhibits in the appendix.

The computations of tables B and C, representing more than 1300 different calculations to periods of eight decimals, besides additions and subtractions "too numerous to mention," were all made by Isaac Smith, Accountant of the Bank Department, and their perfect accuracy has been very carefully and thoroughly tested.

The transcripts of cash transactions were made from the returns of savings banks, and prepared for the printer under my direction by Clarence W. Olcott, who also wrote out from my dictation the provisions of the various charters.

The results of the calculations for tables B and C, were tabulated with great care, by A. H. Dennis, Esq., who also rendered other valuable service.

The cheerful alacrity with which all my demands upon their time, whether in office hours or otherwise, were answered, merits and receives my grateful thanks.

And finally, and chiefly, to yourself, for placing at my disposal the services above acknowledged, for leaving to me the utmost freedom of action, both as regards the time and the method of prosecuting my labors, for your cordial sympathy with the purposes to be accomplished, for your hearty co-operation, and for your confidence, at all times, so generous and unreserved, am I indebted for any measure of success that has waited on my endeavor.

That this work, wrought under your auspices, may serve to identify your administration with the inception of a higher and more stable prosperity, and of a broader and more harmonious practical development of the great provident system of savings banks in our State, is a hope, most ardently cherished by

Your obedient servant,

EMERSON W. KEYES,

Dept. Superintendent.

JANUARY 1, 1868.

APPENDIX.

(A.)

A Statement of the Cash Transactions of Savings Banks during the year 1866, *and of their Assets on a given day within the present year, as found upon an examination, and verified according to the form on page* 24, *together with other facts of interest concerning these institutions, and critical or explanatory comments.*

These statements are in general literal transcripts from the returns made by the savings banks in response to my inquiries. In a few instances items have been transposed in order to give them their proper relation, and a few have been condensed, where a detailed enumeration was merely unnecessary repetition. As a rule, however, they stand in the order and are expressed in the terms in which they were received.

To apprehend the full force of many facts appearing in these statements, they should be studied in connection with the reports of these institutions for the 1st of January last, made for the same period covered by the cash transactions here given. Some inconsistences would appear upon such examination, some puzzling questions would be resolved and perhaps more suggested; but the necessity for a more thorough and detailed exposition of their condition, and of the processes by which that condition is reached, will be forced upon the conviction of every candid mind.

The comments are designed primarily to explain some point proper or necessary to be understood, and which could not appear among the facts or statistics returned without breaking their continuity—as in the case of the Institution for Savings of Merchants' Clerks; or to reveal the causes of reported conditions by directing attention to the methods of business under which such results could be reached.

I have not hesitated, however, to criticise where practices at variance with the principles upon which savings banks should be conducted have been revealed.

As a rule, any savings bank that is not distinguished by special comment is distinguished without it, as it is an indication that its exhibit is itself the best commentary that could be passed upon it.

The order of arrangement adopted is the same as in the last report on savings banks, to the Legislature, alphabetically by cities where these have more than one savings bank, and then alphabetically for other localities, including cities having but one savings bank.

Alphabetically by counties would be a better arrangement, but for the purpose of making reference to the last report, the present order is preferred.

ALBANY SAVINGS BANK.

CASH TRANSACTIONS DURING THE YEAR 1866.

Receipts.

Cash on hand 1st January, 1866, before the transactions of the day		$302,101 56
Deposited in bank	$302,101 56	
From depositors		953,707 90
From interest on mortgages		10,007 17
From interest on stocks		84,997 00
From premium on gold		2,009 59
From mortgages paid, called in or foreclosed		25,000 00
From redemption of stocks		5,000 00
From repayment of loans		7,000 00
Bonus from Commercial Bank		3,000 00
Excess of receipts over payments		11,164 88
		$1,403,988 10

Payments.

Interest		$76,174 65
To depositors, cash		925,534 45
Loans on bond and mortgage		21,000 00
Cash on hand 31st December, 1866, after the transactions of the day*		
Deposited in bank	$381,279 00	381,279 00
		$1,403,988 10

* $42,000 estimated interest due depositors Jan. 1, 1867, deducted from cash on hand.

Assets of the Albany Savings Bank on the 1st day of July, 1867.

	Par value.	Cost.
Bonds and mortgages		$151,800 00
United States bonds and treasury notes	$140,000	142,892 00
New York State bonds	528,500	532,841 00
Bonds of other States	282,490	274,658 00
Bonds of cities in this State	342,400	345,033 00
Bonds of counties in this State	309,300	311,730 00
Cash in bank		411,202 10
		$2,170,156 10

Examination made and verified by 1st vice-president and secretary.

Other Facts—None given.

Remarks.

The Albany Savings Bank, the second chartered institution of the kind in the State, has an agreement with the Commercial National Bank to transact the business through its machinery, pay all expenses, pay the dividends of depositors, and a bonus of $3,000 per annum to the savings bank, supposed to be credited to account of surplus. In return it receives the interest on all investments, except of surplus, and has the use of the large balance of cash in reserve. The profits in favor of the Commercial Bank appear from the cash transactions to be over $11,000 a year, besides the use of over $300,000 more. Some of the trustees of the savings bank, I have good reason to believe, are not satisfied with this arrangement. It is to be hoped they will before long, become a majority, and institute a better order of things.

ALBANY CITY SAVINGS INSTITUTION.

CASH TRANSACTIONS DURING THE YEAR 1866.

Receipts.

Cash on hand 1st January, 1866, before the transactions of the day	$122,434 97
From depositors	166,589 05
From interest on deposits in banks	13,091 76

From mortgages paid, called in or foreclosed	$25,359 47
From redemption of stocks	12,500 00
	$339,975 25

PAYMENTS.

To depositors	$166,633 84
Cash on hand 31st December, 1866, after the transactions of the day	173,341 41
	$339,975 25

ASSETS OF THE ALBANY CITY SAVINGS INSTITUTION ON THE 1ST DAY JANUARY, 1867.

Bonds and mortgages	$36,942 28
	Cost.
New York State bonds	52,000 00
Bonds of cities in this State, and county bonds	64,000 00
Cash in bank	180,452 36
	$333,394 64

Examinations made and verified by the treasurer.

OTHER FACTS.

Number of trustees authorized by charter, twenty.

Number of trustees who are directors in any bank of issue where deposits of this institution are kept, eight.

Investments yielding no revenue, none.

Average amount kept on deposit in bank, $138,736.

Regular meetings of the board, by charter, monthly. But two held during the year at which a quorum was present.

Number constituting a quorum, eight.

Average attendance at two meetings held during 1866, nine.

Loans on bond and mortgage are effected on authority of the vote of at least seven members of the board.

Purchases or sales of stocks, the same.

Temporary loans, the same.

Deposits in banks of discount, the same.

Examinations of books, for proof of accuracy and fidelity, and assets, are made by the secretary weekly.

Remarks.

This Savings Bank has an arrangement with the Albany City National Bank, similar to that of the Albany Savings Bank with the Commercial, except that *all* the net profits go to the National Bank. The savings bank has no surplus.

ALBANY EXCHANGE SAVINGS BANK.

CASH TRANSACTIONS DURING THE YEAR 1866.

Receipts.

Cash on hand, 1st January, 1866, before the transactions of the day		$76,538 15
Deposited in bank	$76,538 15	
From depositors		98,196 84
From interest on stocks		3,889 24
From interest on deposits in bank		844 23
		$179,468 46

Payments.

To depositors		$75,229 29
For purchase of stocks and bonds		20,300 00
(Par value thereof, $20,000)		
For taxes and assessments		544 23
Cash on hand, 31st December, 1866, after the transactions of the day:		
Deposited in bank	$83,394 94	83,394 94
		$179,468 46

Assets of the Albany Exchange Savings Bank on the 1st Day of July, 1867.

	Par value.	Cost.
United States bonds and treasury notes	$60,000	$60,806 00
New York State bonds	7,000	7,045 00
Bonds of cities in this State	1,000	1,000 00
Bonds of Albany county, in this State	1,000	1,000 00
Cash in bank		33,252 07
		$103,103 07

Examination made and verified by the treasurer.

Other Facts.

Number of trustees authorized by charter, twenty.

Number of trustees who are directors in any bank of issue where deposits of this institution are kept, seven.

Investments yielding no revenue, none.

Average amount kept on deposit in bank, with interest, $80,171.

Regular meetings of the board, quarter yearly.

Number constituting a quorum, eleven.

Average attendance at regular meetings during 1866, twelve.

Loans on bond and mortgage are effected by vote of the board, on recommendation of committee.

Purchases or sales of stocks, the same.

Temporary loans, none made.

Deposits in banks of discount are made by authority of the board.

Examination of books, for proof of accuracy and fidelity, and assets, are made by a committee, appointed by the board, annually.

Remarks.

The business of this savings bank is done for it by the Albany Exchange National Bank, which, of course, makes the most it can out of the operation. Since January, 1867, its investments have exceeded its deposits in bank. See assets, p. 181.

MECHANICS' AND FARMERS' SAVINGS BANK.

CASH TRANSACTIONS DURING THE YEAR 1866.

Receipts.

Cash on hand 1st January, 1866, before the transactions of the day		$46,984 97
Deposited in bank	$3,784 50	
Deposited in vault	43,200 47	
From depositors		848,186 09
From interest on mortgages From interest on stocks From interest on loans From interest on deposits in bank		53,083 87
From sales of stocks		307,000 00
		$1,255,254 93

PAYMENTS.

To depositors		$724,154 36
For purchase of stocks and bonds		371,810 00
For taxes and assessments		2,947 99
Cash on hand 31st December, 1866, after the transactions of the day:		
Deposited in banks	$142,950 63	
Deposited in vault	13,391 95	
		156,342 58
		$1,255,254 93

ASSETS OF THE MECHANICS' AND FARMERS' SAVINGS BANK ON THE 25TH DAY OF JUNE, 1867.

	Par value.
United States bonds, treasury notes and compound interest notes	$216,100
New York State bonds	505,000
Other securities, Cleveland, C. & C. R. R. bonds	181,000
New York Central R. R. bonds	1,500
Cash in bank, National M. & Farmers	129,310
	$1,032,910

Examined and verified by a committee of three trustees.

OTHER FACTS.

Number of trustees authorized by charter, eleven.

Number of trustees who are directors in any bank of issue where deposits of this institution are kept, nine.

Investments yielding no revenue, none.

Average amount kept on deposit in bank with interest, $23,434.

Regular meetings of the board, quarter yearly.

Number constituting a quorum, five.

Average attendance at regular meetings during 1866, four.

Loans on bond and mortgage, none.

Purchases or sales of stocks are effected on authority of the board.

Temporary loans, none.

Deposits in banks of discount are made by authority of the board.

Examinations of books, for proof of accuracy and fidelity, and assets, are made by the officers of the National Mechanics' and Farmers' Bank, and by a committee of the board at their pleasure.

Remarks.

The Mechanics' and Farmers' Savings Bank and the National Mechanics' and Farmers' Bank, are one and the same institution, in so far as this, that the trustees of the one are the directors of the other. The business is all done by the National Bank. What per cent of the net profits the latter receives does not appear, but it is presumed to be its full share. The fault in all the above cases is not with the *banks*, whose *business* it is to make money, but with the *system* that allows savings banks to be used for such purpose.

AUBURN SAVINGS INSTITUTION.

CASH TRANSACTIONS DURING THE YEAR 1866.

Receipts.

Cash on hand 1st January, 1866, before the transactions of the day		$64,277 94
Deposited in bank	$62,020 95	
Deposited in vault	2,256 99	
From depositors		1,098,539 91
From interest on mortgages		6,166 49
From interest on stocks and gold premiums		25,408 99
From interest on loans		14,287 27
From interest on deposits in bank		2,977 88
From mortgages paid, called in or foreclosed		14,225 00
From repayment of loans		107,507 81
From sales of stocks and county bonds		22,900 00
From rents		120 00
From exchange		447 30
		$1,356,858 59

Payments.

To depositors		$1,017,449 72
Loans on bonds and mortgage		16,050 00
Loans on stocks and other securities		123,945 29
For purchase of stocks and bonds		36,090 17
Par value thereof	$35,300 00	
For repairs		45 63
For salaries		4,600 00
For suits at law		15 10

For printing, advertising, stationery and blank books,		$94 40
For fuel and lights		50 94
For taxes and assessments		4,224 59
For incidental expenses per petty cash		484 87
For charged profit and loss		2,550 00
Cash on hand 31st December, 1866, after the transactions of the day:		
Deposited in bank	$150,414 28	
Deposited in vault	843 60	
		151,257 88
		$1,356,858 59

Assets of the Auburn Savings Institution on the 1st day of July, 1867.

	Par value.	Cost.
Bonds and mortgages		$128,920 00
United States bonds and treasury notes	$373,120	373,120 00
New York State bonds	16,000	16,000 00
Bonds of counties in this State	96,700	96,700 00
Loans on stocks and other securities, available fund,		71,976 75
Other securities		47,810 82
Real estate, $5,000 charged to interest account.		
Cash in bank		118,690 23
Cash in vault		2,670 78
		$855,888 58

Examined and verified by two trustees.

Other Facts.

Number of trustees authorized by charter, thirteen.

Number of trustees who are directors in any bank of issue where deposits of this institution are kept, five.

Investments yielding no revenue; loans amounting to $3,550.

Average amount kept on deposit in bank with interest, $83,764.

Regular meetings of the board, semi-annually.

Number constituting a quorum, seven.

Average attendance at regular meetings during 1866, ten.

Loans on bond and mortgage are effected on authority of the finance committee.

Purchases or sales of stocks, the same.

Temporary loans, the same.

Deposits in banks of discount are made in four different banks, on consultation with board.

Examinations of books, for proof of accuracy and fidelity, and assets, are made by the auditing committee in January and July of each year.

Remarks.

In the semi-annual report for July, the items bonds of counties, $96,700, and other securities, $47,810.82, which here appear as investments belonging to the savings bank, are there stated as collateral for loans only. The feature of its business which I regard as most liable to criticism, is the free use made of the provision authorizing an available fund of $100,000 to be kept on deposit, or otherwise, as the trustees may direct. With $118,000 on deposit in bank, I am at loss to understand where the authority is found for loans to the amount of even $71,000, as stated above, to say nothing of the character of the collaterals—as personal, manufacturing stock, gas stock, water works stock, and the like. They are *presumed* to be good, but savings banks should not rest on *presumptions*.

MUTUAL SAVINGS BANK OF AUBURN.

CASH TRANSACTIONS DURING THE YEAR 1866.

Receipts.

Cash on hand 1st January, 1866, before the transactions of the day		$8,963 70
Deposited in bank	$8,145 00	
Deposited in vault	818 70	
From depositors		485,853 63
From interest on mortgages From interest on stocks From interest on loans From interest on deposits in bank From premium on gold		12,017 40
From mortgages paid, called in or foreclosed		500 00
From repayment of loans		73,644 45
From sales of stocks		10,800 00
		$591,779 18

Payments.

To depositors		$324,885 80
Loans on bond and mortgage		10,675 00
Loans on stocks and other securities		148,655 37
For purchase of stocks and bonds		90,150 00
For salaries		550 00
For printing, advertising, stationery and blank books		75 75
For taxes and assessments		192 08
For incidental expenses per petty cash		215 95
Cash on hand 31st December, 1866, after the transactions of the day:		
Deposited in bank	$14,273 05	
Deposited in vault	2,106 18	
		16,379 23
		$591,779 18

Assets of the Mutual Savings Bank of Auburn on the 1st day of July, 1867.

	Par value.	Cost.
Bonds and mortgages		$13,937 93
United States bonds and treasury notes	$93,000	93,000 00
New York State bonds	5,000	5,000 00
Bonds of counties in this State { Cayuga	26,000	26,500 00
Monroe	300	
Loans on stocks and other securities, available fund		54,293 63
Loans on personal securities, available fund		36,894 02
Cash in bank		6,100 00
Cash in vault		3,627 32
		$239,352 09

Examined and verified by two trustees.

Other Facts.

Number of trustees authorized by charter, seventeen.

Number of trustees who are directors in any bank of issue where deposits of this institution are kept, four.

Investments yielding no revenue, none.

Average amount kept on deposit in bank with interest, not stated.

Regular meetings of the board, quarter yearly.

Number constituting a quorum, president or vice-president and six trustees.

Average attendance at regular meetings during 1866, eight.

Loans on bond and mortgage are effected on authority of loaning committee.

Purchases or sales of stocks, the same.

Temporary loans, the same.

Deposits in banks of discount are made by authority of the board.

Examinations of books, for proof of accuracy and fidelity, and assets, are made by examining committee, and reported to the board at each regular meeting.

Remarks.

The business of this savings bank is carried on in the Auburn City National Bank, but is kept entirely distinct from the affairs of that institution. The available fund which it is authorized to keep is one-fourth of its deposits, or less than $60,000 on its present business; yet its total available fund, including cash in bank and vault, is $100,914.97, or nearly half its total assets. More than one-seventh of its funds are loaned on personal security alone.

BROOKLYN SAVINGS BANK.

CASH TRANSACTIONS DURING THE YEAR 1866.

Receipts.

Cash on hand 1st January, 1866, before the transactions of the day		$129,643 82
Deposited in bank	$70,000 00	
Deposited in vault	59,643 82	
From depositors		2,606,756 32
From interest on mortgages		65,086 46
From interest on stocks		272,388 28
From interest on loans		957 95
From interest on deposits in banks and trust companies		4,300 70
From premium on gold		26,159 00
From mortgages paid, called in or foreclosed		130,050 00
From redemption of stocks		189,000 00
From repayment of loans		45,000 00

From sales of stocks		$169,162 50
From rents		1,340 00
From sundry small balances		602 78
From U. S. Treasurer, N. Y.		540,000 00
From trust companies, N. Y.		250,000 00
		$4,430,447 81

PAYMENTS.

To depositors		$2,413,063 04
Loans on bond and mortgage		440,150 00
Loans on stocks and other securities		104,000 00
For purchase of stocks and bonds		594,316 14
(Par value thereof, $585,000.)		
For repairs		60 00
For salaries		24,836 00
For printing, advertising, stationery and blank books		857 50
For fuel and lights		322 50
For taxes and assessments		59,536 69
For incidental expenses per petty cash		1,659 00
For insurance premium		66 60
For short cash and overdrafts		400 00
For deposit with U. S. Treasurer, N. Y.		140,000 00
For deposit with trust companies, N. Y.		500,000 00
Cash on hand 31st December, 1866, after the transactions of the day:		
Deposited in bank	$59,363 85	
Deposited in vault	91,816 49	
		151,180 34
		$4,430,447 81

ASSETS OF THE BROOKLYN SAVINGS BANK ON THE FIRST DAY OF JANUARY, 1867.

	Par value.	Cost.
Bonds and mortgages		$1,224,950 00
U. S. bonds and treasury notes	$1,070,000	1,050,000 00
New York State bonds	569,500	559,000 00
Bonds of other States	1,020,000	886,550 00
Bonds of cities in this State	1,286,500	1,226,850 00
Bonds of counties in this State	718,000	678,000 00

Loans on stocks and other securities, available fund,	$104,000 00
Other securities	118,014 04
Real estate	10,000 00
Cash in banks and trust companies	309,363 85
Cash in vault	91,816 49
	$6,258,544 38

Examined and verified by two trustees.

Other Facts.

Number of trustees authorized by charter, twenty-seven.

Number of trustees who are directors in any bank of issue where deposits of this institution are kept, four.

Investments yielding no revenue, none.

Average amount kept on deposit in bank, with interest, $90,000.

Regular meetings of the board, quarter yearly.

Number constituting a quorum, president or vice-president, and five trustees.

Average attendance at regular meetings during 1866, twelve.

Loans on bond and mortgage are effected on authority of the funding committee.

Purchases or sale of stocks, the same.

Temporary loans are made by authority of the same, and officers of the bank.

Deposits in banks of discount are made by authority of the same, or by the board.

Examinations of books, for proof of accuracy and fidelity, and assets, are made by a committee of trustees in January and July.

Remarks.

Of the bonds of other States all but $99,000 (par value) are of northern States, and all, it would seem, produce an income. Its condition and character can be seen from the foregoing statements and from statistics in Tables B and C, and require no comment.

DIME SAVINGS BANK OF BROOKLYN.

CASH TRANSACTIONS DURING THE YEAR 1866.

Receipts.

Cash on hand 1st January, 1866, before the transactions of the day		$59,341 01
Deposited in bank	$52,187 87	
Deposited in vault	7,153 14	
From depositors		1,890,459 96
From interest on mortgages		25,516 54
From interest on stocks		114,085 76
From interest on loans		1,738 32
From interest on deposits in bank		291 30
From premium on gold		13,913 34
From mortgages paid, called in or foreclosed		28,150 00
From redemption of stocks		133,604 70
From repayment of loans		105,000 00
From sales of stocks		132,810 00
From rents		2,013 64
		$2,506,924 57

Payments.

Interest to depositors	$104,525 56
To depositors	1,142,894 38
Loans on bond and mortgage	204,650 52
Loans on stocks and other securities	90,500 00
For purchase of stocks and bonds	848,514 83
For building or construction account For repairs For furniture and fixtures	5,781 06
For salaries	17,186 49
For suits at law	188 63
For printing, advertising, stationery and blank books	968 33
For fuel and lights	789 47
For taxes and assessments	15,279 65
For incidental expenses per petty cash	517 59
For insurance	100 00
For extra allowance to clerks	465 00

Cash on hand 31st December, 1866, after the transactions of the day:		
Deposited in bank	$31,697 42	
Deposited in vault	13.893 97	
		$45,591 39
Accrued interest and premium on stocks purchased, and profit and loss items		28,971 67
		$2,506,924 57

ASSETS OF THE DIME SAVINGS BANK OF BROOKLYN, ON THE 1ST DAY OF FEBRUARY, 1867.

Bonds and mortgages	$598,800 00
	Par value.
United States bonds and treasury notes	1,596,150 00
New York State bonds	90,000 00
Bonds of cities in this State	234,427 36
Bonds of counties in this State (Kings)	83,000 00
Loans on U. S. stocks and other securities, available fund	3,600 00
Real estate annual rental value, about $6,000, cost	60,000 00
Cash in bank	1,904 47
Cash in vault	3,638 65
Accrued interest to January 1, not yet available	8,234 78
	$2,679,755 26

Examined and verified by three trustees.

OTHER FACTS.

Number of trustees authorized by charter, thirty-one.

Number of trustees who are directors in any bank of issue where deposits of this institution are kept, none.

Investments yielding no revenue, none.

Average amount kept on deposit in bank with interest, $40,000.

Regular meetings of the board, monthly.

Number constituting a quorum, seven.

Average attendance at regular meetings during 1866, thirteen.

Loans on bond and mortgage are effected by authority of the board, on recommendation of the funding committee.

Purchases or sales of stock are effected by vote of the funding committee, confirmed by the board of trustees.

Temporary loans are made by treasurer and secretary, confirmed by the funding committee and board of trustees.

Deposits in banks of discount are made by authority of funding committee as to depository, and by the teller as to amount.

Examinations of books, for proof of accuracy and fidelity and assets, are made by attending committee daily or monthly, and by the examining committee annually.

DIME SAVINGS BANK OF WILLIAMSBURGH.

CASH TRANSACTIONS DURING THE YEAR 1866.

RECEIPTS.

Cash on hand 1st January, 1866, before the transactions of the day		$26,642 30
Deposited in bank	$15,053 55	
Deposited in vault	11,588 75	
From depositors		487,547 29
From interest on mortgages		126 07
From interest on stocks		15,291 03
From interest on loans		409 27
From interest on deposits in bank		449 78
From premium on gold		204 48
From repayment of loans		5,225 00
From sales of stocks		106,200 00
		$642,095 22

PAYMENTS.

To depositors	$289,810 27
Loans on bond and mortgage	36,450 00
Loans on stocks and other securities	19,425 00
For purchase of stocks and bonds	249,362 40
(Par value thereof $250,322 40)	
For repairs	75 12
For rent	650 00
For salaries	3,131 31
For printing, advertising, stationery and blank books	934 32
For fuel and lights	127 62
For taxes and assessments	1,408 19
For incidental expenses per petty cash	45 95
For rent of bank safe	28 00

Cash on hand 31st December, 1866, after the transactions of the day:		
Deposited in bank	$35,899 27	
Deposited in vault	4,747 77	
		$40,647 04
		$642,095 22

Assets of the Dime Savings Bank of Williamsburgh, on the Fourteenth Day of June, 1867.

	Par value.	Cost.
Bonds and mortgages		$55,450 00
U. S. bonds and treasury notes	$100,250	$102,047 63
Bonds of cities in this State	237,100	236,440 00
Bonds of Kings county, in this State	15,000	15,005 00
Loans on stock and other securities, available fund,		18,700 00
Cash in bank		32,580 55
Cash in vault		4,442 58
		$464,665 76

Examined and verified by two trustees.

Other Facts.

Number of trustees authorized by charter, twenty-three.

Number of trustees who are directors in any bank of issue where deposits of this institution are kept, none.

Investments yielding no revenue, none.

Average amount kept on deposit in bank with interest, $38,375.

Regular meetings of the board, monthly.

Number constituting a quorum, eight.

Average attendance at regular meetings during 1866, eleven.

Loans on bond and mortgage are effected on authority of finance committee.

Purchases of sales of stocks, the same.

Temporary loans are made by authority of the president and secretary.

Deposits in banks of discount are made by authority of the secretary.

Examinations of books, for proof of accuracy and fidelity, and assets, are made by the auditing committee monthly.

EAST BROOKLYN SAVINGS BANK.

CASH TRANSACTIONS DURING THE YEAR 1866.

Receipts.

Cash on hand 1st January, 1866, before the transactions of the day		$12,431 95
Deposited in bank	$5,879 88	
Deposited in vault	6,552 07	
From depositors		214,558 80
From interest on mortgages		4,525 05
From interest on stocks		9,506 00
From interest on deposits in bank		80 35
From premium on gold		1,452 29
From mortgages paid, called in or foreclosed		5,200 00
For sales of stocks		2,000 00
		$249,754 44

Payments.

To depositors		$167,826 93
Loans on bond and mortgage		28,250 00
For purchase of stocks and bonds		40,627 85
For repairs		89 75
For rent		400 00
For salaries		2,788 00
For printing, advertising, stationery and blank books		148 04
For fuel and lights		117 53
For taxes and assessments		1,116 72
For incidental expenses for petty cash		107 85
Cash on hand 31st December, 1866, after the transactions of the day:		
Deposited in bank	$3,272 92	
Deposited in vault	5,018 85	
		8,291 77
		$249,754 44

Assets of the East Brooklyn Savings Bank, on the 31st Day of May, 1867.

	Par value.	Cost.
Bonds and mortgages		$88,200 00
U. S. bonds and treasury notes	$158,000 00	158,000 00
Bonds of cities in this State	30,900 45	30,900 45

Cash in bank	$443 03
Cash in vault	5,681 80
	$283,225 28

Examined and verified by treasurer and accountant.

Other Facts.

Number of trustees authorized by charter, seventeen.

Number of trustees who are directors in any bank of issue where deposits of this institution are kept, none.

Investments yielding no revenue, none.

Average amount kept on deposit in bank with interest, $1,500.

Regular meetings of the board, monthly.

Number constituting a quorum, seven.

Average attendance at regular meetings during 1866, ten.

Loans on bond and mortgage are effected by the funding committee.

Purchases or sales of stocks are effected by the president and treasurer, under direction of the board of trustees.

Temporary loans; none made.

Deposits in banks of discount are made by the treasurer.

Examinations of books, for proof of accuracy and fidelity, and assets, are made by the examining committee semi-annually.

Remarks.

The investments, both as regards their quality and the proportions of the different kinds, could hardly be improved.

EMIGRANT SAVINGS BANK OF BROOKLYN.

CASH TRANSACTIONS DURING THE YEAR 1866.

Receipts.

Cash on hand 1st January, 1866, before the transactions of the day		$13,062 40
Deposited in bank	$12,833 06	
Deposited in vault	229 34	
From depositors		111,256 17
From interest on mortgages		1,263 97
From interest on stocks		3,432 14
From interest on loans		2 78

From interest on deposits in bank		$611 61
From premium on gold		139 50
From mortgages paid, or called in		1,000 00
From redemption of stocks		27,000 00
From repayment of loans		2,007 50
From sales of stocks (5-20's)		10,000 00
From rents		175 20
		$169,951 27

PAYMENTS.

To depositors		$83,884 97
Loans on bond and mortgage		55,100 00
Loans on stocks and other securities		9,000 00
For purchase of stocks and bonds		9,870 56
(Par value thereof	$10,000 00)	
For furniture and fixtures		210 00
For rent		750 00
For salaries		1,630 00
For printing, advertising, stationery and blank books, For fuel and lights		243 95
For taxes and assessments		210 33
For incidental expenses per petty cash		134 72
For other expenses, enumerated below :		
Painting sign	$10 00	
Insurance of furniture	18 75	
		28 75
Cash on hand 31st December, 1866, after the transactions of the day :		
Deposited in bank	$8,181 46	
Deposited in vault	706 53	
		8,887 99
		$169,951 27

ASSETS OF THE EMIGRANT SAVINGS BANK OF BROOKLYN ON THE 1ST DAY OF JANUARY, 1867.

Bonds and mortgages	$69,300 00
	Cost.
United States bonds and treasury notes	12,000 00
Bonds of cities in this State	7,000 00

Cash in bank	$8,181 46
Cash in vault	706 53
Furniture and fixtures	1,786 72
	$98,974 71

Examined and verified by the comptroller of the institution.

Other Facts.

Number of trustees authorized by charter, twenty-eight.

Number of trustees who are directors in any bank of issue where deposits of this institution are kept, none.

Investments yielding no revenue, none.

Average amount kept on deposit in bank with interest, not stated.

Regular meetings of the board, twice each month.

Number constituting a quorum, nine.

Average attendance at regular meetings during 1866, not stated.

Loans on bond and mortgage are effected on authority of finance committee, approved by the board.

Purchases or sales of stocks, the same.

Temporary loans, the same.

Deposits in banks of discount, the same.

Examinations of books, for proof of accuracy and fidelity, and assets, are made daily by auditing committee; semi-annually by president and secretary.

Remarks.

The large per cent. invested in bond and mortgage will attract attention, not to mention the small per cent. in furniture and fixtures, which, if deducted, would leave the liabilities greater than the assets. Yet the institution pays six per cent. dividends! But it is young, and we hope will improve with age.

GERMAN SAVINGS BANK OF BROOKLYN.

(Commenced business June 30, 1866.)

CASH TRANSACTIONS DURING THE YEAR 1866.

Receipts.

From depositors	$184,099 13
From interest on mortgages	333 69
From interest on stocks	2,625 00
From interest on loans	238 58
From interest on deposits in bank	401 78

From premium on gold, &c.		$57 73
From mortgages paid, called in or foreclosed		1,535 50
		$189,291 41

PAYMENTS.

To depositors		$44,808 26
Loans on bond and mortgage		42,325 00
Loans on stocks and other securities		10,000 00
For purchase of stocks and bonds		76,754 92
(Par value thereof	$75,880 00)	
Back interest	874 92	
For furniture and fixtures		939 85
For rent		210 00
For printing, advertising, stationery and blank books		534 35
For fuel and lights		55 79
For other expenses, enumerated below		142 90
Stove and putting up	$46 30	
Stamps	9 87	
Sign and other painting	76 00	
Sundries	10 73	
Cash on hand 31st December, 1866, after the transactions of the day:		
Deposited in bank	$12,819 56	
Deposited in vault	699 15	
		13,518 71
Error to balance		1 63
		$189,291 41

ASSETS OF THE GERMAN SAVINGS BANK OF BROOKLYN ON THE 1ST DAY OF JANUARY, 1867.

Bonds and mortgages	$40,789 50
	Par value.
United States bonds and treasury notes	880 00
Bonds of cities in this State	75,000 00
Loans on stocks and other securities, available fund,	10,000 00
Cash in bank	12,819 56
Cash in vault	699 15
	$140,188 21

Examined and verified by two trustees.

Other Facts.

Number of trustees authorized by charter, twenty-one.

Number of trustees who are directors in any bank of issue where deposits of this institution are kept, none.

Investments yielding no revenue, none.

Average amount kept on deposit in bank with interest, $22,000.

Regular meetings of the board, monthly.

Number constituting a quorum, eleven.

Average attendance at regular meetings during 1866, fourteen.

Loans on bond and mortgage are effected on authority of finance committee.

Purchases or sales of stocks, the same.

Temporary loans, the same. The above are all reported to the board.

Deposits in banks of discount are made by authority of the board of trustees.

Examinations of books, for proof of accuracy and fidelity, and assets, are made by examining committee twice each year.

Remarks.

As will be seen, this is a young institution, but its trustees take pride in it, and notwithstanding reverses elsewhere detailed, are determined to make it a success, and I believe will do so.

KINGS COUNTY SAVINGS INSTITUTION.

CASH TRANSACTIONS DURING THE YEAR 1866.

Receipts.

Cash on hand 1st January, 1866, before the transactions of the day		$26,798 20
Deposited in bank	$22,856 89	
Deposited in vault	3,941 31	
From depositors		587,173 70
From interest on mortgages From interest on stocks From interest on loans		34,851 15
From interest on deposits in bank		1,468 53
From premium on gold		1,691 00
From redemption of stocks From repayment of loans		24,550 00
From sales of stocks		185,245 99
		$861,778 57

Payments.

To depositors		$393,967 26
Loans on bond and mortgage		82,000 00
Loans on stocks and other securities		3,800 00
For purchase of stocks and bonds		279,517 82
For rent		700 00
For salaries		2,966 66
For printing, advertising, stationery and blank books		600 37
For fuel and lights		166 78
For taxes and assessments		4,550 57
For incidental expenses per petty cash		305 80
Real estate for bank use		20,384 99
Cash on hand 31st December, 1866, after the transactions of the day:		
Deposited in bank	$65,183 26	
Deposited in vault	7,635 06	
		72,818 32
		$861,778 57

Assets of the Kings County Savings Institution on the 10th Day of January, 1867.

	Par value.	Cost.
Bonds and mortgages		$109,300 00
U. S. bonds and treasury notes	$40,000 00	$40,000 00
New York State bonds	100,000 00	98,500 00
Bonds of other States	10,000 00	9,300 00
Bonds of cities in this States	346,952 64	338,000 00
Loans on stocks and other securities, available fund,		10,900 00
Other securities		17,553 00
Real estate		20,000 00
Cash in bank		65,183 26
Cash in vault		7,635 06
		$716,371 32

Examined and verified by the president and a trustee.

Other Facts.

Number of trustees authorized by charter, sixteen.

Number of trustees who are directors in any bank of issue where deposits of this institution are kept, none.

Investments yielding no revenue, none.

Average amount kept on deposit in bank with interest, $20,000.

Regular meetings of the board, monthly.

Number constituting a quorum, seven.

Average attendance at regular meetings during 1866, ten.

Loans on bond and mortgage are effected on authority of finance committee, confirmed by the board.

Purchases or sales of stocks, the same.

Temporary loans, the same.

Deposits in banks of discount, the same.

Examinations of books, for proof of accuracy and fidelity, and assets, are made by the examining committee, semi-annually; by attending committee, daily, and by president and secretary.

LONG ISLAND SAVINGS BANK OF BROOKLYN.

(Commenced business April 12, 1866.)

CASH TRANSACTIONS DURING THE YEAR 1866.

Receipts.

From depositors	$151,294 82
From interest on mortgages to Dec. 31, 1866	1,005 92
From interest on stocks	582 50
From interest on loans	40 00
From interest on deposits in bank	271 58
From premium on gold	173 78
From repayment of loans	3,247 50
	$156,616 10

Payments.

To depositors		$23,907 52
Loans on bond and mortgage		62,200 00
For purchase of stocks and bonds		45,464 61
(Par value thereof	$45,000)	
For building or construction account For repairs For furniture and fixtures		1,885 95
For rent		700 00
For salaries		661 56
For printing, advertising, stationery and blank books,		1,253 60

For fuel and lights		$33 47
For incidental expenses per petty cash		13 75
Cash on hand 31st December, 1866, after the transactions of the day:		
Deposited in bank	$17,690 21	
Deposited in vault	2,805 43	
		20,495 64
		$156,616 10

ASSETS OF THE LONG ISLAND SAVINGS BANK OF BROOKLYN, ON THE 1ST DAY OF JULY, 1867.

	Par value.	Cost.
Bonds and mortgages		$132,200 00
United States bonds and treasury notes,	$59,100 00	63,071 87
Bonds of counties in this State	39,213 00	49,676 74
Kings county bonds	10,000 00	
Cash in bank		25,800 02
Cash in vault		1,240 78
		$271,989 41

Examined and verified by president and treasurer.

OTHER FACTS.

Number of trustees authorized by charter, twenty.

Number of trustees who are directors in any bank of issue where deposits of this institution are kept, none known.

Investments yielding no revenue, none.

Average amount kept on deposit in bank with interest, $15,000.

Regular meetings of the board, monthly.

Number constituting a quorum, seven.

Average attendance at regular meetings during 1866, eleven.

Loans on bond and mortgage are effected on authority of funding committee.

Purchases or sales of stocks, the same.

Temporary loans, the same.

Deposits in banks of discount, the same.

Examinations of books for proof of accuracy and fidelity and assets, are made by examining committee monthly.

REMARKS.

Too large a proportion of bonds and mortgages for great emergencies. Otherwise satisfactory.

SOUTH BROOKLYN SAVINGS INSTITUTION.

CASH TRANSACTIONS DURING THE YEAR 1866.

RECEIPTS.

Cash on hand 1st January, 1866, before the transactions of the day		$97,119 09
Deposited in bank	$85,770 30	
Deposited in vault	11,348 79	
From depositors		1,143,412 12
From interest on mortgages From interest on stocks From interest on loans		112,195 65
From interest on deposits in bank		1,912 76
From premium on gold		13,980 75
From mortgages paid		22,250 00
From redemption of stocks		203,000 00
From repayment of loans		101,800 00
From rents		1,887 50
From insurance repaid, tenants for fuel, exchange of stocks and sundries		418 80
		$1,697,976 67

PAYMENTS.

To depositors		$988,499 40
Loans on bond and mortgage		42,500 00
Loans on stocks and other securities		135,600 00
For purchase of stocks and bonds		427,978 25
(Par value thereof	$426,000)	
For repairs		510 18
For furniture and fixtures		108 77
For salaries		12,760 00
For suits at law		94 11
For printing, advertising, stationery and blank books		705 78
For fuel and lights		452 94
For taxes and assessments		11,937 33
For incidental expenses per petty cash		388 14
For accrued interest paid on stocks above named		3,620 27
Cash on hand 31st December, 1866, after the transactions of the day:		

Deposited in bank	$60,331 53	
Deposited in vault	12,489 97	
		$72,821 50
		$1,697,976 67

ASSETS OF THE SOUTH BROOKLYN SAVINGS INSTITUTION ON THE 31ST DAY OF JANUARY, 1867.

Bonds and mortgages	$262,500 00
	Par value.
United States bonds and treasury notes	1,000,000 00
New York State bonds	100,000 00
Bonds of other States (Ohio)	50,000 00
Bonds of cities in this State (Brooklyn)	408,000 00
Bonds of counties in this State (Kings)	69,000 00
Loans on stocks, available fund	140,900 00
Real estate, standing on ledger at	5,000 00
Cash in banks	29,917 96
Cash in vault	1,619 16
	$2,066,937 12

Examined and verified by three trustees.

OTHER FACTS.

Number of trustees authorized by charter, twenty-six.

Number of trustees who are directors in any bank of issue where deposits of this institution are kept, none.

Investments yielding no revenue, none.

Average amount kept on deposit in bank with interest, $47,819.

Regular meetings of the board, monthly.

Number constituting a quorum, eight.

Average attendance at regular meetings during 1866, thirteen.

Loans on bond and mortgage are effected on authority of finance committee.

Purchases or sales of stocks are effected on authority of the board when the amount exceeds $50,000; by the finance committee for smaller amounts.

Temporary loans are made by authority of finance committee.

Deposits in banks of discount are made by authority of finance committee and officers of the institution.

Examinations of books, for proof of accuracy and fidelity, are made by an examining committee of three trustees, monthly, and of the assets annually or semi-annually.

Remarks.

The condition of this institution is better than is represented—not a very common error—by reason of its real estate being worth more than the nominal sum of $5,000, at which it stands on their books. It yields an income of nearly $2,000 per annum in rents. See cash transactions—receipts.

WILLIAMSBURGH SAVINGS BANK.

CASH TRANSACTIONS DURING THE YEAR 1866.

Receipts.

Cash on hand 1st January, 1866, before the transactions of the day		$119,824 81
Deposited in bank	$16,677 37	
Deposited in vault	103,147 44	
From depositors		2,818,900 22
From interest on mortgages		55,554 21
From interest on stocks		261,575 48
From interest on loans		17,504 89
From interests on deposits in bank		3,607 18
From premium on gold		62,458 40
From mortgages paid, called in or foreclosed		92,634 04
From redemption of stocks		403,199 83
From repayment of loans		173,225 00
From sales of stocks		287,191 25
From rents		750 00
From gain on sales of U. S. stocks		14,598 58
		$4,311,023 89

Payments.

To depositors		$2,614,901 13
Loans on bond and mortgage		380,581 15
Loans on stocks and other securities		104,206 34
For purchase of stocks and bonds		911,967 50
(Par value thereof	$949,300 00)	
For building or construction account		152 00
For repairs		79 67

For furniture and fixtures		$97 40
For interest		6,534 12
For salaries		23,165 64
For insurance		99 05
For printing, advertising, stationery and blank books		947 05
For fuel and lights		339 91
For taxes and assesments		44,868 52
For incidental expenses per petty cash		552 22
For internal revenue stamps		250 00
For New York State Bank Department		42 89
For loss on spurious money and short cash		341 62
Cash on hand 31st December, 1866, after the transactions of the day:		
Deposited in bank	$141,566 78	
Deposited in vault	80,330 90	
		221,897 68
		$4,311,023 89

Assets of the Williamsburgh Savings Bank on the 1st day of January, 1867.

	Par value.	Cost.
Bonds and mortgages		$973,155 03
U. S. bonds and treasury notes	$2,531,900 00	2,531,900 00
New York State bonds	500,000 00	500,000 00
Bonds of cities in this State	940,629 50	906,629 50
Bonds of counties in this State	526,500 00	521,500 00
Loans on stocks and other securities, available fund,		223,156 34
Real estate, annual rental value, $3,000		42,543 92
Cash in bank		141,566 78
Cash in vault		80,330 90
		$5,920,782 47

Examined and verified by three trustees.

Other Facts.

Number of trustees authorized by charter, eighteen.

Number of trustees who are directors in any bank of issue where deposits of this institution are kept, seven.

Investments yielding no revenue, real estate taken to secure debt, $10,811.06.

Average amount kept on deposit in bank with interest, $57,403.

Regular meetings of the board, monthly.

Number constituting a quorum, eight.

Average attendance at regular meetings during 1866, eleven.

Loans on bond and mortgage are effected on authority of the board, on report of funding committee.

Purchases or sales of stocks are made by the cashier, under direction of the funding committee, upon the authority of resolutions of the board.

Temporary loans are made by funding committee, approved by the president or a vice-president.

Deposits in banks of discount are made by authority of the board.

Examinations of books, for proof of accuracy and fidelity, are made by the attending committee once a month; and of the assets and books by examining committee at least twice in each year.

Remarks.

This institution never declares dividends until the profits out of which they are to be paid are ascertained. The right way.

BUFFALO SAVINGS BANK.

CASH TRANSACTIONS DURING THE YEAR 1866.

Receipts.

Cash on hand 1st January, 1866, before the transactions of the day		$90,653 73
Deposited in bank	$38,727 43	
Deposited in vault	51,926 30	
From depositors		1,888,911 60
From interest on mortgages		33,298 86
From interest on stocks		86,700 79
From interest on loans		21,956 36
From interest on deposits in bank		5,203 26
From premium on gold		10,817 20
From mortgages paid, called in or foreclosed		41,150 00
From redemption of stocks		270,875 00
From repayment of loans		1,170,000 00
From sales of real estate		310 00
From sales of stocks		230,500 00
From rents		149 96

From premium on exchange, of stocks		$15,338 83
From United States District Court, and exchange		97 74
		$3,865,963 33

PAYMENTS.

To depositors		$1,504,534 83
Loans on bond and mortgage		89,775 00
Loans on stocks and other securities		667,602 75
For purchase of stocks and bonds		1,163,041 84
(Par value thereof	$1,142,500)	
For building or construction account		75,664 67
For furniture and fixtures		32 70
For rent		225 00
For salaries		10,000 00
For printing, advertising, stationery and blank books		427 82
For fuel and lights		160 62
For taxes and assessments		13,952 78
For incidental expenses per petty cash		525 56
Cash on hand 31st December, 1866, after the transactions of the day:		
Deposited in bank	$259,542 52	
Deposited in vault	80,497 24	
		340,039 76
		$3,865,963 33

ASSETS OF THE BUFFALO SAVINGS BANK ON THE 1ST DAY OF AUGUST, 1867.

Bonds and mortgages	$599,526 92
	Par value.
United States bonds and treasury notes	809,100 00
New York State bonds	506,000 00
Bonds of cities in this State (Buffalo)	140,600 00
Bonds of counties in this State (Erie)	150,000 00
Loans on stocks and other securities, available fund,	155,700 00
Other securities, U. S. compound interest notes	11,239 34
Real estate, cost	132,849 49
Cash in bank	207,898 63
Cash in vault	52,906 79
	$2,765,821 17

Examined and verified by two trustees.

Other Facts.

Number of trustees authorized by charter, eighteen.

Number of trustees who are directors in any bank of issue where deposits of this institution are kept, none.

Investments yielding no revenue, none.

Average amount kept on deposit in bank with interest, $189.129.

Regular meetings of the board, monthly.

Number constituting a quorum, ten.

Average attendance at regular meetings during 1866, eleven.

Loans on bond and mortgage are effected on authority of unanimous vote of trustees.

Purchases or sales of stocks are effected on authority of eight affirmative votes of trustees.

Temporary loans are made by president and secretary under avthority of a resolution of the board.

Deposits in banks of discount are made by authority of unanimous resolution of the board.

Examinations of books, for proof of accuracy and fidelity, and assets, are made by auditing committee at their pleasure. In practice twice a year. Also under provisions of charter by the board of supervisors of the county of Erie, annually.

Remarks.

The loans on stocks are nearly all United States. A fair proportion on Erie county. None on fancy stocks. Deposits fairly distributed among several banks.

EMIGRANT SAVINGS BANK OF BUFFALO.

CASH TRANSACTIONS DURING THE YEAR 1866.

Receipts.

Cash on hand 1st January, 1866, before the transactions of the day		$40,721 82
Deposited in bank	$28,992 27	
Deposited in vault	11,729 55	
From depositors		279,439 00
From interest on mortgages		334 91
From interest on stocks From interest on loans From premium on gold		3,940 64

From mortgages paid, called in or foreclosed		$800 00
From interest on deposits in bank		1,331 44
		$326,567 81

PAYMENTS.

To depositors		$242,387 40
Loans on bond and mortgage		6,200 00
For purchase of stocks and bonds		3,930 00
(Par value thereof	$3,930 00	
For repairs		63 69
For furniture, fixtures and safe		1,056 49
For rent		300 00
For salaries		1,836 00
For printing, advertising, stationery and blank books		97 67
For fuel and lights		44 86
For taxes and assessments		614 72
For incidental expenses per petty cash		74 25
Cash on hand 31st December, 1866, after the transactions of the day:		
Deposited in bank	$47,078 79	
Deposited in vault	22,883 94	
		69,962 73
		$326,567 81

ASSETS OF THE EMIGRANT SAVINGS BANK, OF BUFFALO, ON THE 1ST DAY OF OCTOBER, 1867.

	Par value.	Cost.
Bonds and mortgages		$20,940 00
U. S. bonds and treasury notes	$33,400 00	33,400 00
Bonds of cities in this State (Buffalo)	1,000 00	1,000 00
Bonds of counties in this State (Erie)	30,000 00	30,000 00
Loans on stocks and other securities, available fund		5,431 92
Other securities		7,842 10
Cash in bank		32,225 16
Cash in vault		23,842 02
		$154,681 20

Not verified.

OTHER FACTS.

Number of trustees authorized by charter, sixteen.

Number of trustees who are directors in any bank of issue where deposits of this institution are kept, none.

Investments yielding no revenue, none.

Average amount kept on deposit in bank with interest, $26,625.

Regular meetings of the board, monthly.

Number constituting a quorum, nine.

Average attendance at regular meetings during 1866, eleven.

Loans on bond and mortgage are effected on authority of a vote of majority of the trustees.

Purchases or sales of stocks, the same.

Temporary loans, the same.

Deposits in banks of discount are made by authority of a committee appointed by the board.

Examinations of books, for proof of accuracy and fidelity, and assets, if made, are not stated.

Remarks.

This institution labors under the disadvantage of having to compete with three older and stronger savings banks in the same city. In order to attract deposits it has to declare dividends as high as theirs. To do this last year, it credited interest to depositors, $6,122.52, out of $5,592.43 received. The amount kept on deposit in bank at five per cent interest, and in vault without interest, is much too large. Half of it would be better, and a third of it added to investments in bond and mortgage, would help its condition materially.

ERIE COUNTY SAVINGS BANK.

CASH TRANSACTIONS DURING THE YEAR 1866.

Receipts.

Cash on hand 1st January, 1866, before the transactions of the day		$199,794 68
Deposited in bank	$156,701 28	
Deposited in vault	43,093 40	
From depositors		4,311,052 89
From interest on mortgages		26,893 89
From interest on stocks		125,919 00
From interest on loans		20,988 94
From interest on deposits in banks		9,043 98
From premium on gold		14,902 66
From mortgages paid, called in or foreclosed		29,596 39
From redemption of stocks		346,965 00
From repayment of loans		306,240 94

From sales of stocks		$130,530 00
From rents		134 10
From exchange account		34 06
From suspense account		1,665 19
		$5,523,761 72

PAYMENTS.

To depositors		$3,939,039 62
Loans on bond and mortgage		120,588 97
Loans on stocks and other securities		205,923 37
For purchase of stocks and bonds		900,085 22
(Par value thereof	$869,705 41)	
For building or construction account		69,780 67
For repairs		14 83
For furniture and fixtures		36 33
For rent		2,175 00
For salaries		10,261 33
For printing, advertising, stationery and blank books,		703 17
For fuel and lights		169 54
For taxes and assessments		18,524 28
For incidental expenses, per petty cash		435 06
For suspense account		735 83
Cash on hand 31st December, 1866, after the transactions of the day:		
Deposited in bank	$197,532 58	
Deposited in vault	57,755 92	
		255,288 50
		$5,523,761 72

ASSETS OF THE ERIE COUNTY SAVINGS BANK, ON THE 1ST DAY OF JANUARY, 1867.

Bonds and mortgages	$452,157 63
	Par value.
U. S. bonds and treasury notes	1,682,840 00
New York State bonds	400,000 00
Bonds of other States	99,085 00
Bonds of cities in this State	126,898 90
Bonds of towns in this State	10,000 00
Loans on stocks and other securities, available fund,	159,267 00
Other securities	49,400 00

Real estate, cost	$115,939 59
Cash in bank	197,532 58
Cash in vault	57,755 92
	$3,350,876 62

Examined and verified by the president and secretary.

Other Facts.

Number of trustees authorized by charter, twenty.

Number of trustees who are directors in any bank of issue where deposits of this institution are kept, one.

Investments yielding no revenue. Banking houses in course of construction and real estate on foreclosure.

Average amount kept on deposit in bank with interest, $233,-133, at six per cent.

Regular meetings of the board, monthly.

Number constituting a quorum, eight.

Average attendance at regular meetings during 1866, twelve.

Loans on bond and mortgage are effected on authority of the vote of eight members of the board.

Purchases or sales of stocks are effected on authority of the board of trustees.

Temporary loans are made by president, as authorized by board of trustees.

Deposits in banks of discount are made by order of the board of trustees.

Examinations of books, for proof of accuracy and fidelity, and assets, are made by the president, monthly; by committees of the board occasionally.

Remarks.

Six per cent interest on balance in bank, is very good to have while we *do* have it. But I can not get over a feeling of suspicion of the bank that *tries* to afford to *pay* that rate for its deposits. It certainly leaves them but a small margin for profit in legitimate banking business, after paying the half per cent government tax.

WESTERN SAVINGS BANK OF BUFFALO.

CASH TRANSACTIONS DURING THE YEAR 1866.

Receipts.

Cash on hand 1st January, 1866, before the transactions of the day		$104,163 59
Deposited in bank	$78,591 64	
Deposited in vault	25,571 95	
From depositors		1,119,933 22
From interest on mortgages From interest on stocks From interest on loans From interest on deposits in bank From premium on gold		42,158 93
From mortgages paid, called in or foreclosed		4,225 00
From redemption of stocks		21,200 00
From profits from interest		3,101 17
		$1,294,781 91

Payments.

To depositors		$1,050,294 23
Loans on bond and mortgage		48,250 00
Loans on stocks and other securities		5,183 67
For purchase of stocks and bonds		75,000 00
(Par value thereof	$75,000 00)	
For furniture and fixtures		673 28
For rent		1,000 00
For salaries		3,000 00
For printing, advertising, stationery and blank books		60 00
For fuel and lights		62 10
For taxes and assessments		2,855 40
For incidental expenses per petty cash		274 04
Cash on hand 31st December, 1866, after the transactions of the day:		
Deposited in bank	$103,527 81	
Deposited in vault	4,601 38	
		108,129 19
		$1,294,781 91

Assets of the Western Savings Bank of Buffalo, on the 1st day of January, 1867.

Bonds and mortgages	$102,257 14
	Par value.
U. S. bonds and treasury notes	331,000 00
Bonds of cities in this State	9,000 00
Bonds of Erie county in this State	62,000 00
Cash in bank	103,527 81
Cash in vault	4,601 38
	$612,386 33

Examined and verified by the president and secretary.

Other Facts.

Number of trustees authorized by charter, twenty-one.

Number of trustees who are directors in any bank of issue where deposits of this institution are kept, none.

Investments yielding no revenue, none.

Average amount kept on deposit in bank, with interest, $113,213, at six per cent.

Regular meetings of the board, monthly.

Number constituting a quorum, eight.

Average attendance at regular meetings during 1866, nine.

Loans on bond and mortgage are effected on authority of a majority vote of a quorum of trustees.

Purchases or sales of stocks, the same.

Temporary loans, the same.

Deposits in banks of discount, the same.

Examinations of books, for proof of accuracy and fidelity, and assets, are made by committee of trustees annually.

Remarks.

The same will apply here that was said of the Erie County Savings Bank.

ATLANTIC SAVINGS BANK, NEW YORK.

CASH TRANSACTIONS DURING THE YEAR 1866.

RECEIPTS.

Cash on hand 1st January, 1866, before the transactions of the day		$146,084 62
Deposited in bank	$115,568 57	
Deposited in vault	30,516 05	
From depositors		1,161,454 71
From interest on mortgages From interest on stocks From interest on loans		83,077 47
From premium on stocks		6,323 62
From mortgages paid, called in or foreclosed		13,100 00
From redemption of stocks		50,000 00
From sales of stocks		225,000 00
From repayment of loans		468,764 38
From rents		1,239 85
		$2,185,044 65

PAYMENTS.

To depositors		$803,123 54
Loans on bond and mortgage		244,971 75
Loans on stocks and other securities		835,787 00
For purchase of stocks and bonds		148,434 00
(Par value thereof	$146,000)	
Overcredited premiums, 1866		375 50
For legal expenses, etc		154 47
For salaries		10,362 00
All expenses other than those enumerated above		10,921 00
Cash on hand 31st December, 1866, after the transactions of the day		130,385 39
Error to balance		530 00
		$2,185,044 65

ASSETS OF THE ATLANTIC SAVINGS BANK ON THE 1ST DAY OF JANUARY, 1867.

	Par value.	Cost.
Bonds and mortgages		$504,740 16
United States bonds and treasury notes	$417,000 00	422,900 00
New York State bonds	25,000 00	25,000 00
Bonds of counties in this State (Westchester)	1,000 00	1,000 00
Loans on stocks and other securities, available fund	422,212 00	422,212 00
Real estate, annual rental value, including the part occupied by this bank	4,000 00	33,000 00
Cash in bank		120,014 80
Cash in vault		10,370 59
		$1,539,237 55

Examined and verified by three trustees.

OTHER FACTS.

Number of trustees authorized by charter, thirty-four.

Number of trustees who are directors in any bank of issue where deposits of this institution are kept, six.

Investments yielding no revenue, none.

Average amount kept on deposit in bank with interest, $270,000.

Regular meetings of the board, monthly.

Number constituting a quorum, eight.

Average attendance at regular meetings during 1866, eleven.

Loans on bond and mortgage are effected on authority of the board.

Purchases or sales of stock, the same.

Temporary loans are made by authority of the officers of the bank.

Deposits in banks of discount are made by the secretary in banks designated by the board.

Examinations of books, for proof of accuracy and fidelity, and assets, are made by examining committee twice a year, and by treasurer as to assets monthly.

REMARKS.

A more detailed statement of the cash transactions, of expenses especially, would have been desirable. The available fund stated above for 1st January, was much reduced on the 1st July, and the collaterals were all first class.

THE BANK FOR SAVINGS IN THE CITY OF NEW YORK.

CASH TRANSACTIONS DURING THE YEAR 1866.

Receipts.

Cash on hand 1st January, 1866, before the transactions of the day		$583,880 52
Deposited in bank	$543,185 24	
Deposited in vault	40,695 28	
From depositors		4,084,463 95
From interest on mortgages		186,805 37
From interest on stocks		678,807 27
From interest on deposits in bank		12,170 04
From premium on gold		106,402 48
From mortgages paid, called in or foreclosed		136,500 00
From redemption of stocks		175,000 00
From sales of real estate		28,500 00
From rents		2,000 00
		$5,994,529 63

Payments.

To depositors		$4,131,330 79
Loans on bond and mortgage		292,000 00
For purchase of stocks and bonds		940,187 50
(Par value thereof	$927,000)	
For building or construction account		74 65
For repairs		278 61
For furniture and fixtures		360 84
For salaries		39,457 49
For suits at law		2,706 50
For printing, advertising, stationery and blank books,		1,775 65
For fuel and lights		763 87
For taxes and assessments		106,839 17
For incidental expenses per petty cash		1,405 07
For loss at counter		79 18
For new safe		1,100 00
For accrued interest on stocks purchased		3,452 50
For extra clerks		1,415 20

Cash on hand 31st December, 1866, after the transactions of the day:		
Deposited in bank	$413,948 17	
Deposited in vault	57,354 44	
		$471,302 61
		$5,994,529 63

ASSETS OF THE BANK FOR SAVINGS IN THE CITY OF NEW YORK, ON THE 1ST DAY OF JANUARY, 1867.

Bonds and mortgages	$3,183,100 00
	Par value.
United States bonds and treasury notes	5,723,600 00
New York State bonds	2,411,500 00
Bonds of other States	1,211,982 09
Bonds of city of New York	2,429,653 00
Real estate	50,000 00
Cash in bank	413,948 17
Cash in vault	57,354 44
	$15,481,137 70

Examined and verified by two trustees.

OTHER FACTS.

Number of trustees authorized by charter, twenty-eight.

Number of trustees who are directors in any bank of issue where deposits of this institution are kept, not stated.

Investments yielding no revenue, not stated.

Average amount kept on deposit in bank with interest, estimated at $400,000.

Regular meetings of the board, monthly.

Number constituting a quorum, six.

Average attendance at regular meetings during 1866, not stated.

Loans on bond and mortgage are effected on authority of the board on report of committee of loans on mortgage.

Purchases or sales of stocks are effected by funding committee on authority of the board.

Temporary loans, none made.

Deposits in banks of discount, are made by authority not stated.

Examinations of books, for proof of accuracy and fidelity, and assets, are made by examining committee twice a year.

Remarks.

This institution is one of the *impregnables*, as it should be, being the pioneer. Of the bonds of other States held by it, about $200,000 are of Tennessee and Kentucky. The remainder are Northern States bonds.

BOWERY SAVINGS BANK.

CASH TRANSACTIONS DURING THE YEAR 1866.

Receipts.

Cash on hand 1st January, 1866, before the transactions of the day		$954,659 94
Deposited in bank	$75,654 38	
Deposited in vault	879,005 56	
From depositors		8,027,670 00
From interest on mortgages		183,663 05
From interest on stocks		712,333 98
From interest on loans		28,877 52
From interest on deposits in bank		1,085 47
From premium on gold		152,753 35
From mortgages paid, called in or foreclosed		200,800 00
From redemption of stocks		410,500 00
From repayment of loans		1,456,800 00
From reimbursement for substitute furnished in 1864		193 75
From sale of old building materials		110 85
		$12,129,447 91

Payments.

To depositors		$8,272,604 59
Loans on bond and mortgage		417,200 00
Loans on stocks and other securities		741,000 00
For purchase of stocks and bonds		765,172 83
(Par value thereof	$753,000 00)	
For building or construction account		78,163 38
For repairs		533 64
For furniture and fixtures		6,665 57
For salaries		73,748 55
For suits at law		230 00

For printing, advertising, stationery and blank books		$4,001 43
For fuel and lights		2,550 44
For taxes and assesments		80,751 94
For incidental expenses per petty cash		5,911 67
For interest in exchange for United States stock,		1,695 63
For deficit in cash. Counterfeit bills and claims allowed		1,504 87
Cash on hand 31st December, 1866, after the transactions of the day:		
Deposited in bank	$186,132 81	
Deposited in vault	1,391,580 56	1,577,713 37
		$12,129,447 91

Assets of the Bowery Savings Bank on the 1st Day of January, 1867.

Bonds and mortgages	$3,260,333 00
	Par value.
United States bonds and treasury notes	7,325,500 00
New York State bonds	661,500 00
Bonds of other States	1,355,400 00
Bonds of cities in this State	2,656,419 00
Bonds of counties in this State	230,000 00
Loans on stocks and other securities, available fund	41,000 00
Real estate, cost	150,000 00
Cash in bank	186,132 81
Cash in vault	1,391,580 56
	$17,257,865 37

Examined and verified by five trustees.

Other Facts.

Number of trustees authorized by charter, forty-three.

Number of trustees who are directors in any bank of issue where deposits of this institution are kept, eight.

Investments yielding no revenue, none.

Average amount kept on deposit in bank, with interest, estimated at $175,000.

Regular meetings of the board, monthly.

Number constituting a quorum, six.

Average attendance at regular meetings during 1866, twenty-seven.

Loans on bond and mortgage are effected by funding committee approved by board of trustees.

Purchases or sales of stocks, the same.

Temporary loans, the same.

Deposits in banks of discount, the same.

Examinations of books, for proof of accuracy and fidelity, and assets, are made by attending committee for cash funds monthly, by yearly committee for general transactions and assets, once a year.

Remarks.

This is the largest institution in the State. It will be seen by the statement of cash transactions, that more than $16,000,000 were received from and paid to depositors in 1866; a sum nearly equal to the entire assets of the institution, and twice the amount received and paid by any other savings bank, and many times larger than by any but one. This will explain the greater proportionate expense attending its business. I hardly need say that its success is merited.

BROADWAY SAVINGS INSTITUTION.

CASH TRANSACTIONS DURING THE YEAR 1866.

Receipts.

Cash on hand 1st January, 1866, before the transactions of the day		$131,397 32
Deposited in bank	$79,831 57	
Deposited in vault	51,565 75	
From depositors		703,676 28
From interest on mortgages		9,887 55
From interest on stocks		59,775 00
From interest on loans		4,547 02
From interest on deposits in bank		2,490 13
From premium on gold		9,821 25
From mortgages paid, called in or foreclosed		36,500 00
From repayment of loans		207,200 00
From sales of stocks		3,256 87
		$1,168,551 42

PAYMENTS.

To depositors		$622,748 62
Loans on bonds and mortgages		41,600 00
Loans on stocks and other securities		177,250 00
For purchase of stocks and bonds		225,885 62
(Par value thereof	$221,000)	
For repairs		39 50
For rent		2,250 00
For salaries		8,349 96
For printing, advertising, stationery and blank books,		510 55
For fuel and lights		25 56
For taxes and assessments		7,989 22
For incidental expenses per petty cash		31 46
Cash on hand 31st December, 1866, after the transactions of the day:		
Deposited in bank	$67,325 12	
Deposited in vault	14,545 81	
		81,870 93
		$1,168,551 42

ASSETS OF THE BROADWAY SAVINGS INSTITUTION ON THE 31ST DAY OF DECEMBER, 1866.

	Par value.	Cost.
Bonds and mortgages		$154,000 00
U. S. bonds and treasury notes	$550,000	544,940 00
New York State bonds	50,000	49,350 00
Bonds of cities in this State	568,000	567,160 00
Loans on stocks and other securities, available fund,		45,550 00
Cash in bank		67,325 12
Cash in vault		14,545 81
		$1,442,870 93

Examined and verified by two trustees.

OTHER FACTS.

Number of trustees authorized by charter, twenty-three.

Number of trustees who are directors in any bank of issue where deposits of this institution are kept, five.

Investments yielding no revenue, none.

Average amount kept on deposit in bank with interest, $71,146.

Regular meetings of the board, monthly.

Number constituting a quorum, seven.

Average attendance at regular meetings during 1866, nine.

Loans on bond and mortgage are effected on authority of unanimous vote of trustees.

Purchases or sales of stock are effected on authority of the finance committee.

Temporary loans, the same.

Deposits in banks of discount, the same.

Examinations of books, for proof of accuracy and fidelity, and assets, are made by examining committee twice in each year.

CITIZENS' SAVINGS BANK.

CASH TRANSACTIONS DURING THE YEAR 1866.

Receipts.

Cash on hand 1st January, 1866, before the transactions of the day		$155,980 36
Deposited in bank	$107,591 34	
Deposited in vault	48,389 02	
From depositors		3,143,269 52
From interest on mortgages		39,629 60
From interest on stocks		108,622 22
From interest on loans		13,951 82
From interest on deposits in bank		7,775 76
From premium on gold		27,783 87
From mortgages paid, called in or foreclosed		43,500 00
From redemption of stocks		42,845 00
From repayment of loans		599,000 00
From rents		4,460 89
		$4,186,809 04

Payments.

To depositors		$1,693,031 70
Loans on bond and mortgage		555,832 00
Loans on stocks and other securities		615,500 00
For purchase of stocks and bonds		916,453 96
(Par value thereof	$880,000)	
For repairs		2,636 34

For furniture and fixtures		$1,613 65
For salaries		17,400 07
For printing, advertising, stationery and blank books		4,077 26
For fuel and lights		423 95
For taxes and assessments		10,195 72
For incidental expenses per petty cash		759 56
For accrued interest on stocks purchased		6,903 87
For dues credited depositors for interest		93,453 40
Cash on hand 31st December, 1866, after the transactions of the day:		
Deposited in bank	$176,737 21	
Deposited in vault	91,790 35	
		268,527 56
		$4,186,809 04

Assets of the Citizens' Savings Bank on the 1st Day of January, 1867.

	Par value.	Cost.
Bonds and mortgages		$890,982 00
United States bonds and treasury notes	$1,580,000	1,580,000 00
New York State bonds	50,000	50,000 00
Bonds of other States	40,000	38,300 00
Bonds of counties in this State	94,900	91,821 22
Loans on stocks and other securities, available fund		286,250 00
Real estate		80,000 00
Cash in bank		176,737 21
Cash in vault		91,790 35
		$3,285,880 78

Examined and verified by two trustees.

Other Facts.

Number of trustees authorized by charter, thirty.

Number of trustees who are directors in any bank of issue where deposits of this institution are kept, three.

Investments yielding no revenue, none.

Average amount kept on deposit in bank with interest, estimated at $150,000.

Regular meetings of the board, monthly.

Number constituting a quorum, eight.

Average attendance at regular meetings during 1866, fifteen.

Loans on bond and mortgage are effected on authority of a unanimous vote at a regular meeting upon a favorable report of loan committee.

Purchases or sales of stocks are effected on authority of finance committee.

Temporary loans the same.

Deposits in banks of discount, the same.

Examinations of books, for proof of accuracy and fidelity, and assets, are made by a trial balance from depositors' ledger twice a year; by comparison of pass-books with ledgers whenever presented. Whole transactions examined twice a year by auditing committee.

Remarks.

The July report has an item of $116,000 loaned on S. A. Navigation Stock or bonds. It may be very good, but has a sort of "South Sea" odor about it.

DRY DOCK SAVINGS INSTITUTION.

CASH TRANSACTIONS DURING THE YEAR 1866.

Receipts.

Cash on hand 1st January, 1866, before the transactions of the day		$484,639 81
Deposited in bank	$257,102 61	
Deposited in vault	227,537 20	
From depositors		3,272,937 00
From interest on mortgages		68,881 96
From interest on stocks		223,033 96
From interest on loans		22,359 54
From interest on deposits in bank		7,540 69
From premium on gold		42,123 24
From mortgages paid, called in or foreclosed		215,900 00
From redemption of stocks		237,500 00
From repayment of loans		422,384 25
From discount on stocks purchased		28,923 00
		$5,026,223 45

Payments.

To depositors	$2,922,323 98
Loans on bond and mortgage	392,900 00

Loans on stocks and other securities		$3,650 00
For purchase of stocks and bonds		971,400 00
(Par value thereof $971,400)		
For repairs		934 24
For salaries		16,583 01
For print'g, advertising, stationery and blank books,		1,468 26
For fuel and lights		668 16
For taxes and assessments		27,436 97
For incidental expenses per petty cash		551 97
For premium on U. S. bonds purchased		8,156 25
For accrued interest on stock purchased		417 77
Cash on hand 31st December, 1866, after the transactions of the day:		
Deposited in bank	$479,757 87	
Deposited in vault	199,954 97	
		679,712 84
		$5,026,223 45

Assets of the Dry Dock Savings Institution, on the 1st Day of January, 1867.

	Par value.	Cost.
Bonds and mortgages		$994,150 00
U. S. bonds and treasury notes	$1,891,600	1,891,600 00
New York State bonds	110,000	110,000 00
Bonds of cities in this State	1,029,100	1,929,100 00
Bonds of towns in this State	72,350	72,350 00
Loans on stocks and other securities, available fund.		45,700 00
Real estate		52,681 35
Cash in bank		479,757 87
Cash in vault		199,954 97
		$5,775,294 19

Examined and verified by three trustees.

Other Facts.

Number of trustees authorized by charter, fifteen.

Number of trustees who are directors in any bank of issue where deposits of this institution are kept, none.

Investments yielding no revenue, none.

Average amount kept on deposit in bank with interest, $335,-250.

Regular meetings of the board, monthly.

Number constituting a quorum, seven.

Average attendance at regular meetings during 1866, thirteen.

Loans on bond and mortgage are effected on authority of board of trustees, on recommendation of funding committee.

Purchases or sales of stocks, the same.

Temporary loans, the same.

Deposits in banks of discount, the same.

Examinations of books, for proof of accuracy and fidelity, and of assets, are made by committee of three trustees once a year.

EAST RIVER SAVINGS INSTITUTION.

CASH TRANSACTIONS DURING THE YEAR 1866.

RECEIPTS.

Cash on hand 1st January, 1866, before the transactions of the day		$94,810 87
Deposited in bank	$82,579 93	
Deposited in vault	12,230 94	
From depositors		1,096,468 35
From interest on mortgages		18,408 12
From interest on stocks		111,016 37
From interest on loans		2,523 65
From interest on deposits in bank		3,158 76
From premium on gold		19,114 25
From mortgages paid, called in or foreclosed		37,700 00
From redemption of stocks		1,000,000 00
From repayment of loans		225,200 00
From sales of real estate		4,650 00
From sales of stocks		121,277 50
From rents		4,266 06
From suspense, being difference in cash over		581 08
		$2,739,175 01

PAYMENTS.

To depositors		$1,000,659 75
Loans on bond and mortgage		180,300 00
Loans on stocks and other securities		350,000 00
For purchase of stocks and bonds		983,523 13
(Par value thereof	$978,500 00)	

For repairs		$711 96
For salaries		14,075 00
For printing, advertising, stationery and blank books		1,206 83
For fuel and lights		246 97
For taxes and assessments, and insurance		13,799 12
For incidental expenses per petty cash		200 13
Back interest on stocks and bonds		7,950 00
Exchange of 7-30's for 5-20's		591 74
Cash on hand 31st December, 1866, after the transactions of the day:		
Deposited in bank	$177,227 70	
Deposited in vault	8,682 68	
		$185,910 38
		$2,739,175 01

ASSETS OF THE EAST RIVER SAVINGS INSTITUTION ON THE 1ST DAY OF JANUARY, 1867.

	Par value.	Cost.
Bonds and mortgages		$382,425 00
U. S. bonds and treasury notes	$1,044,900 00	1,064,139 53
Bonds of other States	156,300 00	143,393 00
Bonds of cities in this State	169,000 00	168,890 00
Loans on stocks and other securities, available fund,		203,450 00
Real estate costs $45,089.53; market value $70,000; value on books		30,000 00
Cash in bank		177,227 70
Cash in vault		8,682 68
		$2,178,207 91

Examined by committee and verified by chairman.

OTHER FACTS.

Number of trustees authorized by charter, twenty-eight.

Number of trustees who are directors in any bank of issue where deposits of this institution are kept, none.

Investments yielding no revenue, none.

Average amount kept on deposit in bank, with interest, $94,202.

Regular meetings of the board, monthly.

Number constituting a quorum, five.

Average attendance at regular meetings during 1866, thirteen.

Loans on bond and mortgage are effected on authority of finance committee.

Purchases or sales of stocks, the same.

Temporary loans, the same.

Deposits in banks of discount, the same.

Examinations of books, for proof of accuracy and fidelity, and assets, are made by examining committee usually once a month.

EMIGRANT INDUSTRIAL SAVINGS BANK.

CASH TRANSACTIONS DURING THE YEAR 1866.

RECEIPTS.

Cash on hand 1st January, 1866, before the transactions of the day		$242,736 21
Deposited in bank	$207,733 02	
Deposited in vault	35,003 20	
From depositors		3,293,628 90
From interest on mortgages		98,255 24
From interest on stocks		217,107 42
From interest on deposits in bank		3,828 82
From premium on gold		11,631 23
From mortgages paid		129,589 91
From redemption of stock		153,800 00
From rents		8,000 00
From money found (being a sum found on floor of the bank, for which no owner has yet appeared),		249 00
		$4,158,826 74

PAYMENTS.

To depositors		$2,992,503 40
Loans on bond and mortgage		340,806 00
For purchase of stocks and bonds		440,412 00
(Par value thereof	$436,550 00)	
For salaries		12,150 02
For suits at law For printing, advertising, stationery and blank books, For fuel and lights For taxes and assessments For incidental expenses per petty cash		5,369 37
For internal revenue, United States		41,899 19

Cash on hand 31st December, 1866, after the transactions of the day:		
Deposited in bank	$272,040 54	
Deposited in vault	53,646 22	
		$325,686 76
		$4,158,826 74

ASSETS OF THE EMIGRANT INDUSTRIAL SAVINGS BANK ON THE 1ST DAY OF JUNE, 1867.

	Par value.	Cost.
Bonds and mortgages		$1,706,962 25
U. S. bonds and treasury notes	$1,423,750 00	1,418,887 81
New York State bonds	600,000 00	599,337 50
Bonds of other States	234,800 00	226,586 95
Bonds of cities in this State	1,502,600 00	1,517,188 75
Bonds of counties in this State (Westchester)	65,000 00	65,000 00
Real estate, annual rental value, we receive $8,000, the property would probably let for $20,000.		
Cash in bank		18,650 89
Cash in vault		24,361 88
		$5,576,976 03

Examined and verified by two trustees.

OTHER FACTS.

Number of trustees authorized by charter, eighteen.

Number of trustees who are directors in any bank of issue where deposits of this institution are kept, two.

Investments yielding no revenue, none.

Average amount kept on deposit in bank with interest, $165,131.

Regular meetings of the board, monthly.

Number constituting a quorum, five, including a president and vice-president; seven without.

Average attendance at regular meetings during 1866, eight.

Loans on bond and mortgage are effected on authority of finance committee.

Purchases or sales of stocks are effected on authority of board of trustees.

Temporary loans, none made.

Deposits in banks of discount are made by the comptroller in banks designated by the trustees.

Examinations of books, for proof of accuracy and fidelity, and assets, are made by comptroller daily, finance committee weekly, and by a special investigating committee twice in each year.

FRANKLIN SAVINGS BANK.

CASH TRANSACTIONS DURING THE YEAR 1866.

RECEIPTS.

Cash on hand 1st January, 1866, before the transactions of the day		$5,361 80
Deposited in bank	$2,391 80	
Deposited in vault	2,970 00	
From depositors		284,361 75
From interest on mortgages		850 56
From interest on stocks		11,530 00
From mortgages paid, called in or foreclosed		3,000 00
From redemption of stocks		40,623 89
From sales of stocks		13,903 15
		$359,631 15

PAYMENTS.

To depositors		$176,665 40
Loans on bond and mortgage		33,500 00
For purchase of stocks and bonds		134,736 63
(Par value thereof	$131,750)	
For interest on special loans		3 17
For rent		800 00
For salaries		*2,500 00
For printing, advertising, stationery and blank books,		815 40
For fuel and lights		85 05
For taxes and assessments		753 86
For incidental expenses per petty cash		375 66
Repaid trustees for moneys advanced in fitting up and establishing bank		271 68
Paid associated savings banks		100 00

* $1,000 paid secretary for services rendered previously to the year 1866.

Cash on hand 31st December, 1866, after the transactions of the day:

Deposited in bank	$6,237 40	
Deposited in vault	2,786 90	
		$9,024 30
		$359,631 15

ASSETS OF THE FRANKLIN SAVINGS BANK ON THE 1ST DAY OF JUNE, 1867.

	Par value.	Cost.
Bonds and mortgages		$37,500 00
U. S. bonds and treasury notes	$173,380 00	$176,638 34
New York State bonds	5,000 00	4,925 00
Bonds of cities in this State	34,000 00	33,830 41
Cash in bank		4,956 73
Cash in vault		2,163 92
		$260,014 40

Examined and verified by two trustees.

OTHER FACTS.

Number of trustees authorized by charter, twenty-five.

Number of trustees who are directors in any bank of issue where deposits of this institution are kept, none.

Investments yielding no revenue, none.

Average amount kept on deposit in bank, 5,357.

Regular meetings of the board, monthly.

Number constituting a quorum, seven.

Average attendance at regular meetings during 1866, eleven.

Loans on bond and mortgage are effected on authority of a unanimous vote of trustees.

Purchases or sales of stocks are effected on authority of a vote of trustees, not more than two dissenting.

Temporary loans, none made.

Deposits in banks of discount are made by authority of the board of trustees.

Examinations of books for proof of accuracy and fidelity and assets, are made by a special committee appointed for the purpose, twice in each year.

REMARKS.

Among the payments in cash transactions, note the item of $271.68, repaid trustees for moneys advanced for fitting and furnishing the institution at its organization, six years before. That is the way the first expenses incident to organization should always be paid. They should never come out of the deposits, but be advanced by trustees, and repaid from surplus earnings. I am glad to be able to say, however, that such practice is not peculiar to this institution.

GERMAN SAVINGS BANK IN NEW YORK.

CASH TRANSACTIONS DURING THE YEAR 1866.

RECEIPTS.

Cash on hand 1st January, 1866, before the transactions of the day		$287,014 43
Deposited in bank	$220,387 95	
Deposited in vault	66,626 48	
From depositors		2,814,062 59
From interest on mortgages		63,076 63
From interest on stocks		172,465 52
From interest on loans		19,420 23
From interest on deposits in bank		6,768 82
From premium on gold		6,356 54
From mortgages paid		104,533 00
From redemption of stocks		100,000 00
From repayment of loans		728,500 00
From sales of stocks		110,950 00
From rents, interest account		5,350 00
From premium on stocks sold		4,078 07
		$4,422,575 83

PAYMENTS.

To depositors		$3,247,986 77
Loans on bond and mortgage		110,033 00
Loans on stocks and other securities		232,500 00
For purchase of stocks and bonds		248,500 00
(Par value thereof	$250,000)	
For repairs		79 84
For salaries		19,920 00

For suits at law		$112 50
For printing, advertising, stationery and blank books,		1,999 44
For fuel and lights		415 97
For taxes and assessments		25,346 01
For incidental expenses per petty cash		837 98
For fire insurance		193 50
For loss to depositors		268 35
Cash on hand 31st December, 1866, after the transactions of the day:		
Deposited in bank	$477,399 57	
Deposited in vault	56,982 90	
		534,382 47
		$4,422,575 83

ASSETS OF THE GERMAN SAVINGS BANK, ON THE 28TH DAY OF MARCH, 1867.

	Par value.	Cost.
Bonds and mortgages		$972,400 00
U. S. bonds and treasury notes	$1,479,500	1,473,375 00
New York State bonds	100,000	100,000 00
Bonds of other States	183,500	183,221 88
Bonds of cities in this State	870,005	849,554 25
Loans on stocks and other securities, available fund		197,400 00
Real estate		65,000 00
Cash in bank		388,437 79
Cash in vault		18,552 44
		$4,247,941 36

Examined and verified by three trustees.

OTHER FACTS.

Number of trustees authorized by charter, twenty-five.

Number of trustees who are directors in any bank of issue where deposits of this institution are kept, none.

Investments yielding no revenue, not stated.

Average amount kept on deposit in bank with interest, estimated at $350,000.

Regular meetings of the board, monthly.

Number constituting a quorum, eight.

Average attendance at regular meetings during 1866, twenty.

Loans on bond and mortgage are effected on authority of the finance committee, confirmed by the board.

Purchases or sales of stock the same.

Temporary loans, the same.

Deposits in banks of discount, the same.

Examination of books, for proof of accuracy and fidelity, and assets, are made by auditing committee quarter yearly.

GREENWICH SAVINGS BANK.

CASH TRANSACTIONS DURING THE YEAR 1866.

RECEIPTS.

Cash on hand 1st January, 1866, before the transactions of the day		$313,311 92
Deposited in bank and Trust Co.	$288,715 65	
Deposited in vault	24,596 27	
From depositors		1,921,314 19
From interest on mortgages		123,351 23
From interest on stocks		173,519 07
From interest on loans		6,469 16
From interest on deposits in bank and Trust Co.		3,709 93
From premium on gold		17,738 83
From mortgages paid, called in or foreclosed		232,335 00
From redemption of stocks		1,220,000 00
From repayment of loans		70,000 00
From bonus in exchange of 100,000 U. S. Stocks of 1871, for 100,000 U. S. stock of 6's 5–20		5,500 00
From suspense account, check not presented,	$30 00	
From suspense account, am't not claimed	34 87	
		64 87
		$4,087,314 20

PAYMENTS.

To depositors		$1,941,534 62
Loans on bonds and mortgages		557,100 00
Loans on stocks and other securities		260,000 00
For purchase of stock and bonds		715,513 42
(Par value thereof	$718,000)	
For repairs		221 39

For premium of insurance		$8 10
For salaries		23,896 64
For printing, advertising, stationery and blank books,		610 10
For fuel and lights		324 57
For taxes and assessments, and city tax		994 50
For incidental expenses per petty cash		680 40
For United States tax		37,629 10
For bank porter robbed by policeman*		6,000 00
Cash on hand 31st December, 1866, after the transactions of the day:		
Deposited in banks and Trust Co	$463,524 62	
Deposited in vault	79,276 74	
		542,801 36
		$4,087,314 20

ASSETS OF THE GREENWICH SAVINGS BANK, ON THE 27TH DAY OF NOVEMBER, 1867.

	Par value.	Cost.
Bonds and mortgages		$1,860,183 00
U. S. bonds and treasury notes	$1,097,500	1,109,151 71
New York State bonds	394,671	423,690 30
Bonds of other States	159,000	168,107 25
Bonds of cities in this State	906,900	910,033 88
Loans on stocks and other securities, available fund,		90,000 00
Other securities		79,302 67
Cash in banks and U. S. Trust company		427,567 80
Cash in vault		17,682 89
		$5,085,719 50

Examined and verified by two trustees.

OTHER FACTS.

Number of trustees authorized by charter, thirty-three.

Number of trustees who are directors in any bank of issue where deposits of this institution are kept, three.

Investments yielding no revenue, $50,000 Missouri bonds; redemption of payment anticipated.

Average amount kept on deposit in banks and Trust Co's, with interest, $300,000

* A curious incident in police annals, as well as in the experience of savings banks!

Regular meetings of the board, monthly.

Number constituting a quorum, five, if the president be one; otherwise a majority of the board.

Average attendance at regular meetings during 1866, twelve.

Loans on bond and mortgage are effected on authority of funding committee, who report action to the board.

Purchases or sales of stock, the same.

Temporary loans, the same.

Deposits in banks of discount, the same.

Examinations of books, for proof of accuracy and fidelity, and assets, are made by a standing committee semi-annually. The depositors' accounts are examined and compared with ledgers and proved by trial balance twice in each year by a person specially employed for that purpose.

HARLEM SAVINGS BANK.

CASH TRANSACTIONS DURING THE YEAR 1866.

RECEIPTS.

Cash on hand 1st January, 1866, before the transactions of the day		$5,102 19
Deposited in bank	$4,459 26	
Deposited in vault	642 93	
From depositors		124,053 39
From interest on mortgages		140 00
From interest on stocks		4,286 33
From interest on deposits in bank		347 52
From sales of stocks		31,350 00
From rents		220 00
		$165,499 43

PAYMENTS.

To depositors	$93,063 45
Loans on bonds and mortgages	49,000 00
For purchase of stock and bonds	14,100 00
For repairs	32 00
For rent	585 00
For salaries	262 50
For printing, advertising, stationery and blank books	197 56

For fuel and lights		$74 43
For taxes and assessments		55 50
For incidental expenses per petty cash		77 98
For interest paid on assigned mortgages		356 53
Cash on hand 31st December, 1866, after the transactions of the day:		
Deposited in bank	$5,807 40	
Deposited in vault	1,887 08	
		7,694 48
		$165,499 43

ASSETS OF THE HARLEM SAVINGS BANK ON THE 3D DAY OF JUNE, 1867.

	Par value.	Cost.
Bonds and mortgages		$67,500 00
U. S. bonds and treasury notes	$11,000 00	11,000 00
New York State bonds	6,000 00	6,000 00
Other securities, compound interest notes		850 00
Cash in bank		11,814 57
Cash in vault		781 43
		$97,946 00

Examined and verified by two trustees.

OTHER FACTS.

Number of trustees authorized by charter, twenty-eight.

Number of trustees who are directors in any bank of issue where deposits of this institution are kept, two.

Investments yielding no revenue, none.

Average amount kept on deposit in bank with interest, estimated at $10,000.

Regular meetings of the board, monthly.

Number constituting a quorum, eight.

Average attendance at regular meetings during, 1866, ten.

Loans on bond and mortgage are effected on authority of the board on report of finance committee.

Purchases or sales of stocks are effected on authority of the board of trustees.

Temporary loans, the same.

Deposits in banks of discount, the same.

Examinations of books, for proof of accuracy and fidelity, and assets, are made by a committee of trustees semi-annually.

Remarks.

This institution appears to be conducted, as it should be, in the main on principles of safety and prudence, the only criticism to be made on investments relating to the large amount on bond and mortgage. It would seem, however, as though such an institution in Harlem ought to have a larger line of deposits than is here indicated. The report for 1st July, however, shows a moderate but healthy growth. It has no surplus without including safe and furniture among the assets.

INSTITUTION FOR THE SAVINGS OF MERCHANTS' CLERKS.

CASH TRANSACTIONS DURING THE YEAR 1866.

Receipts.

Cash on hand 1st January, 1866, before the transactions of the day		$87,476 66
Deposited in bank	$76,159 48	
Deposited in vault	11,317 18	
From depositors		1,023,934 18
From interest on mortgages		19,744 77
From interest on stocks and treasury notes		86,225 15
From interest on loans		70 35
From interest on deposits in bank		2,086 31
From premium on gold		13,702 83
From mortgages paid, called in or foreclosed		27,050 00
From redemption of stocks		56,118 00
From sales of real estate		2,978 55
From sales of stocks		295,862 81
From rents		3,831 37
From return premium of insurance		1 20
From profit and loss		8 51
		$1,619,090 69

Payments.

To depositors		$873,750 21
Loans on bond and mortgage		53,500 00
For purchase of stocks and bonds		595,141 50
(Par value thereof	$579,150 00)	
For repairs		654 97
For furniture and fixtures, and safe for securities		2,445 97
For salaries		10,700 16
For printing, advertising, stationery and blank books,		861 16
For fuel and lights		172 65
For taxes and assessments, including U. S. taxes		12,102 99
For interest accrued on 7-30 treasury notes		2,901 00
For insurance		84 00
For extra compensation to clerks		500 00
For express charges		100 50
For Bank Department		13 48
For profit and loss		105 00
For sundries		821 25
Cash on hand 31st December, 1866, after the transactions of the day:		
Deposited in bank	$52,084 40	
Deposited in vault	13,151 45	
		65,235 85
		$1,619,090 69

Assets of the Institution for the Savings of Merchants' Clerks on the 11th Day of June, 1867.

	Par value.	Cost.
Bonds and mortgages		$259,550 00
U. S. bonds and treasury notes	$846,600 00	828,558 00
Bonds of other States	513,540 37	451,656 01
Bonds of cities in this State (New York)	361,554 00	360,183 89
Loans on stocks and other securities, available fund,		1,000 00
Real estate, annual rental value, exclusive of bank accommodations	$4,350 00	167,903 64
Cash in banks		40,948 26
Cash in vault		8,168 18
		$2,117,967 98

Examined and verified by two trustees.

Other Facts.

Number of trustees authorized by charter, twenty-four.

Number of trustees who are directors in any bank of issue where deposits of this institution are kept, none.

Investments yielding no revenue, $25,000 Missouri bonds; resumption of payment anticipated.

Average amount kept on deposit in bank with interest, $49,100.

Regular meetings of the board, monthly.

Number constituting a quorum, five, if one be an officer of the board.

Average attendance at regular meetings during 1866, seven.*

Loans on bond and mortgage are effected on authority of the board of trustees, on report of bond and mortgage committee.

Purchases or sales of stocks are effected on judgment of finance committee, authorized by the board of trustees.

Temporary loans, the same.

Deposits in banks of discount are made by authority of the board of trustees.

Examinations of books, for proof of accuracy and fidelity, and assets, are made by the examining committee twice in each year, or oftener in their discretion.

Remarks.

The real estate includes a building recently purchased under chapter 550, Laws of 1867, and to which the institution will remove as soon as alterations are completed. This building, of course, yields no income at present.

IRVING SAVINGS INSTITUTION.

CASH TRANSACTIONS DURING THE YEAR 1866.

Receipts.

Cash on hand 1st January, 1866, before the transactions of the day		$186,976 09
Deposited in bank	$88,033 00	
Deposited in vault	98,943 09	
From depositors		824,033 55

* This bank has *ex-officio* members who rarely attend meetings.

From interest on mortgages From interest on stocks From interest on loans From interest on deposits in bank From premium on gold	$113,937 60
From mortgages paid, called in or foreclosed	52,500 00
From redemption of stock	629,310 00
From repayment of loans	23,800 00
From rents	1,003 19
	$1,832,060 43

PAYMENTS.

To depositors		$685,318 68
Loans on bond and mortgage		72,300 00
Loans on stocks and other securities		32,600 00
For purchase of stocks and bonds		743,950 00
For repairs		173 80
For salaries		9,600 00
For printing, advertising, stationery and blank books		2,124 56
For fuel and lights		116 25
For taxes and and assessments		8,609 95
For incidental expenses per petty cash, and other expenses		1,388 49
For interest paid		92,426 62
Cash on hand 31st December, 1866, after the transactions of the day:		
Deposited in bank	$55,725 78	
Deposited in vault	127,726 30	
		183,452 08
		$1,832,060 43

ASSETS OF THE IRVING SAVINGS INSTITUTION ON THE 1ST DAY OF JANUARY, 1867.

	Par value.	Cost.
Bonds and mortgages		$301,300 00
U. S. bonds and treasury notes	$918,080 00	918,080 00
Bonds of cities in this State (N. Y. city)	$250 000 00	250,000 00
Loans on stocks and other securities, available fund U. S. bonds)		13,750 00

Interest earned on investments 31st Dec. 1866	$24,048 95
Real estate, valuation $40,000, cost	24,000 00
Cash in bank	55,725 78
Cash in vault	127,726 30
	$1,714,631 03

Examined and verified by three trustees.

Other Facts.

Number of trustees authorized by charter, twenty-nine.

Number of trustees who are directors in any bank of issue where deposits of this institution are kept, three.

Investments yielding no revenue, none.

Average amount kept on deposit in bank with interest, about $50,000.

Regular meetings of the board, monthly.

Number constituting a quorum, eight.

Average attendance at regular meetings during 1866, twelve.

Loans on bond and mortgage are effected on authority of unanimous vote of the finance committee.

Purchases or sales of stocks, the same.

Temporary loans, the same.

Deposits in banks of discount, the same.

Examinations of books, for proof of accuracy and fidelity, and assets, are made annually by a committee of the board.

MANHATTAN SAVINGS INSTITUTION.

CASH TRANSACTIONS DURING THE YEAR 1866.

Receipts.

Cash on hand 1st January, 1866, before the transactions of the day		$282,206 74
Deposited in bank	$241,667 03	
Deposited in vault	40,539 71	
From depositors		3,164,720 62
From interest on mortgages, stocks, loans and deposits in bank		250,587 76
From premium on gold		21,694 59
From mortgages paid, called in or foreclosed		171,018 60
From redemption of stocks		150,000 00

From repayment of loans		$420,067 00
From sales of stocks		77,283 50
From rents		11,179 99
From other sources, enumerated below		2,600 65
Back interest on N. Y. State stock	$687 05	
Back interest on U. S. 7 3-10 notes	1,913 60	
		$4,551,359 45

PAYMENTS.

To depositors		$2,753,808 13
Loan on bond and mortgage		527,845 44
Loans on stocks and other securities		407,525 00
For purchase of stocks and bonds		301,382 50
(Par value thereof	$303,000)	
For repairs		1,404 16
For furniture and fixtures		1,231 00
For converting U. S. coupon bonds into registered		287 50
For salaries, including additional salaries to employees for 1865		32,384 50
For U. S. tax on dividends, deposits, &c.		31,597 56
For print'g, advertising, stationery and blank books,		3,574 09
For fuel and lights		427 31
For taxes and assessments		1,737 50
For incidental expenses per petty cash		751 35
For other expenses enumerated below		2,868 60
For part of the expenses of representing savings banks before Congressional committee on taxation	$850 00	
For bank interest on Brooklyn city bonds	105 00	
For bank interest on U. S. 7 3-10 notes	1,913 60	
Cash on hand 31st December, 1866, after the transactions of the day:		
Deposited in banks and Trust Co.	$450,334 84	
Deposited in vault	34,199 97	
		$484,534 81
		$4,551,359 45

Assets of the Manhattan Savings Institution, on the 1st Day of January, 1867.

	Par value.	Cost.
Bonds and mortgages		$1,189,400 44
U. S. bonds and treasury notes	$1,358,000	1,358,000 00
New York State bonds	350,000	350,000 00
Bonds of other States	60,000	50,800 00
Bonds of cities in this State	926,700	926,630 00
Loans on stock and other securities, available fund,		348,870 12
Real estate, annual rental value	$18,000	104,017 01
Cash in bank and Union Trust Co.		450,334 84
Cash in vault		34,199 97
		$4,812,252 38

Examined and verified by three trustees.

Other Facts.

Number of trustees authorized by charter, thirty-three.

Number of trustees who are directors in any bank of issue where deposits of this institution are kept, seven.

Investments yielding no revenue, Missouri, North Carolina and Louisiana bonds, $49,000.

Average amount kept on deposit in bank with interest, $270,509.

Regular meetings of the board, monthly.

Number constituting a quorum, eight.

Average attendance at regular meetings during 1866, sixteen.

Loans on bond and mortgage are effected on authority of the board of trustees.

Purchases or sales of stocks, the same.

Temporary loans, not stated.

Deposits in banks of discount are made by authority of board of trustees.

Examinations of books, for proof of accuracy and fidelity, and assets, are made by officers in charge and weekly attending committee, daily; by finance committee, at sundry times during the year; and by special examining committee once a year.

Remarks.

It will be seen that the real estate of this institution is one of its best paying investments.

MARKET SAVINGS BANK.

CASH TRANSACTIONS DURING THE YEAR 1866.

Receipts.

Cash on hand 1st January, 1866, before the transactions of the day		$27,425 37
Deposited in bank	$17,006 46	
Deposited in vault	10,418 91	
From depositors		981,432 35
From interest on mortgages		704 50
From interest on stocks		11,743 04
From interest on loans		8,560 67
From interest on deposits in bank		1,205 86
From premium on gold		3,298 02
From redemption of stocks		1,400 00
From repayment of loans		1,248,553 50
From sales of stocks		772,147 95
		$3,056,471 26

Payments.

To depositors		$703,943 51
Loans on bond and mortgage		4,500 00
Loans on stocks and other securities		1,687,901 27
For purchase of stocks and bonds		514,683 80
(Par value thereof	$487,360)	
For repairs		950 74
For furniture and fixtures		520 70
For rent		1,600 00
For salaries		3,641 33
For suits at law		160 00
For printing, advertising, stationery and blank books,		1,955 97
For fuel and lights		139 88
For taxes and assessments		1,618 34
For incidental expenses per petty cash		360 83
Cash on hand 31st December, 1866, after the transactions of the day:		
Deposited in bank	$58,913 47	
Deposited in vault	75,581 42	
		$134,494 89
		$3,056,471 26

ASSETS OF THE MARKET SAVINGS BANK ON THE 1ST DAY OF JANUARY, 1867.

	Par value.	Cost.
Bonds and mortgages		$14,600 00
U. S. bonds and treasury notes	$660 00	659 69
Loans on stocks and other securities, available fund,		446,847 77
Cash in bank		58,913 47
Cash in vault		75,581 42
		$596,602 35

Examined and verified by three trustees.

OTHER FACTS.

Number of trustees authorized by charter, thirty-seven.

Number of trustees who are directors in any bank of issue where deposits of this institution are kept, none.

Investments yielding no revenue, none.

Average amount kept on deposit in bank with interest, $94,259.

Regular meetings of the board, monthly.

Number constituting a quorum, seven.

Average attendance at regular meetings during 1866, nine.

Loans on bond and mortgage are effected on report of finance committee, approved by the board.

Purchases or sales of stocks, the same.

Temporary loans are made by the president and secretary on approval of the board.

Deposits in banks of discount are made by authority of a resolution of the board.

Examinations of books, for proof of accuracy and fidelity, and assets, are made by the finance committee semi-annually; and by a special committee once a year.

REMARKS.

This savings bank was organized in 1863, since which time it has not, at all times, been practicable to make investments in the best securities, except at a considerable premium. It is a matter of some surprise, however, that the rare opportunity to invest in the N. Y. State seven per cent bounty loan was not improved. It is but just to say, however, that loans made are on good securities, the larger amount being upon U. S. stocks.

MECHANICS' AND TRADERS' SAVINGS INSTITUTION.

CASH TRANSACTIONS DURING THE YEAR 1866.

RECEIPTS.

Cash on hand 1st January, 1866, before the transactions of the day		$189,726 65
Deposited in bank	$169,726 65	
Deposited in vault	20,000 00	
From depositors		1,272,796 82
From interest on mortgages		25,237 88
From interest on stocks		110,361 88
From interest on loans		427 39
From interest on deposits in bank		3,605 31
From premium on gold		17,504 99
From mortgages paid		13,000 00
From redemption of stocks		454,477 75
From repayment of loans		60,000 00
From stocks		141,525 00
		$2,288,663 67

PAYMENTS.

To depositors	$999,354 07
Loans on bond and mortgage	327,000 00
Loans on stocks and other securities	66,000 00
For purchase of stocks and bonds	740,407 51
(Par value thereof $710,900 00)	
For building or construction account	15,593 20
For repairs	110 69
For salaries	15,253 72
For suits at law	2,235 00
For printing, advertising, stationery and blank books	964 97
For fuel and lights	329 86
For taxes and assessments	13,665 69
For incidental expenses per petty cash	771 24
For insurance	125 00
For express	98 35

For accrued interest on stocks at time of purchase..		$2,294 27
Cash on hand 31st December, 1866, after the transactions of the day:		
Deposited in bank	$84,460 10	
Deposited in vault	20,000 00	
		104,460 10
		$2,288,663 67

ASSETS OF THE MECHANICS' AND TRADERS' SAVINGS INSTITUTION ON THE 1ST DAY OF JANUARY, 1867.

	Par value.	Cost.
Bonds and mortgages		$502,800 00
U. S. bonds and treasury notes	$1,400,000 00	1,424,921 88
Bonds of other States	230,600 00	189,023 50
Bonds of cities in this State	28,000 00	27,965 00
Bonds of counties in this State	45,900 00	44,423 13
Loans on stocks and other securities, available fund		6,000 00
Real estate		46,107 40
Cash in bank		84,460 10
Cash in vault		20,000 00
		$2,345,701 01

Examined by three trustees and verified by two.

OTHER FACTS.

Number of trustees authorized by charter, thirty.

Number of trustees who are directors in any bank of issue where deposits of this institution are kept, two.

Investments yielding no revenue, $10,000 North Carolina bonds.

Average amount kept on deposit in bank with interest, $93,722.

Regular meetings on the board, monthly.

Number constituting a quorum, ten.

Average attendance at regular meetings during 1866, twenty.

Loans on bond and mortgage are effected on authority of the finance committee.

Purchases or sales of stocks, the same.

Temporary loans, the same.

Deposits in banks of discount are made by authority of the board of trustees.

Examinations of books, for proof of accuracy and fidelity, and assets, are made by examining committee monthly.

Remarks.

The examinations of books and assets in this institution are very thorough. A committee of three trustees examine and check every deposit and draft ticket, and every entry, through all the books, count all the assets and cash, and make their report monthly to the board.

A liberal salary has been voted by the board to the members of this committee, which has given rise to an unhappy controversy in the institution. It is doubtful whether so thorough a work could be ensured without compensation. At the same time the principle of gratuitous service by trustees is a good one, if it can be enforced. Besides, are not the members of such committee still trustees, and discharging the duties of trustees while engaged in this examination, and "as such" are they not prohibited by the charter of the institution from "receiving any pay for their services?" The questions involved are by no means free from difficulties.

METROPOLITAN SAVINGS BANK.

CASH TRANSACTIONS DURING THE YEAR 1866.

Receipts.

Cash on hand 1st January, 1866, before the transactions of the day		$149,136 21
Deposited in bank	$120,212 48	
Deposited in vault	28,923 73	
From depositors		1,373,825 43
From interest on mortgages		25,869 17
From interest on stocks		72,932 05
From interest on loans		16,618 54
From interest on deposits in bank		6,196 08
From premium on gold		12,173 55
From mortgages paid, called in or foreclosed		21,500 00
From repayment of loans		851,152 97
From sales of stocks		981,987 52
From rents		133 33
		$3,511,524 85

Payments.

To depositors		$877,674 87
Loans on bond and mortgage		360,600 00
Loans on stocks and other securities		1,024,820 57
For purchase of stocks and bonds		990,137 80
(Par value thereof	$975,050 00)	
For building or construction account		90,800 00
For repairs and furniture and fixtures		658 69
For rent		525 00
For salaries		11,380 23
For printing, advertising, stationery and blank books,		2,754 94
For fuel and lights		152 84
For taxes and assessments		10,725 87
For incidental expenses per petty cash		484 44
Cash on hand 31st December, 1866, after the transactions of the day:		
Deposited in bank	$107,978 30	
Deposited in vault	32,831 30	
		140,809 60
		$3,511,524 85

Assets of the Metropolitan Savings Bank on the First Day of January, 1867.

	Par value.	Cost.
Bonds and mortgages		$582,000 00
U. S. bonds and treasury notes	$600,000 00	640,895 42
New York State bonds	125,000 00	125,000 00
Bonds of other States	80,000 00	75,396 92
Bonds of cities in this State	80,300 00	78,640 00
Loans on stocks and other securities, available fund,		364,076 00
Real estate		134,100 00
Cash in bank		107,978 30
Cash in vault		32,831 30
		$2,140,917 94

Examined by committee and verified by chairman.

Other Facts.

Number of trustees authorized by charter, twenty-three.

Number of trustees who are directors in any bank of issue where deposits of this institution are kept, none.

Investments yielding no revenue, none.

Average amount kept on deposit in bank with interest, $150,000.

Regular meetings of the board, monthly.

Number constituting a quorum, eight.

Average attendance at regular meetings during 1866, fourteen.

Loans on bond and mortgage are effected on authority of the finance committee.

Purchases or sales of stocks, the same.

Temporary loans, the same.

Deposits in banks of discount are made by authority of the board of trustees.

Examinations of books, for proof of accuracy and fidelity, and assets, are made by a committee of trustees monthly.

Remarks.

The loans of this institution are chiefly on U. S. stocks, and all, except one sum of $8,900 on Jersey City bonds, are on securities, in which they are authorized by law to invest. The July report shows a large increase of assets in U. S. stocks.

NEW YORK SAVINGS BANK.

CASH TRANSACTIONS DURING THE YEAR 1866.

Receipts.

Cash on hand 1st January, 1866, before the transactions of the day		$21,439 25
Deposted in bank	$17,798 15	
Deposited in vault	3,641 10	
From depositors		476,662 18
From interest on mortgages		3,215 05
From interest on stocks		24,650 78
From interest on loans		4,572 25
From interest on deposits in bank		435 75
From premium on gold		2,764 39
From mortgages paid, called in or foreclosed		2,900 00
From redemption of stocks		6,901 34
From repayment of loans		133,600 00
From furniture and fixtures		89 00
From return of taxes		71 89
		$677,301 88

Payments.

To depositors		$295,074 75
Loans on bond and mortgage		103,000 00
Loans on stocks and other securities		200,000 00
For purchase of stocks and bonds		42,942 74
(Par value thereof	$45,000 00)	
For furniture and fixtures		2,414 88
For rent		906 25
For salaries		3,206 95
For printing, advertising, stationery and blank books		875 85
For fuel and lights		79 79
For taxes and assessments		1,682 69
For incidental expenses per petty cash		177 49
For profit and loss of previous years		2,592 86
For interest on stock investments		218 75
Cash on hand 31st December, 1866, after the transactions of the day:		
Deposited in bank	$16,590 02	
Deposited in vault	7,538 86	
		24,128 88
		$677,301 88

Assets of the New York Savings Bank on the 28th Day of May, 1867.

	Par value.	Cost.
Bonds and mortgages		$233,000 00
U. S. bonds and treasury notes	$293,000 00	291,500 00
New York State bonds	10,000 00	10,000 00
Bonds of other States	15,000 00	14,500 00
Bonds of cities in this State	100,000 00	100,000 00
Loans on stock and other securities, available fund,		27,100 000
Cash in bank		74,222 77
Cash in vault		3,067 22
		$753,380 99

Examined and verified by three trustees.

Other Facts.

Number of trustees authorized by charter, seventeen.

Number of trustees who are directors in any bank of issue where deposits of this institution are kept, none.

Investments yielding no revenue, none.

Average amount kept on deposit in bank with interest, $10,700.

Regular meetings of the board, monthly.

Number constituting a quorum, eight.

Average attendance at regular meetings during 1866, seven.

Loans on bond and mortgage are effected on authority of the board of trustees.

Purchases or sales of stocks are effected by the finance committee with the approval of the board.

Temporary loans, the same.

Deposits in banks of discount, the same.

Examinations of books, for proof of accuracy and fidelity, and assets, are made by the finance committee monthly; and in detail by the president and secretary twice in each year.

Remarks.

The loans of this institution are not very considerable in amount, and its investments are good. But the loans are made under that convenient provision of an available fund, at the discretion of the trustees, and are mostly upon securities that are never authorized for savings bank investments. They are good marketable bank stocks, city railroad stocks, insurance stocks, gas company stocks, and the like, and are taken at a good margin. They could hardly lose on *all* of them; and even if they should, the amount of such loans is less than their surplus.

NORTH RIVER SAVINGS BANK.

(Commenced business December 16th, 1866.)

CASH TRANSACTIONS DURING THE YEAR 1866.

Receipts.

From depositors		$12,022 60
		$12,022 60

Payments.

To depositors		$395 00
Cash on hand 31st December, 1866, after the transactions of the day:		
Deposited in bank	$7,507 00	
Deposited in vault	4,120 60	
		11,627 60
		$12,022 60

Remarks.

Of course, commencing so late in the year, it could have little to report January, 1867, but that little is very good.

SEAMENS' BANK FOR SAVINGS.

CASH TRANSACTIONS DURING THE YEAR 1866.

Receipts.

Cash on hand 1st January, 1866, before the transactions of the day		$371,112 74
Deposited in bank	$371,112 74	
From depositors		2,616,440 39
From interest on mortgages		171,780 29
From interest on stocks		395,039 12
From interest on deposits in bank		13,121 80
From premium on gold*		330,740 70
From mortgages paid, called in or foreclosed		279,650 00
From redemption of stocks		1,169,197 13
From sales of real estate		145 00
From sales of stocks		1,160,679 41
From rents		6,662 50
Amount refunded by bounty commissioners		1,065 50
		$6,515,634 58

Payments.

To depositors		$3,111,583 86
Loans on bond and mortgage		613,000 00
For purchase of stocks and bonds		2,290,713 15
(Par value thereof	$2,221,000)	
For building or construction account		1,198 33
For repairs		544 01
For salaries		29,951 42
For suits at law†		2,181 09
For printing, advertising, stationery and blank books,		1,324 36
For fuel and lights		503 40
For taxes and assessments, U. S., State and city, including $26,372.30, for 1865		72,689 40
For incidental expenses per petty cash		737 07

* A large portion of this amount received for redemption of United States stocks.

† Includes fee of counsel at Washington to reduce United States tax.

For counterfeit bills	$140 00
Cash on hand 31st December, 1866, after the transactions of the day	391,068 49
	$6,515,634 58

Assets of the Seamen's Bank for Savings, in the City of New York, on the 2d day of January, 1867.

	Par value.	Cost.
Bonds and mortgages		$2,499,300 00
U. S. bonds and treasury notes	$3,243,000 00	2,749,860 93
New York State bonds	539,046 00	538,306 00
Bonds of other States	1,838,910 11	1,834,762 97
Bonds of cities in this State	1,160,150 00	1,160,150 00
Real estate, annual rental value	6,662 50	98,434 42
Cash in bank		391,068 49
		$9,271,882 81

Examined and verified by four trustees.

Other Facts.

Number of trustees authorized by charter, twenty-seven.

Number of trustees who are directors in any bank of issue where deposits of this institution are kept, none.

Investments yielding no revenue, none.

Average amount kept on deposit in bank with interest, $429,500.

Regular meetings of the board, monthly.

Number constituting a quorum, five.

Average attendance at regular meetings during 1866, ten.

Loans on bond and mortgage are effected by the funding committee empowered by the board.

Purchases or sales of stocks, the same.

Temporary loans: "This bank does not make them, and thinks no savings institution should."

Deposits in banks of discount are made by authority of the board.

Examinations of books, for proof of accuracy and fidelity, and assets, are made by auditing committee twice in each year.

Remarks.

This is another of the old pioneers, and is worthy of its title. Its view concerning temporary loans, as above expressed, is characteristic. The theory of the institution is, that it should *own*, and not merely have a *contingent interest* in its securities. A strong institution that can afford to keep its reserve in its vault or in bank, may do this; but younger and weaker institutions that have to keep a larger ratio of their assets available, can not always invest readily, nor can they afford to keep their available fund at low interest in bank. Hence the occasional expediency of call loans.

SIXPENNY SAVINGS BANK.

CASH TRANSACTIONS DURING THE YEAR 1866.

Receipts.

Cash on hand 1st January, 1866, before the transactions of the day		$19,735 41
Deposited in bank	$13,123 57	
Deposited in vault	6,611 84	
From depositors		439,496 01
From interest on mortgages		12,199 87
From interest on stocks		8,540 04
From interest on deposits in bank		949 40
From premium on gold		6,478 62
From mortgages paid, called in or foreclosed		19,000 00
From sales of stocks		18,750 00
		$525,149 35

Payments.

To depositors		$314,671 86
Loans on bond and mortgage		28,540 00
Loans on stocks and other securities		600 00
For purchase of stocks and bonds		123,531 41
(Par value thereof	$121,350)	
For repairs		544 88
For furniture and fixtures		315 86
For rent		1,250 00
For salaries		2,734 29

For print'g, advertising, station'y and blank books		
For fuel and lights		
For taxes and assessments		$5,866 37
For incidental expenses per petty cash		
For other expenses		
Cash on hand 31st December, 1866, after the transactions of the day:		
Deposited in bank	$34,551 22	
Deposited in vault	12,543 46	
		47,094 68
		$525,149 35

ASSETS OF THE SIXPENNY SAVINGS BANK ON THE 31ST DAY OF JULY, 1867.

	Cost.	Par value.
Bonds and mortgages		$203,780 50
U. S. bonds and treasury notes	$249,457 91	243,700 00
New York State bonds	7,280 00	7,000 00
Bonds of other States	28,766 00	39,000 00
Bonds of cities in this State	46,410 00	49,000 00
Loans on stocks and other securities, available fund		30,750 00
Cash in bank		71,334 84
Cash in vault		6,822 87
		$651,388 21

Examined and verified by two trustees.

OTHER FACTS.

Number of trustees authorized by charter, thirty-nine.

Number of trustees who are directors in any bank of issue where deposits of this institution are kept, four.

Investments yielding no revenue, none.

Average amount kept on deposit in bank with interest, $13,406.

Regular meetings of the board, monthly.

Number constituting a quorum, seven.

Average attendance at regular meetings during 1866, not stated.

Loans on bond and mortgage are effected on authority of the board of trustees, after approval by the finance committee, the president and counsel for the bank.

Purchases or sales of stock, the same.

Temporary loans, the same.

Deposits in banks of discount, the same.

Examinations of books for proof of accuracy and fidelity and assets, are made by a committee of trustees, at least twice in each year, and are subject to continual inspection by the finance committee.

THIRD AVENUE SAVINGS BANK.

CASH TRANSACTIONS DURING THE YEAR 1866.

Receipts.

Cash on hand 1st January, 1866, before the transactions of the day		$175,787 83
Deposited in bank	$61,027 03	
Deposited in vault	114,760 80	
From depositors		3,409,346 30
From interest on mortgages		19,596 00
From interest on stocks		125,192 20
From interest on loans		34,576 01
From interest on deposits in bank		5,809 63
From premium on gold		3,509 53
From mortgages paid, called in or foreclosed		35,538 08
From redemption of stocks		308,000 00
From repayment of loans		1,432,747 49
From sales of stocks		786,500 00
From rents		1,449 96
		$6,338,053 03

Payments.

To depositors		$2,015,355 11
Loans on bonds and mortgage		352,350 00
Loans on stocks and other securities		2,532,363 12
For purchase of stocks and bonds		1,120,347 97
(Par value thereof	$1,170,000)	
For repairs		829 40
For furniture and fixtures		140 00
For rent		250 00
For salaries		16,744 06
For printing, advertising, stationery and blank books,		4,860 25
For fuel and lights		358 59
For N. Y. taxes and assessments, and internal revenue tax		7,908 07

For incidental expenses per petty cash		$1,547 08
For other expenses		2,850 00
For insurance		70 00
Cash on hand 31st December, 1866, after the transactions of the day:		
Deposited in bank	$172,621 78	
Deposited in vault	109,457 60	
		282,079 38
		$6,338,053 03

ASSETS OF THE THIRD AVENUE SAVINGS BANK, ON THE 1ST DAY OF JULY, 1867.

	Par value.	Cost.
Bonds and mortgages		$840,550 00
U. S. bonds and treasury notes	$838,500	855,312 50
New York State bonds	363,000	329,750 00
Bonds of other States	263,000	240,685 00
Bonds of cities and counties in the State of New Jersey	141,500	127,887 50
Bonds of counties in this State	100,000	100,000 00
Loans on stocks and other securities, available fund,		1,497,300 00
Other securities	$178,000	159,000 00
Real estate, annual rental value	6,000	60,000 00
Cash in bank		278,726 40
Cash in vault		133,007 68
		$4,622,219 08

Examined and verified by three trustees.

OTHER FACTS.

Number of trustees authorised by charter, twenty-two.

Number of trustees who are directors in any bank of issue where deposits of this institution are kept, two.

Investments yielding no revenue, none.

Average amount kept on deposit in bank with interest, $172,126.

Regular meetings of the board, monthly.

Number constituting a quorum, eight.

Average attendance at regular meetings during 1866, fourteen.

Loans on bond and mortgage are effected on authority of the board of trustees.

Purchases or sales of stock, the same.

Temporary loans, the same.

Deposits in banks of discount, the same.

Examinations of books, for proof of accuracy and fidelity, and assets, are made by attending committee at least once a month, also by a special committee when directed by the board.

Remarks.

The theory of this very flourishing institution is, that in order to be ready for the *grand crisis* that is sure to come sometime, when depositors will besiege their doors in droves, they must have a large proportion of their funds *available*, and there is no available form for so large a sum but call loans. The above loans are made on all kinds of stock securities, principally railroad, bank, and Atlantic and Pacific Mail, but at a good—I was about to say *safe*—margin, if anything that *can* fail may be called "*good*" *for savings banks.*

Under the clause authorizing loans on bond and mortgage—they have a small amount in securities, such as city railroad bonds, that no savings bank is, or should be, *authorized* to invest in.

UNION DIME SAVINGS BANK.

CASH TRANSACTIONS DURING THE YEAR 1866.

Receipts.

Cash on hand 1st January, 1866, before the transactions of the day		$201,274 03
Deposited in bank	$172,928 73	
Deposited in vault	28,345 30	
From depositors		2,246,149 29
From interest on mortgages		37,030 16
From interest on stocks / From interest on loans		75,538 52
From interest on deposits in banks		8,799 19
From premium on gold		10,891 82
From mortgages paid		46,899 99
From redemption of stocks		192,874 78
From repayment of loans		193,370 00
From sales of stocks		190,000 00

From rents		$2,125 00
From premium on sale of stocks, etc.		3,904 18
		$3,208,856 96

PAYMENTS.

To depositors		$1,308,257 86
Loans on bond and mortgage		540,100 00
Loans on stocks and other securities		216,500 00
For purchase of stocks and bonds		699,778 99
(Par value thereof	$696,000)	
For building or construction account		52,438 88
For repairs		451 81
For rent		1,750 00
For salaries		15,000 00
For suits at law, examination of title and counsel fees,		353 80
For printing, advertising, stationery and blank books,		3,322 21
For fuel and lights		214 47
For taxes and assessments		7,922 21
For incidental expenses per petty cash		360 00
For sundry expenses		693 50
Cash on hand 31st December, 1866, after the transactions of the day:		
Deposited in bank	$327,811 22	
Deposited in vault	33,902 01	
		361,713 23
		$3,208,856 96

ASSETS OF THE UNION DIME SAVINGS BANK ON THE 1ST DAY OF JANUARY, 1867.

Bonds and mortgages	$884,624 68
	Cost.
U. S. bonds and treasury notes	1,000,000 00
New York State bonds	240,000 00
Bonds of counties in this State (Richmond)	20,000 00
Loans on stocks and other securities, available fund,	45,685 00
Furniture and safes	2,000 00
Real estate	88,238 88

Cash in bank	$327,811 22
Cash in vault	33,902 01
	$2,642,261 79

Examined and verified by two trustees.

Other Facts.

Number of trustees authorized by charter, thirty-four.

Number of trustees who are directors in any bank of issue where deposits of this institution are kept, five.

Investments yielding no revenue, none.

Average amount kept on deposit in bank with interest, $223,650.

Regular meetings of the board, monthly.

Number constituting a quorum, nine.

Average attendance at regular meetings during 1866, fifteen.

Loans on bond and mortgage are effected on authority of finance committee approved by the board.

Purchases or sales of stock, the same.

Temporary loans are made by officers of the bank approved by the finance committee.

Deposits in banks of discount are made by the officers of the institution.

Examinations of books, for proof of accuracy and fidelity, and assets, are made by the officers of the bank monthly, and by a committee of three trustees annually.

UP TOWN SAVINGS BANK.

(Commenced business 2d July, 1866.)

CASH TRASACTIONS DURING THE YEAR 1866.

Receipts.

From depositors	$229,368 54
From interest on mortgages From interest on stocks From interest on loans	1,765 51
From premium on gold	358 12
From repayment of loans	2,500 00
From rents	572 00
	$234,564 17

Payments.

To depositors		$116,020 35
Loans on bond and mortgage		18,900 00
Loans on stocks and other securities		7,650 00
For purchase of stocks and bonds		45,531 25
(Par value thereof	$45,000)	
For furniture aud fixtures		4,919 18
For rent		700 00
For salaries		1,124 50
For printing, advertising, stationery and blank books		597 36
For fuel and lights		71 00
For incidental expenses per petty cash		160 65
Cash on hand 31st December, 1866, after the transactions of the day:		
Deposited in bank	$21,283 13	
Deposited in vault	17,606 75	
		38,889 88
		$234,564 17

Assets of the Up Town Savings Bank on the 1st Day of January, 1867.

	Par value.	Cost.
Bonds and mortgages		$18,900 00
U. S. bonds and treasury notes	$25,000 00	26,331 25
Bonds of cities in this State	20,000 00	19,200 00
Add difference of rate		800 00
Loans on stocks and other securities, available fund		5,150 00
Office furniture, safe, &c		4,907 93
Interest accrued on investments		539 04
Cash in bank		21,283 13
Cash in vault		17,606 75
		$114,718 10

Examined and verified by four trustees.

Other Facts.

Number of trustees authorized by charter, twenty-two.

Number of trustees who are directors in any bank of issue where deposits of this institution are kept, one.

Investments yielding no revenue, none.

Average amount kept on deposit in bank with interest, $15,000.

Regular meetings of the board, monthly.

Number constituting a quorum twelve.

Average attendance at regular meetings during 1866, nine. (Quorum too large.)

Loans on bond and mortgage are effected on authority of the funding committee.

Purchases or sales of stocks, the same.

Temporary loans the same.

Deposits in banks of discount, the same.

Examinations of books for proof of accuracy and fidelity and assets, are made by auditing committee every three months.

MONROE COUNTY SAVINGS BANK.

CASH TRANSACTIONS DURING THE YEAR 1866.

RECEIPTS.

Cash on hand 1st January, 1866, before the transactions of the day		$172,412 22
Deposited in bank	$92,196 25	
Deposited in vault	80,215 97	
From depositors		2,378,104 37
From interest on mortgages		26,270 91
From interest on stocks		63,394 24
From interest on loans		7,402 64
From interest on deposits in bank		3,963 99
From premium on gold		11,190 85
From mortgages paid, called in or foreclosed		55,195 00
From redemption of stocks		2,800 00
From repayment of loans		78,522 50
From sales of stocks		235,000 00
From rents		300 00
Furniture account charged to profit and loss in '66		2,519 34
		$3,037,076 06

PAYMENTS.

To depositors	$1,980,284 09
Loans on bond and mortgage	260,162 00
Loans on stocks and other securities	135,410 00

For purchase of stock and bonds		$335,400 00
(Par value thereof $355,400)		
For repairs		503 63
For rent		450 00
For salaries		7,400 00
For suits at law		391 79
For printing, advertising, stationery and blank books		652 35
For fuel and lights		286 20
For taxes and assessments		6,536 72
For incidental expenses, per petty cash		761 26
For exchanges, &c.		284 28
For interest paid to depositors in 1866		85,159 27
Cash on hand 31st December, 1866, after the transactions of the day:		
Deposited in bank	$104,661 39	
Deposited in vault	98,733 08	
		203,394 47
		$3,037,076 06

ASSETS OF THE MONROE COUNTY SAVINGS BANK ON THE 8TH DAY OF JULY, 1867.

	Par value.	Cost.
Bonds and mortgages		$639,418 00
U. S. bonds and treasury notes	$685,000 00	685,000 00
New York State bonds	100,000 00	100,000 00
Bonds of cities in this State	152,500 00	152,500 00
Bonds of Monroe county	145,800 00	145,800 00
Loans on stocks and other securities, available fund		137,665 74
Real estate		29,065 61
Cash in bank		70,320 00
Cash in vault		64,919 40
		$2,024,688 75

Examined and verified by three trustees.

OTHER FACTS.

Number of trustees authorized by charter, twenty-one.

Number of trustees who are directors in any bank of issue where deposits of this institution are kept, three.

Investments yielding no revenue, none.

Average amount kept on deposit in bank with interest, $100,000.

Regular meetings of the board, monthly.

Number constituting a quorum, eight.

Average attendance at regular meetings during 1866, fifteen.

Loans on bond and mortgage are effected on authority of unanimous vote of trustees at a regular meeting.

Purchases or sales of stocks, are effected on authority of a majority vote of the trustees.

Temporary loans, the same.

Deposits in banks of discount, the same.

Examinations of books, for proof of accuracy and fidelity, and assets, are made by a committee of trustees, semi-annually.

ROCHESTER SAVINGS BANK.

CASH TRANSACTIONS DURING THE YEAR 1866.

Receipts.

Cash on hand 1st January, 1866, before the transactions of the day		$164,122 19
Deposited in bank	$61,470 49	
Deposited in vault	102,651 70	
From depositors		1,640,593 37
From interest on mortgages and loans		89,142 29
From interest on stocks		44,394 47
From interest on deposits in bank		2,249 60
From premium on gold		7,473 87
From mortgages paid, called in or foreclosed		115,112 52
From repayment of loans		29,570 00
From sales of real estate		1,020 00
From sales of stocks		130,650 00
From premium on stocks sold		5,190 20
From premium on exchange		87 37
		$2,229,605 88

Payments.

To depositors	$1,568,983 25
Loans on bond and mortgage	330,125 00
Loans on stocks	12,100 00

For purchase of stocks and bonds		$5,500 00
(Par value thereof	$5,500 00)	
For repairs		821 75
For furniture and fixtures, including new vault locks,		1,519 57
For salaries		9,740 91
For suits at law		121 28
For printing, advertising, stationery and blank books,		417 52
For fuel and lights		348 70
For taxes and assessments, incl. internal revenue		7,947 84
For incidental expenses per petty cash		172 52
For interest on deposits		90,807 43
For real estate purchased under foreclosure		1,674 63
For postage and rev. stamps, express and insurance,		465 27
Cash on hand 31st December, 1866, after the transactions of the day:		
Deposited in bank	$108,456 22	
Deposited in vault	90,403 99	
		198,860 21
		$2,229,605 88

ASSETS OF THE ROCHESTER SAVINGS BANK ON THE 1ST DAY OF JANUARY, 1867.

	Par value.	Cost.
Bonds and mortgages		$1,327,958 00
U. S. bonds and treasury notes	$343,000 00	343,000 00
Bonds of other States	379,000 00	336,400 00
Bonds of Rochester city, in this State,	54,000 00	53,760 00
Bonds of Monroe county, in this State,	70,000 00	70,000 00
Loan on stocks, available fund		46,800 00
Other securities, accrued interest on loans payable January, 1867		37,900 80
Real estate		39,680 00
Cash in bank		108,456 22
Cash in vault		90,403 99
		$2,454,359 01

Examined and verified by two committees—one for assets other than loans; the other for loans and the securities therefor.

Other Facts.

Number of trustees authorized by charter, fifteen.

Number of trustees who are directors in any bank of issue where deposits of this institution are kept, none.

Investments yielding no revenue, $147,000, Missouri State bonds.

Average amount kept on deposit in bank with interest, $58,000.

Regular meetings of the board, monthly.

Number constituting a quorum, seven.

Average attendance at regular meetings during 1866, eight.

Loans on bond and mortgage are effected on authority of loaning committee, subject to approval of board.

Purchases or sales of stocks, the same.

Temporary loans, the same.

Deposits in banks of discount, the same.

Examinations of books, for proof of accuracy and fidelity, and assets, are made by a committee of trustees annually.

ONONDAGA COUNTY SAVINGS BANK.

CASH TRANSACTIONS DURING THE YEAR 1866.

Receipts.

Cash on hand 1st January, 1866, before the transactions of the day		$177,153 08
Deposited in bank	$151,816 29	
Deposited in vault	25,336 79	
From depositors		3,084,870 27
From interest on mortgages and stock loans		44,205 82
From interest on stocks		44,293 18
From error interest account, January 1, 1866		3,667 90
From interest deposits in bank		7,090 00
From premium on gold		6,159 88
From premium on government stocks		1,664 31
From mortgages paid, called in or foreclosed		130,223 11
From repayment of loans		154,700 00
From sales of stocks		34,650 00
From rents		2,379 20
From overdrafts, January 1, 1866, since paid		4,917 46
From unpaid interest, January 1, 1866		35,165 91
From insurance		98 95
		$3,731,239 07

PAYMENTS.

To depositors		$2,837,973 04
Loans on bond and mortgage		218,294 27
Loans on stocks and other securities		78,496 50
For purchase of stocks and bonds		321,353 43
(Par value thereof	$316,710)	
For repairs		269 64
For furniture and fixtures		1,462 80
For rent		1,625 03
For salaries		7,851 06
For printing, advertising, stationery and blank books		1,064 03
For fuel and lights		204 09
For taxes and assessments (government)		7,553 93
For taxes, State, county and city		450 07
For incidental expenses per petty cash		487 80
For insurance, stamps, expressage, &c		1,497 99
For unpaid interest, January 1, 1867		35,118 00
For interest paid depositors		66,924 49
Cash on hand 31st December, 1866, after the transactions of the day:		
Deposited in bank	$113,859 62	
Deposited in vault	36,753 28	
		150,612 90
		$3,731,239 07

ASSETS OF THE ONONDAGA COUNTY SAVINGS BANK ON THE 1ST DAY OF JANUARY, 1867.

	Par value.	Cost.
Bonds and mortgages		$562,540 47
U. S. bonds, treasury notes and compounds,	$376,010	376,010 00
Bonds of cities in this State	5,000	5,000 00
Loans on stocks and other securities, available fund,		184,818 50
Other securities		330,400 00
Real estate		25,500 00
Cash in bank		113,859 62
Cash in vault		36,753 28
		$1,634,881 87

Examined and verified by two trustees.

Other Facts.

Number of trustees authorized by charter, seventeen.

Number of trustees who are directors in any bank of issue where deposits of this institution are kept, none.

Investments yielding no revenue, banking house in process of construction.

Average amount kept on deposit in bank with interest, $118,584.

Regular meetings of the board, monthly.

Number constituting a quorum, a majority of trustees, if not less than seven.

Average attendance at regular meetings during 1866, eleven.

Loans on bond and mortgage are effected on authority of the affirmative vote of at least seven trustees, a quorum being present.

Purchases or sales of stocks, the same.

Temporary loans, the same.

Deposits in banks of discount, the same.

Examinations of books, for proof of accuracy and fidelity, and assets, are made by special committee of the board, once a year, but at no regular time.

Remarks.

The "other securities" mentioned above are all bonds of counties in this State, and should have been so stated. Otherwise they might be supposed to be *anything* which the lax provisions of the law sometimes permit to work into the assets of savings banks. The loans of this institution are chiefly on local salt and other stocks, having a value at home, but little known abroad. They are taken at a wide margin from their par or home market value.

SYRACUSE SAVINGS INSTITUTION.

CASH TRANSACTIONS DURING THE YEAR 1866.

Receipts.

Cash on hand 1st January, 1866, before the transactions of the day		$90,661 22
Deposited in bank	$71,290 29	
Deposited in vault	19,370 93	
From depositors		1,389,325 90
From interest on mortgages		15,117 09
From interest on stocks		33,626 68

From interest on loans	$9,574 89
From interest on deposits in bank	3,574 39
From premium on gold	3,180 25
From mortgages paid	19,398 00
From repayment of loans	47,024 75
From sales of stocks	35,200 00
From rents	2,851 28
From certificates surrendered	10,439 58
From sold old vault	400 00
From charges for drawing mortgages	253 99
From premium on drafts, &c	87 44
	$1,660,715 46

PAYMENTS.

To depositors		$1,399,828 53
Loans on bond and mortgage		26,303 00
Loans on stocks and other securities		91,625 16
For purchase of stocks and bonds		55,485 00
For repairs		360 58
For law suits		75 00
For interest on mortgage on banking house		232 50
For salaries		4,699 92
For insurance		96 00
For printing, advertising, stationery and blank books		416 12
For fuel and lights		129 77
For taxes and assessments		5,767 74
Paid H. Gifford for services and buying banking house		2,000 00
Accrued interest paid on 7-30 bonds		1,756 19
Premium and commission on $50,000, 7-30's		2,875 00
Cash on hand 31st December, 1866, after the transactions of the day:		
Deposited in bank	$60,140 96	
Deposited in vault	8,923 99	
		69,064 95
		$1,660,715 46

ASSETS OF THE SYRACUSE SAVINGS INSTITUTION, ON THE 1ST DAY OF JANUARY, 1867.

	Par value.	Cost.
Bonds and mortgages		$203,430 31
U. S. bonds and treasury notes	$248,900	248,320 63

Bonds of the Syracuse Water Company	$4,000 00
Bonds of cities in this State	5,000 00
Bonds of counties in this State (Onondaga)	246,500 00
Loans on stocks and other securities, available fund	173,460 41
Real estate (the bank building)	15,500 00
Cash in bank	60,140 96
Cash in vault	8,923 99
	$965,276 30

Verified by the president and treasurer from an examination made in the month of April, 1866.

Other Facts.

Number of trustees authorized by charter, eighteen.

Number of trustees who are directors in any bank of issue where deposits of this institution are kept, seven.

Investments yielding no revenue, none.

Average amount kept on deposit in bank with interest, $50,000.

Regular meetings of the board, twice in each month.

Number constituting a quorum, eight.

Average attendance at regular meetings during 1866, nine.

Loans on bond and mortgage are effected on authority of a vote of the trustees, not more than two dissenting.

Purchases or sales of stocks are effected on authority of affirmative vote of at least seven trustees.

Temporary loans, the same.

Deposits in banks of discount are made by authority of a majority of trustees.

Examinations of books, for proof of accuracy and fidelity, and assets, are made by the president and secretary at their convenience.

Remarks.

The loans of this institution are upon the same general class of securities as those of the Onondaga County Savings Bank.

An examination of securities could not be made for the above statement, by reason of their being in a bank safe, the combination to which was lost at the time the statement was prepared.

CENTRAL SAVINGS BANK OF TROY.

CASH TRANSACTIONS DURING THE YEAR 1866.

Receipts.

Cash on hand 1st January, 1866, before the transactions of the day		$55,696 91
Deposited in bank	$55,696 91	
From depositors		32,062 93
From interest on deposits in banks		2,175 33
		$89,935 17

Payments.

To depositors		$33,631 52
Cash on hand 31st December, 1866, after the transactions of the day:		
Deposited in bank	$56,303 65	
		56,303 65
		$89,935 17

Assets of the Central Savings Bank of Troy, on the 18th Day of October, 1867.

Cash in bank	$64,316 87
	$64,316 87

Examined and verified by two trustees.

Other Facts.

Number of trustees authorized by charter, fifteen.

Number of trustees who are directors in any bank of issue where deposits of this institution are kept, nine.

Investments yielding no revenue, none.

Average amount kept on deposit in bank with interest, the whole amount of deposits.

Regular meetings of the board, quarter yearly.

Number constituting a quorum, a majority of trustees.

Average attendance at regular meetings during 1866, seven.

Loans on bond and mortgage, none made.

Purchases or sales of stocks, none.

Temporary loans, none.

Deposits in banks of discount are made by authority of the board, a majority of whom are directors in the bank where the deposits are kept.

Examinations of books, for proof of accuracy and fidelity, and assets, are made by special committees of the board quarterly.

MANUFACTURERS' SAVINGS BANK OF TROY.

CASH TRANSACTIONS DURING THE YEAR 1866.

Receipts.

Cash on hand 1st January, 1866, before the transactions of the day		$67,094 40
Deposited in bank	$67,094 40	
From interest on loans		839 72
From interest on deposits in bank		531 21
		$68,465 33

Payments.

To depositors		$45,740 90
Cash on hand 31st December, 1866, after the transactions of the day:		
Deposited in bank	$22,724 43	
		22,724 43
		$68,465 33

Assets of the Manufacturers' Savings Bank of Troy, on the 17th day of September, 1867.

Cash in bank	14,390 92
	$14,390 92

Examined and verified by the secretary and treasurer.

Other Facts.

Number of trustees authorized by charter, thirteen. Four vacancies.

Number of trustees who are directors in any bank of issue where deposits of this institution are kept, all of them.

Investments yielding no revenue, none.

Average amount kept on deposit in bank, with interest, the whole amount of depcsits.

Regular meetings of the board, quarter yearly.

Number constituting a quorum, not stated.

Average attendance at regular meetings during 1866, not stated.

Loans on bond and mortgage, none made.

Purchases or sales of stocks, none.

Temporary loans, none.

Deposits in banks of discount are made by the board, all of whom are directors in the bank where deposits are kept.

Examinations of books, for proof of accuracy and fidelity, and assets, are made by accountant and treasurer at their discretion.

MUTUAL SAVINGS BANK OF TROY.

CASH TRANSACTIONS DURING THE YEAR 1866.

Receipts.

Cash on hand 1st January, 1866, before the transactions of the day		$97,142 11
Deposited in bank	$97,142 11	
From depositors		83,573 78
From interest on stocks From interest on loans From interest on deposits in bank		4,724 07
		$185,439 96

Payments.

To depositors		$65,329 71
For purchase of stocks and bonds		64,000 00
(Par value thereof	$64,000)	
Cash on hand 31st December, 1866, after the transactions of the day:		
Deposited in bank	$56,110 25	
		56,110 25
		$185,439 96

Assets of the Mutual Savings Bank of Troy on the 1st Day of July, 1867.

	Par value.	Cost.
United States bonds and treasury notes	$55,000 00	55,000 00
New York State bonds	25,000 00	25,000 00
Cash in bank		56,110 25
		$136,110 25

Examined and verified by one trustee.

Other Facts.

Number of trustees authorized by charter, nine.

Number of trustees who are directors in any bank of issue where deposits of this institution are kept, seven.

Investments yielding no revenue, none.

Average amount kept on deposit in bank with interest, $95,355.

Regular meetings of the board, not stated.

Average attendance at regular meetings during 1866, not stated.

Loans on bond and mortgage are effected on authority of board of trustees.

Purchases or sales of stock, the same.

Temporary loans, the same.

Deposits in banks of discount, the same.

Examinations of books, for proof of accuracy and fidelity, and assets, are made by committee of trustees semi-annually.

STATE SAVINGS BANK OF TROY.

CASH TRANSACTIONS DURING THE YEAR 1866.

Receipts.

Cash on hand 1st January, 1866, before the transactions of the day		$98,605 97
Deposited in bank	$96,038 64	
Deposited in vault	2,567 33	
From depositors		44,285 40
From interest on stocks		5,406 55
From interest on deposits in bank		3,000 00
From redemption of stocks		103,100 00
		$254,397 92

Payments.

To depositors		$71,034 15
For purchase of stocks and bonds		85,000 00
(Par value thereof	$85,000)	
For salaries		300 00
Cash on hand 31st December, 1866, after the transactions of the day:		
Deposited in bank	$94,825 05	
Deposited in vault	3,238 72	
		98,063 77
		$254,397 92

ASSETS OF THE STATE SAVINGS BANK OF TROY ON THE 19TH DAY OF JUNE, 1867.

	Par value.
United States bonds and treasury notes	$13,500 00
New York State bonds	25,000 00
Bonds of counties in this State (Rensselaer)	2,000 00
Cash in bank	98,523 51
Cash in vault	981 52
	$140,005 03

Examined and verified by three trustees.

OTHER FACTS.

Number of trustees authorized by charter, fifteen.

Number of trustees who are directors in any bank of issue where deposits of this institution are kept, thirteen.

Investments yielding no revenue, none.

Average amount kept on deposit in bank with interest, $95,000.

Regular meetings of the board, monthly.

Number constituting a quorum, five.

Average attendance at regular meetings during 1866, five.

Loans on bond and mortgage, none made.

Purchases or sales of stocks are effected on authority of the board of trustees.

Temporary loans, none made.

Deposits in banks of discount are made by authority of board of trustees, a majority of whom are directors in the bank where deposits are kept.

Examinations of books, for proof of accuracy and fidelity, and assets, are made by a committee of trustees semi-annually.

REMARKS.

Of these four last institutions, two have not a single feature of a savings bank, and the other two not enough to justify the name. They are nothing more than National banks of issue and discount, paying an interest on deposits. I believe they are very good banks, but they are *not* savings banks.

TROY SAVINGS BANK.

CASH TRANSACTIONS DURING THE YEAR 1866.

Receipts.

Cash on hand 1st January, 1866, before the transactions of the day		$288,258 73
Deposited in bank	$279,188 42	
Deposited in vault	9,070 31	
From depositors		745,713 31
From interest on mortgages		16,031 93
From interest on stocks		75,032 50
From interest on deposits in bank		12,743 85
From premium on gold		16,052 76
From mortgages paid, called in or foreclosed		5,400 00
From redemption of stocks		20,000 00
From premium on stocks		2,287 50
From sales of stocks		50,000 00
From rents		2,172 00
From other sources not enumerated		11 50
		$1,233,704 08

Payments.

To depositors		$693,394 49
Loans on bond and mortgage		105,740 00
For repairs		658 45
For salaries		4,623 00
For printing, advertising, stationery and blank books		362 51
For fuel and lights		163 37
For taxes and assessments		10,985 40
For incidental expenses, per petty cash		1 82
For revenue stamps, night police, &c.		439 62
Cash on hand 31st December, 1866, after the transactions of the day:		
Deposited in bank	$404,562 71	
Deposited in vault	12,772 71	
		417,335 42
		$1,233,704 08

Assets of the Troy Savings Bank, on the 1st day of April, 1867.

	Par value.	Stand on the books at
Bonds and mortgages		$302,286 00
United States bonds and treasury notes	$600,000	575,289 11
New York State bonds	130,000	130,000 00
Bonds of cities in this State (Troy)	445,500	376,515 00
Bonds of counties in this State (Rensselaer)	70,000	70,000 00
Real estate		20,000 00
Cash in four banks		524,894 35
Cash in vault		37,424 44
		$2,036,408 90

Examined and verified by two trustees, except as to cash in vault.

Other Facts.

Number of trustees authorized by charter, nineteen.

Number of trustees who are directors in any bank of issue where deposits of this institution are kept, eleven.

Investments yielding no revenue, none.

Average amount kept on deposit in bank with interest, $340,000.

Regular meetings of the board, twice a year.

Number constituting a quorum, five for regular meetings; eleven for special meetings.

Average attendance at regular meetings during 1866, eleven.

Loans on bond and mortgage are effected on authority of mortgage loan committee.

Purchases or sales of stocks are effected on authority of a resolution of the board.

Temporary loans, none made.

Deposits in banks of discount are made by resolution of the board, under contract for a period of three years.

Examinations of books, for proof of accuracy and fidelity, and assets, are made by examining committee twice in each year.

Remarks.

This is the only real savings bank in Troy, and the only one entitled to recognition as such. Its deposits in bank are very large—larger, it seems to me, than is necessary or desirable, but otherwise its exhibit is highly creditable and satisfactory.

CENTRAL CITY SAVINGS INSTITUTION.

CASH TRANSACTIONS DURING THE YEAR 1866.

RECEIPTS.

Cash on hand 1st January, 1866, before the transactions of the day		$3,360 73
Deposited in bank	$2,354 84	
Deposited in vault	1,005 89	
From depositors		131,314 43
From interest on mortgages		2,399 93
From interest on stocks		4,186 68
From interest on loans		1,529 99
From interest on deposits in bank		166 32
From premium on gold		516 06
From mortgages paid, called in or foreclosed		1,625 00
From redemption of stocks		29,630 00
From repayment of loans		21,800 00
		$196,529 14

PAYMENTS.

To depositors		$111,975 46
Loans on bonds and mortgages		16,150 00
Loans on stocks and other securities		36,361 48
For purchase of stocks and bonds		20,700 00
For furniture and fixtures		70 00
For rent		350 00
For salaries		1,500 00
For suits at law		150 00
For printing, advertising, stationery and blank books,		225 00
For fuel and lights		55 00
For taxes and assessments		678 80
For incidental expenses per petty cash		31 00
Cash on hand 31st December, 1866, after the transactions of the day:		
Deposited in bank	$6,409 75	
Deposited in vault	1,872 65	
		8,282 40
		$196,529 14

Assets of the Central City Savings Institution on the 1st Day of July, 1867.

	Par value.	Cost.
Bonds and mortgages		$50,723 12
U. S. bonds and treasury notes	$20,000	20,200 00
Loans on stocks, woolen, mining and express		8,200 00
Loans on other securities, chiefly personal		42,676 34
Real estate		5,235 05
Cash in bank		10,480 11
Cash in vault		3,181 58
Due, and not included under either of above heads,		944 01
		$141,640 21

Examined and verified by three trustees.

Other Facts.

Number of trustees authorized by charter, thirteen.

Number of trustees who are directors in any bank of issue where deposits of this institution are kept, one.

Investments yielding no revenue, none.

Average amount kept on deposit in bank with interest, $4,150.

Regular meetings of the board, monthly.

Number constituting a quorum, seven.

Average attendance at regular meetings during 1866, eight.

Loans on bond and mortgage are effected by finance committee, on unanimous approval of the board at a regular meeting.

Purchases or sales of stocks, the same.

Temporary loans, the same.

Deposits in banks of discount, the same.

Examinations of books, for proof of accuracy and fidelity, and assets, are made by a committee of trustees appointed by the board for that purpose, semi-annually, and oftener if required.

Remarks.

The securities for loans have a local character that I believe is creditable; but I would much prefer to see public stocks or municipal securities in their place. The securities of a savings bank should be such that the very mention of them, anywhere in the State, will reveal their substantial character. This can not be where local securities constitute, as above, a very large proportion of the total assets.

NATIONAL SAVINGS BANK OF UTICA.

(Commenced business in 1866.)

CASH TRANSACTIONS DURING THE YEAR 1866.

Receipts.

From depositors		$467,909 61
From interest on mortgages		253 06
From interest on stocks		4,480 84
From interest on loans		527 01
From interest on deposits in bank		457 99
From redemption of stocks		12,000 00
From sales of stocks		112,483 90
		$598,112 42

Payments.

To depositors		$148,559 74
Loans on bond and mortgage		16,628 50
Loans on stocks and other securities		27,100 00
For purchase of stocks and bonds		351,401 44
Cash on hand 31st December, 1866, after the transactions of the day:		
Deposited in bank	$49,784 47	
Deposited in vault	4,638 27	
		54,422 74
		$598,112 42

Assets of the National Savings Bank of Utica on the 1st Day of July, 1867.

	Par value.	Cost.
Bonds and mortgages		$25,628 50
United States bonds and treasury notes	$258,043 18	262,695 01
Bonds of cities in this State	102,500 00	102,500 00
Loans on stocks and other securities, available fund		16,582 85
Other securities		1,392 50
Cash in bank		57,494 85
Cash in vault		4,357 03
		$470,650 74

Examined and verified by two trustees.

Other Facts.

Number of trustees authorized by charter, twenty-nine.

Number of trustees who are directors in any bank of issue where deposits of this institution are kept, none. Such being prohibited by charter.

Investments yielding no revenue, none.

Average amount kept on deposit in bank with interest, $20,000 during part of the year the bank was in operation.

Regular meetings of the board, monthly.

Number constituting a quorum, seven.

Average attendance at regular meetings during 1866, nine.

Loans on bond and mortgage are effected on authority of finance committee, with unanimous approval of the board.

Purchases or sales of stock are effected on authority of the finance committee.

Temporary loans, the same.

Deposits in banks of discount, the same.

Examinations of books, for proof of accuracy and fidelity, and assets, are made by special committee of trustees appointed twice in each year for that purpose.

THE SAVINGS BANK OF UTICA.

CASH TRANSACTIONS DURING THE YEAR 1866.

Receipts.

Cash on hand 1st January, 1866, before the transactions of the day		$116,064 95
Deposited in bank	$109,452 63	
Deposited in vault	6,612 32	
From depositors		1,036,407 98
From interest on mortgages		27,256 69
From interest on stocks and loans		56,042 00
From interest on deposits in bank		3,595 08
From premium on gold		8,725 34
From mortgages paid, called in or foreclosed		25,604 31
From redemption of stocks		24,000 00
From repayment of loans		1,200 00
From sales of real estate		482 60
From rents		200 00
From difference in exchange of U. S. 5-20's		12,343 35

From New York State stocks	$500 00
From contracts, $661; interest bearing notes, $1,810 (United States)	2,471 00
From sundry items	156 29
	$1,315,049 59

PAYMENTS.

To depositors		$877,249 93
Loans on bond and mortgage		30,150 00
For purchase of stocks and bonds		159,433 97
(Par value thereof	$153,000 00)	
For repairs		49 44
For furniture and fixtures		221 14
For salaries		5,736 34
For print'g, advertising, stationery and blank books,		178 68
For fuel and lights		193 72
For taxes and assessments		10,558 03
For incidental expenses per petty cash		369 76
For attorneys, $231; interest bearing notes, $350		581 00
For extra services in bank		475 52
For sundries, counterfeit money, &c		531 70
Cash on hand 31st December, 1866, after the transactions of the day:		
Deposited in bank	$227,763 28	
Deposited in vault	1,557 08	
		229,320 36
		$1,315,049 59

ASSETS OF THE SAVINGS BANK OF UTICA, ON THE 1ST DAY OF JANUARY, 1867.

Bonds and mortgages	$349,834 00
	Par value.
U. S. bonds and treasury notes	466,000 00
New York State bonds	167,000 00
Bonds of other States	350,000 00
Bonds of cities in this State	34,000 00
Other securities	4,950 00

Real estate, cost	$7,821 66
Cash in bank	227,763 28
Cash in vault	1,557 08
	$1,608,926 02

Interest due but unpaid at this date, *and not included in statement*, $10,263.95.

Examined and verified by two trustees.

Other Facts.

Number of trustees authorized by charter, fifteen.

Number of trustees who are directors in any bank of issue where deposits of this institution are kept, four.

Investments yielding no revenue, none.

Average amount kept on deposit in bank with interest, $150,000.

Regular meetings of the board, semi-annually.

Number constituting a quorum, five.

Average attendance at regular meetings during 1866, eleven.

Loans on bond and mortgage are effected on authority of finance committee.

Purchases or sales of stocks, the same.

Temporary loans, none made.

Deposits in banks of discount are made by treasurer in banks designated by the board.

Examinations of books, for proof of accuracy and fidelity, and of assets, are made by a committee appointed annually.

CHAUTAUQUA COUNTY SAVINGS BANK.

This bank was opened for deposits September 17, 1866.

CASH TRANSACTIONS DURING THE YEAR 1866.

Receipts.

From depositors	$48,900 50
From interest on mortgages	31 80
From interest on stocks	69 69
From repayment of loans	4,373 17
From exchanges and commissions	14 36
	$53,389 52

Payments.

To depositors		$23,859 55
Loans on bond and mortgage		6,459 70
Loans on stocks and other securities		15,161 93
For purchase of stocks and bonds		362 60
(Par value thereof	$340 00)	
For furniture and fixtures		959 82
For rent		50 40
For salaries		175 00
For printing, advertising, stationery and blank books		178 58
For fuel and lights		9 25
For incidental expenses per petty cash		4 44
For internal revenue stamps		100 00
Cash on hand 31st December, 1866, after the transactions of the day:		
Deposited in bank	$1,678 17	
Deposited in vault	4,390 08	
		6,068 25
		$53,389 52

Assets of the Chautauqua Savings Bank on the 1st Day of July, 1867.

	Par value.	Cost.
Bonds and mortgages		$10,524 66
U. S. bonds and treasury notes	$4,700 00	5,006 00
Loans on stocks and other securities, available fund,		800 00
Other securities		8,782 28
Cash in bank		1,648 99
Cash in vault		1,045 25
		$27,807 18

Examined and verified by a committee of two, except as to cash in vault.

Other Facts.

Number of trustees authorized by charter, nine.

Number of trustees who are directors in any bank of issue where deposits of this institution are kept, none.

Investments yielding no revenue, none.

Average amount kept on deposit in bank, during part of the year the bank was in operation, $800.

Regular meetings of the board, monthly.

Number constituting a quorum, five.

Average attendance at regular meetings during 1866, four.

Loans on bond and mortgage are effected on authority of the president, vice-president, secretary and executive committee.

Purchases or sales of stocks, the same.

Temporary loans, the same.

Deposits in banks of discount, the same.

Examinations of books, for proof of accuracy and fidelity, and assets, are made by a committee of trustees whenever required.

CHENANGO COUNTY SAVINGS BANK.

CASH TRANSACTIONS DURING THE YEAR 1866.

RECEIPTS.

Cash on hand 1st January, 1866, before the transactions of the day		$85,728 48
Deposited in bank	$85,728 48	
From depositors		141,567 22
		$227,295 70

PAYMENTS.

To depositors		$146,453 29
Cash on hand 31st December, 1866, after the transactions of the day:		
Deposited in bank	$80,842 41	
		$80,842 41
		$227,295 70

ASSETS OF THE CHENANGO COUNTY SAVINGS BANK ON THE 17TH DAY OF OCTOBER, 1867.

Bonds and mortgages	$9,750 00
Bonds of counties in this State (Chenango)	21,000 00
Cash in bank	25,665 70
	$56,415 70

Examined and verified by three trustees.

Other Facts.

Number of trustees authorized by charter, fifteen.

Number of trustees who are directors in any bank of issue where deposits of this institution are kept, five.

Investments yielding no revenue, none.

Average amount kept on deposit in bank with interest, $61,161.

Regular meetings of the board, quarter yearly.

Number constituting a quorum, seven.

Average attendance at regular meetings during 1866, not stated.

Loans on bond and mortgage are effected on authority of trustees.

Purchases or sales of stocks, the same.

Temporary loans, the same.

Deposits in banks of discount, the same. During 1866 the whole amount of deposits was kept in bank.

Examinations of books, for proof of accuracy and fidelity, and assets, are not made with any regularity.

Remarks.

The business is done by the Bank of Chenango. All reports previous to the above represent the assets as wholly in cash, deposited in the Bank of Chenango. It is in effect that part of the Bank of Chenango that pays four per cent interest on ordinary deposits.

COHOES SAVINGS INSTITUTION.

CASH TRANSACTIONS DURING THE YEAR 1866.

Receipts.

Cash on hand 1st January, 1866, before the transactions of the day		$93,470 35
Deposited in bank	$90,053 53	
Deposited in vault	3,416 82	
From depositors		208,909 45
From interest on mortgages		502 00
Mortgages paid		1,200 00
Errors and profit and loss		1,324 95
		$305,406 75

Payments.

To depositors		$180,007 40
Loans on bond and mortgage		2,300 00

All other payments unknown, being made by National Bank of Cohoes.

Cash on hand 31st December, 1866, after the transactions of the day:		
Deposited in bank	$111,972 06	
Deposited in vault	11,127 29	
		123,099 35
		$305,406 75

Assets of the Cohoes Savings Institution on the 10th day of December, 1867.

	Par value.	Cost.
Bonds and mortgages		$7,200 00
U. S. bonds and treasury notes	$100,500	$101,500 00
Loans on stocks and other securities, available fund,		35,000 00
Cash in bank		106,499 37
Cash in vault		424 44
		$250,623 81

Examined and verified by the vice-president and treasurer.

Other Facts.

Number of trustees authorized by charter, nineteen.

Number of trustees who are directors in any bank of issue where deposits of this institution are kept, five.

Investments yielding no revenue, none.

Average amount kept on deposit in bank with interest, estimated at $100,000.

Regular meetings of the board, not stated.

Number constituting a quorum, not stated.

Remarks.

The trustees of this institution, finding themselves much embarrassed in making desirable investments, by reason of the restrictions in their charter concerning loans on bond and mortgage, have made arrangements with the National Bank of Cohoes to transact the business. All the interest from investments is received by the National Bank, which makes up any deficiency in the amount necessary to pay expenses and five per cent to depositors. Hence the incompleteness in the statement of cash transactions. It is not a profitable arrangement for either the National or the Savings Bank. Removal of unnecessary restrictions concerning loans on bond and mortgage would enable the Savings bank to cut loose from the National bank, and do a more safe and prosperous business on its own account.

CORTLAND SAVINGS BANK.

(Commenced business September 25, 1866.)

CASH TRANSACTIONS DURING THE YEAR 1866.

Receipts.

From depositors		$28,482 71
From interest on mortgages		1 52
From interest on loans		13 14
From repayment of loans		4,000 00
		$32,497 37

Payments.

To depositors		$7,353 89
Loans on bond and mortgage		130 00
Loans on stocks and other securities		5,950 00
For purchase of stocks and bonds		7,600 00
(Par value thereof	$7,600 00)	
For furniture and fixtures		11 02
For printing, advertising, stationery and blank books,		99 13
For fuel and lights		4 00
For incidental expenses per petty cash		12 94
For interest paid on county bonds bought previous to January 1, 1867		304 62
Cash on hand 31st December, 1866, after the transactions of the day:		
Deposited in bank	$10,871 97	
Cash on hand	159 80	
		11,031 77
		$32,497 37

ASSETS OF THE CORTLAND SAVINGS BANK ON THE 25TH DAY OF JULY, 1867.

	Par value.	Cost.
Bonds and mortgages		$130 00
U. S. bonds and treasury notes	$400 00	418 00
Bonds of counties in this State (Cortland)		12,500 00
Loans on stocks and other securities, available fund, (government and county bonds)		7,039 00
Cash in bank		112 43
Cash in vault		4,071 45
		$24,270 88

Examined and verified by two trustees.

OTHER FACTS.

Number of trustees authorized by charter, twenty.

Number of trustees who are directors in any bank of issue where deposits of this institution are kept, one.

Investments yielding no revenue, none.

Average amount kept on deposit in bank during part of the year bank was organized, $6,772.00.

Regular meetings of the board, twice in each month.

Number constituting a quorum, eleven.

Average attendance at regular meetings during 1866, eleven.

Loans on bond and mortgage are effected on authority of the board.

Purchases or sales of stocks are effected on authority of the secretary and treasurer.

Temporary loans, the same.

Deposits in banks of discount are made by authority of the board.

Examinations of books, for proof of accuracy and fidelity, and assets, are made by auditing committee annually.

FISHKILL SAVINGS INSTITUTE.

CASH TRANSACTIONS DURING THE YEAR 1866.

RECEIPTS.

Cash on hand 1st January, 1866, before the transactions of the day	$1,987 74

Deposited in bank	$1,987 74	
Deposited in vault		
From depositors		$58,684 00
From interest on mortgages		781 00
From interest on stocks		8,277 50
From premium on gold		2,732 00
From redemption of stocks		300 00
		$72,762 24

PAYMENTS.

To depositors		$48,196 32
Loans on bond and mortgage		
Loans on stocks and other securities		
For purchase of stocks and bonds		7,558 75
(Par value thereof	$8,000)	
For fixtures (safe)		1,800 00
For rent		400 00
For salaries		1,196 00
For printing, advertising, stationery and blank books,		218 10
For taxes and assessments		647 53
For incidental expenses per petty cash		121 36
From interest advanced		30 00
Cash on hand 31st December, 1866, after the transactions of the day:		
Deposited in bank	$12,594 18	
Deposited in vault		
		12,594 18
		$72,762 24

ASSETS OF THE FISHKILL SAVINGS INSTITUTE, ON THE 12TH DAY OF DECEMBER, 1867.

	Par value.	Cost.
Bonds and mortgages		$17,100 00
U. S. bonds and treasury notes	$128,500 00	128,072 85
New York State bonds	35,000 00	34,358 75
Bonds of cities in this State	15,100 00	15,037 50

Loans on stocks and other securities, available fund,	$5,000 00
Other resources, safe	1,800 00
Cash in bank	29,666 67
	$231,035 77

Examined and verified by Isaac Smith, of Bank Department.

Remarks.

Failing to get any return from the above institution, Isaac Smith, accountant in the Bank Department, was deputed to visit and examine its affairs, under authority of the act of 1857 in relation to savings banks. He made a thorough examination of the books and assets and of the credit of the savings bank in the National Bank of Fishkill. The fact of those assets being in possession of the Fishkill Savings Institute on the 12th day of December, is therefore established.

The business of the institution is carried on by the National Bank of Fishkill, but not in the interest of that bank. The assets have uniformly been kept quite closely invested; but the restrictions of their charter in regard to loans on bond and mortgage, have, during the last year, resulted in a largor accumulation of cash on hand than usual.

But the savings bank, from its intimate connection with the bank of discount, suffers, as *secondary* interests always do, from at least partial neglect.

HUDSON CITY SAVINGS INSTITUTION.

CASH TRANSACTIONS DURING THE YEAR 1866.

Receipts.

Cash on hand 1st January, 1866, before the transactions of the day		$19,291 26
Deposited in bank	$15,794 90	
Deposited in vault	3,496 36	
From depositors		145,916 00

From interest on mortgages / From interest on stocks / From interest on loans / From interest on deposits in banks / From premium on gold	$19,616 00
From mortgages paid, called in or foreclosed	1,500 00
From sales of stocks	29,168 00
From deposits, error, in 1865	200 00
	$215,691 26

PAYMENTS.

To depositors		$143,711 16
Loans on bond and mortgage		5,000 00
Loans on stocks and other securities		21,034 34
For purchase of stocks and bonds		2,000 00
For building or construction account		10,924 62
For rent		1,600 00
For printing, advertising, stationery, blank books, and expenses		558 67
For taxes and assessments		1,121 21
Cash on hand 31st December, 1866, after the transactions of the day:		
Deposited in bank	$19,443 90	
Deposited in vault	10,297 37	
		29,741 27
		$215,691 27

ASSETS OF THE HUDSON CITY SAVINGS INSTITUTION, ON THE 1ST DAY OF JULY, 1867.

	Par value.	Cost.
Bonds and mortgages		$59,740 55
United States bonds and treasury notes	$136,000	139,216 50
Bonds of other States	20,000	12,796 00
Bonds of cities in this State	28,700	28,700 00
Bonds of counties in this State (Columbia)		27,000 00
Loans on stocks and other securities, available fund		34,355 00
Other securities (U. S.)		5,800 00
Real estate		14,878 03
Cash in bank		12,387 02

Cash in vault	$11,304 14
Office furniture, &c	1,200 00
	$347,377 24

Verified from examination by president and two trustees, except as to cash on hand.

Other Facts.

Number of trustees authorized by charter, thirteen.

Number of trustees who are directors in any bank of issue where deposits of this institution are kept, four.

Investments yielding no revenue, none.

Average amount kept on deposit in bank, $9,000.

Regular meetings of the board, monthly, but not always held for want of quorum.

Number constituting a quorum, eight.

Average attendance at regular meetings during 1866, not stated.

Loans on bond and mortgage are effected on authority of the whole board, or by finance committee authorized by the board.

Purchases or sales of stock the same.

Temporary loans are made by authority of the finance committee. Deposits in banks of discount are made by the treasurer at his discretion.

Examinations of books for proof of accuracy and fidelity and assets, are made by examining committee twice in each year.

JEFFERSON COUNTY SAVINGS BANK.

CASH TRANSACTIONS DURING THE YEAR 1866.

Receipts.

Cash on hand 1st January, 1866, before the transactions of the day		$12,486 32
Deposited in bank	$11,435 53	
Deposited in vault	1,050 79	
From depositors		73,923 53
From interest on mortgages		2,815 17
From interest on stocks		4,561 41
From premium on gold		358 44
From mortgages paid, called in or foreclosed		2,865 91

From redemption of stocks		$5,014 50
From repayment of loans		1,054 60
From sales of stocks		22,000 00
		$125,079 88

PAYMENTS.

To depositors		$97,957 97
For purchase of stocks and bonds		1,254 60
(Par value thereof	$1,254 60)	
For repairs		14 68
For furniture and fixtures		3 40
For rent		550 00
For salaries		900 00
For printing, advertising, stationery and blank books,		48 75
For fuel and lights		65 87
For taxes and assessments		327 24
For incidental expenses, per petty cash		57 18
For cashier's check		20 00
For interest to depositors		5,198 96
Cash on hand 31st December, 1866, after the transactions of the day:		
Deposited in bank	$15,336 11	
Deposited in vault	3,345 12	
		18,681 23
		$125,079 88

ASSETS OF THE JEFFERSON COUNTY SAVINGS BANK, ON THE 1ST DAY OF JANUARY, 1867.

	Par value.	Cost.
Bonds and mortgages		$35,818 64
U. S. bonds and treasury notes	$20,200 00	20,286 00
New York State bonds	10,000 00	10,000 00
Bonds of counties in this State (Jefferson)	18,200 00	16,553 60
Bonds of towns in this State	5,934 50	5,934 50
Cash in bank		15,336 11
Cash in vault		3,345 12
		$107,273 97

Examined and verified by the president and one trustee.

Other Facts.

Number of trustees, seventeen.

Number of trustees who are directors in any bank of issue where deposits of this institution are kept, seven.

Investments yielding no revenue, none.

Average amount kept on deposit in bank, with interest, $11,143.

Regular meetings of the board, quarter yearly.

Number constituting a quorum, seven.

Average attendance at regular meetings during 1866, eight.

Loans on bond and mortgage are effected on authority of executive committee, subject to approval of the board.

Purchases or sales of stocks, the same.

Temporary loans, the same.

Deposits in banks of discount, the same.

Examinations of books, for proof of accuracy and fidelity, and assets, not stated.

MECHANICS' SAVINGS BANK OF FISHKILL, ON HUDSON.

(Commenced business in 1866.)

CASH TRANSACTIONS DURING THE YEAR 1866.

Receipts.

From depositors	$48,167 29
From interest on stocks	760 90
	$48,928 19

Payments.

To depositors		$9,641 39
Loans on bond and mortgage		7,225 00
Loans on stocks and other securities		20,200 00
For purchase of stocks and bonds		1,242 45
For furniture and fixtures		100 46
For interest to depositors		262 06
Cash on hand, 31st December, 1866, after the transactions of the day:		
Deposited in bank	$4,069 19	
Compound interest notes in vault	6,187 65	
		10,256 84
		$48,928 19

Assets of the Mechanics' Savings Bank of Fishkill on the 14th Day of September, 1867.

	Par value.	Cost.
Bonds and mortgages		$27,075 00
United States bonds and treasury notes	$18,500	19,542 45
Other securities, expense account		21 00
Cash in bank		1,544 90
Cash in vault (compound interest notes)		6,827 49
		$55,010 84

Examined and verified by two trustees.

Other Facts.

Number of trustees authorized by charter, twenty-five.

Number of trustees who are directors in any bank of issue where deposits of this institution are kept, five.

Investments yielding no revenue, none.

Average amount kept on deposit in bank with interest, estimated at $1,000.

Regular meetings of the board, monthly.

Number constituting a quorum, nine.

Average attendance at regular meetings during 1866, not stated.

Loans on bond and mortgage are effected on authority of seven trustees.

Purchases or sales of stocks, the same.

Temporary loans, the same.

Deposits in banks of discount, not stated.

Examinations of books, for proof of accuracy and fidelity, and assets, are made by executive committee; how often, not stated.

NEWBURGH SAVINGS BANK.

CASH TRANSACTIONS DURING THE YEAR 1866.

Receipts.

Cash on hand 1st January, 1866, before the transactions of the day		$36,233 94
Deposited in bank	$36,233 94	
From depositors		385,653 10
From interest on mortgages		11,013 66
From interest on stocks		33,128 13
From interest on loans		1,008 77

From interest on deposits in bank		$610 38
From premium on gold		4,426 78
From mortgages paid, called in or foreclosed		33,688 31
From sales of stocks		140,300 00
		$646,063 07

PAYMENTS.

To depositors		$372,466 69
Loans on bond and mortgage		56,175 00
Loans on stocks and other securities		170,340 00
For purchase of stocks and bonds		4,459 55
For building or construction account		18,297 00
For rent		425 00
For salaries		4,100 00
For printing, advertising, stationery and blank books		782 41
For fuel and lights		15 50
For taxes and assessments		4,456 34
Cash on hand 31st December, 1866, after the transactions of the day:		
Deposited in bank	$14,545 58	
		14,545 58
		$646,063 07

ASSETS OF THE NEWBURGH SAVINGS BANK ON THE 1ST DAY OF JULY, 1867.

Bonds and mortgages	$189,278 69
	Cost.
U. S. bonds and treasury notes	455,370 00
New York State bonds	30,000 00
Bonds of other States (Ohio)	5,500 00
Bonds of cities in this State	69,000 00
Bonds of towns in this State	40,000 00
Loans on stocks and other securities, available fund	11,500 00
Other securities	10,000 00
Real estate	33,619 80
Cash in bank	24,284 42
	$868,552 91

Examined by three, and verified by two trustees.

Other Facts.

Number of trustees authorized by charter, twenty-two.

Number of trustees who are directors in any bank of issue where deposits of this institution are kept, eight.

Investments yielding no revenue, $1,500.

Average amount kept on deposit in bank with interest, estimated at $30,000.

Regular meetings of the board, monthly.

Number constituting a quorum, eight.

Average attendance at regular meetings during 1866, thirteen.

Loans on bond and mortgage are effected on authority of the board.

Purchases or sales of stocks, the same.

Temporary loans the same.

Deposits in banks of discount, the same.

Examinations of books, for proof of accuracy and fidelity, and assets, are made by a committee of trustees twice in each year.

NEW ROCHELLE SAVINGS BANK.

(Commenced business 1866.)

CASH TRANSACTIONS DURING THE YEAR 1866.

Receipts.

From depositors	$14,231 50
From interest on stocks	377 53
From premium on gold	55 95
	$14,664 98

Payments.

To depositors	$4,891 63
Loans on stocks and other securities	7,826 76
For furniture and fixtures	64 37
For express	40
For printing, advertising, stationery and blank books,	130 00
Cash on hand 31st December, 1866, after the transactions of the day:	

Deposited in bank	$518 82	
Deposited in vault	1,233 00	
		$1,751 82
		$14,664 98

ASSETS OF THE NEW ROCHELLE SAVINGS BANK ON THE 1ST DAY OF JANUARY, 1867.

	Par value.	Cost.
United States bonds and treasury notes	$7,600 00	7,826 76
Cash in bank		518 82
Cash in vault		1,233 00
		$9,578 58

Examined and verified by the treasurer.

OTHER FACTS.

Number of trustees authorized by charter, thirteen.

Number of trustees who are directors in any bank of issue where deposits of this institution are kept, none.

Investments yielding no revenue, none.

Average amount kept on deposit in bank with interest, not stated. (Must be small.)

Regular meetings of the board, monthly.

Number constituting a quorum, seven.

Average attendance at regular meetings during 1866, eight.

Loans on bond and mortgage are effected on authority of at least five trustees.

Purchases or sales of stocks, the same.

Temporary loans, the same.

Deposits in banks of discount, the same.

Examinations of books, for proof of accuracy and fidelity, and assets, are made by examining committee once a year.

NIAGARA COUNTY SAVINGS BANK.

CASH TRANSACTIONS DURING THE YEAR 1866.

RECEIPTS.

Cash on hand 1st January, 1866, before the transactions of the day		$304 66
Deposited in vault	$304 66	

From depositors	$11,037 59
From interest on mortgages and stocks	72 90
From mortgages paid, called in or foreclosed	100 00
From sales of stocks	500 00
	$12,015 15

Payments.

To depositors		$9,256 56
For purchase of stocks and bonds		1,700 00
(Par value thereof	$1,804 00)	
For printing, advertising, stationery and blank books; For fuel and lights; For taxes and assessments; For incidental expenses per petty cash; For other expenses		17 90
For interest paid during the year		187 14
Cash on hand 31st December, 1866, after the transactions of the day:		
Deposited in vault	$853 55	
		853 55
		$12,015 15

Assets of the Niagara County Savings Bank on the 1st day of January, 1867.

	Par value.	Cost.
Bonds and mortgages		$325 00
United States bonds and treasury notes	$2,915 00	2,750 00
Bonds of counties in this State (Niagara)		1,500 00
Other securities expense account		112 84
Cash in vault		853 55
		$5,541 39

Examined and verified by the secretary.

Other Facts.

Number of trustees authorized by charter, nine.

Number of trustees who are directors in any bank of issue where deposits of this institution are kept, none.

Investments yielding no revenue, none.

Average amount kept on deposit in bank with interest, none.

Regular meetings of the board, monthly, but not regularly held. President and secretary manage the business.

Number constituting a quorum, five.

Average attendance at regular meetings during 1866, not stated.

Loans on bond and mortgage are effected on authority of the president.

Purchases or sales of stocks are effected on authority of the president and secretary, or either of them.

Temporary loans; none made.

Deposits in banks of discount; none.

Examinations of books, for proof of accuracy and fidelity, and assets, are made by officers of the bank twice in each year.

Remarks.

The city of Lockport and surrounding country ought to give a better support to a savings bank than is indicated by the above. Instead of $5,000 of deposits there should be $500,000.

ONEIDA SAVINGS BANK.

(Organized April 1, 1866.)

CASH TRANSACTIONS DURING THE YEAR 1866.

Receipts.

From depositors	$103,829 66
From interest on mortgages	395 78
From interest on stocks	666 43
From interest on loans	9 15
From mortgages paid, called in or foreclosed	820 00
From repayment of loans	694 00
From sales of stocks	3,000 00
From premiums on stocks sold	186 50
	$109,601 52

Payments.

To depositors	$28,474 21
Loans on bond and mortgage	22,692 34
Loans on stocks and other securities	10,811 00
For purchase of stocks and bonds	39,346 33
For furniture and fixtures	48 50
For salaries	150 00

For printing, advertising, stationery and blank books		$112 86
For incidental expenses per petty cash		12 86
For exchange		48 39
Cash on hand 31st December, 1866, after the transactions of the day:		
Deposited in bank	$7,898 68	
Deposited in vault	6 35	
		7,905 03
		$109,601 52

ASSETS OF THE ONEIDA SAVINGS BANK ON THE FIRST DAY OF JULY, 1867.

	Par value.	Cost.
Bonds and mortgages		$28,007 84
U. S. bonds and treasury notes	$9,350 00	9,808 50
New York State bonds	8,000 00	8,226 25
Bonds of counties in this State	3,400 00	3,400 00
Bonds of towns in this State		1,063 52
Furniture		48 50
Cash in vault		11 85
		$50,566 46

Examined and verified by two trustees.

OTHER FACTS.

Number of trustees authorized by charter, seventeen.

Number of trustees who are directors in any bank of issue where deposits of this institution are kept, two.

Investments yielding no revenue, none.

Average amount kept on deposit in bank, $5,757, during part of the year the bank was in operation.

Regular meetings of the board, monthly.

Number constituting a quorum, nine.

Average attendance at regular meetings during 1866, nine.

Loans on bond and mortgage are effected on authority of an affimative vote of at least seven trustees.

Purchases or sale of stocks, the same, except sometimes referred to finance committee, with power.

Temporary loans, the same.

Deposits in banks of discount, the same.

Examinations of books, for proof of accuracy and fidelity, and assets, are made by special committee appointed by the board; how frequently, not stated.

Remarks.

Proportion of bond and mortgage rather large, though in an agricultural region there is usually less fluctuation in the circumstances of depositors than in manufacturing and commercial districts, and this fact may justify a somewhat larger proportion of unconvertible assets.

OSWEGO CITY SAVINGS BANK.

CASH TRANSACTIONS DURING THE YEAR 1866.

Receipts.

Cash on hand 1st January, 1866, before the transactions of the day		$72,384 61
Deposited in bank	$60,714 09	
Deposited in vault	11,670 52	
From depositors		479,719 60
From interest on mortgages		2,804 96
From interest on stocks		12,205 53
From interest on loans		1,339 89
From interest on deposits in bank		1,746 00
From premium on gold, exchange, discount, &c		153 83
From mortgages paid, called in or foreclosed		2,201 00
From repayment of loans		13,784 00
From sales of stocks		14,900 00
Amount received on accrued interest account		16,667 15
Amount received from city and county warrants paid by the city and county treasurers		5,023 23
		$622,929 80

Payments.

To depositors		$494,379 01
Loans on bond and mortgage		13,900 00
Loans on stocks and other securities		7,855 00
For purchase of stocks and bonds		2,260 00
(Par value thereof	$2,260)	
For rent		200 00
For salaries		3,850 00

For printing, advertising, stationery and blank books,		$120 31
For fuel and lights		76 11
For taxes and assessments		1,217 99
For incidental expenses per petty cash		159 87
For accrued interest account		17,070 93
For city and county treasury warrants		11,499 90
For interest paid depositors		11,938 20
Cash on hand 31st December, 1866, after the transactions of the day:		
Deposited in bank	$51,804 45	
Deposited in vault	6.598 03	
		58,402 48
		$622,929 80

Assets of the Oswego City Savings Bank on the 1st day of January, 1867.

	Par value.	Cost.
Bonds and mortgages		$44,875 00
U. S. bonds and treasury notes	$96,550 00	$96,550 00
Bonds of counties in this State	61,300 00	61,300 00
Loans on stocks and other securities, available fund,		16,871 00
Other securities		21,829 35
Cash in bank		51,804 45
Cash in vault		6,598 03
Interest accrued and due this day		7,368 95
		$307,196 78

Examined and verified by two trustees.

Other Facts.

Number of trustees authorized by charter, eleven.

Number of trustees who are directors in any bank of issue where deposits of this institution are kept, five.

Investments yielding no revenue, none.

Average amount kept on deposit in bank with interest, $33,840.

Regular meetings of the board, quarter-yearly.

Number constituting a quorum, five.

Average attendance at regular meetings during 1866, nine.

Loans on bond and mortgage are effected on authority of loan committee, or of the board.

Purchases or sales of stock, the same.

Temporary loans, the same.

Deposits in banks of discount, the same.

Examinations of books, for proof of accuracy and fidelity, and assets, are made by the examining committee, semi-annually.

PEEKSKILL SAVINGS BANK.

CASH TRANSACTIONS DURING THE YEAR 1866.

RECEIPTS.

Cash on hand 1st January, 1866, before the transactions of the day		$11,067 76
Deposited in bank	$9,067 76	
Deposited in vault	2,000 00	
From depositors		174,712 65
From interest on mortgages		1,502 78
From interest on stocks		11,690 30
From interest on loans		21 20
From interest on deposits in bank		115 31
From premium on gold		3,681 58
From mortgages paid, called in or foreclosed		4,800 00
From repayment of loans		1,000 00
For sales of stocks		21,940 20
On exchange of U. S. 5-20's		847 50
Interest on town bonds		695 00
Interest on corporation Peekskill bonds		84 00
Interest on county bonds		1,540 00
		$233,698 28

PAYMENTS.

To depositors		$135,897 57
Loans on bond and mortgage		27,000 00
Loans on stocks and other securities		5,000 00
For purchase of stocks and bonds		47,629 00
(Par value thereof	$45,000 00)	
For rent		150 00
For salaries		1,200 00
For printing, advertising, stationery and blank books		191 25
For fuel and lights		15 75
For taxes and assessments		1,282 81

For incidental expenses for petty cash		$37 86
For interest paid on assignment of mortgages to bank		173 48
Cash on hand 31st December, 1866, after the transactions of the day:		
Deposited in bank	$13,120 56	
Deposited in vault	2,000 00	
		15,120 56
		$233,698 28

Assets of the Peekskill Savings Bank, on the 1st Day of January, 1867.

	Par value.	Cost.
Bonds and mortgages		$47,800 00
U. S. bonds and treasury notes	$206,000	$206,000 00
New York State bonds	10,000 00	10,000 00
Bonds of counties in this State		22,000 00
Loans on stocks and other securities, available fund,		4,000 00
Other securities		600 00
Cash in bank		13,120 56
Cash in vault		2,000 00
		$305,520 56

Examined and verified by president and accountant.

Other Facts.

Number of trustees authorized by charter, twenty-four.

Number of trustees who are directors in any bank of issue where deposits of this institution are kept, none.

Investments yielding no revenue, none.

Average amount kept on deposit in bank, $10,638.

Regular meetings of the board, monthly.

Number constituting a quorum, seven.

Average attendance at regular meetings during 1866, nine.

Loans on bond and mortgage are effected on authority of bond and mortgage committee.

Purchases of sales of stocks are effected on authority of funding committee.

Temporary loans, the same.

Deposits in banks of discount are made by authority of funding committee or treasurer.

Examinations of books, for proof of accuracy and fidelity and assets, are made by a committee appointed from the board once in each year.

PORT CHESTER SAVINGS BANK.

CASH TRANSACTIONS DURING THE YEAR 1866.

Receipts.

Cash on hand 1st January, 1866, before the transactions of the day		$8,719 55
Deposited in bank	$8,463 55	
Deposited in vault	256 00	
From depositors		94,382 92
From interest on mortgages		1,444 88
From interest on loans, on call		59 42
From interest on deposits in bank		683 10
From mortgages paid, called in or foreclosed		2,500 00
From redemption of stocks		22,035 70
From repayment of loans		100 00
From sales of stocks		26,612 50
From accrued interest on bond and mortgage		115 62
		$156,653 69

Payments.

To depositors		$68,840 34
Loans on bond and mortgage		19,440 00
Loans on stocks and other securities		1,000 00
For purchase of stocks and bonds		48,457 48
(Par value thereof	$47,000 00)	
For salaries		350 00
For printing, advertising, stationery and blank books,		201 26
For fuel and lights		60 09
For taxes and assessments		234 37
Accrued interest on bond and mortgage		91 62
Cash on hand 31st December, 1866, after the transactions of the day:		
Deposited in bank	$17,188 31	
Deposited in vault	790 22	
		$17,978 53
		$156,653 69

ASSETS OF THE PORT CHESTER SAVINGS BANK, ON THE 24TH DAY OF AUGUST, 1867.

	Par value.	Cost.
Bonds and mortgages		$41,925 00
U. S. bonds and treasury notes	$10,000 00	10,387 50
Bonds of towns in this State	19,000 00	18,900 00
Other securities		1,535 64
Cash in bank		23,586 71
Cash in vault		621 39
		$96,956 24

Examined and verified by two trustees.

OTHER FACTS.

Number of trustees authorized by charter, sixteen.

Number of trustees who are directors in any bank of issue where deposits of this institution are kept, three.

Investments yielding no revenue, none.

Average amount kept on deposit in bank with interest, $18,440.

Regular meetings of the board, monthly.

Number constituting a quorum, seven.

Average attendance at regular meetings during 1866, eight.

Loans on bond and mortgage are effected on authority of finance committee.

Purchases or sales of stocks, the same.

Temporary loans, the same.

Deposits in banks of discount are made by authority of the act of incorporation. Section 6.

Examinations of books, for proof of accuracy and fidelity, and assets, are made by the examining committee annually.

REMARKS.

This savings bank commenced business in 1865. It was originated by the proprietors of extensive manufacturing works in the village, for the benefit of their workmen. Such beneficent enterprise is most praiseworthy, and that it is properly appreciated is evident from the very considerable deposits made in the first year of its operation. There are many villages in the State where the same enterprising spirit would be attended by equally favorable results.

POUGHKEEPSIE SAVINGS BANK.

CASH TRANSACTIONS DURING THE YEAR 1866.

RECEIPTS.

Cash on hand 1st January, 1866, before the transactions of the day		$28,877 04
Deposited in bank	$27,877 04	
Deposited in vault	1,000 00	
From depositors		387,888 10
From interest on mortgages		28,081 15
From interest on stocks, including premium		39,853 20
From interest on loans		2,794 91
From interest on deposits in bank		163 91
From mortgages paid, called in or foreclosed		62,276 00
From redemption of stocks		55,300 00
From repayment of loans		14,500 00
		$619,734 31

PAYMENTS.

To depositors		$354,953 65
Loans on bond and mortgage		199,087 96
Loans on stocks and other securities		1,900 00
For purchase of stocks and bonds		6,000 00
For repairs		59 52
For salaries		3,500 00
For printing, advertising, stationery and blank books,		482 50
For fuel and lights		83 00
For taxes and assessments		4,427 70
For incidental expenses per petty cash		647 00
For other expenses, insurance		49 25
Cash on hand 31st December, 1866, after the transactions of the day:		
Deposited in bank	$47,543 73	
Deposited in vault	1,000 00	
		48,543 73
		$619,734 31

Assets of the Poughkeepsie Savings Bank, on the 1st day of January, 1867.

Bonds and mortgages	$567,876 36
	Par value.
United States bonds and treasury notes	216,000 00
New York State bonds	30,000 00
Bonds of cities in this State (Poughkeepsie)	115,700 00
Bonds of counties in this State	145,400 00
Loans on stocks and other securities, available fund,	44,650 00
Other securities, Hudson River railroad, 1st and 2d bonds	12,000 00
Real estate, cost	5,000 00
Cash in bank	47,543 73
Cash in vault	1,000 00
	$1,185,170 09

Examined and verified by two trustees of two different committees.

Other Facts.

Number of trustees authorized by charter, eleven.

Number of trustees who are directors in any bank of issue where deposits of this institution are kept, one.

Investments yielding no revenue, none.

Average amount kept on deposit in bank, with interest, $15,463.

Regular meetings of the board, semi-annually.

Number constituting a quorum, six.

Average attendance at regular meetings during 1866, not stated.

Loans on bond and mortgage are effected by loaning committee, ratified by the board.

Purchases or sales of stocks, the same.

Temporary loans, none made.

Deposits in banks of discount are made by authority of the board.

Examinations of books, for proof of accuracy and fidelity, and assets, are made by committees of trustees appointed by the board, who report semi-annually.

Remarks.

The amount loaned on bond and mortgage is larger than I would favor, though partially offset by the fair proportion of United States and New York State stocks, which are easily convertible, usually without loss. The Hudson River railroad bonds are *good* as any such securities can be, but are not the kind for savings banks, nor do I find any authority under which the above are held.

QUEENS COUNTY SAVINGS BANK.

CASH TRANSACTIONS DURING THE YEAR 1866.

Receipts.

Cash on hand 1st January, 1866, before the transactions of the day		$11,591 29
From depositors		76,806 59
From interest on mortgages		1,383 00
From interest on stocks		8,835 05
From interest on loans		45 20
From premium on gold		1,139 66
From redemption of stocks		22,500 00
From repayment of loans		2,500 00
		$124,800 79

Payments.

To depositors		$47,000 31
Loans on bond and mortgage		29,200 00
Loans on stocks and other securities		2,500 00
For purchase of stocks and bonds		35,756 50
For rent		150 00
For salaries		656 25
For printing, advertising, stationery and blank books		105 98
For fuel and lights		10 96
For taxes and assessments		589 30
For incidental expenses per petty cash (janitor)		12 00
Cash on hand 31st December, 1866, after the transactions of the day:		
Deposited in bank	$3,858 89	
Deposited in vault	4,960 60	
		8,819 49
		$124,800 79

ASSETS OF THE QUEENS COUNTY SAVINGS BANK ON THE TWENTY-EIGHTH DAY OF OCTOBER, 1867.

	Par value.	Cost.
Bonds and mortgages		$60,900 00
U. S. bonds and treasury notes	$76,000 00	76,000 00
New York State bonds	30,000 00	29,775 00
Bonds of cities in this State (New York and Brooklyn)	14,000 00	13,960 00
Bonds of counties in this State (Queens)	10,000 00	10,000 00
Cash in bank		11,289 04
Cash in vault		851 62
		$202,775 66

Examined and verified by one member of finance committee.

OTHER FACTS.

Number of trustees authorized by charter, twenty-four.

Number of trustees who are directors in any bank of issue where deposits of this institution are kept, not stated.

Investments yielding no revenue, none.

Average amount kept on deposit in bank, estimated at $10,000.

Regular meetings of the board, monthly.

Number constituting a quorum, six.

Average attendance at regular meetings during 1866, not stated.

Loans on bond and mortgage are effected on authority of finance committee.

Purchases or sales of stocks, the same.

Temporary loans, the same.

Deposits in banks of discount, not stated.

Examinations of books, for proof of accuracy and fidelity, and assets, are made by a committee of three trustees appointed twice in each year.

RHINEBECK SAVINGS BANK.

CASH TRANSACTIONS DURING THE YEAR 1866.

RECEIPTS.

Cash on hand 1st January, 1866, before the transactions of the day		$2,645 72
Deposited in bank	$2,645 72	

From depositors	$21,976 46
From interest on stocks	3,072 50
From interest on deposits in bank	246 09
	$27,940 77

PAYMENTS.

To depositors		$14,000 94
For purchase of stocks and bonds		5,000 00
For salaries		200 00
For taxes and assessments		274 53
For incidental expenses per petty cash		8 50
Cash on hand 31st December, 1866, after the transactions of the day:		
Deposited in bank	$8,456 80	
		8,456 80
		$27,940 77

ASSETS OF THE RHINEBECK SAVINGS BANK ON THE 1ST DAY OF JULY, 1867.

	Par value.	Cost.
U. S. bonds and treasury notes	$5,000 00	
Bonds of cities in this State	10,000 00	$52,500 00
Bonds of counties in this State	35,000 00	
Cash in bank		2,274 36
		$54,774 36

Examined and verified by two trustees.

OTHER FACTS.

Number of trustees authorized by charter, twenty.

Number of trustees who are directors in any bank of issue where deposits of this institution are kept, two.

Investments yielding no revenue, none.

Average amount kept on deposit in bank with interest, $5,000.

Regular meetings of the board, monthly.

Number constituting a quorum, seven.

Average attendance at regular meetings during 1866, seven.

Loans on bond and mortgage are effected on authority of finance committee.

Purchases or sales of stocks, the same.

Temporary loans, the same.

Deposits in banks of discount, the same.

Examinations of books, for proof of accuracy and fidelity, and assets, are made by examining committee, twice in each year.

ROME SAVINGS BANK.

CASH TRANSACTIONS DURING THE YEAR 1866.

Receipts.

Cash on hand 1st January, 1866, before the transactions of the day		$54,552 30
Deposited in bank	$53,917 47	
Deposited in treasurer's hands	634 83	
From depositors		223,163 52
From interest on mortgages		12,973 30
From interest on stocks		1,400 00
From interest on loans		4,594 94
From interest on deposits in banks		669 18
From mortgages paid, called in or foreclosed		14,143 59
From repayment of loans		35,675 42
From sales of stocks and county bonds		24,805 12
		$371,977 37

Payments.

To depositors	$206,917 41
Loans on bond and mortgage	70,523 66
Loans on stocks and other securities	56,514 20
For salaries	1,900 00
For printing, advertising, stationery and blank books,	156 50
For taxes and assessments	2,792 49
For incidental expenses per petty cash	35 98
Cash on hand 31st December, 1866, after the transactions of the day	33,137 13
	$371,977 37

Assets of the Rome Savings Bank on the 1st Day of July, 1867.

Bonds and mortgages	$236,583 85
	Cost.
New York State bonds	40,000 00
Loans on stocks and other securities, available fund,	92,925 35

Accrued interest	$10,996 48
Cash in bank	26,105 39
Cash in treasurer's hands	782 62
	$407,393 69

Examined and verified by president and treasurer.

OTHER FACTS.

Number of trustees authorized by charter, thirteen.

Number of trustees who are directors in any bank of issue where deposits of this institution are kept, six.

Investments yielding no revenue, none.

Average amount kept on deposit in bank with interest, $22,544.

Regular meetings of the board, monthly, but seldom held.

Number constituting a quorum, seven.

Average attendance at regular meetings during 1866, not stated.

Loans on bond and mortgage are effected on authority of the finance committee.

Purchases or sales of stocks, the same.

Temporary loans, the same.

Deposits in banks of discount, the same.

Examinations of books for proof of accuracy and fidelity, and assets, are made by finance committee twice in each year.

REMARKS.

The large amount of bond and mortgage investment is supposed to be offset by the correspondingly large amount held available. The securities for loans are nearly all personal. I believe, from the statement made to me by the treasurer, that they are uniformly perfectly good, but I am not thereby reconciled to the principle of admitting securities that *may be—not good.*

SAG HARBOR SAVINGS BANK.

CASH TRANSACTIONS DURING THE YEAR 1866.

RECEIPTS.

Cash on hand 1st January, 1866, before the transactions of the day		$3,304 04
H. G. Reeve	$815 00	
Deposited in bank	1,410 54	
Deposited in vault	1,078 50	

From depositors	$37,827 05
From interest on mortgages	3,520 87
From interest on stocks	2,128 17
From interest on loans, offset rent	60 00
From interest on deposits in bank	39 15
From premium on gold	236 88
From mortgages paid, called in or foreclosed	3,125 00
From sales of stocks	6,518 99
From rents	18 75
	$56,778 90

PAYMENTS.

To depositors		$25,477 15
Loans on bond and mortgage		18,050 00
For purchase of stocks and bonds		6,892 88
(Par value thereof	$6,800)	
For furniture and fixtures		175 00
For rent		60 00
For salaries		500 00
For printing, advertising, stationery and blank books		49 91
For fuel and lights		15 00
For taxes and assessments		540 85
For incidental expenses per petty cash		250 37
Cash on hand 31st December, 1866, after the transactions of the day:		
Deposited in bank	$4,677 01	
Deposited in vault	90 73	
		4,767 74
		$56,778 90

ASSETS OF THE SAG HARBOR SAVINGS BANK ON THE 1ST DAY OF JANUARY, 1867.

Bonds and mortgages	$65,745 37
	Cost.
United States bonds and treasury notes	33,550 00
Loans on stocks and other securities, available fund, accrued interest	1,768 89

Cash in bank	$4,677 01
Cash in vault	90 73
	$105,832 00
Less coupons stolen	135 00
	$105,697 00

Examined and verified by the president and treasurer.

Other Facts.

Number of trustees authorized by charter, thirty.

Number of trustees who are directors in any bank of issue where deposits of this institution are kept, none.

Investments yielding no revenue, none.

Average amount kept on deposit in bank with interest, $1,500.

Regular meetings of the board, quarter yearly.

Number constituting a quorum, ten.

Average attendance at regular meetings during 1866, fifteen.

Loans on bond and mortgage are effected on authority of the funding committee.

Purchases or sales of stocks, the same.

Temporary loans, the same.

Deposits in banks of discount are made by the president and treasurer.

Examinations of books, for proof of accuracy and fidelity, and assets, are made by a special committee annually.

Remarks.

The large proportion of bond and mortgage investments of this savings bank may, perhaps, be sustained by the rural character of the community, and the fact that the balance of securities are governments and cash. This institution met with quite a severe loss from robbery by burglars soon after its organization. That it should recover from its embarrassment, continue to do business, and accumulate a surplus of four per cent, and all in six years from its commencement, speaks well for its management.

SCHENECTADY SAVINGS BANK.

CASH TRANSACTIONS DURING THE YEAR 1866.

Receipts.

Cash on hand 1st January, 1866, before the transactions of the day	$226,428 36
From depositors	149,966 03
From interest on mortgages	6,267 14
From interest on stocks	3,500 00
From interests on deposits in bank	4,043 74
From premium on gold	1,174 69
From mortgages paid, called in or foreclosed	12,605 00
	$403,984 96

Payments.

To depositors	$179,133 38
Loans on bond and mortgage	4,100 00
For repairs	5 00
For furniture and fixtures	48 00
For rent	300 00
For salaries	2,300 00
For printing, advertising, stationery and blank books	28 50
For taxes and assessments	1,795 45
For incidental expenses per petty cash	853 36
For internal revenue stamps	40 00
For Bank Department draft	3 16
Cash on hand 31st December, 1866, after the transactions of the day	215,378 11
	$403,984 96

Assets of the Schenectady Savings Bank on the 28th Day of October, 1867.

	Par value.	Cost.
Bonds and mortgages		$87,233 43
U. S. bonds and treasury notes	$50,000	50,386 42
New York State bonds	10,000	8,832 95
Cash in bank		242,901 35
Cash in vault		698 00
		$390,052 15

Examined and verified by president and accountant.

Other Facts.

Number of trustees authorized by charter, thirteen.

Number of trustees who are directors in any bank of issue where deposits of this institution are kept, seven.

Investments yielding no revenue, none.

Average amount kept on deposit in bank with interest, $204,165.

Regular meetings of the board, not stated.

Number constituting a quorum, not stated.

Average attendance at regular meetings during 1866, not stated.

Loans on bond and mortgage are effected on authority of funding committee.

Purchases or sales of stocks, the same.

Temporary loans, none made.

Deposits in banks of discount are made by authority of the board, a majority of whom are directors in the bank where deposits are kept.

Examinations of books, for proof of accuracy and fidelity, and assets, not stated.

Remarks.

The business of the institution is carried on, in and by the Schenectady Bank, whose directors form a majority of the board of trustees. The effect is seen, in the large amount kept in bank. The average amount for the year 1866 is stated above; also, in cash transactions, the total amount of interest received by the savings bank on that deposit. It will be found to be less than two per cent. Such is the general tendency of all savings banks when officered and conducted by banks of issue; the principal advantage inures to the latter.

SING SING SAVINGS BANK.

CASH TRANSACTIONS DURING THE YEAR 1866.

Receipts.

Cash on hand 1st January, 1866, before the transactions of the day	$4,871 37
From depositors	90,509 26
From interest on mortgages	1,191 50
From interest on stocks	7,480 02
From interest on loans	145 58
From premium on gold	1,091 15

From mortgages paid, called in or foreclosed		$685 00
From redemption of stocks		2,000 00
From repayment of loans		4,000 00
From exchanging 5-20 bonds, and discount on U. S. bonds		1,039 50
		$113,013 38

PAYMENTS.

To depositors		$39,652 67
Loans on bond and mortgage		8,800 00
Loans on stocks and other securities		4,000 00
For purchase of stocks and bonds		56,629 34
(Par value thereof	$56,000 00)	
For rent		150 00
For salaries		300 00
For printing, advertising, stationery and blank books,		36 00
For taxes and assesments		655 24
For incidental expenses per petty cash		3 75
Cash on hand 31st December, 1866, after the transactions of the day		2,786 38
		$113,013 38

ASSETS OF THE SING SING SAVINGS BANK ON THE 1ST DAY OF JULY, 1867.

	Par value.	Cost.
Bonds and mortgages		$28,888 00
U. S. bonds and treasury notes	$153,000 00	153,000 00
New York State bonds	24,000 00	24,000 00
Bonds of cities in this State	20,000 00	20,000 00
Cash in vault		6,464 53
		$232,352 53

Examined and verified by three trustees.

OTHER FACTS.

Number of trustees authorized by charter, twelve.

Number of trustees who are directors in any bank of issue where deposits of this institution are kept, none.

Investments yielding no revenue, none.

Average amount kept on deposit in bank with interest, not stated; must be small.

Regular meetings of the board, monthly.

Number constituting a quorum, six.

Average attendance at regular meetings during 1866, eight.

Loans on bond and mortgage are effected on authority of an affirmative vote of at least six trustees.

Purchases or sales of stocks, the same.

Temporary loans, the same.

Deposits in banks of discount, the same.

Examinations of books, for proof of accuracy and fidelity, and assets, are made by a committee of trustees semi-annually.

SKANEATELES SAVINGS BANK.

(Commenced business after 1st January, 1866.)

CASH TRANSACTIONS DURING THE YEAR 1866.

Receipts.

From depositors	$93,045 01
From interest on mortgages	49 00
From interest on stocks	207 57
From interest on loans	42 88
From interest on deposits in bank	161 12
From repayment of loans	3,500 00
From exchange	26 09
	$97,031 67

Payments.

To depositors	$41,030 01
Loans on bond and mortgage	9,000 00
Loans on stocks and other securities	17,700 00
For purchase of stocks and bonds	21,097 75
(Par value thereof $21,500)	
For furniture and fixtures	38 25
For printing, advertising, stationery and blank books	147 73
For fuel and lights	14 63
For taxes and assessments	20 98
For incidental expenses per petty cash	32 38

Cash on hand 31st December, 1866, after the transactions of the day:		
Deposited in bank	$7,723 53	
Deposited in vault	226 41	
		$7,949 94
		$97,031 67

ASSETS OF THE SKANEATELES SAVINGS BANK ON THE 1ST DAY OF JULY, 1867.

	Par value.	Cost.
Bonds and mortgages		$17,100 00
U. S. bonds and treasury notes	$400 00	$400 00
Bonds of counties in this State		19,000 00
Bonds of towns in this State		6,000 00
Loans on stocks and other securities, available fund		16,125 00
Fixtures		451 91
Cash in bank		16,261 91
Cash in vault		711 56
		$76,050 38

Examined and verified by two trustees.

OTHER FACTS.

Number of trustees authorized by charter, fifteen.

Number of trustees who are directors in any bank of issue where deposits of this institution are kept, five.

Investments yielding no revenue, none.

Average amount kept on deposit in bank with interest, $5,000.

Regular meetings of the board, quarter yearly.

Number constituting a quorum, eight.

Average attendance at regular meetings during 1866, ten.

Loans on bond and mortgage are effected on authority of loan committee and attorney.

Purchases or sales of stocks are effected on authority of loan committee.

Temporary loans, the same.

Deposits in banks of discount, the same.

Examinations of books, for proof of accuracy and fidelity, and assets, are made by examining committee at each regular meeting.

SOUTHOLD SAVINGS BANK.

CASH TRANSACTIONS DURING THE YEAR 1866.

Receipts.

Cash on hand 1st January, 1866, before the transactions of the day		$21,482 44
Deposited in vault	$21,482 44	
From depositors		102,607 68
From interest on mortgages		7,881 64
From interest on stocks		5,243 34
From interest on loans		451 92
From premium on gold		1,893 09
From mortgages paid, called in or foreclosed		6,611 00
From repayment of loans		30,506 63
From sales of real estate		3,300 00
From sales of stocks		2,452 77
From rents		21 50
From other sources		8 79
		$182,460 80

Payments.

To depositors		$72,744 69
Loans on bond and mortgage		57,868 00
Loans on stocks and other securities		30,828 16
For purchase of stocks and bonds		12,438 00
(Par value thereof	12,400 00)	
For salaries		600 00
For printing, advertising, stationery and blank books,		35 50
For taxes and assessments		1,201 57
For incidental expenses per petty cash		110 59
For other expenses, enumerated below		76 11
Finance committee, $43.30; accrued interest on mortgages, &c., bought, $23.81; examining committee, $6,00; bank note reporter, $3.00.		
Cash on hand 31st December, 1866, after the transactions of the day:		
Deposited in vault	$6,558 18	
		6,558 18
		$182,460 80

Assets of the Southold Savings Bank, on the 27th Day of August, 1867.

	Par value.	Cost.
Bonds and mortgages		$190,157 10
U. S. bonds and treasury notes	$95,200	93,502 50
New York State bonds	7,000	7,245 00
Bonds of cities in this State	10,000	9,387 50
Loans on stocks and other securities		3,000 00
Personal securities, available fund		7,548 57
Cash in vault		3,714 33
		$314,555 00

Examined and verified by four trustees.

Other Facts.

Number of trustees authorised by charter, twenty-one.

Number of trustees who are directors in any bank of issue where deposits of this institution are kept, none.

Investments yielding no revenue, none.

Average amount kept on deposit in bank with interest, none.

Regular meetings of the board, quarter yearly.

Number constituting a quorum, eight.

Average attendance at regular meetings during 1866, fifteen.

Loans on bond and mortgage are effected by finance committee, authorized by the board.

Purchases or sales of stocks, the same, but special authority required.

Temporary loans are made by authority of the board.

Deposits in banks of discount, none.

Examinations of books, for proof of accuracy and fidelity, and assets, are made by examining committee semi-annually, or oftener.

Remarks.

The same feature of large bond and mortgage investments appears here, that we have observed in other savings banks in agricultural districts.

The institution is a fine illustration of what may be done with a savings bank in a strictly rural neighborhood.

ULSTER COUNTY SAVINGS INSTITUTION.

CASH TRANSACTIONS DURING THE YEAR 1866.

RECEIPTS.

Cash on hand 1st January, 1866, before the transactions of the day		$12,103 79
Deposited in bank	$12,103 79	
From depositors		275,847 08
From interest on mortgages From interest on stocks From interest on loans From interest on deposits in bank From premium on gold		32,757 76
From mortgages paid, called in or foreclosed		22,828 79
From repayment of loans		27,050 00
		$370,587 42

PAYMENTS.

To depositors		$226,621 44
Loans on bond and mortgage		49,150 14
Loans on stocks and other securities		4,950 00
For purchase of stocks and bonds		53,170 00
(Par value thereof	$50,570)	
For furniture and fixtures		625 00
For rent		100 00
For salaries		1,500 00
For printing, advertising, stationery and blank books,		175 00
For taxes and assessments		1,520 89
Cash on hand 31st December, 1866, after the transactions of the day:		
Deposited in bank	$32,774 95	
		32,774 95
		$370,587 42

ASSETS OF THE ULSTER COUNTY SAVINGS INSTITUTION ON THE 1ST DAY OF OCTOBER, 1867.

	Par value.	Cost.
Bonds and mortgages		$346,679 48
U. S. bonds and treasury notes	$259,950 00	264,595 00
Bonds of counties in this State (Ulster)		48,300 00

Loans on stocks and other securities, available fund,	$13,550 00
Real estate	5,000 00
Cash in bank	18,613 43
	$696,737 91

Not verified.

Other Facts.

Number of trustees authorized by charter, twenty-one.

Number of trustees who are directors in any bank of issue where deposits of this institution are kept, six.

Investments yielding no revenue, none.

Average amount kept on deposit in bank, estimated at $15,000.

Regular meetings of the board, quarter yearly.

Number constituting a quorum, five.

Average attendance at regular meetings during 1866, not stated.

Loans on bond and mortgage are effected on authority of finance committee.

Purchases or sales of stock, the same.

Temporary loans, the same.

Deposits in banks of discount are made by authority of the board.

Examinations of books, for proof of accuracy and fidelity, and assets, not stated.

Remarks.

Until this year the books of this institution have been so kept that it was absolutely impossible to get from them, with any certainty, the facts called for by me. The statement of cash transactions is, therefore, reliable as an approximate estimate only, the balances being forced. Under the direction of a new financial officer there is the assurance of a different state of affairs in the future. From what I saw while at the institution I am confident that this assurance will be realized.

WESTCHESTER COUNTY SAVINGS BANK.

CASH TRANSACTIONS DURING THE YEAR 1866.

Receipts.

Cash on hand 1st January, 1866, before the transactions of the day		$13,313 90
Deposited in bank	$10,345 85	
Deposited in vault	2,968 05	

From depositors	$224,534 64
From interest on mortgages From interest on stocks From interest on loans From deposits in bank From premium on gold	21,655 98
From mortgages paid, called in or foreclosed	20,458 96
From redemption of stocks	36,500 00
From repayment of loans	1,500 00
From estate of Elijah Yerks and suspense account	106 90
	$318,070 38

PAYMENTS.

To depositors		$136,201 67
Loans on bond and mortgage		58,858 96
Loans on stocks and other securities		1,500 00
For purchase of stocks and bonds		46,485 80
(Par value thereof	$46,500)	
For repairs For furniture and fixtures		446 58
For salaries		1,593 15
For printing, advertising, stationery and blank books		221 28
For fuel and lights		76 47
For taxes and assessments		1,674 65
For incidental expenses per petty cash		13 06
Cash on hand 31st December, 1866, after the transactions of the day:		
Deposited in bank	$65,802 66	
Deposited in vault	5,196 10	
		70,998 76
		$318,070 38

ASSETS OF THE WESTCHESTER COUNTY SAVINGS BANK ON THE 17TH DAY OF JUNE, 1867.

	Par value.	Cost.
Bonds and mortgages		$122,687 29
U. S. bonds and treasury notes	$50,000	50,000 00
New York State bonds	25,000	25,000 00
Bonds of cities in this State	71,594	71,199 00
Bonds of counties in this State	37,500	37,500 00
Loans on stocks and other securities, available fund		1,750 00

Real estate, cost		$4,000 00
Cash in bank		63,364 40
Cash in vault		3,942 83
		$379,443 52

Examined and verified by two trustees.

Other Facts.

Number of trustees authorized by charter, twenty-three.

Number of trustees who are directors in any bank of issue where deposits of this institution are kept, not stated.

Investments yielding no revenue, none.

Average amount kept on deposit in bank, estimated at $50,000.

Regular meetings of the board, monthly.

Number constituting a quorum, eight.

Average attendance at regular meetings during 1866, not stated.

Loans on bond and mortgage are effected on authority of a vote of the board.

Purchases or sales of stocks, the same.

Temporary loans, the same.

Deposits in banks of discount, the same.

Examinations of books, for proof of accuracy and fidelity, and assets, are made by examining committee semi-annually.

YONKERS SAVINGS BANK.

CASH TRANSACTIONS DURING THE YEAR 1866.

Receipts.

Cash on hand 1st January, 1866, before the transactions of the day		$19,430 90
Deposited in bank	$18,131 79	
Deposited in vault	1,299 11	
From depositors		253,718 76
From interest on mortgages		2,767 63
From interest on stocks		15,647 56
From interest on loans		502 74
From interest on deposits in bank		684 63
From premium on gold		3,617 04
From mortgages paid, called in or foreclosed		10,450 00
From redemption of stocks		17,000 00

From repayment of loans	$6,855 00
From rents	119 00
	$330,793 26

Payments.

To depositors		$213,297 88
Loans on bond and mortgage		25,800 00
Loans on stocks and other securities		8,210 00
For purchase of stock and bonds		28,700 00
(Par value thereof	$28,700)	
For building or construction account		12,405 67
For repairs		2 95
For furniture and fixtures		19 00
For rent		250 00
For salaries		1,699 92
For printing, advertising, stationery and blank books		284 75
For fuel and lights		51 68
For taxes and assessments		1,400 41
For incidental expenses, per petty cash		24 79
Cash on hand 31st December, 1866, after the transactions of the day:		
Deposited in bank	$35,596 42	
Deposited in vault	3,049 79	
		38,646 21
		$330,793 26

Assets of the Yonkers Savings Bank on the 6th day of September, 1867.

	Par value.	Cost.
Bonds and mortgages		$45,440 00
U. S. bonds and treasury notes	$160,000 00	162,822 50
New York State bonds	25,000 00	25,000 00
Bonds of other States	17,000 00	15,368 75
Bonds of counties in this State (Westchester)	78,200 00	78,200 00
Loans on stocks and other securities, available fund		2,200 00
Other securities		8,000 00
Real estate		29,952 86

Cash in bank	$20,794 25
Cash in vault	452 57
	$388,230 93

Examined and verified by treasurer and clerk.

Other Facts.

Number of trustees authorized by charter, forty-one.

Number of trustees who are directors in any bank of issue where deposits of this institution are kept, nine.

Investments yielding no revenue, none.

Average amount kept on deposit in bank with interest, $17,115.

Regular meetings of the board, monthly.

Number constituting a quorum, eleven.

Average attendance at regular meetings during 1866, thirteen.

Loans on bond and mortgage are effected on authority of affirmative vote of at least eleven trustees, not more than two trustees dissenting.

Purchases or sales of stocks, the same.

Temporary loans, the same.

Deposits in banks of discount, the same.

Examinations of books, for proof of accuracy and fidelity, and assets, are made by examining committee semi-annually.

(B.)

Analytical statement of the condition of Savings Banks in this State on the 1*st of January*, 1867.

The bases for the following calculations were derived wholly from the annual reports of savings banks made to the Bank Department, January 1, 1867.

The statement comprises the following:

1. The per cent of surplus to total assets.
2. Excess of deposits over withdrawals during the year 1866.
3. Excess of withdrawals over deposits during the year 1866.
4. Interest received in 1866.
5. Interest credited to depositors in 1866.
6. Per cent of interest received in 1866 calculated upon the assets reported January 1, 1866.
7. Per cent of interest credited to depositors in 1866 calculated upon the same basis.
8. Per cent of interest received in 1866 calculated upon the assets reported January 1, 1867.
9. Per cent of interest credited to depositors in 1866 calculated upon the same basis.

[Concerning the last four items it will be seen that only approximates can be obtained, for the reason that the assets on which interest is received is a continually changing amount. To estimate on the assets reported at the beginning of the year, the deposits meantime increasing, will give as a result a higher rate of interest than is received. On the other hand, to estimate on the assets at the end of the year, is to include some investments on which no interest or but little has been received, and will show a less per cent than is in fact realized. The reverse conditions will appear where the deposits of a savings bank are diminishing instead of increasing. Perhaps a fairer average might be obtained by taking the assets reported on the 1st of July of the year for which the per cent is estimated. But these are not tabulated, and, besides, a better comparison can be made by a calculation upon the assets at both the beginning and end of the period. Hence the calculation in the manner stated.]

10. Per cent of investments in bond and mortgage.
11. Per cent of investments in U. S. stocks and treasury notes.
12. Per cent of investments in New York State stocks.
13. Per cent of investments in city, county and town bonds.
14. Per cent of investments in bonds of other States.
15. Per cent of investments in other securities.
16. Per cent of assets deposited in banks.
17. Per cent of assets in cash on hand.
18. Per cent of assets loaned on stock or other securities.
19. Per cent of assets otherwise invested.

The calculations in this table were very carefully made, being carried to eight decimals, and thoroughly tested by accurate proofs.

By dropping the remote decimals, as was necessary for practical use, something of this perfect accuracy is, of course, sacrificed; but the results will be found to be as nearly perfect as it is possible to state them in hundredths per cent.

(B.)

	No. 1. Per cent of surplus to assets.	No. 2. Excess of deposits over withdrawals in 1866.	No. 3. Excess of withdrawals over deposits in 1866.	No. 4. Interest received in 1866.	No. 5. Interest credited, 1866.	No. 6. Per cent of interest received on assets, as reported Jan. 1, 1866.	No. 7. Per cent of interest credited on assets, as reported Jan. 1, 1866.	No. 8. Per cent of interest received on assets, as reported Jan. 1, 1867.	No. 9. Per cent of interest credited on assets, as reported Jan. 1, 1867.
CITY OF ALBANY.									
Albany Savings Bank	04.67	$28,173 45	....	$90,683 93	$76,174 65	04.38	03.68	04.15	03.48
Albany City Savings Bank	....	....	$44 79	13,528 77	13,528 77	04.23	04.23	04.06	04.06
Albany Exchange Savings Bank	00.50	23,811 78	....	3,889 24	3,785 02	03.65	03.55	02.91	02.84
Mechanics and Farmers' Savings Bank	01.62	13,141 51	....	50,383 87	37,024 20	05.99	04.40	04.85	03.56
CITY OF AUBURN.									
Auburn Savings Institution	05.36	81,090 19	....	49,407 92	39,950 42	06.59	05.33	05.70	04.61
Mutual Savings Bank of Auburn	01.48	168,886 67	....	12,017 40	7,918 84	16.22	10.69	04.88	03.22
CITY OF BROOKLYN.									
Brooklyn Savings Bank	06.67	193,693 28	....	345,595 10	258,601 51	05.94	04.44	05.63	04.21
Dime Savings Bank of Brooklyn	04.99	747,565 58	....	155,545 26	104,505 52	08.62	05.79	06.11	04.10
Dime Savings Bank of Williamsburgh	02.18	197,737 02	....	16,425 70	9,566 42	08.59	05.00	04.10	02.39
East Brooklyn Savings Bank	03.23	46,731 87	....	13,928 07	9,914 76	06.66	04.74	05.24	03.73
Emigrant Savings Bank	00.64	28,441 14	....	6,055 14	4,084 79	08.89	06.00	06.02	04.06
German Savings Bank	00.61	140,258 93	....	2,724 13	968 06	....	....	01.93	00.68
Kings County Savings Institution	04.83	194,206 44	....	36,986 76	30,367 54	07.67	06.30	05.08	04.17
Long Island Savings Bank	01.05	127,387 30	....	3,272 95	1,900 83	....	....	02.50	01.45
South Brooklyn Savings Institution	07.31	154,912 72	....	125,317 50	84,522 99	07.10	04.79	06.13	04.13
Williamsburgh Savings Bank	08.53	203,999 09	....	338,241 76	259,698 91	06.29	04.83	05.71	04.39
CITY OF BUFFALO.									
Buffalo Savings Bank	06.92	384,376 77	....	173,413 04	119,617 81	08.00	05.52	06.47	04.46

Emigrant Savings Bank	00.19	37,051 60		5,592 43	6,122 52	04.78	05.24	03.51	03.84
Erie County Savings Bank	06.51	372,013 27		193,308 45	131,611 27	06.81	04.64	05.77	03.93
Western Savings Bank	05.05	69,638 99		19,069 65	14,673 79	03.73	02.87	03.11	02.40
CITY OF NEW YORK.									
Atlantic Savings Bank	05.37	358,330 17		74,344 22	55,208 63	06.71	04.98	04.85	03.60
Bank for Savings	08.03		46,866 84	877,782 68	570,202 50	05.97	03.88	05.67	03.68
Bowery Savings Bank	09.61		344,934 59	925,960 02	753,957 26	05.50	04.48	05.36	04.37
Broadway Savings Institution	09.32	80,927 66		76,699 70	60,194 71	05.92	04.64	05.23	04.10
Citizens' Savings Bank	04.95	1,450,237 82		197,763 27	93,453 40	10.86	05.13	05.89	02.78
Dry Dock Savings Institution	05.71	350,613 02		342,862 39	243,792 09	07.72	04.79	06.80	04.22
East River Savings Institution	10.73	95,808 60		139,372 96	88,152 46	07.10	04.49	06.42	05.06
Emigrant Industrial Savings Bank	05.63	303,098 33		344,633 06	248,362 32	06.73	04.85	05.99	04.32
Franklin Savings Bank	02.57	107,696 35		12,380 56	6,500 47	09.64	05.06	04.96	02 60
German Savings Bank	03.30		433,924 18	267,081 20	185,585 18	05.97	04.15	06.28	04.36
Greenwich Savings Bank	07.96		20,220 43	312,379 84	207,577 36	06.35	04.22	06.05	04.02
Harlem Savings Bank	01.18	30,980 94		4,993 85	2,582 81	11.93	06.17	06.53	03.38
Institution for the Savings of Merchants' Clerks	10.96	150,183 97		115,253 08	106,335 39	06.59	06.08	05.65	05.22
Irving Savings Institution	06.63	138,714 87		114,940 79	75,172 75	07.41	04.84	06.80	04.45
Manhattan Savings Institution	04.32	410,912 49		250,587 76	200,348 24	05.97	04.77	05.21	04.16
Market Savings Bank	01.97	277,488 84		19,088 45	14,751 18	06.36	04.92	03.20	02.47
Mechanics' and Traders' Savings Institution	05.84	273,442 75		156,990 45	111,427 52	07.55	05.36	06.46	04.58
Metropolitan Savings Bank	06.78	496,150 56		135,469 19	78,292 23	08.91	05.15	06.31	03.65
New York Savings Bank	05.72	181,587 43		35,422 48	23,156 40	08.02	05.24	05.45	03.56
North River Savings Bank		11,627 60							
Seamen's Bank for Savings	09.85		495,143 47	622,375 03	412,802 64	06.72	04.45	06.71	04.45
Sixpenny Savings Bank	01.80	139,453 88		23,303 47	14,629 73	07.58	04.76	05.22	03.27
Third Avenue Savings Bank	03.72	1,393,991 19		199,612 72	128,447 81	08.17	05.26	04.95	03.18
Union Dime Savings Institution	06.06	782,111 39		122,194 09	82,003 33	07.27	04.88	04.62	03.10
Up-Town Savings Bank		113,348 19		1,765 51	1,369 91			01.53	01.19
CITY OF ROCHESTER.									
Monroe County Savings Bank	06.11	397,820 28		102,241 78	83,797 63	06.09	04.99	04.90	04.01
Rochester Savings Bank	08.25	71,610 12		135,786 36	90,807 43	05.69	03.81	05.53	03.70
CITY OF SYRACUSE.									
Onondaga County Savings Bank	07.60	246,897 23		99,256 90	66,924 49	07.05	04.75	05.94	04.01
Syracuse Savings Institution	06.99		1,228 59	65,020 15	38,175 68	07.00	04.11	06.68	03.92
CITY OF TROY.									
Central Savings Bank		606 74		2,175 33	2,175 33	03.90	03.90	03.86	03.86
Manufacturers' Savings Bank			44,379 97	1,370 93	1,370 93	02.00	02.00	06.03	06.03

B—Continued.

	No. 1. Per cent of surplus to assets.	No. 2. Excess of deposits over withdrawals in 1866.	No. 3. Excess of withdrawals over deposits in 1866.	No. 4. Interest received in 1866.	No. 5. Interest credited, 1866.	No. 6. Per cent of interest received on assets, as reported Jan. 1, 1866.	No. 7. Per cent of interest credited on assets, as reported Jan. 1, 1866.	No. 8. Per cent of interest received on assets, as reported Jan. 1, 1867.	No. 9. Per cent of interest credited on assets, as reported Jan. 1, 1867.
Mutual Savings Bank	....	$18,244 07	....	$4,724 07	$4,724 07	04.37	04.37	03.60	03.60
State Savings Bank	00.16	....	$8,212 59	7,229 42	7,139 45	04.19	04.14	04.71	04.65
Troy Savings Bank	02.89	52,318 82	....	103,808 28	84,435 11	05.76	04.69	05.48	04.46
CITY OF UTICA.									
Central City Savings Institution	01.22	40,185 84	....	5,285 48	3,665 47	05.87	04.07	04.05	02.81
National Savings Bank of Utica	00.35	315,470 11	....	5,718 91	3,879 76	....	....	01.78	01.21
Savings Bank of Utica	08.88	222,576 00	....	86,993 77	61,412 95	06.33	04.47	05.37	03.79
OTHER LOCALITIES.									
Chautauqua County Savings Bank, Fredonia	00.02	25,296 36	....	145 23	134 25	....	....	00.57	00.52
Chenango County Savings Bank, Norwich	00.85	....	4,886 07	2,427 39	1,259 66	02.83	01.47	03.00	01.56
Cohoes Saving Institution, Cohoes	....	28,902 05	....	6,996 17	6,996 17	03.90	03.90	03.34	03.34
Corning Savings Bank, Corning (closing)	53.50	....	567 88	51 85	9 98	17.00	03.28	16.06	03.09
Cortland Savings Bank, Cortland	....	21,128 82	....	14 66	....	....	....	00.07	....
Elmira Savings Bank, Elmira (closing)	19.44	....	....	....	....	....	....	....	....
Fishkill Savings Institute, Fishkill	15.71	10,487 68	....	9,058 50	6,627 02	05.71	04.18	05.00	03.66
Hudson City Savings Institution, Hudson	08.97	2,205 15	....	19,616 00	12,008 38	06.40	03.92	06.01	03.68
Jefferson County Savings Bank, Watertown	06.33	....	24,034 44	7,735 02	5,198 96	05.75	03.87	06.90	04.64
Mechanics' Savings B'k of Fishkill-on-Hudson	01.28	38,525 00	....	760 90	262 06	....	....	01.95	00.67
Newburgh Savings Bank, Newburgh	09.57	13,186 41	....	35,728 17	30,906 13	04.42	03.82	04.17	03.60
New Rochelle Savings Bank, New Rochelle	01.60	9,339 87	....	433 48	276 16	....	....	04.43	02.82
Niagara County Savings Bank, Lockport	04.47	1,759 82	....	72 90	187 14	01.88	04.82	01.32	03.37
Oneida Savings Bank, Oneida	00.72	75,939 96	....	366 96	58 60	....	....	00.48	00.08

Oswego City Savings Bank, Oswego	04.63	....	14,659 41	19,357 48	11,938 20	06.02	03.71	06.30	03.89
Peekskill Savings Bank, Peekskill	07.49	38,815 08	....	19,330 17	10,696 14	07.66	04.24	06.33	03.50
Port Chester Savings Bank, Port Chester	00.91	25,542 58	....	4,124 58	2,445 01	11.27	06.68	06.35	03.76
Poughkeepsie Savings Bank, Poughkeepsie	09.14	32,935 45	....	71,399 79	43,938 18	06.56	04.04	06.04	03.72
Queens County Savings Bank, Flushing	07.22	29,806 28	....	11,646 62	10,810 34	08.54	07.93	06.65	06.17
Rhinebeck Savings Bank, Rhinebeck	02.34	7,975 52	....	3,318 59	2,016 52	07.22	04.39	05.90	03.58
Rome Savings Bank, Rome	06.38	16,246 11	....	20,272 25	13,688 97	05.72	03.86	05.24	03.54
Sag Harbor Savings Bank, Sag Harbor	04 04	14,644 84	....	5,682 46	4,696 98	06.53	05.40	05.37	04.43
Schenectady Savings Bank, Schenectady	02.94	....	29,166 71	13,810 88	14,934 35	03.61	03.90	03.80	04.11
Sing Sing Savings Bank, Sing Sing	07.57	57,560 64	....	8,576 86	6,704 05	06.55	05.12	04.49	03.51
Skaneateles Savings Bank, Skaneateles	01.94	52,229 39	....	2,103 26	1,071 32	....	....	03.95	02.01
Southold Savings Bank, Southold	05.09	24,862 99	....	13,576 90	13,024 92	06.07	05.83	05.05	04.84
Ulster County Savings Institution, Kingston	03.92	69,435 63	....	34,249 05	21,056 93	07.03	04.32	06.14	03.78
Westchester County Savings Bank, Tarrytown	05.21	106,616 18	....	21,715 08	18,283 21	07.83	06.59	05.67	04.77
Yonkers Savings Bank, Yonkers	06.96	40,420 88	....	23,485 57	11,910 15	08.08	04.10	06.70	03.40
	06.96	12,469,416 45	$1,468,269 96	$8,054,311 99	$5,678,493 02	06.47	04.56	05.68	04.00

B—Continued.

	No. 10. Per cent of bonds and mortgages.	No. 11. Per cent of U. S. stocks and treasury notes.	No. 12. Per cent of New York State stocks	No. 13. Per cent of city, county and town bonds.	No. 14. Per cent of bonds of other States.	No. 15. Per cent of other securities.	No. 16. Per cent of assets deposited in banks.	No. 17. Per cent of assets in cash on hand.	No. 18. Per cent of assets loan'd on stocks & other securities.	No. 19. Per cent of assets otherwise invested.
CITY OF ALBANY.										
Albany Savings Bank	06.88	06.54	24.38	30.44	12.39	....	19.37	....	....	....
Albany City Savings institution	11.08	....	15.60	19.20	....	....	54.12	....	....	....
Albany Exchange Savings Bank	....	37.48	....	....	....	....	62.52	....	....	....
Mechanics' and Farmers' Savings Bank	....	27.94	20.02	....	19.44	17 56	13.76	01.29	....	....
CITY OF AUBURN.										
Auburn Savings Institution	12.38	39.25	01.84	17.50	....	06.97	17.35	00.10	04.60	....
Mutual Savings Bank of Auburn	04.68	37.84	04.06	11.50	....	20.80	05.80	00.86	14.45	....
CITY OF BROOKLYN.										
Brooklyn Savings Bank	19.95	17.10	09.10	31.02	14.44	....	05.04	01.49	01.69	00.16
Dime Savings Bank of Brooklyn	19.75	59.72	03.52	11.08	....	....	01.24	00.54	00.35	03.79
Dime Savings Bank of Williamsburgh	09.09	15.03	....	61.41	....	....	08.96	01.18	04.32	....
East Brooklyn Savings Bank	31.08	54.18	....	11.62	....	....	01.23	01.89	....	....
Emigrant Savings Bank	68.94	11.94	....	....	....	....	08.14	00.70	06.96	03.31
German Savings Bank	28.90	00.62	....	53.14	....	....	09.08	00.49	07.08	00.67
Kings County Savings Institution	15.02	05.50	13.75	47.69	01.37	....	08.96	01.05	01.50	05.15
Long Island Savings Bank	47.60	10.05	....	24.74	....	....	13.54	02.15	01.91	....
South Brooklyn Savings Institution	12.92	43.93	04.89	20.89	02.45	....	02.95	00.61	04.62	01.74
Williamsburgh Savings Bank	16.95	51.21	....	24.12	....	....	02.39	01.36	03.26	00.72
CITY OF BUFFALO.										
Buffalo Savings Bank	18.42	30.73	18.88	11.27	....	....	09.68	03.00	04.00	04.02
Emigrant Savings Bank	06.68	21.92	....	19.46	....	....	29.55	14.36	....	08.03
Erie County Savings Bank	13.49	50.22	11.94	07.04	....	01.47	05.89	01.72	04.75	03.46

Western Savings Bank	16.70	54.05	....	11.59	....	....	16.90	00.75	....	....
City of New York.										
Atlantic Savings Bank	32.92	27.19	01.63	00.06	....	....	07.83	00.68	27.53	02.15
Bank for Savings	20.56	36.97	15.58	15.69	07.83	....	02.67	00.37	....	00.32
Bowery Savings Bank	18.89	42.45	03.83	16.72	07.85	....	01.08	08.06	00.24	00.87
Broadway Savings Institution	10.50	37.15	03.36	38.67	....	....	04.59	00.99	03.10	01.62
Citizens' Savings Bank	26.55	49.45	01.51	02.83	01.19	....	05.27	02.73	08.53	01.94
Dry Dock Savings Institution	17.21	32.75	01.90	34.65	....	....	08.31	03.46	00.79	00.91
East River Savings Institution	17.61	48.11	....	07.78	07.20	....	08.16	00.40	09.37	01.38
Emigrant Industrial Savings Bank	26.51	23.01	....	27.25	14.51	....	04.73	00.93	....	03.05
Franklin Savings Bank	17.04	63.46	02.14	13.74	....	....	02.50	01.12	....	....
German Savings Bank	22.59	36.30	02.43	18.42	04.05	....	11.26	01.34	02.06	01.53
Greenwich Savings Bank	36.25	21.27	08.23	13.70	03.08	....	04.96	01.54	06.01	04.96
Harlem Savings Bank	64.09	15.50	07.87	....	....	....	07.59	02.46	....	02.48
Institution for the Savings of Merchants' Clerks	14.27	41.82	....	17.67	19.92	....	02.55	00.64	00.05	03.07
Irving Savings Institution	17.82	54.30	....	14.79	....	....	03.30	07.55	00.81	01.42
Manhattan Savings Institution	24.72	28 22	07.27	19.25	01.05	....	05.20	00.71	07.25	06.32
Market Savings Bank	02.45	00.11	....	....	....	....	09.87	12.67	74.90	....
Mechanics' and Traders' Savings Institution	20.69	57.60	....	03.04	09.49	....	03.47	09.82	00.25	04.64
Metropolitan Savings Bank	27.28	29.35	06.05	03.82	03.73	....	05.03	01.53	16.96	06.25
New York Savings Bank	19.62	40.42	01.53	15.33	02.30	....	02.54	01.15	15.88	01.23
North River Savings Bank	....	....	....	....	....	....	64.56	35.44	....	....
Seamens' Bank for Savings	26.95	29.66	05.80	12.51	19.79	....	04.22	....	....	01.06
Sixpenny Savings Bank	38.09	43.73	01.12	03.69	02.24	....	07.73	02.81	00.53	....
Third Avenue Savings Bank	13.89	19.54	09.00	02.48	C6.31	04.41	04.28	02.71	36.11	01.26
Union Dime Savings Institution	33.48	37.85	09.08	00.76	....	....	12.41	01.28	01.73	03.41
Up-Town Savings Bank	16.47	22.95	....	17.43	....	04.49	18.55	15.35	....	04.75
City of Rochester.										
Monroe County Savings Bank	25.63	32.81	04.79	15.96	....	....	05.01	04.73	08.54	02.52
Rochester Savings Bank	54.11	13.97	....	05.04	13.71	....	04.42	03.68	01.91	03.16
City of Syracuse.										
Onondaga County Savings Bank	33.68	22.51	....	19.60	....	10.25	06.82	02.20	00.82	04.11
Syracuse Savings Institution	20.92	25.53	....	25.86	....	04.29	06.18	00.92	13.96	02.34
City of Troy.										
Central Savings Bank	....	....	....	....	....	....	100.00	....	....	....
Manufacturers' Savings Bank	....	....	....	....	....	....	100.00	....	....	....
Mutual Savings Bank	....	38.13	19.07	....	....	....	42.80	....	....	....

B—Continued.

	No. 10. Per cent of bonds and mortgages.	No. 11. Per cent of U. S. stocks and treasury notes.	No. 12. Per cent of New York State stocks	No. 13. Per cent of city, county and town bonds.	No. 14. Per cent of bonds of other States.	No. 15. Per cent of other securities.	No. 16. Per cent of assets deposited in banks.	No. 17. Per cent of assets in cash on hand.	No. 18. Per cent of assets loaned on stocks and other securities.	No. 19. Per cent of assets otherwise invested.
State Savings Bank	....	08.79	26.05	01.95	....	....	61.77	01.43	....	—
Troy Savings Bank	16.03	30.40	06.87	23.59	....	....	21.38	00.67	....	01.06
CITY OF UTICA.										
Central City Savings Institution	33.44	15.68	....	....	....	31.28	01.44	04.92	08.05	05.19
National Savings Bank of Utica	05.19	38.10	....	31.27	....	08.46	15.53	01.45	....	....
Savings Bank of Utica	21.60	28.77	10.31	02.10	21.61	00.30	1 . 7	00.10	....	01.12
OTHER LOCALITIES.										
Chautauqua County Savings Bank, Fredonia	25.29	01.45	....	....	....	33.44	06.59	18.12	....	14.98
Chenango County Savings Bank, Norwich	....	....	....	....	....	....	100.00	....	....	....
Cohoes Savings Institution, Cohoes	02.96	38.22	....	....	....	....	53.51	05.32	....	....
Corning Savings Bank, Corning (closing)	....	....	....	....	....	....	94.03	....	....	05.96
Cortland Savings Bank, Cortland	00.61	....	....	35.96	....	09.22	51.45	00.75	....	01.97
Elmira Savings Bank, Elmira (closing)	28.89	....	....	....	....	55.55	15.55	....	....	....
Fishkill Savings Institute, Fishkill	06.79	67.06	05.52	08.50	....	....	06 95	....	....	05.18
Hudson City Savings Institution, Hudson	15.04	45.01	....	16.84	....	....	05.80	03.	09.67	04.57
Jefferson County Savings Bank, Watertown	31.96	19.72	08.92	21.53	....	....	13.68	01.29	....	02.88
Mechanics' Savings Bank of Fishkill-on-Hudson	26.45	43.81	....	....	....	....	10.42	15.86	....	03.43
Newburgh Savings Bank, Newburgh	22.33	53.76	03.50	12.95	00.64	01.17	01.70	....	01.82	02.13
New Rochelle Savings Bank, New Rochelle	....	80.08	....	....	....	....	05.31	12.61	....	02.00
Niagara County Savings Bank, Lockport	05.86	49.62	....	27.06	....	....	....	15.40	....	02.03
Oneida Savings Bank, Oneida	28.44	21.41	11.34	14.65	....	....	10 36	00.02	13.37	00.39
Oswego City Savings Bank, Oswego	14.61	31.43	....	19.95	....	07.10	16.86	02.15	05.49	02.40
Peekskill Savings Bank, Peekskill	15.64	67.42	03.27	07.40	....	....	84.29	00.65	01.31	....
Port Chester Savings Bank, Port Chester	52.10	15.40	....	....	....	....	26.47	01.59	01.38	03.03

Poughkeepsie Savings Bank, Poughkeepsie	47.91	18.22	02.53	22.03	....	01.01	04.01	00.08	03.77	00.43
Queens County Savings Bank, Flushing	20.77	49.08	17.12	07.99	....	....	02.20	02.83	....	....
Rhinebeck Savings Bank, Rhinebeck	....	09.35	....	74.82	....	....	15.82	....	....	....
Rome Savings Bank, Rome	61.81	....	10.33	....	....	16.58	08.56	....	....	02.72
Sag Harbor Savings Bank, Sag Harbor	62.12	31.70	....	....	....	....	04.42	00.09	....	01.67
Schenectady Savings Bank, Schenectady	24.30	13.74	02.75	....	....	....	59.20	....	....	....
Sing Sing Savings Bank, Sing Sing	13.75	70.66	03.14	10.99	....	....	....	01.46	....	....
Skaneatelas Savings Bank, Skaneateles	16.90	10.70	....	29.66	....	....	14.20	01.87	26.66	....
Southold Savings Bank, Southold	58.05	31.43	02.58	01.47	....	01.33	....	02.42	01.18	01.53
Ulster County Savings Institution, Kingston	39.32	38.17	....	09.34	....	....	06.34	....	02.99	03.84
Westchester County Savings Bank, Tarrytown	33.01	13.05	06.52	27.33	....	....	16.75	01.78	00.46	01.09
Yonkers Savings Bank, Yonkers	12.39	45.65	07.13	14.47	....	02.28	10.16	00.87	02.54	04.50
	21.96	34.39	06.18	16.35	06.30	00.67	06.09	02.25	03.93	01.87

(C.)

The following Table exhibits a Comparative Statement of Income or Earnings, and of outlay for Expenses and Dividends, of Savings Banks during the year 1866, *as ascertained from their Annual Reports* 1*st January*, 1866 *and* 1867, *and the Statement of Cash Transactions made for this examination.*

The facts disclosed are as follows:

1. The income or gross profits during the year, estimated from statement of cash transactions.

2. Payments on account of expenses estimated from the same statement.

3. Dividends or interest credited to depositors as stated in the reports 1st January, 1867.

4. Total payments or outlay for the year found by adding together the items in columns 2 and 3.

5. The net profit or loss to the institution for the year as found by taking the difference between columns 1 and 4. Where the income exceeds the outlay, it is, of course, profit, and is not marked. It should appear in the increase of surplus over what was reported the previous year. If the outlay exceeds the income, it is, of course, loss, and is marked —. It should appear in a corresponding diminution of surplus as reported the previous year.

6. For the purpose of comparison with what should be the net profit or loss, as found from the foregoing bases, the actual net profit or loss of each institution for the year, as found in the difference of surplus reported in 1866 and 1867, is given in column 6. A reported increase is not marked; a reported decrease is marked—.

7. Is the total difference between the estimated net profit or loss, found in column 5, and the actual net profit or loss reported in column 6.

To make the table still more plain, I will illustrate by an example, and select for the purpose that institution that exhibits the greatest difference between the estimated and actual profit—The Seamen's Bank for Savings:

Its income from interest, premiums, rents, etc., was		$817,344 41
Its expenses	$108,070 75	
Its dividends	412,802 64	
Total outlay		520,873 39
Difference or net profit		$396,471 02

That is, we look to see the surplus as reported 1st January, 1866, augmented by the above sum in the report for 1867. But on comparing the report for 1866 with that for 1867, we find that the surplus, as reported in the latter, is but $89,987.38 greater than in 1866. The difference between this actual net profit and the estimated net profit, is $306,483.64, and appears in column 7.

The question naturally arises, what has become of this princely sum of $396,471.02 of profits, of which we find but $89,987.38 augmenting the resources of the institution!

Suspicious minds might at once start grave accusations upon such an exhibit as this. What a placer for an inquisitorial investigating committee!

But I have purposely selected for illustration an institution whose officers and trustees stand high in the community, and to whom no taint or suspicion of dishonesty attaches.

The solution of the mystery is found in the fact that all sources of actual profit or actual loss to a savings bank are not reported. Large items are swallowed up in premiums on stocks purchased, and in other ways that never appear, except in final results. But the fact that through the medium of these *unknown quantities* there is *opportunity* for the gratification of cupidity and avarice, without risk of de ection, is impressive in its suggestion of the necessity for a more thorough disclosure of the operations of these institutions through their reports.

It will be noticed that in a few instances the actual profit is greater than the estimated.

Where the estimated result is a profit, and the actual is a loss, the difference is of course found by *adding* the items in 5 and 6.

The subject receives further illustration and comment in the body of this report.

(C.)

	No. 1. Receipts of income during year 1866.	No. 2. Payments for expenses during year 1866.	No. 3. Payments of interest, or interest credited depositors in 1866.	No. 4. Total payments in 1866.	No. 5. Estimated net profits or losses in 1866, to be added to or deduct'd from surplus reported Jan. 1, 1866. Losses m'ked —.	No. 6. Actual net profits or losses, as appearing from differences in surplus as reported in 1866 and 1867. Losses, —.	No. 7. Differences between estimated and actual profits or losses.
CITY OF ALBANY.							
Albany Savings Bank	$100,013 76	....	$76,174 65	$76,174 65	$23,899 11	$10,753 72	$13,085 39
Albany City Savings Institution	13,091 76	....	13,528 77	13,528 77	—437 01	....	437 01
Albany Exchange Savings Bank	4,733 47	$544 23	3,785 02	4,329 25	404 22	—740 01	1,144 23
Mechanics' and Farmers' Savings Bank	53,083 87	2,947 99	37,024 20	39,972 19	13,111 68	10,741 03	2,370 65
CITY OF AUBURN.							
Auburn Savings Institution	47,287 93	12,065 53	39,950 42	52,015 95	—4,728 02	—3,016 45	1,711 57
Mutual Savings Bank of Auburn	12,017 40	1,033 78	7,918 84	8,952 62	3,064 78	3,064 78	....
CITY OF BROOKLYN.							
Brooklyn Savings Bank	370,835 17	87,738 29	258,601 51	346,339 80	24,495 37	—132,334 53	156,829 90
Dime Savings Bank of Brooklyn	157,558 90	41,276 22	104,505 52	145,781 74	11,777 16	—5,548 10	17,325 26
Dime Savings Bank of Williamsburgh	16,480 63	6,400 51	9,566 42	15,966 93	513 70	2,410 88	1,897 18
East Brooklyn Savings Bank	22,763 69	4,757 89	9,914 76	14,672 65	8,091 04	163 64	7,927 40
Emigrant Savings Bank of Brooklyn	5,450 00	3,207 75	4,084 79	7,292 54	—1,842 54	644 32	2,486 86
German Savings Bank of Brooklyn	3,656 78	1,882 89	968 06	2,850 95	805 83	869 13	63 30
Kings County Savings Institution	38,010 68	9,290 18	30,367 54	39,657 72	—1,647 04	15,356 41	17,003 45
Long Island Savings Bank	2,073 78	4,548 33	1,900 83	6,449 16	—4,375 38	1,372 12	5,747 50
South Brooklyn Savings Institution	130,395 46	30,577 52	84,522 99	115,100 51	15,294 95	—4,646 40	19,941 35
Williamsburgh Savings Bank	416,048 74	77,318 09	259,698 91	377,017 00	79,031 74	77,899 08	1,132 66
CITY OF BUFFALO.							
Buffalo Savings Bank	173,413 04	25,324 48	119,617 81	144,942 29	28,470 75	6,767 19	21,703 56
Emigrant Savings Bank of Buffalo	5,606 99	4,087 68	6,122 52	10,210 20	—4,603 21	—7,840 07	3,236 86
Erie County Savings Bank	199,581 82	33,055 37	131,611 27	164,666 64	34,915 18	8,419 57	26,495 61
Western Savings Bank of Buffalo	45,260 10	7,924 82	14,673 70	22,598 61	22,661 49	3,101 17	19,560 32

City of New York.							
Atlantic Savings Bank	90,640 94	21,812 97	55,208 63	77,021 60	13,619 34	11,195 92	2,423 42
Bank for Savings in the City of New York	986,185 16	156,181 58	570,202 50	726,384 08	259,801 08	250,088 31	9,712 77
Bowery Savings Bank	1,079,017 97	175,898 11	753,957 2[illegible]	929,855 37	149,162 60	27,825 06	121,337 54
Broadway Savings Bank	86,520 95	19,196 25	60,194 71	79,390 96	7,129 99	—1,239 17	8,369 16
Citizens' Savings Bank	202,224 16	37,106 55	93,453 40	130,559 95	71,664 21	84,808 87	13,144 66
Dry Dock Savings Institution	392,862 39	47,662 61	243,792 09	291,454 70	101,407 69	92,833 67	8,574 02
East River Savings Institution	159,068 29	30,240 01	88,152 46	118,392 47	40,675 82	25,627 06	15,048 76
Emigrant Industrial Savings Bank	339,071 71	59,418 58	248,362 32	307,780 90	31,290 81	94,072 12	62,781 31
Franklin Savings Bank	12,380 56	5,704 82	6,500 47	12,205 29	175 26	4,536 06	4,360 80
German Savings Bank of New York	277,515 81	49,173 59	185,585 18	234,758 77	42,757 04	27,757 04	15,000 00
Greenwich Savings Bank	330,353 09	70,364 80	207,577 36	277,942 16	52,410 93	—38,784 65	91,195 58
Harlem Savings Bank	4,993 85	1,284 97	2,582 81	3,867 78	1,126 07	868 54	257 53
Institution for the Savings of Merchants' Clerks	125,670 49	28,562 13	106,335 34	134,897 52	—9,227 03	32,157 25	41,384 28
Irving Savings Institution	114,940 79	22,013 05	75,172 75	97,185 80	17,754 99	501 12	17,253 87
Manhattan Savings Institution	283,462 34	73,957 47	200,348 24	274,305 71	9,156 63	2,123 10	7,033 53
Market Savings Bank	25,512 09	10,947 79	14,751 18	25,698 97	—186 88	4,337 27	4,524 15
Mechanics' and Traders' Savings Institution	157,137 45	33,554 52	111,427 52	144,982 04	12,155 41	—33,176 78	45,332 19
Metropolitan Savings Bank	133,922 72	26,682 01	78,292 23	104,974 24	28,948 48	52,928 53	23,980 05
New York Savings Bank	35,799 11	11,936 76	23,156 40	35,093 16	705 95	3,915 77	3,209 82
North River Savings Bank	....	....	....	....	....	....	....
Seamen's Bank for Savings	917,344 41	108,070 75	412,802 64	520,873 39	396,471 02	89,987 38	306,483 64
Sixpenny Savings Bank	28,167 90	10,711 40	14,629 73	25,341 13	2,826 77	—34 43	2,861 20
Third Avenue Savings Bank	190,133 33	35,557 45	128,447 81	164,005 26	26,128 07	69,632 63	43,504 56
Union Dime Savings Institution	138,288 87	30,068 00	82,003 33	112,071 33	26,217 54	24,816 66	1,311 41
Up-Town Savings Bank	2,337 51	7,572 69	1,369 91	8,942 60	—6,605 09	....	6,605 09
City of Rochester.							
Monroe County Savings Bank	115,041 97	17,266 23	83,797 63	101,063 86	13,978 11	12,417 56	1,560 55
Rochester Savings Bank	148,537 80	21,555 36	90,807 43	112,362 79	36,175 01	592 29	35,582 72
City of Syracuse.							
Onondaga County Savings Bank	110,433 19	22,466 44	66,924 49	89,390 93	21,042 26	15,545 08	5,497 18
Syracuse Savings Institution	65,814 73	13,777 63	38,175 68	51,953 31	13,861 42	17,712 20	3,850 78
City of Troy.							
Central Savings Bank	2,175 33	....	2,175 33	2,175 33	....	....	....
Manufacturers' Savings Bank	1,370 93	....	1,370 93	1,370 93	....	....	....
Mutual Savings Bank of Troy	4,724 07	....	4,724 07	4,724 07	....	....	....
State Savings Bank	8,406 55	300 00	7,139 45	7,439 45	967 10	—51 57	1,018 67
Troy Savings Bank	105,991 78	17,234 17	84,435 11	101,669 28	4,322 50	—46,322 24	50,644 74

C—Continued.

	No. 1. Receipts of income during year 1866.	No. 2. Payments for expenses during year 1866.	No. 3. Payments of interest, or interest credited depositors in 1866.	No. 4. Total payments in 1866.	No. 5. Estimated net profits or losses in 1860 to be added to or deduc'd from surplus reported Jan. 1, 1866. Losses m'ked —	No. 6. Actual net profits or losses, as appearing from differences in surplus as reported in 1866 and 1867. Losses, —.	No. 7. Differences between estimated and actual profits or losses.
City of Utica.							
Central City Savings Institution	$8.798 98	$3,059 80	$3,665 47	$6,725 27	$2,073 71	$215 29	$1,858 42
National Savings Bank of Utica	5,718 91	....	3,879 76	3,879 76	1,839 15	1,126 69	712 46
Savings Bank of Utica	108,178 75	18,545 33	61,412 95	79,958 28	28,220 47	24,092 43	4,128 04
Other Localities.							
Chautauqua County Savings Bank, Fredonia	115 85	1,477 49	134 25	1,611 74	—1,495 89	5 71	1,501 60
Chenango County Savings Bank, Norwich	2,427 39	....	1,259 66	1,259 66	1,167 73	234 74	932 99
*Cohoes Savings Institution, Cohoes	....	....	6,996 17	....	....	....	....
Corning Savings Bank, Corning (closing)	....	....	9 98	9 98	—9 98	98 83	108 81
Cortland Savings Bank, Cortland	14 66	338 07	14 66	352 73	—338 07	....	338 07
Elmira Savings Bank, Elmira (closing)	....	....	....	....	....	—1,103 34	....
*Fishkill Savings Institute, Fishkill	....	....	6,627 02	....	....	5,569 71	....
Hudson City Savings Institution, Hudson	19,618 00	3,279 88	12,008 38	15,288 26	4,329 74	4,746 76	417 02
Jefferson County Savings Bank, Watertown	7,735 02	1,987 12	5,198 96	7,186 08	548 94	1,703 36	1,154 42
Mechanics' Savings Bank, of Fishkill on Hudson	760 90	100 45	262 06	362 51	398 39	498 84	100 45
Newburgh Savings Bank, Newburgh	50,187 72	9,779 25	30,906 13	40,685 38	9,502 34	5,042 79	4,459 55
New Rochelle Savings Bank, New Rochelle	433 48	194 37	276 16	470 53	—37 05	157 32	194 37
Niagara County Savings Bank, Lockport	72 90	17 90	187 14	205 04	—132 14	—114 24	17 90
Oneida Savings Bank, Oneida	1,257 86	372 61	58 60	431 21	826 65	553 57	273 08
Oswego City Savings Bank, Oswego	18,250 21	5,624 28	11,938 20	17,562 48	687 73	164 23	523 50
Peekskill Savings Bank, Peekskill	20,177 67	2,877 67	10,696 14	13,573 81	6,603 86	3,641 58	2,962 28
Port Chester Savings Bank, Port Chester	2,187 40	845 72	2,445 01	3,290 73	—1,103 33	351 35	1,454 68
Poughkeepsie Savings Bank, Poughkeepsie	70,893 17	9,248 97	43,938 18	53,187 15	17,706 02	17,755 27	49 25
Queens County Savings Bank, Flushing	11,402 91	1,512 39	10,810 34	12,322 73	—919 82	2,485 36	3,405 18

Rhinebeck Savings Bank, Rhinebeck	3,318 59	483 03	2,016 52	2,499 55	819 04	319 04	500 00
Rome Savings Bank, Rome....................	19,637 42	4,884 97	13,688 97	18,573 94	1,063 48	2,705 85	1,642 37
Sag Harbor Savings Bank, Sag Harbor.........	6,003 32	1,591 13	4,696 98	6,298 11	—294 29	1,704 06	1,998 35
Schenectady Savings Bank, Schenectady	14,985 57	5,373 47	14,934 35	20,307 82	—5,322 25	—5,218 02	104 23
Sing Sing Saving Bank, Sing Sing	10,947 75	1,144 99	6,704 05	7,849 04	3,098 71	1,031 94	2,066 77
Skaneateles Savings Bank, Skaneateles	486 66	253 97	1,071 32	1,325 29	—838 63	2,469 37	3,308 00
Southold Savings Bank, Southold.............	15,500 28	2,076 07	13,024 92	15,100 99	399 29	3,137 59	2,738 28
Ulster County Savings Institution, Kingston....	32,757 75	3,920 89	21,056 93	24,977 82	11,700 82	—1,164 59	12,865 41
Westchester County Savings Bank, Tarrytown..	*21,762 88	4,025 19	18,283 21	22,308 40	—545 52	—936 26	390 74
Yonkers Savings Bank, Yonkers.........	23,338 60	3,733 50	11,910 15	15,643 65	7,694 95	7,622 09	72 86

* Statement not obtained in season for estimate.

(D.)

Summary of opinions of Officers of Savings Banks, in answer to series of questions submitted for their consideration.

It is of course impossible to tabulate the opinions received, and the following seems to be the best form in which they can be presented. It was wholly optional with savings bank officers to give or withhold their opinions upon any or all of the points suggested.

I had two objects in view in soliciting these opinions. First, it seemed no more than courtesy, not to say justice, to the institutions to be affected by the general legislation proposed, that they should be consulted upon leading points which such legislation should embrace.

Second, the experience, observation and thought of gentlemen connected with these institutions, would be of material service to me in the formation or modification of my own opinions, to be presented for your approval in the form of the act proposed.

As was to be expected, very many institutions more recently organized, or having but a limited business, have not deemed an expression of any opinion important. The greater number, however, have responded, and some with evident thoughtful preparation.

I cannot sufficiently express my obligation to the gentlemen who have thus favored me with their views, from which I have derived great assistance in a clearer understanding of the workings of these institutions, and of their practical needs from consistent and well considered legislation. Not less gratifying is the evidence which the expression of these opinions affords of the deep and abiding interest which the directors of these institutions take in their trust, and of the zeal and intelligence which they bring to the discharge of their responsible duties.

Differences of opinion in matters of policy were to be expected; but without exception, all appear to be animated by one spirit of devotion to the interests committed to their keeping, and of desire to promote the highest prosperity and surest success of this great provident agency in our State.

Opinions.

What number of trustees is best for a thorough and efficient working organization?

Perhaps upon no question has there been expressed a greater variety of opinions than upon the above. As a rule, each institution prefers its own charter number, which is natural and proper, though a few have found that number inconvenient, and would be glad of a change. About thirty institutions express no opinion; of the remainder much the greater number favor as a minimum fifteen or less, and as a maximum twenty-one.

There has been no uniformity in legislation upon it. I can hardly conceive of an instance in which more than twenty-one would be desirable. I have more doubt concerning the lowest number that it would be safe and expedient to entrust with these powers. My convictions, rather than the weight of authority, incline to seven.

What provisions of law are desirable in defining or limiting the constituency of the board?

The general opinion expressed favors freedom in this direction. To citizens, residents of this State and of the county where the institution is located, seems to be all the restriction required. The question of personal character and fitness can best be disposed of in each particular case as it comes up.

Would efficiency of organization be promoted by removal of restriction that no person shall be a trustee in two or more institutions; or otherwise?

This provision in the present law is applicable only to the counties of New York and Kings. It would have little practical force elsewhere. Very few report any inconveniences arising from it, and there are to my mind valid reasons why it should be retained.

Does the provision that no trustee shall be at the same time a director in a bank of discount where the savings institution has deposits, impair the efficiency of organization?

This provision also applies only to the counties of New York and Kings. In those counties the weight of opinion is decidedly in favor of retaining the provision. Outside of those localities little interest was expressed, for the reason, doubtless, that the existing provision does not apply to them.

The object of such a prohibition obviously is to prevent savings banks from being controlled in the matter of their deposits by any bank or banks of discount. And yet, in the face of this plain and worthy intent, the Legislature has since chartered whole boards of directors as trustees of savings banks! In the cities where the provision applies, not one savings bank is controlled by a bank of discount: in localities where it does not apply, savings banks are thus controlled, and frequently to their injury. The practical question relates, therefore, not so much to retaining the present provision as to extending its application to other localities. The general subject is elsewhere discussed.

What acts or omissions of duty should be prescribed by law creating a vacancy, which the Board should be authorized or directed to declare?

The provisions of existing law, relating to absence from regular meetings for six successive months, are generally regarded as sufficient. This, however, only subjects trustees to the liability of removal. I would have the vacancy created absolutely so as to require action by the Board to restore to the forfeited place.

By whom should vacancies in office be filled?

The opinion is nearly or quite unanimous that vacancies should be filled by the Board.

Should offices be designated by law, or left to discretion of the Board?

The leading offices as of president and vice-president may properly be designated by law; others by the board, according to their requirements. Such is the prevailing opinion, and such is the prevailing tenor of existing charters.

Should the offices of secretary, treasurer, cashier, teller, attorney, surveyor, &c., be held by members of the Board or by others?

Most institutions would have this left entirely to the discretion of the board. Not a few would have it depend upon whether they were salaried offices or not; if salaried, would have such offices held by others. This view of the question is properly considered in the next succeeding question.

Should members of the Board acting in any possible capacity for the Board, receive compensation for their services?

Here, too, is found a decided diversity of opinion. Only sixty-four institutions answer the question, and these as follows:

Yes	23
No	15
Yes, with some qualifications	14
No, with qualifications	10
Indefinite	2

The qualifications are various, most of them relating to duties which trustees may do in the way of special or professional service for which compensation ought to be allowed. Some would only allow compensation as the law of some localities now does, to the president of the board. Where any assent, in any form or under any circumstances is expressed, I have included it above with the absolute or qualified affirmatives. A qualified negative, however, as the question is stated, is almost equivalent to an affirmative. Generally, the older institutions deprecate any departure from the original theory and practice of strictly gratuitous service. The subject is fully considered elsewhere.

Should there be legislative prohibition against the practice of letting any contracts for labor or material for the institution to members of the Board?

Opinions upon this are variable. I have not found any abuses growing out of a want of such prohibition, and in view of the limited opportunity for such abuses am of opinion that no legislation upon the subject is required.

Should there be a statutory provision prohibiting members or officers of the Board from receiving commissions from the institution, or from parties with whom the institution has dealings?

Most respond to this affirmatively, but regard the present provision common to all charters prohibiting trustees from receiving any pay or emolument for their services as covering the case. It does, doubtless, the first part, and the last it is doubtless impracticable to reach by legislation.

Should the Legislature prescribe the frequency of regular meetings, or is that better left to the discretion of the Board?

The general opinion is that this should be left entirely to the discretion of the board of trustees. Except that the law should require regular meetings as often as quarter-yearly, I concur in that opinion.

Should quorum be prescribed by law, and what number or proportion of members should constitute a quorum?

The majority of answers favor a quorum fixed by law, and most very justly regard the proper number to constitute a quorum as depending upon the number of trustees; a majority of a small body being not too large, while a less proportion of a large body would be quite large enough. In providing for a minimum and maximum number of trustees, a sliding scale must be adopted for a quorum.

Is the law at present too rigid or too lax, relative to the investments which may be made by savings banks?

If too rigid, in what respect should the power be extended?

If too lax, to what should investments be limited?

These questions may properly be considered together. Most savings banks regard the law at present as about right. Twelve find the limitations to which they are subjected too rigid. Most of these relate to special restrictions of their charters in the matter of loans upon bond and mortgage. Some that are prohibited from investing in stocks of other States, or in bonds of any but some particular city, would have this restriction removed. One or two would have the provision for investments enlarged, so as to embrace town and village bonds. A few mention county bonds as among the securities in which they would be glad to invest, overlooking the fact, that the acts of 1863 and 1864, fully meet their wishes in this respect. One institution would include bank stock among the authorized investments. Some very properly deprecate the singular provision in the act of 1853, that restricts investments to securities below par.

Ten regard the law at present too lax, having reference it is presumed to provisions elsewhere criticised in this report.

Some regard the provisions of law at present as too variable, and I quite agree with them.

Would it not be well to limit by law the proportion of aggregate deposits to be invested in bond and mortgage?

Twenty-six savings banks make no answer to the above, thirty-three would leave it wholly to the discretion of the trustees, and twenty-five regard some limit as desirable and proper. Of the latter, the proportion to which they would limit this class of investments varies from fifteen to seventy-five per cent of the assets. One-third of the assets is the prevailing proportion however.

My own views are elsewhere very fully set forth.

Is it desirable to limit the proportion of investment in different classes of stocks?

Almost universally answered no.

Is it practicable to secure interest on the deposits made by savings banks in banks of discount?

It is found to be so very generally, and the prevailing rate of interest is four per cent.

Is the limit of 20 per cent of deposits greater or less than is desirable?

As this provision, like some others to which these inquiries relate, applies only to New York and Kings counties, the answers to it are mostly from those counties. Thirty-four savings banks make no response. Of those that express an opinion, twenty-six regard twenty per cent as about the proper proportion of deposits to authorize to be kept in bank, twelve consider it much more than is necessary, four find that proportion too small, four would fix no limit by law but leave it all to the discretion of trustees, and four give a qualified answer.

Is the limit of $100,000 that may be made in one bank too great or too small?

Here opinions differ according to experience and wants. Very few savings banks can keep a sufficient amount of their deposits in cash, to be much inconvenienced by the above limitation. A few, however, are embarrassed by it. Most of those that express any opinion corcerning it, regard some ratio to the capital of the deposit bank as preferable to any fixed sum.

Would not call loans on United States or New York State stocks exclusively, with 10 per cent margin from par value, or from market value when less than par, be as safe as a deposit in banks, and be as available, and more profitable?

Nearly all the answers to the above are to the effect that such a provision is wholly impracticable for the reason that such securities cannot be got for call loans, and time loans not being available on demand, could not, of course, take the place of cash in bank.

Some are opposed to loans upon securities of any description, but the negative answers to the inquiry relate chiefly to its impracticability upon the grounds above stated.

What limitations concerning dividends to depositors is it practicable to prescribe by law, and what should be left to the discretion of trustees?

Thirty-five savings banks would vest the entire discretion in the trustees.

Twenty favor some limitation, but a few of these favor a provision, if any, that shall require uniformity or equality of dividends to all classes of depositors. These would, of course, be satisfied with a removal of all restrictions upon the discretion of trustees, Most of the twenty, however, would have some positive restriction placed upon this discretion. Some earnestly favor the enforcement of the provision in the act of 1853, requiring the rate of dividends upon five hundred dollars and under to be one per cent more than upon larger deposits. Several mention the limitation of dividends to actual earnings less expenses, as desirable, others favor the limitation of dividends to five per cent until a certain surplus is acquired, others would require one per cent to be added annually to surplus until fifteen per cent is accumulated, others would require all extra dividends to be made to depositors of $1,000 or less, others make a special point of making all dividends uniform in rate without regard to amount.

What surplus in gross or proportional to deposits, is safe to the institution and just to the depositors?

A very few institutions would have no surplus but divide all profits to depositors—that is all after expenses which, in such cases, would generally prove to be the larger share. A small number regard five per cent as ample. The majority favor ten per cent probably for the reason that they are familiar with that rate from existing provisions of law. Quite a large number, however, are in favor of fifteen per cent, and a few regard 20 per cent as not too high.

What limit should the statute prescribe to the amount that may be received on deposit from one individual?

Most answers to the above are to the effect, that the whole subject should be left to the discretion of each savings bank respectively. Very many favor the more general limit of charters, which is $5,000. Some charters have a less amount—as $3,000 and $2,000, which limits have their advocates.

The president of one institution urges, with much force, the propriety of requiring all savings banks to receive deposits as small as ten cents. His connection with an institution that receives the smallest sums on deposit, has given him opportunities for observing the beneficial effects of this policy, that entitle his opinions to respectful consideration.

Does the law at present sufficiently protect the deposits of married women made in their own name, and do they sufficiently protect savings banks from suits at law regarding such deposits on complaint of husbands?

In every instance but one this question is answered affirmatively. The exception will be considered under the following:

If not, what further provisions are necessary in this regard?

Knowing that the Third Avenue Savings Bank had procured an amendment to its charter designed to afford better protection to the institution from adverse claims to any deposit, for my better information and satisfaction, in view of the generally expressed conviction of the sufficiency of the present provisions of law, I addressed a note to the attorney of that institution, asking him for a statement of his views upon the necessity for such amendment, and wherein it was preferable to remedies already provided.

I give his answer, in full, as the best exposition of the question: "I consider the amendment to our charter referred to by you, a very simple and inexpensive mode of reaching a judicial decision upon conflicting claims to the same fund. It was designed to avoid multiplicity of actions and a consequent consumption of the fund in costs.. Our depositors are generally poor, or operatives with moderate means, and controversies usually arise as to the ownership of small amounts. In such cases, ours being charitable institutions, it was deemed desirable to reach a decision with the least loss possible. We consider the following some of the advantages of our amendment over the previous provisions of law applicable to such cases. First, it relieves the bank from the necessity of paying the fund into court, and with it, costs to the time of such payment. There is no reason why the bank should be mulcted in costs even to that extent, nor to avoid the payment of those costs, should it be compelled or induced to decide between conflicting claimants. Second, it leaves the fund on deposit, drawing interest, the same as other deposits, during the litigation, intact and without diminution for commissions or fees. The bank is retained as co-defendant, simply as receiver or custodian of the fund, pending the litigation, subject to the final decision of the court upon the rights of the claimants. Costs as against the bank are in the discretion of the court, and the court would not impose costs upon the bank, except it were guilty of laches. Third, it avoids the necessity of a new suit of interpleader, and the appointment of a receiver and application for an injunction, all of these being in effect accomplished in the original action on a simple motion upon a notice of five days. Fourth, under the Code, without the advantages of our amendment, all these would be necessary. An adverse claimant cannot be brought in on motion, unless it appear on the face of the complaint, that a final determination of the action brought cannot be obtained without the presence of other parties. A case of this kind occurred, which suggested the application for the amendment. A wife deposited moneys in our bank. The husband came to the bank and demanded the money, alleging that it was his money; had been taken from him by the wife surreptitiously. The bank refusing to pay, he brought suit against the bank as sole defendant. On a motion to make the wife a party, the court decided that it was not necessary to a final determination of the question of the liability of the bank *to him.* If he did not succeed in proving his case, he could not get judgment; thus forcing the bank to commence a second action against husband and wife, with the consequent expense for costs, &c., or else to take the responsibility of defending the original action, and be subjected to another by the wife upon her claim. It has been our policy to avoid litigation as much as possible, and to husband the fund in such cases, and we think this provision of our charter is eminently efficient for that purpose. I am sure if the other boards had given it their attention, with that effect of it in view, they would agree with us that it should be retained.

"Respectfully yours, W. B. HARRISON."

The amendment referred to will be found sec. 4, chap. 783, Laws of 1867.

Is not uniformity in the powers and privileges conferred, and in the duties imposed on saving institutions, especially in the cities of New York and Brooklyn, important for the highest good of all?

With one or two exceptions answered in the affirmative, and often with much emphasis.

Is the effect of multiplying these institutions salutary or otherwise?

The question was stated too indefinitely. Reference was had, of course, to multiplying these institutions in cities already well provided. Restricted to this meaning, the answers are uniformly affirmative. The institution of savings banks, where none have been organized, is altogether approved.

Opinions on points not enumerated.

The following are the opinions in full as rendered under the above head. There will be found among them many valuable suggestions, and I could have selected quite as many more, from answers to other inquiries, which I have been obliged to pass by with brief and general reference. They have not, however, been lost sight of in the forming of my own conclusions, and to this extent they have fulfilled their office.

The following, as all others, have generally been prepared under the direction of one or more officers or trustees, hence are not to be regarded as an authoritative exposition of the boards of trustees. Wherever the name of the officers has been given as the authority for the opinion expressed, I have inserted it.

Opinions.

"This savings bank is, in fact, managed by the officers of the National Mechanics' and Farmers' Bank, and no savings can, by any legal enactments, be placed on a footing of more perfect security to depositors. It has the safety of its investments not only, but the capital and surplus of the National Mechanics' and Farmers' Bank, with the double liability of its stockholders. The National Mechanics' and Farmers' Bank guarantees all investments. Where savings bank deposits are wholly deposited in a bank of discount and deposit, as in some instances in this city, with banks of undoubted credit, it would be diffiult to find other investments equally safe, and equally available, and of equally unvarying value. In New York and Brooklyn the large and most cautiously managed banks will not allow interest to savings banks, or if so, only at a low rate and on a very moderate amount. Savings banks, therefore, must form this consideration, even if their enormous deposits did not suggest its importance, seek diversified investments."—*Mechanics' and Farmers' Savings Bank.*

COMMENTS.

In view of the very decided position I have taken throughout this report, against the policy of intimate connection between savings banks and banks of issue, I deemed it no more than just that the other side should be heard through one of its most esteemed and trustworthy advocates. The general theory maintained, I have combatted to the best of my ability in previous pages, and will not, therefore, encumber this report with a repetition of my views. A few issues of *fact*, however, it is proper to notice.

1. That other investments than bank deposits, equally available, safe and unvarying in value, cannot be found, is, I think, disproved, by the fact that in Syracuse, Rochester, Buffalo and other cities, they *are* found in sufficient quantities, and sufficiently reliable to serve every purpose which a savings bank requires of its investments.

2. "The large and most cautiously managed banks" in New York and Brooklyn *do* allow interest, varying from three to four per cent on savings bank deposits (the latter the prevailing rate), and on very large balances; as why should they not, as they are the most unvarying deposits they have. They allow all that it is prudent to allow. If any bank in Albany allows more, I fail to see where the better security is found in such practice.

3. Of the thirty-five savings banks in New York and Brooklyn, thirteen reported January 1, 1867, less deposits than the Mechanics' and Farmers'; should they be *attaches* of banks of discount because their narrower line of deposits does not require diversified investments?

It is proper to say further, that I regard the deposits in no savings bank in the State, as more secure than those in the Mechanics' and Farmers'. But in view of the 36th section of the National Banking Law, my confidence does not rest upon the guarantee of investments by the National Bank.

"Provision should be made for a close scrutiny as to fitness of a board of trustees, in establishing a savings bank. Perhaps the names should be submitted to the Department, and an acceptance required from them with a promise to discharge the duties devolving on them."

Illustration is given of the laxity of trustees in attending meetings; also of the manner in which boards are frequently constituted by the use of reputable names with which to secure the favor of the Legislature; when incorporated, the best men never attend meetings, or perhaps resign, and the business falls into the hands of a clique in the interest of the treasurer, secretary or other managing officer.

"If quarterly meetings are prescribed, trustees should be allowed, say two dollars each, for attendance, and failure to attend two consecutive meetings without satisfactory excuse in writing, should vacate office in discretion of the board."

Names of subsequent, as well as first trustees, should be submitted to Department for approval.

"The law should prescribe the population to justify a savings bank, and give Department power to determine upon the necessity or otherwise of increasing the number."—*Auburn Savings Institution.*

"A single institution should not be allowed to monopolize a large line of deposits at low interest in a growing place. It bears hard on the poorer classes, and takes away an encouragement to industry."—*Mutual Savings Bank, Auburn.*

COMMENTS.

This is the *other side of that* question, and exceedingly well put. My views upon it will be found at length in the body of the *report.*

"Give the right to deal with married women and minors to any extent, and without restrictions, leaving it to the husbands, parents, guardians and creditors to redress themselves through the courts."

"The right to lend money on call upon public securities, should be at least 90 per cent of their *market* value, provided the interest thereon has been punctually paid for at least three years previous to making such loan; and the right to purchase at market price under the same provisions."

"Deposits in good National or State banks or trust companies (making as now such deposits a first lien as far as possible), upon interest, better in practice than lending on coupon bonds which you are bound to return, thus avoiding the risk of theft."—*Brooklyn Savings Bavks.*

COMMENTS.

1. Was not the Farmers' and Citizens' National Bank considered "good" when the above was written?

2. Deposits in National banks are not a "*first lien*" on their assets. It is only to State banks that that salutary provision applies.

"No dividend should be allowed of interest not earned and realized.

"A fixed time should be adopted for allowance of deposits, commencing at each quarter day, and not 10, 15 and 20 days, as is now practiced.

"Savings banks having $100,000 surplus should be allowed to receive chancery and litigated funds by order of courts, public funds by order of treasurers and boards of trustees of corporations.

"The published report of the savings banks by the Superintendent should contain a full statement ot the several kinds of stock and bond investments and securities for call loans held by each bank, as set forth in their returns to him in their several schedules, and the rate of interest they pay respectively, that the Legislature, the depositors and the public may know the true character of security under which their deposits are held.

"The accrued interest and dividend should always be included in the returns to the Superintendent, and, in published accounts, to give the real condition of the institution.

"To reduce the number of trustees to 24, let vacancies lapse as they occur."—*Dime Savings Bank, Brooklyn*, WM. W. EDWARDS, *Treasurer*, and J. W. HUNTER, *Secretary.*

"The original design of savings banks should be kept in view, viz:

"To provide places of safety where persons in moderate circumstances can deposit their hard earned savings and receive them again when called for (except in times of panic, notice should be required), with a fair amount of interest.

"Trustees should be men in whom the public have confidence, which should be looked into before a charter is granted.

"Statements or the form of reports should be so changed as to tell the exact condition of the institution."—*German Savings Bank, Brooklyn.*

"There should be a uniform law regulating the days of *grace* given to depositors. As it is now, some give to the 10th, some to the 15th, and others to the 20th and 25th of the month, to draw the interest from the 1st of the month. It should not exceed the 10th."—*Kings County Savings Institution.*

"The object aimed at is to make all deposits in savings banks *perfectly safe* under *all* circumstances. This cannot be done unless a liberal surplus is allowed. Such surplus cannot be accumulated, if all the earnings of each year should be distributed as dividends. Stocks bought in one year may greatly depreciate the next, especially during a panic. Sales of stocks to pay depositors would seldom be necessary, except during a panic or great pressure for money; in such case they must always be sold below their true value. Bonds and mortgages are never *available* in a panic. During the year 1857, our city stocks sold at 75 cents on the dollar, and in 1863, U. S. bonds of 1881 at 90, a difference of over 20 per cent from present value. It is not *impossible* that such prices may again rule, notwithstanding the present prosperous appearances."—*South Brooklyn Savings Bank.*

Required.

"1. A general law allowing temporary loans to be made on all securities the savings banks are permitted to invest in.

"2. A repeal of all laws requiring savings banks to make any reports to, or be subject to any examinations except by the Banking Department.

"3. A repeal of all laws that require the approval of any outside official to an election of a trustee.

"4. A repeal of all laws requiring the approval of any outside official to the sale or transfer of any securities held by the institution."—*Buffalo Savings Bank.*

NOTE.—[The last three paragraphs relate to provisions of the charter of the Buffalo Savings Bank, which allow the interference of the city authorities in the manner suggested.]

"The slight tax to which depositors may be subject in order to maintain a surplus and safety deposit fund, is entirely unimportant in view of its objects, the principle of which is that faith in these institutions should never be shaken."

Comments further and favorably upon the suggestions of the Superintendent, in his last annual report on savings banks concerning a safety deposit fund to be made by contributions from savings banks, and applied for the benefit of depositors of failing institutions. [See Superintendent's Report, 1867.]

"The success of this mighty expedient for awakening industry and securing its avails by economy, must always mainly depend upon the purity and unselfishness of the men who are chosen as administrators."—*Bowery Savings Bank.*

"The most stringent safeguards should be provided against contingencies of loss to depositors; if any are to suffer from mismanagement it should be the trustees or officers causing the loss, and they should be held personally responsible for the violation of any law created for the protection of depositors.

The suggestions of the Superintendent, in his last annual report, concurred in except—

"1. The paying of trustees.

"It is desirable that all benevolent or provident institutions should be managed by the highest class of trustees, rather than by those who seek these positions for their own personal benefit. The law prohibiting trustees from receiving pay or emolument for their services is wise, and should be enforced except the president, when he devotes his entire time to his duties).

"2. The Common Trust Savings Fund.

"To divert the surplus optained by honest and economical management to sustain careless, dishonest, or recklessly managed institutions would be unjust, and tend to destroy public confidence in well-managed institutions, which should enjoy the full benefit of any surplus fund accumulated by their own wise and prudent management for the protection of their own depositors,"—*East River Savings Institution, Chas. A. Whitney, Secretary.*

"The act of April 15, 1853, should be amended. Its first section should be so amended, that the stocks referred to may be purchased at the market price, and that the loans may be made not to exceed 90 per cent of the par or market value; but in no event should loans exceed 90 per cent of par value.

"In the list of items required in the report made on the first day of January of each year, instead of requiring the amount '*received* for interest' during the year, the amount *earned* for the year should be required."—*Greenwich Savings Bank.*

"A uniform law should be passed governing all the savings institutions of the State, but more particularly in large cities.

"They should be confined strictly to the objects for which such institutions were originally designed.

"All special provisions in charters of savings banks conflicting with the general law should be repealed.

"No savings bank should be chartered unless the proposed corporators sign the application for it. They should state the necessity of such institution for the location named, and their willingness to act as trustees; also enter into an obligation that the expenses of the institution, as well as interest that may be allowed depositors, shall be paid from the earnings only and not from deposits.

"The 'Common Trust Savings Fund' suggested in the last report of the Superintendent, is liable to the objection that any losses sustained by improvidence or otherwise, by a carelessly managed institution, would have to be responded to by those that have been well managed. It would be more just that each institution should have the full benefit of its own considerate management, but all trustees should be held personally responsible for any loss occasioned by a violation of a law created for the protection of depositors.

"A diversion of the money deposited or accumulating in savings banks should, under no pretence, be permitted. Public confidence in such institutions would be destroyed by any such authority. Such attempt ought to be, if it is not now, deemed unconstitutional."—*Institution for Savings Merchants' Clerks.*

"The law respecting the security of deposits (of savings banks) in banks of discount should be made broad enough to cover *National banks.* At present the law is believed to apply only to banks organized under the State law."—*Metropolitan Savings Bank*, Isaac T. Smith, *President.*

Query. Can any law of the *State* reach and affect the distribution of the assets of a *National bank?*

"1. Let all the savings banks be subject to the same laws, with no special privileges or prohibitions to any.

"2. Do not enlarge or abridge the number or class of investments or securities, but say, if you please, that at least one-half of the deposits of a savings bank should be in bonds of the United States, or of the State of New York, and the remainder in such as the law now provides.

"3. Make it compulsory on all the savings banks to receive the smallest practicable sum on deposit."—*Sixpenny Savings Bank, New York*, Wm. Miles, *President.*

NOTE.

Opinions upon other subjects of inquiry are given with much fullness and contain many excellent suggestions.

"In cities an additional savings bank for every twenty-five or thirty thousand additional inhabitants would, we think, meet all the public requirements, and better serve the pnblic than a greater number.

"Savings banks should be disconnected from banks of discount, private bankers' or brokers' offices."—*Rochester Savings Bank.*

"A savings bank properly managed, is not merely beneficial to community as furnishing the means and inducements for saving money, but is almost equally so by the character of its loans, and the manner of making them.

"This savings bank has always avoided as far as it could, making loans for speculative purposes. The class of people from whom our deposits mainly come, can always obtain loans from us for building or for regular legitimate business, if they can furnish the requisite security."—*Onondaga County Savings Bank.*

The president of the Syracuse Savings Institution, Hon. E. W. Leavenworth, has rendered me special service in the way of valuable suggestions in several communications. They are not in form convenient for introduction here, but have been attentively considered.

"The duty of periodical personal examinations of each savings bank by the Superintendent of the Bank Department, would be a safeguard against abuses. He should be at liberty to employ a professional accountant should the circumstances indicate the necessity."—*Savings Bank of Utica*, J. C. Spafard, *Assistant Treasurer.*

"To prevent fraudulent organizations of savings banks under a general law, there should be required a deposit fund of $75,000, to be made secure for the protection of depositors. Otherwise, the expenses will have to be paid out of depositors' money."—*Hudson City Savings Institution..*

"When a savings bank has accumulated $2,000,000 of deposits, another should be placed alongside of it. Otherwise, accumulations are too great.

"There are very few points which can be embraced in a general law. It would be a sort of "bed of Procrustes," which might seriously impair the usefulness of some institutions, while benefiting others."—*Oswego City Savings Bank.*

"No difference should be made in the rate of interest allowed to depositors on sums below or above a certain amount."—*Queens County Savings Bank.*

"Savings banks being for the deposits of the poorer classes, who place in them their savings, relying on the supervision of the State that created these depositories, should be authorized with great caution. No set of men, unless known to be of high character, should ever be allowed to have a charter, or be permitted to associate as a savings bank.

"If a general act is passed, there should be power vested in the Superintendent of Banking Department to *refuse* to sanction, and he should exercise the power when the applicants were, in his judgment, acting from unworthy or selfish motives.

Better that no general act should be passed, but that all savings bank charters should be acted on by the legislature of the State, and be subject to the veto of the Governor."—*Rhinebeck Savings Bank.*

REMARKS.

This and the Oswego Savings Bank are the only ones in the State that express an opinion adverse to a general law.

"Require all savings banks to make a quarterly report to the Superintendent, and have it called for as the books of the institution stood on the first day of the month in each quarter, and have the same published in a newspaper."—*Ulster County Savings Bank.* J. E. OSTRANDER, *Treasurer.*

(E.)

By-Laws and Annual Statements, as illustrating efficiency of Internal Administration.

For the purpose of exhibiting the leading features of the internal administration of our savings banks, I desired to introduce extracts or copies in full of the by-laws of some of the leading institutions. But extracts would present too broken and disjointed a view, and copies in full from any considerable number would add too greatly to the bulk of this report.

I have, therefore, selected as a specimen that one which I find to be the most elaborate and complete in every detail of administration.

It is proper to say, that quite uniformly, they seem admirably adapted to the particular requirements of the respective institutions for which they are framed, hence no disparagement of any is to be inferred from the selection of this one as a model of their excellencies.

By-Laws of the Emigrant Industrial Savings Bank.

Board of Trustees.

1. The officers of the board are, a president, two vice-presidents, a secretary, a finance committee of five members, and a semi-annual committee of three members.

2. All the said officers and committees, except the semi-annual committee, shall be elected by ballot from the board of trustees, annually, at the regular meeting in January. Any of them may be removed by a vote of the board, and vacancies happening during the year shall be filled by an election by ballot. The semi-anuual committee shall be appointed by the president, at the regular meetings in June and December, and each member of the board shall serve in succession.

3. As the president, vice-president, secretary and trustees can receive, directly or indirectly, no pay or emolument for their services, none of them shall be responsible for any loss whatever.

4. The regular meetings of the board shall be held on the second Thursday in each month, at the banking house, at half past three P. M., except that in the months of July and January, the meeting shall be held on the third Thursday. Extra meetings may be called by the president, the vice-president, the finance committee, or the comptroller, and the object shall always be notified by the comptroller, at the foot of the notice of such meeting to each trustee, and no other business shall be transacted at the meeting.

5. In case of the absence of the president and vice-presidents, a quorum of the board shall consist of seven members of the board.

6. Any person to be elected a trustee must be nominated at one regular meeting. At the next or any subsequent regular meeting, if the board shall so order, the notices of meeting shall be noted at the foot, "Preliminary Ballot for new Trustee," and at that meeting such ballot shall be taken, the votes being cast "Content" or "Non-Content," and in case two ballots are cast "Non-Content," no further ballot shall be taken, and the name be considered as withdrawn; otherwise he shall be considered as nominated, and his nomination shall be published by the comptroller, as required by the charter, and a final ballot shall be taken at the next regular meeting; and if the person balloted for shall receive a majority of the whole number present and voting, he shall be considered and declared as duly elected, and not otherwise. No preliminary ballot shall be taken in the months of July and August.

7. No money shall be borrowed, or obligation incurred, for or in the name of the bank, nor shall any of the property or securities of the bank be sold, assigned or discharged, by way of pledge, collateral security, or otherwise, without the direct order of the board, duly entered in their minutes, unless specially authorized by the by-laws.

8. No money shall be loaned except upon bond and mortgage, as authorized by the charter. No call loans, or loans upon personal or stock securities, shall be permitted under any circumstances whatever.

9. The order of business of the board shall be as follows:

1. Reading the minutes of the last meeting.

2. Reading the minutes of the finance committee since the last meeting, and passing upon their rules, regulations, or recommendations.

3. Reading the monthly report,

4. Reports of special committees.

5. Communications from comptroller.

6. Communications from the officers of the bank.

7. Motions, suggestions and remarks upon the investments of the bank, present or prospective.

8. Motions, suggestions, or remarks upon the business of the bank and the conduct of its officers.

9. Miscellaneous business.

10. The banking room shall not be used by the officers of the board, or any of the trustees, or any other person, for the transaction of business, or for public affairs, or for any purpose not legitimately connected with the duties and affairs of the bank and the Irish Emigrant Society, as defined by their respective acts of incorporation.

11. The seal, having an impression of the name of the Bank, now in the possession of the President, shall be the seal of the bank.

The Officers.

12. The officers of the bank are either honorary or salaried.

Honorary Officers.

The honorary officers are:

1. The president.
2. The 1st vice-president.
3. The 2d vice-president.
4. The secretary.
5. The chairman of the finance committee.

The President.

13. The duty of the president shall be:

1. To preside at the board, and decide rules of order according to parliamentary usage.

2. To be ex-officio a member of the finance committee.

3. To have the custody of the seal of the bank, and affix it, in cases especially authorized by the board, or by the by-laws.

4. To have the custody of all surety bonds to the bank, except when he shall be a surety, in which case the custody shall be held by the first vice-president.

5. To sign checks upon the deposit banks when specially authorized by the by-laws, by the board, or by the finance committee, as expressed in their minutes respectively.

6. To keep the key of "the president's safe" for stock securities in vault No. 1, and also under lock and key, in some secure place, outside of the bank, duplicate keys of the banking room of the four vaults, and a duplicate record of the securities of the bank, to be made out and amended once a year by the comptroller.

7. To deliver to the comptroller, from time to time, from "the president's safe," coupons for payment and stocks to be paid off, taking his receipt therefor.

8. To execute and deliver to the comptroller, from time to time, satisfaction-pieces of bonds and mortgages paid off, the same being signed by the comptroller as a witness. In case of the payment of the principal, either of bonds and mortgages or stocks, he shall see that the moneys received therefor are receipted on the comptroller's cash blotter, by the cashier, on the day of payment.

The Vice-Presidents.

14. The duty of the first vice-president, the second vice-president, and the chairman of the finance committee, shall be, in case of the absence or inability of the president, to perform his duties in succession.

The Secretary.

15. The duty of the secretary shall be to attend the meetings of the board, and make a draft of the minutes, to be given to the comptroller for engrossment or record. He shall be the organ of communication of the board.

The Finance Committee.

16. The finance committee shall have the general charge and government of the bank, subject to the by-laws and the orders of the board; and especially,

1. The chairman shall make a draft of the minutes of their weekly meeting, to be given to the comptroller for engrossment or record.

2. They have power to make investments out of funds on hand, on bond and mortgage, or in securities authorized by law, and, upon delivery of the same to the president, may authorize checks to be signed therefor; to audit and authorize to be paid the ordinary and current expenditures of the bank, and to decide all questions of doubtful obligation in the ordinary business of the bank; but shall have no power to sell or assign any of the securities of the bank, by the way of pledge or otherwise, or to borrow money or

to loan money, except on bond and mortgage, or to admit or grant the liability of the bank in cases where no legal liability shall exist.

3. They shall audit the weekly report, and examine and compare the same with the cashier's blotter, the accountant's minutes, the comptroller's cash blotter, the cash book, the check books, and the bank deposit books.

4. They shall, from time to time, lay down rules for the government of the bank, not inconsistent with the orders of the board, or of the by-laws, which shall be binding until the next meeting of the board, when, if approved by the board, they shall be of permanent obligation, as by-laws, until revoked by the board.

5. They may call extra meetings of the board, in their discretion.

6. They shall order payments to be made in reduction of mortgages, when, in their judgment, the mortgaged premises are an inadequate security; and they may order mortgages to be paid off or foreclosed, as they may deem advisable.

7. The following shall be their order of business:

1. Reading the minutes of the last meeting.

2. Reading the weekly report of the accountant, and examining the same, as hereinbefore required.

3. Auditing bills against the bank.

4. Application for loans on bond and mortgage, and reports on same.

5. Reports and communications from the comptroller.

6. Reports and communications from other officers of the bank.

7. Investment of moneys on hand.

The Semi-Annual Committee.

17. It shall be the duty of the committee generally to examine the books, accounts, and securities of the bank, and to declare the rate of interest to be paid depositors for the preceding six months, and report to the board, and especially.

1. To examine each stock security, and see that all stocks capable of being registered or filled in to the name of the bank, are so registered or filled in, and in regard to coupon securities, that all the coupons to the date of examination are attached.

2. To examine each bond, and see that the last payment of interest has been duly endorsed thereon.

3. To examine each mortgage, and see that the same has been duly recorded.

4. To examine each policy of insurance, and see that the same

accompanies every loan, unless relieved by the finance committee, as expressed in their minutes, and that the same contains the usual mortgagee clause, or is executed by a company which has signed the contract with the bank.

5. To examine each abstract, and see that every loan on bond and mortgage is accompanied with an abstract of the title, verified by the signature of the attorney and counsel to the board.

6. To examine the bank deposits and check books and ascertain the amount of cash on hand.

7. To examine the report of the accountant, to be presented by the comptroller, and verified by him, showing the condition of the bank, the amount of deposits entitled to interest, and the rate of interest which the profits of the bank permit to be declared.

8. To examine all the account books of the bank, all the vaults and safes, with all the drawers and book cases, and see that the directions of the by-laws have been fulfilled, and that the officers of the bank have performed their duties.

9. To report specially upon each one of the items before enumerated, and to state the result of their examination thereof.

Salaried Officers.

18. The salaried officers of the bank are:

1. The comptroller.
2. The accountant.
3. The cashier.
4. The receiving teller.
5. The 1st bookkeeper.
6. The 2d bookkeeper.
7. The messenger.
8. The porter.

The Comptroller.

19. The comptroller shall be the manager of the bank, subject to the by-laws, the orders of the board and of the finance committee. He shall supervise all the other salaried officers of the bank, and all the books, papers and accounts made or used by them.

1. It shall be his duty to attend the bank during banking hours, and to have no other business or pursuit whatever.

2. To open all letters addressed to or intended for the bank, and do the ordinary correspondence.

3. To have and keep the key of the "safe of bonds, mortgages, policies and abstracts," in vault No. 1.

4. To collect the interest upon bonds and mortgages, noting particularly the name and address of the owner of mortgaged premises, and endorse the payment on the bonds. To send the second notice at the expiration of ten days after payment becomes due, and if not paid within ten days thereafter to send the mortgage to the attorney for foreclosure.

To collect the interest upon stocks, and the principal of bonds and stocks upon maturity.

All payments of every description, except from depositors, shall be made to the comptroller and no other officer; and the comptroller shall, on the day of receipt, deliver the amount received to the cashier, who shall receipt the same on the cash blotter of the comptroller.

5. To keep a cash blotter, and enter thereon all receipts and all payments by him, except those of petty cash, and on the last day of each month enter thereon a list of the collections for the ensuing month, to be furnished by the accountant and revised by himself.

6. To deliver all moneys received by him by mail for deposits to the receiving teller, in the same manner as if he were the depositor. To examine the pass-book to be handed him by the cashier, and, finding the same correct, to return it to the accountant.

7. To determine, before 3 o'clock each day, the amount of cash to be deposited by the cashier, and examine the deposit, enter in a book the items thereof, and verify the ticket for delivery to the porter.

8. To sign, with the president, all checks upon the deposit banks, specially authorized by the by-laws or the board, or the finance committee, entered in their minutes, and not otherwise.

9. To examine and compare, at the close of the bank each day, the cash blotter of the cashier and the entry book of the first bookkeeper, and, in case they agree, certify the fact thereon; in case they disagree, report the fact to the finance committee.

10. At the close of the bank each day, to examine and count the money on hand, and certify the fact and the amount on the blotter of the cashier, and see the same locked up by the cashier, in "the cashier's safe," in vault No. 1. In case the amount shall be found to be incorrect, he shall report the fact to the finance committee.

The following shall be the form of certificate:

"I have compared the preceding account of the cashier of the drafts and deposits with the like account of the first bookkeeper and with the cash blotter of the comptroller, and certify that they agree. I have also counted the cash of the same account on hand, and certify that it is correct and as reported in the vault."

11. To verify the weekly and monthly reports of the accountant—the latter being in the following form:

"I have compared and examined the preceding report with the original entries of receipts and payments by the cashier, with the original entries of receipts by the comptroller, with the check books and bank deposit books, and find that all receipts and payments for the last month are duly entered in the report. I have also examined the cash book, the journal, and the ledger, and find such entries to be duly entered and posted therein, and believe said report to be correct."

12. To issue notices by post for the meetings of the board and for the meetings of the finance committee, and to call extra meetings in his discretion, and to attend these meetings when requested.

13. To keep a book for the registration of bonds, mortgages, policies and stocks, with their numbers and full description, for identification or proof in case of loss by fire, robbery, or otherwise, and to deliver to the president a duplicate copy, to be amended from time to time as may be necessary.

14. To keep a policy or insurance register, and to notify owners of mortgaged premises of the expiration of policies previous thereto; and in case now policies or renewal for the times and by the companies required by the by-laws be not delivered, to cause the premises to be insured on account of the bank, require the mortgagee to pay the premium, and in case of refusal or neglect, to send the bond or mortgage to the attorney and counsel for foreclosure.

15. To request all companies, whose policies are held by the bank, to sign the contract with the bank as mortgages, and in case of refusal, to report the fact to the finance committee. He shall keep in the policy or insurance book a list of companies signing the contract, who shall be known as "the accepted companies," and shall receive no policies, unless executed by such companies, or containing the clauses for the protection of mortgagees. All policies shall expire on the first day either of November or of May.

16. To have charge of the real estate of the bank, its rental, repair, taxes, and insurance.

17. To have charge of the library, and continue it upon the basis now laid in the several departments, to wit: the laws of the United States and of the State, relating to savings banks and emigration,

taxation, revenue, &c.; reports upon the finances of the United States, of the State and of the city, and of such other corporations whose stocks may be held by the bank; the reports of the Bank Superintendent; the reports of the Commissioners of Emigration; the reports, &c., of other savings banks.

18. To take the signatures and descriptions of depositors upon their first deposit; and, in case he be otherwise engaged, shall assign some other officer to do so.

19. To prepare and transmit the reports to the Bank Superintendent, and those to the internal revenue office of the United States, having submitted the same to the finance committee for approval.

20. On the day preceding the meeting of the finance committee and of the board, to prepare a memorandum of the business to be laid before them.

21. To prepare the advertisements of interest, the general advertisements of the bank, and the annual statement to depositors, and see that one copy of such statement be put into every new pass-book issued during the year, and into every old pass-book upon the first deposit in that year.

22. To report to the finance committee any attendance at the bank by any of the salaried officers more than one hour after the closing of the bank, with the name of the officer, the cause of attendance, and its duration, in order that the committee and the board may be informed of the actual operations of the bank and the need of the service.

23. To make to the finance committee or to the board such recommendations or suggestions as he may deem advisable for the due conduct of the bank in any particular, and the investment of its funds, present or prospective.

24. To order all account books and stationery for the use of the bank; and none shall be furnished without his direction.

25. To see that the laws of the State and of the United States affecting savings banks, and the provisions of the act of incorporation and the by-laws are fulfilled.

26. To disburse expenses of petty cash, and, at the first meeting of the finance committee in each month, present the same, with the necessary vouchers, to be audited, and check shall then be ordered to be signed for the amount found to be due.

27. To examine all bills against the bank, and certify the result at foot.

28. To obtain and file every advertisement for the sale of real estate for unpaid taxes and assessments, and see whether any premises, under mortgage to the bank, are effected thereby, and if so, to report to the finance committee.

The Accountant.

20. The accountant shall be the *head bookkeeper* of the bank, and it shall be his duty especially:

1. To examine the footings at the close of each day, on the entry books of deposits and drafts kept by the first bookkeeper, and certify the result.

2. To keep the book known as the "Accountant's Minutes," and to enter therein, at the close of each day, the operations of the day in amounts received and amounts paid.

3. To keep the cash book, journal and ledger, in the forms prescribed by the comptroller and the finance committee—the entries in the cash book to be made daily, in the journal monthly, or as required by the finance committee.

4. To prepare the weekly and monthly reports in the form now or hereafter prescribed by the finance committee, and keep them duly filed in books for that purpose, and have one copy of each under file on the trustees' table.

5. To take charge of pass books not used, and deliver to the receiving teller, from time to time, such as may be wanted.

6. To take charge of all pass books for entry of balance and of interest, and insert the same, after such balance and interest have been entered in the depositors' ledger, and not before; and to deliver the same to the depositors, with the same care as to identity as upon payment of a draft.

7. To take charge of all pass books left for safe keeping in the bank.

8. To take charge of the first and second deposit and draft tickets after they are put in their envelopes for the day by the first bookkeeper; and at the end of each month, to file them in the vault number four, under wrappers, in two or more parcels, properly endorsed.

9. To take charge of closed pass books, and, at the end of each month, to file them in the vault number two, under wrappers, in one or more parcels, properly endorsed.

10. To supervise the entries of deposits and drafts in the depositors' ledger by the second bookkeeper, and check the same.

11. To commence on the 9th of April and ninth of October, his preparations for the July and January interest, and the taking of balances and calculations of interest, and entries of the same in the depositors' ledgers.

12. To have charge of the matter of lost pass-books; to note the loss on the margin of the depositor's name in the signature book; to prepare the affidavit of loss; to deliver the blanks for publication; to receive the proof, and, in his discretion, to issue a new pass-book; to keep a book-register of lost pass-books, with the necessary entries thereon, and to deliver to the receiving teller and cashier the numbers thereof, to be posted before them, for easy reference.

13. To devote constant attention to the agreement of the general ledger and the depositors' ledgers, and to ascertain and devise the best modes of accomplishing the object and preserving the proofs thereof.

14. To keep the check-books on the deposit banks, and fill up the checks thereon, when duly anthorized by the board, the by-laws, or the finance committee.

15. To examine and verify the calculation of interest allowed semi-annually by the deposit banks, and have their accounts balanced on the last day of every month.

16. To examine all claims to deposits, on the part of assignees, administrators, or executors of depositors, determine the identity of the claimant, and file the proofs of title, or, in case of doubt or difficulty, take the direction of the comptroller.

17. To receive or pay no moneys on behalf of the bank.

18. To attend to the closing of the bank by the porter.

The Cashier.

21. It shall be the duty of the cashier,

1. To receive and enter in his cash blotter all payments made to the bank by depositors and by others to the comptroller delivered to him, and shall be responsible for the same.

2. To make all payments to depositors and enter the same in his cash blotter, and shall be responsible for all payments so made, either by mark or by signature, and must personally, by examination or otherwise, determine the right to payment before it is made.

3. To require the depositor at the time of receiving a deposit or paying a draft, to state orally the amount of the deposit or the

amount of the draft, and see that it corresponds with the amount marked by the receiving teller on the ticket and in the pass-book.

4. To prepare, before three o'clock each day, his deposit for the deposit bank, as required by the comptroller.

5. To enter, at the close of each day, in his cash blotter, the amount received from the comptroller, the amount of deposits, the amount of drafts, the amount deposited in the deposit bank, and the amount deposited in "the cashier's safe," in vault No. 1: and at the close of each week and of each month, to enter in the accountant's minutes a resumé of the receipts and payments of the week and of the month respectively.

6. To cash no checks under any circumstances, except those received in the ordiniary business of the bank, nor for any private account of an officer of the bank, or for any account of the bank itself, or for any consideration whatever, use or pay out of the cash in the drawer any sum whatever, except in the regular course of business to depositors or into the deposit banks.

7. Upon the receipt of every check in behalf of the bank, immediately to render the same unnegotiable, by stamping the same "for collection" or "on deposit" with the deposit bank.

8. He shall make no entries of receipt or payment in the depositors' or general ledgers.

9. He shall deliver to the accountant, at the close of each day, the pass-books closed during the day.

The Receiving Teller.

22. It shall be the duty of the receiving teller,

1. To receive all moneys for deposit, count the same, rejecting all that is not bankable, and enter the name of the depositor, the number of his pass-book, and the amount deposited on a deposit ticket, and also in the pass-book, and hand the pass-book with the money and the ticket to the first book-keeper. In the case of a first deposit, he shall ascertain and write on the ticket the description of the depositor.

2. In the case of money to be drawn by a depositor, to enter the name, the number of the pass book, and the amount on a draft ticket, take the mark or the signature of the depositor thereto, examine the pass book for the balance in bank, and, if justified by such balance, enter the amount thereon, and hand the same, with the draft ticket to the first book-keeper. He may require such

balance to be ascertained by the accountant—otherwise he shall be responsible for the calculation.

3. At the close of each day, to enclose the deposit tickets and draft tickets in separate envelopes endorsed of the day, and deliver the same to the accountant for deposit in vault number two.

The First Bookkeeper.

23. It shall be the duty of the first bookkeeper:

"To enter in separate books, from the deposit and draft tickets and pass books received from the receiving teller, the number of the pass book, and the amount deposited or withdrawn; and at the close of each day add up the total of each."

The Second Bookkeeper.

24. It shall be the duty of the second bookkeeper:

"To enter, from the books of the first bookkeeper into the depositors' ledgers, the amount deposited and withdrawn on the preceding day, and check the same with the accountant.

The Porter.

25. It shall be the duty of the porter:

1. To open the banking house every morning and close it every evening; to attend at the bank from the opening to the close, and to visit the bank for inspection every Sunday morning, and the morning of every holiday. He shall not, under any circumstances, leave the banking room during the intermission.

2. To attend in front of the counter, and marshal the depositors, so that they shall be served in their turn, according to the order of time of entering the bank, without favoritism or exception.

3. To receive from the comptroller the deposits for the deposit banks, and make such deposits, putting and keeping the same in a leather satchel duly fastened and slung by a strap from his shoulder, and return to the bank immediately thereafter.

4. To make the fires in the grates and furnaces, keep the glass clean and polished, remove the snow and ice, and keep the sidewalk and the front of the bank clean and in order; to keep the cellar, the water-closets, the wash-basins, the banking room and the desks in perfect order and neatness, without extra expense to the bank, all extra services of every kind being included in his monthly compensation.

5. And to attend upon such errands and execute such other duties as may be required by the comptroller.

General Duties of the Salaried Officers.

26. The salaried officers are also subject to the following rules:

1. No salaried officer shall keep any account with the bank, as a depositor, nor shall he receive or make any deposit, or pay out of his own money or otherwise, any draft in the business of the bank, except during the hours when the bank is regularly open for such purpose; nor shall he act as agent or attorney of any depositor, directly or indirectly, nor receive any pass-book for the purpose of having a deposit made therein or money drawn therefrom, except the receiving teller during the hours of business, and no other business than what strictly appertains to the duties and affairs of the bank shall be transacted or attended to within the banking room by any salaried officer, without the express consent of the finance committee.

2. All salaried officers shall be appointed by the board, and be removable at pleasure. They shall be under the direction of the comptroller, and are to perform their duties faithfully, promptly and correctly.

3. The accountant shall neither receive or pay out moneys on account of the bank, nor shall the cashier make any entries in the depositors' ledgers or in the general ledger of receipts or payments.

4. All salaried officers, except the porter and messenger, shall aid the accountant in entering and taking off balances, and calculating and entering interest in the pass-books and ledger, when unoccupied in their regular duties.

5. They shall attend at the bank every day, Sundays and legal holidays excepted, from 9 A. M. to 5 P. M., and as much longer as may be required by the comptroller to finish the current business of the bank.

6. No officer shall be entitled to any pay on the claim of extra services.

7. No officer, except the comptroller in his discretion, shall disclose to any other person than the depositor, anything in relation to the account of such depositor.

8. It is expected of all officers, in their treatment of depositors, and all others, that their conduct, as well away from the bank as in it, shall be courteous and exemplary, and tend to the credit, respectability and success of the bank.

9. All overdrafts, frauds, mistakes, errors or omissions, whether for or against the bank, discovered, known or suspected by any officer, shall be immediately reported to the comptroller, and by him to the finance committee at its next meeting.

10. Salaries shall be paid on the last day of every month, and checks signed therefor.

11. A copy or draft of every letter, advertisement, circular, report, etc., issued in the name of the bank, shall be preserved in a book for that purpose; and no payments shall be made or paper delivered, without receipt.

12. Smoking is prohibited in the banking room, and the use of tobacco in any form in the banking room is prohibited to the salaried officers of the bank, and also of the Irish Emigrant Society.

13. No receipts, except those of the pass books, and no certificates of deposit, transferable or otherwise, shall be issued by or in the name of the bank.

14. No salaried officer shall do or perform any work or labor for compensation by the Irish Emigrant Society, or by any other association or person, without the direct assent of the finance committee, expressed in their minutes.

15. Every salaried officer, except the messenger, shall execute to the bank and deliver to the president, a surety bond for the faithful performance of his duties, approved by the finance committee: that of the comptroller shall be in the sum of $20,000; that of the accountant and cashier, each, in the sums of $10,000; and that of each of the other officers in the sum of $5,000. Security may be waived, or the amount reduced by the board upon the recommendation of the finance committee.

Vacations, Absences, Suspensions and Removals.

27. 1. A vacation of two weeks, to each salaried officer, except the porter, may be granted at such times, and under such regulations as shall be approved by the comptroller and the finance committee.

2. If any salaried officer wishes or requires to be absent from the bank for a day, or part of a day, application must be made to the comptroller, and permission obtained accordingly. If the absence be desired for a longer period, application must be made to the finance committee, noted in their minutes, and the time of absence deducted from the vacation.

3. If any aid shall be required to perform the duties of any absent officer, the compensation therefor must be paid by him.

4. Any officer may be suspended by the comptroller, who shall report the fact and the cause thereof to the finance committee, at their next meeting. Such suspension shall continue until the final order of the committee on the subject. The comptroller may be suspended by the finance committee, subject to the action of the board.

5. No removal shall be made except by the vote of the board.

6. In case of the vacation, absence or suspension of any officer, the officer next below him in grade shall fulfill his duties *pro tem.*; and his own duties shall be discharged by the officer next below him, and so on, unless, in either case, the comptroller or the finance committee shall otherwise order. The officer *pro tem.* shall be invested with all the powers of the office.

Of the Attorney and Counsel.

28. 1. The attorney and counsel of the board shall attend at the banking house at the completion of loans on bond and mortgage, and the check for the amount of the loan shall be there delivered to the mortgagor by the comptroller, upon the receipt of the bond, mortgage and policy. The comptroller shall deliver the mortgage to the attorney for record.

2. The attorney and counsel shall deliver to the comptroller the abstract, duly signed, within ten days after the completion of the loan; and, in case of omission, the comptroller shall report the fact to the finance committee.

3. The presence of the comptroller being constantly required in the banking house, the attorney and counsel shall, in case of suits or other proceedings requiring confidence with the comptroller, attend upon him at the bank.

Investments and Securities.

29. 1. The finance committee are authorized in their discretion, to purchase for investment out of the funds on hand any of the securities permitted by the act of incorporation, may delegate the power of purchase to any one or more of their number, and upon delivery of such security to the president, checks may be drawn and signed in payment.

2. No purchase of stocks or other securities shall be made, except from known and responsible stock and banking houses, or from known and responsible owners, and, after such purchases, a sale receipt, and not a broker's note, shall be taken, describing

the securities by numbers, so that their genuine character shall be impliedly warranted to the bank; the calculation of the sale receipt shall be verified by the comptroller and submitted to the committee.

3. In the purchase of stocks and other securities, preference shall be given to those which are registered, or capable of being rendered unnegotiable. And in all certificates, &c., in which it is practicable, the name of the bank shall be invariably inserted.

4. All stock securities are under the charge of the president, and shall be kept under his key in "the president's safe," in vault No. 1.

The Vaults and Safes.

30. 1. The four vaults, No. 1 and No. 2, in the banking room, and No. 3 and No. 4, in the basement, shall be used and appropriated as follows:

No. 1, containing "the cashier's safe," "the president's safe," and "the private deposit safe," shall be used for those purposes, and for the custody of the pass books not yet required for use.

No. 2 shall be used for the custody of the closed pass books, and the draft and deposit tickets for the current month, the ledgers and books of account, and other valuable books and papers needed or required in the business of the bank.

No. 3 shall be used and appropriated to the trunks, tin boxes, and other enclosures of private individuals permitted to deposit for safe custody, under the rules of the bank; and

No. 4 shall be used for the closed pass books, and the draft and deposit tickets after the end of each month, and for the custody of the ledgers, account books, and other books and papers of the bank, written up or no longer required for daily use.

2. The accountant shall keep the keys of all the vaults, except those of No. 3, which shall be kept by the comptroller. The key of "the cashier's safe" shall be kept by the cashier, that of "the president's safe" by the president, that of "the bond and mortgage safe" and that of "the private deposit safe" by the comptroller.

3. The president shall keep, in some secure place outside of the bank building, duplicate keys of the banking rooms, vaults and safes.

Of the Business of the Bank.

31. The following shall be the rules for the business of the bank:

1. The bank shall be open for the receiving of money of depositors every day, except Sundays and legal holidays, from 10 A. M. to 5 P. M. The comptroller may, in case of urgency, keep the bank open an hour later.

2. Deposits of one dollar or any number of dollars, may be received, but are not, in the whole, to exceed five thousand dollars from any depositor, without the special direction of the comptroller, who shall report in his minutes the instance and occasion.

3. On making the first deposit, the depositor shall be present, and subscribe his or her name in the book of the bank, as his or her agreement to these regulations "of the business of the bank," a copy of which shall be printed on the pass-book, without which no deposit shall be received under any pretence whatever.

4. All deposits and all payments shall be entered at the time they are made, in the books of the bank, and also in the pass-book of the depositor, who shall then examine the same. The pass-book shall be the voucher of the depositor, and the possession of the pass-book shall be sufficient authority to the bank to warrant any payment made and entered in it; and the bank shall not be liable or called on to make any payment without the presenting of the pass-book at its counter, that the proper entry may be made in it.

5. All deposits must be made in gold or silver, or in bills taken on deposit in the banks of this city, at the option of the depositors; and payments shall be made in the like manner, at the option of the bank.

6. The bank shall be at liberty to return all or any part of any deposit whenever they may think proper.

7. All drafts must be made personally, or by order, in writing, duly authenticated, when the signature is not known to the cashier, and must be accompanied by the pass-book.

8. The bank shall not be liable to pay any moneys to depositors, except on a week's previous notice to the comptroller, at the bank, nor except on the third Monday in January, April, July and October; but moneys may be voluntarily paid by the bank daily, and without such notice, and without thereby waiving the right of the bank to such notice and time of payment.

9. No draft shall be made for less than one dollar, nor for fractional parts of a dollar, unless it be for the whole amount remaining on deposit, or for interest only.

10. All notices in relation to the deposits or depositors, published by order of the board, in one or more of the daily newspapers of the city of New York, six days successively, shall be taken and held to be actual notice to each depositor.

11. All accounts, on which no deposit or draft shall have been made for twenty years, shall cease to be entitled to any further interest after twenty years from the last deposit or draft.

12. Although the bank will endeavor to prevent fraud on its depositors, yet all payments to persons producing the pass-books issued by the bank shall be valid payments to discharge the bank. In the case of lost books the bank will decide as to the person to whom payments shall be made, and without the right of the depositor in such lost book to question the correctness of the payment.

13. On the decease of any depositor, the amount to the credit of the deceased shall be paid to his or her legal representatives.

14. No person shall be entitled to make any claim on the bank upon any contract or act by any officer, agent, or servant of the bank, not in conformity with these by-laws.

15. Interest will be allowed at such rate as, in the judgment of the board of trustees, the business of the bank for the last six months will justify; to be declared before the third Mondays of January and July. It will be allowed as follows: On all sums on deposit for six months next preceding to January 1, and July 1, six months' interest, and no more; on other sums on deposit for three months or more, prior to either of those days, three months' interest and no more. No interest will be allowed on sums drawn between those days, nor on sums less than five dollars, nor on fractional parts of a dollar. The interest will be credited as principal as of the first of January and July, and paid on the third Mondays of those months. All interest, if not withdrawn, shall be entitled to interest as much as an original deposit, of the date 1st of January or 1st of July, as the case may be.

Pass-books.

32. 1. No entries shall be made in the pass-books except of receipts and payments of cash exclusively; and the fact that the pass-book is opened subject to the conditions of the by-laws, shall be written or printed at the head of the book.

2. All pass-books, whether not used, or closed, or left in the bank for safe custody, or for the insertion of interest, are under

the sole and exclusive charge of the accountant, who shall be responsible for the same.

3. No entries shall be made on the last line of a pass-book, except the entry of the balance due, which shall be struck and carried to the next page by the accountant before any entry is made on the succeeding page.

4. No interest, or money as interest, shall be paid, unless the amount due for interest be first entered both on the depositor's ledger and on the pass-book by the accountant or second book-keeper.

5. Upon every entry of interest, the balance shall be struck and entered on the ledger and on the pass-book.

6. More than one account in the name of the same person is permitted, but the practice must not be encouraged.

7. Transfers of money from one account to another, or from the same to a new account, are not permitted, except in the single case of a new pass-book being necessary in consequence of the ledger or old pass-book being written up in full, in which case the transfer shall carry the interest upon the money transferred.

8. No change shall be made in the pass-book, or in the books of the bank, or the names of the depositors, either by erasure or addition, except by the request of the depositor, written in the presence of the receiving teller as a witness, authorizing the same to be done. Such authority shall be filed with the draft tickets of the day, and the date noted on the test-book opposite the name of the original depositor.

9. No trust accounts shall be opened, except those of one person in trust, or for one other person.

10. Accounts on behalf of corporate or unincorporate associations shall not be opened without reference to the comptroller, and when permitted, shall be in their name directly, and not in the name of trustees, and the following declaration, to be signed by the persons opening the account, shall be entered in the test-book, and in the pass-book :

"This account is opened upon the additional condition that deposits under it may be paid out upon checks signed by

until the bank receives notice to the contrary, delivered to the comptroller. Such notice shall be in writing, signed by those claiming to be the chief officers of the association above named, to wit, by the under the seal of the association,

and shall specify those who hereafter are

authorized to draw money. Such notice shall be sufficient warrant for payment."

11. No payments shall be made on any pass-book to any person claiming to be the executor, administrator, receiver, or assignee of a depositor, without reference to the accountant, who shall determine the right to payment, and the identity of the claimant.

12. In the delivery of pass-books to depositors, the accountant shall be assured of the identity of the claimant, as the depositor or his attorney, as fully as if such depositor were drawing money upon a draft.

Lost or Stolen Pass-books.

33. 1. Ordinary cases of lost books shall be determined by the accountant, who shall refer special cases to the comptroller.

2. No new pass-book shall be issued unless the depositor shall make an affidavit of the loss, have the same advertised once a week for six weeks in a daily or weekly paper, and present the proof thereof, with a bond of indemnity. The accountant may, in his discretion, having reference to the amount in bank and the circumstances of the case, abridge the time and limit of publication, and waive the bond of indemnity.

3. The accountant shall keep a book "register of lost books," to be examined from time to time by the receiving teller and the cashier, an abstract thereof to be posted before them, and shall note the notice of loss and the issuing of a new pass-book on the test-book opposite or under the name of the old account.

Counter-claimants of Pass-books.

34. Every claimant for a new pass-book, in cases in which the old pass-book is claimed by another person, or is in his possession, shall be referred to the comptroller, who, in his judgment, may leave the parties to their action at law, or report the facts of the case to the finance committee.

Deposit Banks and Checks upon.

35. 1. All moneys received from depositors, from stock securities, from bonds and mortgages, or from any source whatever, shall be deposited in the deposit banks (selected by the board of the finance committee), on the day of receipt or the succeeding day, except such reasonable amount, determined by the comptroller, as shall be retained in "the cashier's safe" for the daily operations of the bank.

2. No payments, unless to depositors, shall be made under any circumstances, except by check upon the deposit bank, specially authorized by the board or by the finance committee, under authority delegated by the board or by these by-laws. Such checks shall be filled up by the accountant, payable to the person to whom the same may be due, or to his order, and shall be signed by the president and the comptroller.

3. Such checks may, nevertheless, be signed for such amounts, as in the judgment of the comptroller may be necessary to supply the cashier with moneys to pay depositors, in which case the check shall always be drawn to the order of the cashier, and the comptroller and accountant shall see, at the close of the day, that the same has been counted in his cash.

4. The margin of the check-book shall contain, besides a statement of the person, amount, and subject of payment, a reference to the date of the authority therefor, as passed by the board or the finance committee.

5. No check shall, under any circumstances, be signed in blank by either officer authorized to sign the same.

6. The books with the deposit banks, and the check-books, shall be balanced on the last day of every month; and the interest allowed by the deposit banks shall be calculated and allowed on the 30th day of June and the 31st day of December in each year, verified by the accountant.

Deposit of Valuables for Safe Keeping.

36. 1. No deposits of valuables for safe keeping shall be permitted without the direct authority of the comptroller—nor unless the same shall be in a box or envelope under lock or seal, with the name of the depositor, but without any statement of its contents endorsed thereon—nor unless the depositor shall sign a declaration that the same is deposited at his or her risk, and without any responsibility of any kind on the part of the comptroller or of the bank.

2. The comptroller shall enforce the rule in regard to the deposits of that character now on hand as soon as practicable.

3. Such boxes or envelopes shall not, under any circumstances, be opened by the comptroller or any salaried officer; nor shall they or any of them undertake any agency on behalf of such depositors, by sale, collection, or otherwise.

4. Such deposits must not be encouraged. The comptroller, in his discretion, may refuse them, or require them to be withdrawn.

Amendments.

37. 1. The preceding by-laws are hereby adopted, and shall supersede all other by-laws and resolutions heretofore made.

2. No alteration or amendment shall be made thereto in the months of July and August, nor unless the same be proposed at one regular meeting of the board, and adopted at a subsequent meeting; nor unless the notice of meeting, at which the same may be adopted, shall have been noted at the foot thereof, "amendment to by-laws." Such notices shall be sent by the comptroller when ordered by the board.

As further exemplifying efficiency in administration, I subjoin annual statements made by a few savings banks for the information of their depositors or others. Besides the value that attaches to such statements as a means of keeping depositors informed concerning the financial condition of their savings bank, there are many valuable facts and suggestions brought to view, not found in their reports to the bank department.

Other institutions make similar statements, but these are all that I have at hand.

It would be well if all institutions would make similar exhibits for the benefit of their depositors and the general public.

Forty-eighth report of the Bank for Savings in the city of New York, for the year 1866, *to the Honorable the Mayor, Aldermen and Commonalty of the city of New York, pursuant to the act of Incorporation.*

Pursuant to the provisions of "An act to incorporate an association by the name of The Bank for Savings in the city of New York," the trustees now beg leave to present their forty-eighth report, as follows:

First. That the trustees have received from forty-four thousand two hundred and forty-nine depositors, from the first of January to the 31st of December, 1866, the sum of four millions eighty-four thousand four hundred and sixty-three dollars and ninety-five cents, in the following manner:

	From depositors.	Amount.
In the month of January..........	4,496	$410,531 37
In the month of February........	3,325	296,425 59
In the month of March	4,271	505,880 37
In the month of April............	3,063	289,912 59
In the month of May	3,220	334,414 94
In the month of June	4,841	479,090 00

	From depositors.	Amount.
In the month of July	3,798	$358,771 06
In the month of August	3,076	276,576 00
In the month of September	3,411	295,048 21
In the month of October	3,397	288,640 00
In the month of November	2,945	244,100 82
In the month of December	4,406	405,073 00
	44,249	$4,084,463 95

Of which number 10,230 are new accounts opened with the bank, and 34,019 are re-deposits.

44,249

Second. That the sum of four millions one hundred and thirty-one thousand three hundred and thirty dollars and seventy-nine cents has been drawn out by fifty-three thousand five hundred and ninety-nine depositors. Of this number, nine thousand five hundred and sixty-nine have closed their accounts.

	Paid drafts.	Amount.
In the month of January	8,434	$585,175 73
In the month of February	4,701	360,511 75
In the month of March	4,082	381,413 48
In the month of April	4,220	434,197 34
In the month of May	3,794	311,631 67
In the month of June	3,101	206,418 16
In the month of July	7,205	486,538 15
In the month of August	5,266	388,896 26
In the month of September	3,451	280,912 97
In the month of October	3,448	293,950 48
In the month of November	2,847	225,736 20
In the month of December	3,050	175,948 60
	53,599	$4,131,330 79

Third. The depositors opening new accounts have been classed under the following heads of professions and occupations:

Agents	31	Barbers	28
Artists	47	Bartenders	6
Attorneys	13	Blacksmiths	63
Bakers	66	Boarding-house keepers	44

Occupation	Number	Occupation	Number
Boatmen	18	Milliners	28
Boilermakers	18	Moulders	13
Bookbinders	14	Musicians	20
Bookfolders	8	Nurses	44
Butchers	74	Ostlers	49
Cabinetmakers	83	Oystermen	16
Cartmen	106	Painters	48
Carpenters	133	Pedlers	56
Chairmakers	4	Police officers	46
Clergymen	11	Physicians	20
Clerks	234	Porters	74
Coachmakers	27	Printers	31
Coachmen	86	Plumbers	12
Conductors	3	Saddlers	10
Confectioners	16	Sailmakers	3
Coopers	18	Seamen	31
Cutlers	2	Sempstresses	378
Distillers	14	Shoemakers	131
Domestics	1,242	Shopkeepers	42
Druggists	5	Soldiers	10
Engineers	21	Stonecutters	35
Engravers	12	Sugar refiners	12
Farmers	45	Tailors	215
Firemen	10	Tanners	9
Fishermen	2	Tavern keepers	121
Fruiterers	21	Teachers	54
Furrier	1	Tinners	28
Gardeners	42	Tobacconists	28
Glasscutters	13	Turners	9
Grocers	115	Upholsterers	16
Hatters	16	Varnishers	7
Hucksters	11	Washers	97
Jewellers	37	Watchmen	25
Junk-dealers	43	Waiters	136
Laborers	660	Weavers	31
Machinists	97	Sundry trades	54
Masons	81	No occupation, being married women, minors, etc.	4,576
Merchants	48		
Milkmen	26	Total	10,230
Miller	1		

Description of Persons.

Married women	2,658
Single women	1,705
Widows	897
Minors	224
Orphan	1
Colored person	73
Total	$5,558

Fourth. The deposits have been made in the following sums :

From $1 to $5	984
From 5 to 10	2,881
From 10 to 20	6,368
From 20 to 30	5,543
From 30 to 40	3,525
From 40 to 50	5,829
From 50 to 60	2,122
From 60 to 70	1,248
From 70 to 80	1,438
From 80 to 90	636
From 90 to 100	4,938
From 100 to 200	4,533
From 200 to 300	1,595
From 300 to 400	956
From 400 to 500	988
From 500 to 600	183
From 600 to 700	104
From 700 to 800	74
From 800 to 900	65
From 900 to 1,000	239
	44,249

The Bank for Savings in the city of New York in account with JAMES F. DE PEYSTER, *Treasurer.*

1866.	DR.		
Jan. 31.	To cash paid depositors and for sundries,	$843,948	15
Feb. 28.	To cash paid depositors and for sundries,	381,988	53
Mar. 31.	To cash paid depositors and for sundries,	420,676	51
Apr. 30.	To cash paid depositors and for sundries,	564,430	24
May 31.	To cash paid depositors and for sundries,	325,501	53
June 30.	To cash paid depositors and for sundries,	383,678	24
July 31.	To cash paid depositors and for sundries,	698,999	26
Aug. 31.	To cash paid depositors and for sundries,	442,713	34
Sept. 30.	To cash paid depositors and for sundries,	285,624	63
Oct. 31.	To cash paid depositors and for sundries,	362,853	73
Nov. 30.	To cash paid depositors and for sundries,	235,440	34
Dec. 31.	To cash paid depositors and for sundries,	580,245	19
		$5,526,099	69
	Balance carried to new account	471,302	61
		$5,997,402	30

1866.		Cr.		
Jan.	1.	By balance brought down from old acc't,	$583,880	52
Jan.	31.	By cash rec'd from depositors and sundries,	652,233	29
Feb.	28.	By cash rec'd from depositors and sundries,	360,410	86
Mar.	31.	By cash rec'd from depositors and sundries,	447,273	05
Apr.	30.	By cash rec'd from depositors and sundries,	341,049	69
May	31.	By cash rec'd from depositors and sundries,	504,148	31
June	30.	By cash rec'd from depositors and sundries,	513,487	17
July	31.	By cash rec'd from depositors and sundries,	523,379	02
Aug.	31.	By cash rec'd from depositors and sundries,	355,927	84
Sept.	30.	By cash rec'd from depositors and sundries,	338,448	36
Oct.	31.	By cash rec'd from depositors and sundries,	369,535	26
Nov.	30.	By cash rec'd from depositors and sundries,	531,846	54
Dec.	31.	By cash rec'd from depositors and sundries,	475,782	39
			$5,997,402	30
1867.				
Jan.	1.	By balance brought down from old account,	$471,302	61

JAMES F. DEPEYSTER, *Treasurer.*

NEW YORK, *Jan. 2d*, 1867.

The Trustees have deemed it expedient to present the following general view of the institution, from the commencement of its operations in July, 1819, *to January*, 1867.

RECEIPTS.

From.			Depositors.		
July, 1819, to July, 1824,	5 years,	from	29,437	$1,880,556	45
July, 1824, to Jan. 1830,	5½ years,	from	60,820	3,451,915	52
Jan. 1830, to Jan. 1835,	5 years,	from	82,535	4,644,604	70
Jan. 1835, to Jan. 1840,	5 years,	from	92,382	5,951,545	80
Jan. 1840, to Jan. 1845,	5 years,	from	94,033	6,040,867	25
Jan. 1845, to Jan. 1850,	5 years,	from	128,143	8,508,937	31
Jan. 1850, to Jan. 1855,	5 years,	from	181,755	12,334,656	56
Jan. 1855, to Jan. 1860,	5 years,	from	175,356	11,405,112	87
Jan. 1860, to Jan. 1865,	5 years,	from	193,023	14,835,858	92
Jan. 1865, to Jan. 1866,	1 year,	from	44,386	4,355,086	67
Jan. 1866, to Jan. 1867,	1 year,	from	44,249	4,084,463	95
	47½		1,126,119	$77,493,606	00
Deduct amount paid 1,027,567 drafts				74,711,653	56
				$2,781,952	44
Add interest up to and includ'g Jan., 1867, div'nd.				11,456,519	39
Total amount due depositors on 1st January.				$14,238,471	83

PAYMENTS.

From.				Drafts.	
July, 1819, to July,	1824, 5	years, paid	9,684	$800,946	61
July, 1824, to Jan.	1830, 5½	years, paid	39,699	2,994,453	49
Jan. 1830, to Jan.	1835, 5	years, paid	57,807	4.166,534	17
Jan. 1835, to Jan.	1840, 5	years, paid	79,841	6,534,306	57
Jan. 1840, to Jan.	1845, 5	years, paid	73,511	5,276,979	53
Jan. 1845, to Jan.	1850, 5	years, paid	108,797	8,442,326	99
Jan. 1850, to Jan.	1855, 5	years, paid	151,289	12,447,212	50
Jan. 1855, to Jan.	1860, 5	years, paid	171,816	11,466,822	25
Jan. 1860, to Jan.	1865, 5	years, paid	217,294	13,727,870	28
Jan. 1865, to Jan.	1866, 1	year, paid	64,230	4,722,870	38
Jan. 1866, to Jan.	1867, 1	year, paid	53,599	4,131,330	79
	47½		1,027,567	$74,711,635	56

The funds of the institution are invested in and consist of—

1. Bonds and mortgages in the city of New York,	$3,183,100	00
2. Funded debt of the United States, par value..	4,865,500	00
3. United States treasury notes	858,100	00
4. Stocks of the State and city of New York, and other States, par value..................	6,053,135	09
5. Real estate.............................	50,000	00
6. Cash in Manhattan Company and other banks,	471,302	61
7. Interest accrued to 1st Jan., but not received..	274,533	78
	$15,755,671	48

The bank has been in operation 47½ years, during which time it has opened 281,123 accounts, and received altogether from depositors	$77,493,606	00
To which add interest up to January, 1866	11,456,519	39
	$88,950,125,39	
Closed during the same period 225,816 accounts, and paid out............................	74,711,653	56
Leaving 55,307 accounts entitled to this balance,	$14,238,471	83

Which averages about 257 dollars to each account.

MARSHALL S. BIDWELL, *President.*

ROBERT LENOX KENNEDY, *Secretary.*

Statement, January 1*st*, 1867, *of the Seaman's Bank for Savingg. Incorporated* 1829.

ASSETS.

Loans secured by bond and mortgage on improved propety in the cities of New York and Brooklyn, worth double the amount loaned		$2,499,300 00
Stocks.		
Of the State of New York	$539,046 00	
Of the city of New York	1,009,150 00	
Of the city of Brooklyn and Kings county	101,000 00	
Of the city of Utica	50,000 00	
Of the United States	3,243,000 00	
Of the State of Massachusetts,	150,000 00	
Of the State of Rhode Island	300,000 00	
Of the State of Connecticut	600,000 00	
Of the State of New Jersey	139,800 00	
Of the State of Pennsylvania	110,000 00	
Of the State of Ohio	438,110 11	
Of the State Tennessee (guaranteed)	101,000 00	
Cost		$6,205,877 04
Real estate		98,434 42
Cash on deposit in various banks		391,068 49
		$9,194,679 95
Of which is due to depositors, including interest to date		$8,565,481 28

The Seaman's Bank for Savings, of the city of New York, has been established under a charter from the Legislature of this State, in order to provide a safe and advantageous deposit for the surplus earnings of the seafaring community.

It originated in a desire to serve this useful class of men, whose occupation, necessarily calling them so much from home, leaves them but an imperfect opportunity of finding who are trust-worthy; and whose generous and confiding disposition often leads them to place confidence where it is not merited.

The frauds practiced on seamen are notorious; and the losses on the part of masters, officers and men, who leave their money with merchants or landlords, or trust it with friends, are of every day occurrence.

The Legislature has taken great care in the charter of this bank, to make it safe. The trustees, respectable and well known gentlemen, are neither allowed to borrow the money themselves, nor to lend it on individual security; but are required to invest it only in the best public stocks, and in mortgages on real estate in the cities of New York and Brooklyn, worth double the amount loaned. The history of other banks for savings, in this State, has proved that such guards are effectual.

Confidence in the Seamen's Bank for Savings has been shown by the large amount of deposits by officers and seamen in the naval and merchant service, and others, which, since its incorporation, has reached $59,000,000, and of which the bank has now in hand over $9,000,000.

Should any seaman ask what benefit he would derive from depositing his money, the following, among other advantages, may be named:

1st. It will always be a recommendation to a man that he has some money in the bank; and would often secure him a good berth where trustworthy and responsible men were wanted.

2d. A fund in this bank would be a good reliance in sickness or old age. The alms house and hospital are, at the best, but poor retreats; and a man's money is a better friend in the time of need than the good will of even his friends. A small deposit at the termination of every voyage, would, in a few years, be a sum of some magnitude.

Should a depositor wish his family to draw money during his absence, he can leave his book and a written order with them; and they can draw as their wants may require; and the balance may remain in this place of safety, gaining interest.

NEW YORK, *January* 1867.

Nineteenth Annual Report of the Institution for the Savings of Merchants' Clerks, January 1st, 1867.

ASSETS.

United States 6 per cent stock	$331,726 75
United States 5 per cent stock	322,331 25
United States 7 3-10 notes	198,500 00
New York city 5 per cent stock	48,844 56

New York city 6 per cent stock	$311,339 33
Ohio State 6 per cent stock	185,778 21
Indiana 5 per cent stock	130,235 00
Indiana 2½ per cent stock	13,058 80
Missouri 6 per cent stock	17,377 50
Tennessee 6 per cent stock	27,056 50
Tennessee 5 per cent stock	32,637 50
Loans on bond and mortgage on improved real estate in New York and Brooklyn, worth double the amount loaned	290,850 00
Real estate	62,603 64
Loan on State stock	1,000 00
Cash on hand	65,235 85
	$2,038,574 89

Amount due depositors December 31, 1866, $1,815,073.12.

This institution was established for the benefit, as its title implies, of merchants' clerks, but deposits are received from all persons; and as the trustees are desirous of encouraging habits of economy and frugality, they invite small and frequent deposits.

The trustees are restricted from any use of the funds of the institution, No investments are made except in public stocks of the most approved character, and upon bond and mortgage on improved real estate, in the cities of New York and Brooklyn, worth double the amount loaned.

Money deposited on or before the first day of January, April, July and October, will begin to draw interest on those days, and interest is payable semi-annually, on and after the third Mondays of January and July.

Interest is added to the principal each six months, and if uncalled for, draws interest the same as an original deposit.

Married women can deposit money in their own names, and have control of it.

By way of precaution, the trustees, during the years of the war, reduced the rate of interest on deposits in order to secure a reserve fund to save depositors from loss in case of any rapid or serious depreciation of securities. A surplus as large as the law allows having been secured, the trustees have resumed their former rates of interest (viz: six per cent on $500 and under, and five per cent on larger sums), and in addition, have since declared two extra dividends to the permanent depositors, as follows: three per cent. on sums not exceeding $1,000 which have remained undisturbed for three years; two per cent. on similar sums which have remained undisturbed for two years; and one per cent. on similar sums which so remained for one year.

Fifteenth Annual Report of the Irving Savings Institutions to the Depositors.

The trustees have received during the year one thousand eight hundred and sixty-six, from five thousand six hundred and seventy-eight depositors, eight hundred and twenty-four thousand, no hundred and thirty-three dollars and fifty-five cents, viz:

	From depositors.	Amount.
In the month of January	847	$135,888 86
In the month of February	344	34,745 87
In the month of March	429	44,995 06
In the month of April	382	107,700 41
In the month of May	359	49,256 89
In the month of June	493	64,723 74
In the month of July	710	138,768 19
In the month of August	376	40,350 58
In the month of September	445	46,356 91
In the month of October	443	50,167 59
In the month of November	319	36,070 42
In the month of December	481	75,009 03
	5,628	$824,033 55

Of which number, one thousand four hundred and fifteen were new accounts.

Six hundred and eighty-five thousand three hundred and eighteen dollars and sixty-eight cents has been paid to five thousand eight hundred and fifty-nine depositors.

Of which number, eleven hundred and seventy-nine closed their accounts.

	Paid drafts.	Amount.
In the month of January	1,074	$94,125 43
In the month of February	507	66,688 65
In the month of March	455	59,647 60
In the month of April	288	58,460 81
In the month of May	391	57,433 85
In the month June	278	31,624 16

	Paid Drafts.	Amount.
In the month of July	939	$89,315 64
In the month of August	531	81,891 01
In the month of September	343	38,287 33
In the month of October	397	39,446 73
In the month of November	333	35,294 33
In the month of December	323	33,103 14
	5,859	$685,318 68

Received from 5,628 depositors during the year	$824,033 55
Paid to 5,859 depositors during the year	685,318 68
Increase of deposits during the year	$138,714 87

January 1st, 1867.

ASSETS.

Loans secured by bond and mortgages on improved property in the cities of New York and Brooklyn, worth double the amount loaned	$301,300 00
United States loan, 5 per cent	10,000 00
United States treasury notes	347,000 00
United States compound interest notes	18,580 00
United States 5-20 bonds	542,500 00
Stocks of the city of New York—Funded debt	100,000 00
Stocks of the city of New York—Water loan	20,000 00
Stocks of the city of New York—Central Park bond	50,000 00
Stocks of the city of New York—Revenue bond	80,000 00
Stocks of the city of New York—Loan account	13,750 00
Real estate, banking house	24,000 00
Interest earned on investments to Dec. 31, 1866	24,048 15
Cash in Irving Bank	55,725 78
Cash in vault	127,726 30
	$1,714,631 03
Amount due depositors 31st December, 1866	$1,578,536 19

Examined by the committee and report the same correct.

JOHN W. FERDON,
JOSEPH ROGERS,
HARVEY P. FARRINGTON.

WILLIAMSBURGH SAVINGS BANK.

BROOKLYN, *January*, 1867.

REPORT OF EXAMINING COMMITTEE TO JANUARY 1, 1867.

RECEIPTS.

Cash on hand at last report	$237,966 08
Received from depositors since	1,371,779 06
Received for interest	179,202 04
Received on account of stocks	358,000 00
Received on account of bonds and mortgages	47,012 72
Received on account of loans on call	81,100 00
Received on account of rents	375 00
Received on account of profit and loss	36,107 68
	$2,311,542 58

PAYMENTS.

Amount paid to depositors	$1,206,327 16	
Amount paid on account, bonds and mortgages	188,456 75	
Amount paid on stocks	600,280 00	
Amount paid on loans on call	53,546 34	
Amount paid on interest	2,340 22	
Amount paid expenses	25,754 19	
Amount paid internal revenue tax	12,742 03	
Amount paid insurance	99 05	
Amount paid profit and loss	99 16	
Balance in banks and on hand	221,897 68	
		2,311,542 68

The amount to the credit of depositors, July 1, 1866, including the dividend (132,403,76) was	$5,250,481 66
Received from depositors since	1,371,779 06
	$6,622,260 72
Paid to depositors since	1,206,327 16
Amount now to the credit of depositors	$5,415,933 56

The present balance of interest account is			$81,386 81
Interest due and accrued to Jan. 1st			99,123 06
The present balance of rent account is			250 00
Rents due and accrued to Jan. 1st			125 00
Credit balance of profit and loss account			36,028 52
Whole earnings from July 1, 1866 to Jan. 1, 1867			216,913 39
The sums entitled to interest for the six months ending Jan. 1, 1867, amount to	$4,508,765 00		
Interest thereon at 6 per cent per annum is		$135,262 95	
The sums entitled to interest for 3 months, amount to	460,432 00		
Interest thereon at 6 per cent, per annum, is		6,901 74	
Do. to no interest am't to	446,736 56		
Amounts of deposits	$5,415,933 56	Am't of div.	142,164 69
Surplus over the interest due depositors			$74,748 70
From which deduct the balance of expense account, including insurance expired and State tax on surplus			25,803 72
Net surplus			$48,944 98

Balance Sheet of General Ledger, December 31, 1866.

Dr.

Folio.		
5.	Williamsburgh city stocks	$8,629 50
10.	Real estate (Bank)	31,732 86
13.	Rochester city bonds	30,000 00
13.	Monroe county bonds	23,500 00
16.	Insurance	84 17
17.	Kings county bonds	222,000 00
24.	New York city bonds	30,000 00

Folio.		
25.	Brooklyn city bonds	$699,000 00
33.	Bonds and mortgages	973,155 03
40.	United States stocks	2,531,900 00
42.	Real estate on Atlantic street	10,811 06
50.	Richmond county bonds	276,000 00
50.	Albany city bonds	139,000 00
51.	Expenses	25,803 72
54.	New York State stocks	500,000 00
56.	Loans on call	223,156 34
58.	Cash	221,897 68
		$5,946,670 36

Cr.

Folio.		
12.	Reserved fund	$413,071 47
34.	Rents	250 00
45.	Deposits	5,415,933 56
47.	Interest	81,386 81
55.	Profit and loss	36,028 52
		$5,946,670 36

Assets.

Bonds and mortgages, 7 per cent	$973,155 03
Williamsburgh city stocks, 6 per cent	8,629 50
Brooklyn city stocks, 6 per cent, $661,000, cost	638,000 00
Brooklyn city stocks, 7 per cent	61,000 00
New York city stocks, 5 per cent	30,000 00
Rochester city stocks, 7 per cent	30,000 00
Albany city stocks, 6 per cent, $150,000, cost	139,000 00
Kings county stocks, 6 per cent, $227,000, cost	222,000 00
Monroe county stocks, 7 per cent	23,500 00
Richmond county stocks, 7 per cent	276,000 00
United States stocks, 6 per cent	2,431,900 00
United States 7 3-10 per cent	100,000 00
New York State, 7 per cent	500,000 00
Loans on call, 7 per cent	223,156 34
Real estate	42,543 92
Cash	221,897 68
Interest due and accrued	99,123 06

Rents due and accrued	$125 00
Insurance paid and unexpired	84 17
	$6,020,114 70

LIABILITIES.

Balance due depositors January 1st	$5,415,933 56
Dividend payable January 21st	142,164 69
Reserved fund	462,016 45
	$6,020,114 70

The securities have been examined and found correct.

There is $2,086,811 37-100 invested at 7 per cent per annum; $100,000 at 7 3-10 per cent; $2,440,529 50-100 at 6 per cent; $1,038,000 at 6 per cent, which cost and are counted in assets $999,000 and $30,000, 5 per cent.

H. P. FREEMAN,
H. M. WARREN.
C. H. FELLOWS,
Committee.

NOTE.—Full statements like the above, showing the *productive resources* of the institution, by giving the rate of interest which the investments bear, are just what is wanted. The example is worthy of imitation.

Interest as placed to the credit of depositors, by the Williamsburgh Savings Bank.

☞ This Bank has always paid six per cent. per annum on all sums entitled to interest, as follows:

DIVIDENDS.		RATE OF INTEREST PAID.	Amount of interest paid.
Years.	Declared.		
1852....	January 1....	Six per cent., on all sums, from $5 to 5,000	$441 41
	July 1....	Six per cent., on all sums, from $5 to 5,000	1,054 64
1853....	January 1....	Six per cent., on all sums, from $5 to 5,000	2,231 65
	July 1....	Six per cent., on all sums, from $5 to 5,000	3,423 58
1854....	January 1....	Six per cent., on all sums, from $3 to 5,000	5,346 63
	July 1....	Six per cent., on all sums, from $3 to 5,000	6,967 39
1855....	January 1....	Six per cent., on all sums, from $3 to 5,000	8,820 39
	July 1....	Six per cent., on all sums, from $3 to 5,000	9,108 92
1856....	January 1....	Six per cent., on all sums, from $3 to 5,000	10,899 29
	July 1....	Six per cent., on all sums, from $3 to 5,000	12,190 09
1857....	January 1....	Six per cent., on all sums, from $3 to 5,000	15,976 20
	July 1....	Six per cent., on all sums, from $3 to 5,000	18,325 75
1858....	January 1....	Six per cent., on all sums, from $3 to 5,000	19,452 63
	July 1....	Six per cent., on all sums, from $3 to 5,000	21,377 46
1859....	January 1....	Six per cent., on all sums, from $3 to 5,000	26,913 60
	July 1....	Six per cent., on all sums, from $3 to 5,000	32,226 18
1860....	January 1....	Six per cent., on all sums, from $3 to 5,000	39,663 79
	July 1....	Six per cent., on all sums, from $3 to 5,000	43,649 15
1861....	January 1....	Six per cent., on all sums, from $3 to 5,000	49,620 24
	July 1....	Six per cent., on all sums, from $3 to 5,000	49,877 57
1862....	January 1....	Six per cent., on all sums, from $3 to 5,000	51,582 55
	July 1....	Six per cent., on all sums, from $3 to 5,000	55,657 32
1863....	January 1....	Six per cent., on all sums, from $3 to 5,000	65,623 13
	July 1....	Six per cent., on all sums, from $3 to 5,000	74,511 29
1864....	January 1....	Six per cent., on all sums, from $3 to 5,000	90,068 79
	July 1....	Six per cent., on all sums, from $3 to 5,000	101,104 62
1865....	January 1....	Six per cent., on all sums, from $3 to 5,000	113,554 22
	July 1....	Six per cent., on all sums, from $3 to 5,000	117,646 30
1866....	January 1....	Six per cent., on all sums, from $3 to 5,000	127,295 15
	July 1....	Six per cent., on all sums, from $3 to 5,000	132,403 76
1867....	January 1....	Six per cent., on all sums, from $3 to 5,000	142,164 69
			$1,449,478 38

(F.)

Charters, and General Laws in relation to Savings Banks.

I have presented in the following pages, a synopsis of the provisions of the charter of each savings bank in this State organized and doing business on the first of July last. Some of these have made no report to the Department, but as they are in existence and have a future before them, it was deemed expedient to give them a place in a summary of the existing provisions of law relating to these institutions.

The topics will be found arranged in the most convenient order for reference and comparison, no attention having been paid to the order in the original statutes which could only have led to confusion, as any one will see who undertakes to compare any one charter and its amendments, with another. Indeed it has been found no inconsiderable labor, in many instances, to ascertain concerning a single savings bank, from the original and various amendatory chapters, what were the provisions of law finally remaining applicable to it.

It will be understood that these synopses do not embrace all the provisions of any charter. Many details that are common to all, or that are properly left to the entire discretion of trustees, or that pertain to them as bodies corporate only, having no significance to their charter as savings banks, are omitted. In short, I have embraced only such provisions, as in the preparation of a general law, applicable to and governing all these institutions, will necessarily receive most careful consideration, because of their vital importance, and of the effect upon existing institutions, of introducing uniformity where at present so great diversity exists.

I should, however, except the provisions relating to the prohibitions upon trustees, which are cited rather as bearing testimony to the very general uniformity with which the Legislature has guarded the funds of these institutions from encroachment by those in charge.

Of course, too, it must be apparant that the language of the stafute could not, as a rule, be cited, when only a synopsis is given.

Many provisions in relation to loans upon bond and mortgage, are not embraced, such as that the borrower shall pay all expenses —that buildings must be insured and policy assigned to savings bank making the loan, etc.

Particular features of interest are referred to in a note, or sometimes by citation to the statute.

The object has been to give the whole material body of the law, relating to savings banks, as it exists to-day, in the most condensed form for practical use. Hence in these pages will be found a summary of nearly two hundred statutes, running through fifty volumes, and covering over six hundred pages.

As the design above expressed has been to give existing law, of course the provisions are stated as affected by the latest amendments; but as the year and chapter of every charter and of every amendment is given, any points left in doubt, or upon which further information is desired, are rendered easily accessible.

It will also be seen that the provisions of the charters are kept wholly distinct from any modification by restriction or enlargement of the general law.

To have attempted to give a synopsis of the charters, as modified by general statutes, would have added largely to the labor undertaken; have embarrassed the subject with grave doubts, where some judgment must be exercised as to the relative force of the general or the special law; and have rendered the whole subject confused and unintelligible.

I have therefore given all the general laws relating to savings banks in full, as they now stand, modified by their respective amendments.

Provisions of the charter of The Bank for Savings in the city of New York, located in New York; incorporated by chapter 62, Laws of 1819; charter amended by chapter 109, Laws of 1820; chapter 114, Laws of 1827; chapter 96, Laws of 1830; chapter 254, Laws of 1831, and chapter 178, Laws of 1836.

Number of trustees, twenty-eight.

Investments authorized:

Bond and mortgage, one-third value of property, located in the city of New York.

United States and New York State stocks, and stocks of any State in the Union.

Stocks of the city of New York.

Real estate other than under judgment or foreclosure, to an amount not exceeding a clear annual value of five thousand dollars.

Securities on which loans are authorized: On the credit of the corporation of the city of New York, and to the Public School Society of New York, on satisfactory real security.

Provisions under which right to invest in, or to loan upon other securities than those named above, may be claimed: None.

Provisions concerning deposits in bank: Lawful to make temporary deposits in any of the incorporated banks in the city of New York.

Largest amount authorized to receive from one depositor: No limit.

Regulations or restrictions concerning rate of interest to be paid to depositors: Lawful to allow depositors of five hundred dollars or more, one per cent less interest than is allowed to others.

Surplus authorized: Ten per cent on the amount of deposits.

Prohibition concerning receiving pay for services, or borrowing funds:

1. The trustees or managers of said institution shall not, directly or indirectly, receive any pay or emolument for their services. Section 1, chapter 62, Laws of 1819.
2. No president, vice-president, trustee or accountant of the corporation shall, directly or indirectly, borrow or use the funds of the corporation, except to pay necessary current expenses. Section 2, chapter 62, Laws of 1819.

Provisions of the charter of The Albany Savings Bank, located at Albany; incorporated by chapter 100, Laws of 1820; charter amended by chapter 208, Laws of 1827; chapter 199, Laws of 1840, and chapter 483, Laws of 1853.

Number of trustees, nineteen.

Investments authorized:

Bond and mortgage, one-third value of property, unincumbered and productive, located in the city of Albany; or on unincumbered real estate in any part of the State out of the city, double the value of the sum loaned, exclusive of buildings.

United States and New York State stocks, and stocks of any State in the union.

Stocks of any city in this State, or in the stock of any of the banks in the cities of Albany or Troy; chapter 208, Laws of 1827.

Real estate other than under judgment or foreclosure: Not exceeding an annual value of five thousand dollars.

Securities on which loans are authorized: On the credit of the city of Albany, and on the credit of any of the banks in the cities of Albany or Troy.

Provisions under which right to invest in, or to loan upon, other securities than those named above, may be claimed: None.

Provisions concerning deposits in bank: None, except in the form of loans as above.

Largest amount authorized to receive from one depositor: No limit.

Regulations or restrictions concerning rate of interest to be paid to depositors: To be such that depositors shall receive a ratable proportion of all the profits.

Surplus authorized: None.

Prohibition concerning receiving pay for services, or borrowing funds:

1. The trustees or managers of said institution shall not, directly or indirectly, receive any pay or emolument for their services. Section 1, chapter 100, Laws of 1820.
2. No president, vice-president, trustee or accountant shall, directly or indirectly, borrow or use the funds of the corporation, except to pay necessary current expenses. Section 2, chapter 100, Laws of 1820.

Provisions of the charter of the Troy Savings Bank, located at Troy; incorporated by chapter 232, Laws of 1823; charter amended by chapter 276, Laws of 1839; chapter 216, Laws of 1850; chapter 34, Laws of 1859, and chapter 150, Laws of 1861.

Number of Trustees, nineteen.

Investments authorized:

Bond and mortgage, half value of property, in sums not exceeding $5,000 in any one loan, located within this State.

United States and New York State stocks, and stocks of any city in this State.

Real estate other than under judgment or foreclosure: A suitable site and building for the accommodation of the bank.

Securities on which loans are authorized: To any bank in the city of Troy.*

Provisions under which right to invest in, or loan upon, other securities than those named above, may be claimed: None.

Provisions concerning deposits in bank: Same as for loans as above.

Largest amount authorized to receive from one depositor: No limit.

Regulations or restrictions concerning rate of interest to be paid to depositors: To be such that depositors shall receive a ratable proportion of all the profits.

Surplus authorized: Three per cent.

Prohibition concerning receiving pay for services, or borrowing funds:

1. The trustees or managers of said institution shall not, directly or indirectly, receive any pay or emolument for their services. Section 1, chapter 232, Laws of 1823.
2. No president, vice-president, trustee or accountant shall, directly or indirectly, borrow or use the funds of the corporation, except to pay necessary current expenses. Section 2, chapter 232, Laws of 1823. But by section 4, chapter 216, Laws of 1850, the trustees were authorized to pay the president such compensation as they should deem reasonable.

---

*The charter also authorized the trustees to make an agreement with any of the banks, in the city of Troy, to receive deposits and transact the business of the institution.

Provisions of the charter of the Brooklyn Savings Bank, located at Brooklyn, incorporated by chapter 177, Laws of 1827; charter amended by chapter 14; Laws of 1829; chapter 193, Laws of 1832, and chapter 323, Laws of 1838.

Number of trustees, twenty-five.

Investments authorized:

Bond and mortgage, half value of property, and not restricted in location.

United States and New York State stocks, (the statute reads United States or State securities) and stocks of cities of New York and Brooklyn.

Real estate other than under judgment or foreclosure, a banking house not exceeding in value thirty thousand dollars.

Securities on which loans are authorized: On credit of the authorities of New York or Brooklyn.

Provisions under which right to invest in, or to loan upon, other securities than those named above, may be claimed: None.

Provisions concerning deposits in bank: None.

Largest amount authorized to receive from one depositor: No limit.

Regulations or restrictions concerning rate of interest to be paid to depositors: Rate to be as high as profits will, in the opinion of the trustees, justify, but lawful to allow depositors of five hundred dollars or more, one per cent less interest than is allowed to others.

Surplus authorized: Three per cent on the amount of deposits.

Prohibition concerning receiving pay for services, or borrowing funds:

1. The trustees or managers of said institution shall not, directly or indirectly, receive any pay or emolument for their services as such trustees or managers. Section 1, chapter 177, Laws of 1827.

2. No president, vice-president, trustee, accountant or other officer of the corporation shall, directly or indirectly, borrow or use any of the funds of said corporation, except to pay the necessary current expenses. Section 2, chapter 177, Laws of 1827, and section 3, chapter 193, Laws of 1832.

Provisions of the charter of The Seaman's Bank for Savings in the city of New York, located in the city of New York, incorporated by chapter 17, Laws of 1829, charter amended by chapter 309, Laws of 1832, and chapter 126, Laws of 1834.

Number of trustees, twenty-three.

Investments authorized :

Bond and mortgage, half value of property, located in cities of New York or Brooklyn.

United States and New York State stocks, stocks of any State in the Union, and stocks of the city of New York.

Real estate, other than under judgment or foreclosure, not exceeding an annual value of five thousand dollars.

Securities on which loans are authorized : None.

Provisions under which right to invest in, or to loan upon, other securities than those named above, may be claimed : None.

Provisions concerning deposits in bank : Authorized to make temporary deposits in any of the incorporated banks in the city of New York.

Largest amount authorized to receive from one depositor: No limit.

Regulations or restrictions concerning rate of interest to be paid to depositors : Lawful to allow depositors of five hundred dollars or more, one per cent less than is allowed to others.

Surplus authorized : Three per cent. on amount of deposits.

Prohibition concerning receiving pay for services, or borrowing funds :

1. The trustees or managers of the said corporation, shall not directly or indirectly receive any pay or emolument for their services. Section 3, chapter 17, Laws of 1829.
2. No president, vice-president, trustee or other officer of said corporation, shall directly or indirectly borrow or use the funds of the corporation, except to pay the necessary current expenses. Section 7, chapter 17, laws of 1829.

Provisions of the charter of The Poughkeepsie Savings Bank, located at Poughkeepsie; incorporated by chapter 134, Laws of 1831; charter amended by chapter 270, Laws of 1832; and chapter 477, Laws of 1863.

Number of trustees, eleven.

Investments authorized:

Bond and mortgage, half value of property, not restricted in location.

United States and New York State stocks, stocks of any State in the Union, and stocks of any city or county in this State.

Real estate, other than under judgment or foreclosure, not exceeding an annual value of five thousand dollars.

Securities on which loans are authorized: None.

Provisions under which right to invest in, or to loan upon, other securities than those named above, may be claimed: None.

Provisions concerning deposits in bank: Lawful to deposit in any bank in Poughkeepsie or in the city of New York, or with the New York Life Insurance and Trust Company.

Largest amount authorized to receive from one depositor: No limit.

Regulations or restrictions concerning rate of interest to be paid to depositors: Such that depositors shall receive a ratable proportion of all profits.

Surplus authorized: None.

Prohibition concerning receiving pay for services or borrowing funds:

1. The trustees or managers of said corporation shall not directly or indirectly receive any pay or emolument for their services. Section 3, chapter 134, Laws of 1831.
2. No president, vice-president, trustee or other officer of said corporation shall, directly or indirectly, borrow or use the funds of the corporation except to pay the necessary current expenses. Section 7, chapter 134, Laws of 1831; but by section 1, chapter 477, Laws of 1863, the trustees were authorized to pay the president of the bank out of the surplus earnings, such compensation as they should deem reasonable.

Provisions of the charter of the Rochester Savings Bank, located in Rochester; incorporated by chapter 207, Laws of 1831; charter amended by chapter 167, Laws of 1859.

Number of trustees, fifteen.

Investments authorized:

Bond and mortgage, half value of property in sums not exceeding $10,000 to one individual, and located in counties of Monroe, Wayne, Ontario, Genesee, Orleans and Livingston.*

United States and New York State stocks, stocks of the States of Massachusetts, Pennsylvania, Ohio, Michigan, Illinois, Indiana, Missouri, Kentucky, Connecticut and Virginia.

Bonds for the city of Rochester or county of Monroe.

Real estate, other than under judgment or foreclosure, not exceeding an annual value of two thousand dollars.

Securities on which loans are authorized: The same as authorized for investment.

Provisions under which right to invest in, or to loan upon, other securities than those named above, may be claimed: Required to invest in securities named in charter, except an available fund of not exceeding one-third of the amount deposited, which may be kept in reserve in banks of discount on deposit, on interest, or otherwise, in such available form as the trustees may direct, to meet current payments. Sec. 1, chap. 167, Laws of 1859.

Provisions concerning deposits in bank: As above.

Largest amount authorized to receive from one depositor: No limit.

Regulations or restrictions concerning rates of interest to be paid to depositors: Such that depositors shall receive a ratable proportion of all profits of the bank.

Surplus authorized: None.

Prohibition concerning receiving pay for services, or borrowing funds:

1. The trustees or managers of the said corporation shall not, directly or indirectly, receive any pay or emolument for their services. Sec. 3, chap. 207, Laws of 1831.
2. No president, vice-president, trustee or other officer of said corporation shall, directly or indirectly, borrow or use the funds of the corporation, except to pay the necessary current expenses. Sec. 7, chap. 207, Laws of 1831.

---

*By the original charter it was provided that the deposits might be loaned out upon bond and mortgage as the board of managers should deem *amply sufficient*. See section 6, chapter 207, Laws of 1831.

Provisions of the charter of The Greenwich Savings Bank, located in New York; incorporated by chapter 215, Laws of 1833; charter amended by chapter 96, Laws of 1836, and chapter 255, Laws of 1841.

Number of trustees, thirty.

Investments authorized:

Bond and mortgage, half value of property, located in the city of New York.

United States and New York State stocks, stocks of the States of Pennsylvania and Ohio, and stocks of the city of New York.

Real estate, other than under judgment or foreclosure, not exceeding an annual value of five thousand dollars.

Securities on which loans are authorized: To the public School society of New York, on satisfactory real security, and stocks of the State or city of New York.

Provisions under which right to invest in, or to loan upon, other securities than those named above, may be claimed: None.

Provisions concerning deposits in bank: Authorized to make temporay deposits in any of the incorporated banks in the city of New York.

Largest amount authorized to receive from one depositor, $3,000.

Regulations or restrictions concerning rate of interest to be paid to depositors: Lawful to allow depositors of five hundred dollars, or more, one per cent less interest than is allowed to others.

Surplus authorized. Three per cent on the amount of deposits.

Prohibition concerning receiving pay for services, or borrowing funds:

1. The trustees or managers of said corporation shall not, directly or indirectly, receive any pay or emolument for their services. Section 3, chapter 215, Laws of 1833.
2. No president, vice-president, trustee, or other officer of said corporation shall, directly or indirectly, borrow or use the funds of the corporation, except to pay the necessary current expenses. Section 7, chapter 215, Laws of 1833. It is further provided that no trustee or officer shall be a depositor in the bank, except as a trustee, for the benefit of others. Section 4, chapter 96, Laws of 1836.

Provisions of the charter of The Schenectady Savings Bank, located at Schenectady; incorporated by chapter 205, Laws of 1834; charter not amended.

Number of trustees, thirteen.

Investments authorized:

Bond and mortgage, half value of property, exclusive of buildings, not limited as to location.

United States and New York State stocks, and stocks of any other State in the Union.

Real estate, other than under judgment or foreclosure, not exceeding an annual value of five thousand dollars.

Securities on which loans are authorized: None.

Provisions under which right to invest in, or to loan upon, other securities than those named above, may be claimed: None.

Provisions concerning deposits in bank: None.

Largest amount authorized to receive from one depositor: No limit. Total deposits not to exceed $500,000.

Regulations or restrictions concerning rate of interest to be paid to depositors: Lawful to allow depositors of five hundred dollars or more, one per cent less than is allowed to others.

Surplus authorized: None.

Prohibition concerning receiving pay for services, or borrowing funds:

1. The trustees or managers of the said corporation shall not directly or indirectly receive any pay or emolument for their services. Section 3, chapter 205, Laws of 1834.
2. No president, vice-president, trustee or other officer of the said corporation shall directly or indirectly borrow or use the funds of the corporation, except to pay the necessary current expenses. Section 7, chapter 205, Laws of 1834.

Provisions of the charter of The Bowery Savings Bank, located in New York; incorporated by chapter 229, Laws of 1834; charter amended by chapter 7, Laws of 1835; and chapter 347, Laws of 1839.

Number of trustees, forty.

Investments authorized:

Bond and mortgage, half value of property, located in the cities of New York or Brooklyn.

United States and New York State stocks, stocks of the States of Pennsylvania or Ohio, and stocks of the city of New York.

Real estate, other than under judgment or foreclosure, not exceeding an annual value of five thousand dollars.

Securities on which loans are authorized: To the Public School Society of New York, on satisfactory real security, worth thirty per cent more than the amount loaned thereon.

Provisions under which right to invest in, or to loan upon, other securities than those named above, may be claimed: None.

Provisions concerning deposits in bank: Lawful to make temporary deposits in any of the incorporated banks of the city of New York.

Largest amount authorized to receive from one depositor: $3,000.

Regulations or restrictions concerning rate of interest to be paid to depositors: Lawful to allow depositors of five hundred dollars or upwards, one per cent less than the interest allowed others.

Surplus authorized: None.

Prohibition concerning receiving pay for services, or borrowing funds:

1. The trustees of the said corporation shall not, directly or indirectly, receive any pay or emolument for their services. Section 3, chapter 229, Laws of 1834.
2. No president, vice-president, trustee or other officer of the said corporation shall, directly or indirectly, borrow or use the funds of the corporation, except to pay the necessary current expenses. Section 7, chapter 229, Laws of 1834.

It is further provided, that no trustee or officer of said bank shall have any interest in the deposits therein or the profits arising therefrom. Section 2, chapter 7, Laws of 1835.

Provisions of the charter of The Savings Bank of Utica, located at Utica; incorporated by chapter 242, Laws of 1839; charter amended by chapter 304, Laws of 1842; and chapter 223, Laws of 1864.

Number of trustees, fifteen.

Investments authorized:

Bond and mortgage, half value of property, exclusive of buildings, not limited as to location.

United States and New York State stocks, stocks of any other State in the Union, and stocks of the city of Utica.

Real estate, other than under judgment or foreclosure, not exceeding an annual value of two thousand dollars. (See surplus authorized.)

Securities on which loans are authorized: Upon personal security, not exceeding in the aggregate the sum of five thousand dollars, by resolution of a majority of the board.

Provisions under which right to invest in, or to loan upon, other securities than those named above, may be claimed: None.

Provisions concerning deposits in banks: Authorized to make temporary deposits in any of the banks of the city of Utica.

Largest amount authorized to receive from one depositor, $2,000, and in the aggregate not to exceed $2,000,000.

Regulations or restrictions concerning rate of interest to be paid to depositors: Such that depositors shall receive a ratable proportion of profits.

Surplus authorized: Ten per cent and suitable banking house.

Prohibition concerning receiving pay for services, or borrowing funds:

1. The trustees or managers of the said corporation shall not, directly or indirectly, receive any pay or emolument for their services. Section 3, chapter 242, Laws of 1839.

2. No president, vice-president, trustee or other officer of said corporation shall, directly or indirectly, borrow or use the funds of the corporation except to pay the necessary current expenses. Section 7, chapter 242, Laws of 1839; also, section 2, chapter 304, Laws of 1842.

Provisions of the charter of The Buffalo Savings Bank, located at Buffalo; incorporated by chapter 176, Laws of 1846; charter amended by chapter 456, Laws of 1847; chapter 281, Laws of 1849; and chapter 75, Laws of 1857.

Number of trustees, eighteen.

Investments authorized:

Bond and mortgage, half value of property, exclusive of buildings, in sums not exceeding $10,000 to one individual, not restricted in location.

United States and New York State stocks, and stocks of the city of Buffalo and of the county of Erie.

Real estate, other than under judgment or foreclosure, such as may be requisite for the convenient transaction of its business.

Securities on which loans are authorized: None.

Provisions under which right to invest in, or loan upon, other securities than those named above, may be claimed:

1. Trustees shall not invest in other securities than those named in the charter, in opposition to the vote of any trustee. Section 6, chapter 176, Laws of 1846.
2. Required to invest in securities named in charter, except an available fund of not exceeding fifteen per cent. of the total amount of deposits of said bank, which may be kept in deposit, on interest, or otherwise, in such available form as the trustees may direct. Sec. 6, chapter 176, Laws of 1846; and section 2, chapter 75, Laws of 1857.

Provisions concerning deposits in banks: None, except as above.

Largest amount authorized to receive from one depositor: No limit.

Regulations or restrictions concerning rate of interest to be paid to depositors: Such that depositors shall receive a ratable proportion of profits.

Surplus authorized: None.

Prohibition concerning receiving pay for services or borrowing funds:

1. The trustees of said corporation shall not, directly or indirectly, receive any pay or emolument for their services. Section 3, chapter 176, Laws of 1846.
2. No president, vice-president, trustee, officer or servant of said corporation shall, directly or indirectly, borrow the funds of said corporation or its depositors, or in any manner use the same, or any part thereof, except to pay necessary current expenses under the direction of the said board of trustees. Section 6, chapter 176, Laws of 1846.

Provisions of the charter of the East River Savings Institution, located in New York; incorporated by chapter 256, Laws of 1848; charter not amended.

Number of trustees, twenty-eight.

Investments authorized:

Bond and mortgage, half value of property, located in either of the cities of New York or Brooklyn.

United States and New York State stocks, and stocks of the city of New York.

Real estate, other than under judgment or foreclosure, not exceeding an annual value of five thousand dollars.

Securities on which loans are authorized: To the Public School Society of New York, on satisfactory real security worth thirty per cent more than the amount loaned thereon.

Provisions under which right to invest in, or to loan upon, other securities than those named above, may be claimed: None.

Provisions concerning deposits in bank: Authorized to make temporary deposits not exceeding forty thousand dollars, in any of the banks in the city of New York.

Largest amount authorized to receive from one depositor, $3,-000.

Regulations or restrictions concerning rate of interest to be paid to depositors: Lawful to allow to depositors of five hundred dollars or upwards, at least one per cent. less than the interest allowed to others.

Surplus authorized: Ten per cent. on the amount of deposits.

Prohibition concerning receiving pay for services or borrowing funds:

1. The trustees of the said corporation shall not directly or indirectly receive any pay or emolument for their services. Section 3 of charter.
2. No president, vice-president, trustee or other officer of the said corporation shall directly or indirectly borrow or use the funds of the corporation except to pay the necessary current expenses. Section 8 of charter. It is further provided that no trustee or officer shall have any interest in any of the deposits or the profits arising therefrom. Section 7, of charter.

Provisions of the charter of the Institution for the Savings of Merchants' Clerks, located in New York; incorporated by chapter 324, Laws of 1848; charter amended by chapter 550, Laws of 1867.

Number of trustees, twenty-five.

Investments authorized:

Bond and mortgage, half value of property improved, not restricted as to location.

United States and New York State stocks, and stocks of other States of the Union, when approved by three-fourths of the board of trustees.

Stocks of the city of New York.

Real estate, other than under judgment or foreclosure, so much as may be necessary for its own purposes in the transaction of business, not exceeding an annual value of $25,000.

Securities on which loans are authorized: None.

Provisions under which right to invest in, or to loan upon, other securities than those named above, may be claimed: None.

Provision concerning deposits in bank: Authorized to make temporary deposits in any of the incorporated banks of the city of New York.

Largest amount authorized to receive from one depositor: No limit.

Regulations or restrictions concerning rate of interest to be paid to depositors: Left to the discretion of the board.

Surplus authorized: twenty per cent. of the deposits.

Prohibition concerning receiving pay for services, or borrowing funds:

1. The trustees or managers of the said corporation shall not directly or indirectly receive any pay or emolument for their services. Sec. 7, chap. 324, Laws of 1848.
2. No president, vice-president, trustee or other officer of the said corporation shall directly or indirectly borrow or use the funds of the corporation except to pay the necessary current expenses. Sec. 10, chap. 324, Laws of 1848.

See sections 3, 4 and 5 of charter, for unusual provisions concerning election of trustees.

Provisions of the charter of the Dry Dock Savings Institution, located in New York; incorporated by chapter 368, Laws of 1848; charter not amended.

Number of trustees, fifteen.

Investments authorized:

Bond and mortgage, half value of property, located in the city of New York.

United States and New York State stocks.

Stocks of the city of New York.

Real estate, other than under judgment or foreclosure, not exceeding an annual value of five thousand dollars.

Securities on which loans are authorized: Stocks of the State or city of New York.

Provisions under which right to invest in, or to loan upon, other securities than those named above, may be claimed: None.

Provisions concerning deposits in bank: Authorized to make temporary deposits to an amount not exceeding $20,000 in any of the banks of the city of New York.

Largest amount authorized to receive from one depositor: No limit.

Regulations or restrictions concerning rate of interest, to be paid to depositors: Such that depositors shall receive a ratable proportion of the profits.

Surplus authorized: None.

Prohibition concerning receiving pay for services, or borrowing funds:

1. The trustees or managers of the said corporation shall not directly or indirectly receive any pay or emolument for their services. Section 3, of charter.
2. No president, vice-president, trustee or other officer of said corporation, shall directly or indirectly borrow or use the funds of the corporation, except to pay the necessary current expenses. Section 7, of charter.

Provisions of the charter of the Auburn Savings Institution, located at Auburn; incorporated by chapter 92, Laws of 1849; charter amended by chapter 503, Laws of 1864, and chapter 417, Laws of 1865.

Number of trustees, thirteen.

Investments authorized:

Bond and mortgage, three-fifths value of property, exclusive of buildings, in sums not exceeding $5,000 to any one person, and located in this State.

United States and New York State stocks, and stocks of any county in this State.

Real estate, other than under judgment or foreclosure, such as may be requisite for the convenient transaction of its business.

Securities on which loans are authorized: Bonds of any county of this State, authorized by law to be issued.

Provisions under which right to invest in, or to loan upon, other securities than those named above, may be claimed: Required to invest in securities named in charter, except an available fund not exceeding $100,000 which may be kept on deposit, on interest or otherwise, in such available form as said trustees may direct. Section 7, chapter 92, Laws of 1849 as amended by section 1, chapter 503, Laws of 1864.

Provisions concerning deposits in bank: None except as above.

Largest amount authorized to receive from one depositor, $5,000.

Regulations or restrictions concerning rate of interest to be paid to depositors.

Such that depositors shall receive ratable proportion of profits, but the trustees may fix a different rate of interest according to the amount deposited, and the time the same shall remain on deposit, and no interest whatever shall be allowed on any sum less than three dollars, or for the fractional parts of a month. Section 6, chapter 92, Laws of 1849.

Whenever the surplus earnings of said institution shall have reached the sum of thirty thousand dollars, the trustees shall thereafter allow to depositors, keeping open book accounts, interest at the rate of six per cent per annum, provided the earnings of current year, after paying the current expenses shall justify the same. Section 1, chapter 503, Laws of 1864.

In making any extra credit of interest, under the provision in the last clause of section one of said (the above) amendatory act, the trustees of said institution shall have authority to confine such credit, if they shall deem best, to one class of depositors; and the class may be determined by a resolution of the board of trustees, fixing the sum of the account which shall be entitled to such credit of interest. And they may vary the sum so fixed each year if they think proper, but the sum fixed shall not exceed one thousand dollars. They may also discriminate in regard to the time the sum shall have been on deposit; and may make such extra credit of interest applicable to any date anterior to the date of the action authorizing the same. Section 2, chapter 417, Laws of 1865.

Surplus authorized, thirty thousand dollars.*

Prohibition concerning receiving pay for services, or borrowing funds:

1. The trustees of said corporation shall not directly or indirectly receive any pay or emolument for their services. Section 3, chapter 92, Laws of 1849.
2. No president, vice-president, trustee, officer or servant of said corporation shall directly or indirectly borrow the funds of said corporation or its deposits, or in any manner use the same, or any part thereof, except to pay necessary current expenses under the direction of said board of trustees. Section 6, chapter 92, Laws of 1849.

---

*The charter recognizes rather than authorizes the accumulation of such surplus.

Provisions of the charter of The Syracuse Savings Institution, located at Syracuse; incorporated by chapter 179, Laws of 1849; charter amended by chapter 32, Laws of 1857, and chapter 307, Laws of 1867.

Number of trustees, eighteen.

Investments authorized:

Bonds and mortgage, half value of property, in sums not exceeding $10,000 to one individual, and not restricted as to location.

United States and New York State stocks, and stocks of any city in this State.

Real estate, other than under judgment or foreclosure, such as may be requisite for the convenient transaction of its business.

Securities on which loans are authorized: None.

Provisions under which right to invest in, or to loan upon, other securities than those named above, may be claimed:

1. Trustees shall not invest in other securities than those named in the charter, in opposition to the vote of any three trustees. Section 1, chapter 307, Laws of 1867.
2. Required to invest in securities named in charter, except an available fund of not exceeding $25,000, or not exceeding one-third of the deposits, which may be kept on deposit, on interest, or otherwise, or in such available form as the trustees may direct. Section 6, chapter 179, Laws of 1849.

Provisions concerning deposits in bank: None, except as above.

Largest amount authorized to receive from one depositor, $10,000.

Regulations or restrictions concerning rate of interest to be paid to depositors: Such that depositors shall receive a ratable proportion of all profits.

Surplus authorized: None.

Prohibition concerning receiving pay for services or borrowing funds:

1. The trustees of said corporation shall not, as such, directly or indirectly, receive any pay or emolument for their services. Section 3, chapter 179, Laws of 1849.
2. No president, vice-president, trustee, officer or servant of said corporation shall, directly or indirectly, borrow the funds of said corporation or its deposits, or in any manner use the same, or any part thereof, except to pay necessary current expenses, under the direction of said board of trustees. Section 6, chapter 179, Laws of 1849.

Provisions of the charter of The Albany City Savings Institution, located at Albany; incorporated by chapter 119, Laws of 1850; charter not amended.

Number of trustees, twenty.

Investments authorized:

Bond and mortgage, half value of property, exclusive of buildings, in sums not exceeding $5,000 to one individual, and not restricted in location.

United States and New York State stocks, and stocks of any city in this State.

Real estate, other than under judgment or foreclosure, such as may be requisite for the convenient transaction of its business.

Securities on which loans are authorized: None.

Provisions under which right to invest in, or to loan upon, other securities than those named above, may be claimed:

1. Trustees shall not invest in other securities than those named in the charter, in opposition to the vote of any trustee. Section 6, of charter.
2. Required to invest in securities named in charter, except an available fund of not exceeding $100,000, or not exceeding one-third of total deposits, which may be kept on deposit, on interest or otherwise, or in such available form as the trustees may direct. See section 6, of charter.

Provisions concerning deposits in bank: None, except as above.

Largest amount authorized to receive from one depositor, $5,000.

Regulations or restrictions concerning rate of interest to be paid to depositors: Such that depositors may receive a ratable proportion of all the profits.

Surplus authorized: None.

Prohibition concerning receiving pay for services, or borrowing funds:

1. The trustees of said corporation shall not, as such, directly or indirectly receive any pay or emolument for their services. Section 3, of charter.
2. No president, vice-president, trustee, officer or servant of said corporation shall directly or indirectly borrow the funds of said corporation or its deposits, or in any manner use the same, or any part thereof, except to pay necessary current expenses under the direction of said board of trustees. Section 6, of charter.

Provisions of the charter of The Hudson City Savings Institution located, at Hudson; incorporated by chapter 145, Laws of 1850; charter not amended.

Number of trustees, thirteen.

Investments authorized :

Bond and mortgage, half value of property exclusive of buildings, in sums not exceeding $5,000 to one individual and not restricted in location.

United States and New York State stocks, and stocks of any city in this State.

Real estate other than under judgment or foreclosure, such as may be requisite for the convenient transaction of its business.

Securities on which loans are authorized : None.

Provisions under which right to invest in, or to loan upon, other securities than those named above, may be claimed:

1. Trustees shall not invest in other securities than those named in the charter, in opposition to the vote of any trustee. Section 6, of charter.
2. Required to invest in securities named in charter, except an available fund not exceeding $40,000 or not exceeding one-third of total amount of deposits, which may be kept on deposit, on interest, or otherwise, or in such available form as the trustees may direct. Section 6 of charter.

Provisions concerning deposits in bank: None except as above.

Largest amount authorized to receive from one depositor, $5,000.

Regulations or restrictions concerning rate of interest to be paid to depositors; Such that depositors shall receive a ratable proportion of all profits.

Surplus authorized : None.

Prohibition concerning receiving pay for services or borrowing funds:

1. The trustees of said corporation shall not, as such, directly or indirectly receive any pay or emolument for their services. Section 3 of charter.
2. No president, vice-president, trustee, officer or servant of said corporation, shall directly or indirectly borrow the funds of said corporation or its deposits, or in any manner use the same or any part thereof, except to pay necessary current expenses, under the direction of said board of trustees. Section 6 of charter.

Provisions of the charter of The Monroe County Savings Bank, located at Rochester: incorporated by chapter 228, Laws of 1850; charter amended by chapter 152, Laws of 1861; and chapter 91, Laws of 1863.

Number of trustees, twenty-one.

Investments authorized:

Bond and mortgage, half value of property, exclusive of buildings, in sums not exeeeding $10,000 to one individual, and not restricted in location.

United States and New York State stocks, and stocks of any city of this State, or of the county of Monroe.

Real estate other than under judgment or foreclosure, such as may be requisite for the convenient transaction of its business.

Securities on which loans are authorized: None.

Provisions under which right to invest in, or to loan upon, other securities than those named above, may be claimed:

1. Trustees shall not invest in other securities than those named in the charter, in opposition to the vote of any trustee. Section 6, chapter 152, Laws of 1861.
2. Required to invest in securities named in charter, except an available fund of not exceeding $100,000, or not exceeding one-third of the total deposits which may be kept on deposit, on interest or otherwise, or in such available form as the trustees may direct. Section 6, chapter 152, Laws of 1861.

Provisions concerning deposits in bank: None except as above.

Largest amount authorized to receive from one depositor, $5,000.

Regulations or restrictions concerning rate of interest to be paid to depositors: Such that depositors shall receive a ratable proportion of all profits.

Surplus authorized: None.

Prohibition concerning receiving pay for services, or borrowing funds:

1. The trustees of said corporation shall not as such directly or indirectly receive any pay or emolument for their services. Section 3, chapter 228, Laws of 1850.
2. No president, vice-president, trustee, officer or servant of said corporation shall directly or indirectly borrow the funds of the said corporation or its deposits, or in any manner use the same or any part thereof, except to pay necessary expenses under the direction of said board of trustees. Section 6, chapter 228, Laws of 1850.

Provisions of the charter of the Manhattan Savings Institution, located in New York; incorporated by chapter 284, Laws of 1850; charter amended by chapter 314, Laws of 1857; and chapter 456, Laws of 1859.

Number of trustees, thirty-three, and mayor and comptroller of the city of New York, *ex-officio.*

Investments authorized:

Bond and mortgage, half value of property, in sums not exceeding $20,000, and located in this State.

United States and New York State stocks, and stocks of any city in this State.

Real estate, other than under judgment of foreclosure, such as may be requisite for the convenient transaction of its business.

Securities on which loans are authorized: None.

Provisions under which right to invest in, or to loan upon, other securities than those named above, may be claimed:

Required to invest in securities named in charter, except an available fund of not exceeding $100,000, or not exceeding one-third of the total amount of deposits which may be kept on deposit, on interest or otherwise, or in such available form as the trustees may direct. Section 6, chapter 284, Laws of 1850.

Provisions concerning deposits in bank: None except as above.

Largest amount authorized to receive from one depositor, $5,000.

Regulations or restrictions concerning rate of interest to be paid to depositors: Such that depositors shall receive a ratable proportion of all profits.

Surplus authorized: Five per cent of the amount of deposits.

Prohibition concerning receiving pay for services, or borrowing funds:

1. The trustees of said corporation shall not, as such, directly or indirectly receive any pay or emolument for their services. Sec. 3, chap. 284, Laws of 1850.
2. No president, vice-president, trustee, officer or servant of said corporation shall directly or indirectly borrow the funds of the said corporation or its deposits, or in any manner use the same or any part thereof, except to pay necessary expenses under the direction of said board of trustees. Sec. 6, chapter 284, Laws of 1850.

Provisions of the charter of The Emigrant Industrial Savings Bank, located in New York; incorporated by chapter 290, Laws of 1850; charter amended by chapter 278, Laws of 1851.

Number of trustees, eighteen (by original charter); by amendment, twenty-six.

Investments authorized:

Bond and mortgage, half value of property, located in the cities of New York or Brooklyn.

United States and New York State stocks, and stocks of any city in this State, authorized by the Legislature to issue stock.

Real estate, other than under judgment or foreclosure, such as may be necessary for the transaction of its business, not exceeding an annual value of $5,000.

Securities on which loans are authorized: None.

Provisions under which right to invest in, or to loan upon, other securities than those named above, may be claimed: Required to invest in securities named in charter, except an available fund of not exceeding $100,000, or not exceeding one-third of the deposits, which may be kept on deposit, on interest or otherwise, or in such available form as the trustees may direct. Section 3, chapter 278, Laws of 1851.

Provisions concerning deposits in bank: By section 6, chapter 290, Laws of 1850, not exceeding $40,000, in any of the banks in the city of New York.

Largest amount authorized to receive from one depositor, $10,000.

Regulations or restrictions concerning rate of interest to be paid to depositors: Lawful to allow depositors of $500 or upwards, one per cent less than is allowed to others.

Surplus authorized: None.

Prohibition concerning receiving pay for services or borrowing funds:

1. The trustees of the said corporation shall not, directly or indirectly, receive any pay or emolument for their services. Section 3, chapter 290, Laws of 1850.
2. No president, vice-president, trustee or other officer of the said corporation shall, directly or indirectly, borrow or use the funds of said corporation, except to pay the necessary current expenses. Section 8, chapter 290, Laws of 1850. It is further provided that no trustee or officer shall be a depositor in the institution. Sec. 7, ch. 290, Laws of 1850.

Provisions of the charter of The South Brooklyn Savings Institution, located in Brooklyn; incorporated by chapter 299, Laws of 1850; charter amended by chapter 228, Laws of 1859.

Number of trustees, twenty-six.

Investments authorized:

Bond and mortgage, half value of property, in sums not exceeding $20,000 to one individual on the same piece of property, and not restricted in location.

United States and N. Y. State stocks, and stocks of any city or village in this State, authorized by law to be issued.

Real estate, other than under judgment or foreclosure, such as may be requisite for the convenient transaction of its business.

Securities on which loans are authorized: None.

Provisions under which right to invest in, or to loan upon, other securities than those named above, may be claimed:

1. Trustees shall not invest in other securities than those named in the charter, in opposition to the vote of any trustee. Section 6, chapter 299, Laws of 1850.
2. Required to invest in securities named in charter, except an available fund of not exceeding $100,000, or not exceeding one-third of the total amount of deposits, which may be kept on deposit, on interest, or otherwise, or in such available form as the trustees may direct. Section 6, chapter 299, Laws of 1850.

Provisions concerning deposit in bank: None except as above.

Largest amount authorized to receive from one depositor, $5,000.

Regulations or restrictions concerning rate of interest to be paid to depositors: Such that depositors shall receive a ratable proportion of the profits.

Surplus authorized: None.

Prohibition concerning receiving pay for services, or borrowing funds:

1. The trustees of the said corporation shall not, as such, directly or indirectly, receive any pay or emolument for their services. Section 3, chapter 299, Laws of 1850.
2. No president, vice-president, trustee, officer or servant of said corporation, shall, directly or indirectly, borrow the funds of said corporation or its deposits, or in any manner use the same or any part thereof, except to pay necessary expenses under the direction of said board of trustees. Section 6, chapter 299, Laws of 1850.

Provisions of the charter of the Williamsburgh Savings Bank, located at Williamsburgh; incorporated by chapter 109, Laws of 1851; charter amended by chapter 282, Laws of 1862, and chapter 478, Laws of 1867.

Number of trustees, eighteen.

Investments authorized :

Bond and mortgage, half value of property, in sums not exceeding $50,000 to one individual on the same piece of property, and not limited in location.

United States and N. Y. State stocks, and stocks of any city in this State, authorized by the Legislature to be issued.

Real estate, other than under judgment or foreclosure, such as may be requisite for the convenient transaction of its business.

Securities on which loans are authorized : None.

Provisions under which right to invest in, or to loan upon, other securities than those named above, may be claimed :

1. Trustees shall not invest in other securities than those named in the charter, in opposition to the vote of three trustees. Section 6, chapter 109, Laws of 1851.
2. Required to invest in securities named in charter, except an available fund of not exceeding $100,000, or not exceeding one-third of the total amount of deposits, which may be kept on deposit, on interest, or otherwise, in such available form as the trustees may direct. Secton 6, chapter 109, Laws of 1851.

Provisions concerning deposits in bank : None except as above.

Largest amount authorized to receive from one depositor, $5,000.

Regulations or restrictions concerning rate of interest to be paid to depositors : Such that deposits shall receive a ratable proportion of profits.

Surplus authorized : None

Prohibition concerning receiving pay for services, or borrowing funds :

1. The trustees of said corporation shall not, as such, directly or indirectly, receive any pay or emolument for their services. Section 3, chapter 109, Laws of 1851.
2. No president, vice-president, trustee, officer or servant of said corporation shall, directly or indirectly, borrow the funds of said corporation or its deposits, or in any manner use the same or any part thereof, except to pay necessary current expenses under the direction of said board of trustees. Section 6, chapter 109, Laws of 1851.

Provisions of the charter of The Niagara County Savings Bank, located at Lockport; incorporated by chapter 120, Laws of 1851; charter amended by chapter 190, Laws of 1854.

Number of trustees by original charter, 13; by amendment nine.

Investments authorized:

Bond and mortgage, half value of property, in sums not exceeding $5,000 to one individual, and not limited in location.

United States and New York State stocks, and stocks of any city authorized by the legislature of this State.

Real estate, other than under judgment or foreclosue, such as may be requisite for the convenient transaction of its business.

Securities on which loans are authorized: None.

Provisions under which right to invest in, or to loan upon, other securities than those named above, may be claimed:

1. Trustees shall not invest in other securities than those named in the charter, in opposition to the vote of any trustee. Section 6, chapter 120, Laws of 1851.
2. Required to invest in securities named in charter, except an available fund of not exceeding $50,000 or not exceeding one-third of the total amount of deposits, which may be kept on deposit, or interest or otherwise, in such available form as the trustees may direct. Section 6, chapter 120, Laws of 1851.

Provisions concerning deposits in bank: None except as above.

Largest amount authorized to receive from one depositor $5,000.

Regulations or restrictions concerning rate of interest to be paid to depositors: Such that depositors shall receive a ratable proportion of profits.

Surplus authorized, twenty-five thousand dollars.

Prohibition concerning receiving pay for services, or borrowing funds:

1. The trustees of said corporation shall not, as such, directly or indirectly receive any payment or emolument for their services. Section 3, chapter 120, Laws of 1851.
2. No president, vice-president, trustee, officer or servant of said corporation shall directly or indirectly borrow the funds of said corporation or its deposits, or in any manner use the same, or any part thereof, except to pay necessary expenses under the direction of said board of trustees. Section 6, chapter 120, Laws of 1851.

Provisions of the charter of the Cohoes Savings Institution, located at Cohoes; incorporated by chapter 138, Laws of 1851; charter not amended.

Number of trustees, nineteen.

Investments authorized:

Bond and mortgage, half value of property, exclusive of buildings, in sums not exceeding $3,000 to any one individual, and not restricted in location.

United States and New York State stocks, and stocks of any city authorized by the legislature of this State to be issued.

Real estate, other than under judgment or foreclosure, such as may be requisite for the convenient transaction of its business.

Securities on which loans are authorized: None.

Provisions under which right to invest in, or to loan upon, other securities than those named above, may be claimed:

1. Trustees shall not invest in other securities than those named in the charter, in opposition to the vote of any trustees. Section 6 of charter.
2. Required to invest in securities named in charter, except an available fund of not exceeding $25,000, or not exceeding one-third of the total amount of deposits, which may be kept on deposit, on interest or otherwise, or such available form as the trustees may direct. Section 6 of charter.

Provisions concerning deposits in bank: None except as above.

Largest amount authorized to receive from one depositor, $5,000.

Regulations or restrictions concerning rate of interest to be paid to depositors: Such that depositors shall receive a ratable proportion of profits.

Surplus authorized: None.

Prohibition concerning receiving pay for services, or borrowing funds:

1. The trustees of said corporation shall not, as such, directly or indirectly, receive any pay or emolument for their services. Section 3 of charter.
2. No president, vice-president, trustee, officer or servant of said corporation shall, directly or indirectly, borrow the funds of said corporation or its deposits, or in any manner use the same, or any part thereof, except to pay necessary current expenses under the direction of said board of trustees. Section 6 of charter.

Provisions of the charter of The Ulster County Savings Institution, located at Kingston; incorporated by chapter 152, Laws of 1851; charter amended by chapter 388, Laws of 1853; chapter 33, Laws of 1858; chapter 207, Laws of 1863, and chapter 247, Laws of 1867.

Number of trustees, by original charter, twenty-one; by amendment, not less than seven.

Investments authorized:

Bond and mortgage, half value of property, in sums not exceeding $25,000 to any one individual, and when loaned on other than city or village property the value to be exclusive of buildings.

United States and N. Y. State stocks, and stocks of any city authorized by this Legislature of this State to be issued.

Real estate, other than under judgment or foreclosure: Banking house and lot. See sec. 1, chap. 247, Laws of 1867.

Securities on which loans are authorized: None.

Provisions under which right to invest in, or to loan upon, other securities than those named above, may be claimed:

1. Trustees shall not invest in other securities than those named in the charter, unless by an affirmative vote of at least nine trustees. Sec. 2, chap. 247, Laws of 1867.
2. Required to invest in securities named in charter, except an available fund of not exceeding $50,000, or not exceeding one-third of the total amount of deposits, which may be kept on deposit, on interest or otherwise, in such available form as the trustees may direct. Section 1, chapter 207, Laws of 1863.

Provisions concerning deposits in bank: None except as above.

Largest amount authorized to receive from one depositor, $5,000.

Regulations or restrictions concerning rate of interest to be paid to depositors: Lawful to allow different rates of interest on sums of $500 and less, and on sums over $500.

Surplus authorized, twenty-five thousand dollars.

Prohibition concerning receiving pay for services, or borrowing funds:

1. The trustees of said corporation shall not, as such, directly or indirectly, receive any payment or emolument for their services. Sec. 3, chap. 152, Laws of 1851.
2. No president, vice-president, trustee, officer or servant of said corporation shall, directly or indirectly, borrow the funds of said corporation or its deposits, or in any manner use the same or any part thereof, except to pay necessary expenses under the direction of said board of trustees. Section 6, chapter 152, Laws of 1851.

Provisions of the charter of the Broadway Savings Institution, located in New York; incorporated by chapter 245, Laws of 1851; charter amended by chapter 316, Laws of 1853.

Number of trustees, twenty-three.

Investments authorized :

Bond and mortgage, half value of property, in sums not exceeding $10,000, and not restricted in location.

United States and N. Y. State stocks, and stocks of any city authorized by the Legislature of this State to be issued.

Real estate, other than under judgment or foreclosure, such as may be requisite for the convenient transaction of its business.

Securities on which loans are authorized : None.

Provisions under which right to invest in, or to loan upon, either securities than those named above, may be claimed :

1. Trustees shall not invest in other securities than those named in the charter, in opposition to the vote of any trustee. Section 6, chapter 245, Laws of 1851.
2. Required to invest in securities named in charter, except an available fund of not exceeding $100,000, or not exceeding one-third of the total amount of deposits, which may be kept on deposit, on interest or otherwise, in such available forms as the trustees may direct. Section 6, chapter 245, Laws of 1851.

Provisions concerning deposits in bank : None.

Largest amount authorized to receive from one depositor, $5,000.

Regulations or restrictions concerning rate of interest to be paid to depositors : Such that depositors shall receive a ratable proportion of profits.

Surplus authorized : None.

Prohibition concerning receiving pay for services, or borrowing funds :

1. The trustees of said corporation shall not, as such, directly or indirectly, receive any pay or emolument for their services. Section 3, chapter 245, Laws of 1851.
2. No president, vice-president, trustee, officer or servant of said corporation shall, directly or indirectly, borrow the funds of said corporation or its deposits, or in any manner use the same or any part thereof, except to pay necessary current expenses, under the direction of said board of trustees. Sec. 6, chap. 245, Laws of 1851.

Provisions of the charter of The Central City Savings Institution, located at Utica; incorporated by chapter 265, Laws of 1851; charter amended by chapter 335, Laws of 1864.

Number of trustees, thirteen.

Investments authorized:

Bond and mortgage, half value of property, exclusive of buildings, in sums not exceeding $5,000 to any one individual, not restricted in location; or in the city of Utica to the amount of one-half appraised value, including the buildings, insured for two-thirds the amount loaned.

United States and New York State stocks, and stocks of any city authorized by the Legislature of this State to be issued.

Real estate, other than under judgment or forclosure, such as may be requisite for the convenient transaction of its business.

Securities on which loans are authorized: None.

Provisions under which right to invest in, or to loan upon, other securities than those named above, may be claimed:

1. Trustees shall not invest in other securities than those named in the charter, in opposition to the vote of any three trustees. Section 6, chapter 265, Laws of 1851.
2. Required to invest in securities named in charter, except an available fund of not exceeding $50,000, or not exceeding one-third of the total amount of deposits, which may be kept on deposit, on interest or otherwise, or in such available form as the trustees may direct. Section 6, chapter 265, Laws of 1851.

Provisions concerning deposits in bank: None, except as above.

Largest amount authorized to receive from one depositor, $5,000.

Regulations or restrictions concerning rate of interest to be paid to depositors: Such that depositors shall receive a ratable proportion of profits.

Surplus authorized: None.

Prohibition concerning receiving pay for services, or borrowing funds:

1. The trustees of said corporation, shall not as such, directly or indirectly, receive any pay or emolument for their services. Section 3, chapter 265, Laws of 1851.

2. No president, vice-president, trustee, officer or servant of said corporation, shall directly or indirectly borrow the funds or deposits of said corporation, or in any manner use the same or any part thereof, except to pay necessary current expenses under the direction of said board of trustees. Section six, chapter 265, Laws of 1851; see section 15, chapter 265, Laws of 1851, for personal liability of trustees for losses.

Provisions of the charter of The Rome Savings Bank, located at Rome; incorporated by chapter 324, Laws of 1851; charter amended by chapter 150, Laws of 1865.

Number of trustees, thirteen.

Investments authorized:

Bond and mortgage, half value of property, exclusive of buildings, in sums not exceeding $5,000 and not restricted in location.

United States and New York State stocks, and stocks of any city authorized by the Legislature of this State to be issued.

Real estate, other than under judgment or foreclosure, such as may be requisite for the convenient transaction of its business.

Securities on which loans are authorized: None.

Provisions under which right to invest in, or to loan upon, other securities than those named above, may be claimed:

1. Trustees shall not invest in other securities than those named in the charter, in opposition to the vote of any trustee. Section 6, chapter 324, Laws of 1851.
2. Required to invest in securities named in charter, except an available fund of not exceeding $25,000, or not exceeding one-third of total amount of deposits, which may be kept on deposit, on interest or otherwise, or in such available form as the trustees may direct. Section 6, chapter 324, Laws of 1851.

Provisions concerning deposits in bank: None except as above.

Largest amount authorized to receive from one depositor, $1,000 by original charter; by amendment no limit.

Regulations or restrictions concerning rate of interest to be paid to depositors: Such that depositors shall receive a ratable proportion of profits.

Surplus authorized: None.

Prohibition concerning receiving pay for services, or borrowing funds:

1. The trustees of said corporation shall not as such, directly or indirectly receive any pay or emolument for their services. Sec. 3, chap. 324, Laws of 1851.
2. No president, vice-president, trustee, officer or servant of said corporation, shall directly or indirectly, borrow the funds of said corporation or its deposits, or in any manner use the same or any part thereof, except to pay necessary current expenses, under the direction of said board of trustees. Sec. 6, chap. 324, Laws of 1851.

Provisions of the charter of The Irving Savings Institution, located in New York; incorporated by chapter 370, Laws of 1851; charter amended by chapter 970, Laws of 1867.

Number of trustees, twenty-nine.

Investments authorized:

Bond and mortgage, half value of property, in sums not exceeding $50,000 to any one individual, and not limited in location.

United States and New York State stocks, and stocks of any city authorized by the Legislature of this State to be issued.

Real estate, other than under judgment or foreclosure, such as may be requisite for the convenient transaction of its business.

Securities on which loans are authorized: None.

Provisions under which right to invest in, or to loan upon, other securities than those named above may be claimed:

1. Trustees shall not invest in other securities than those named in the charter, in opposition to the vote of any two trustees. Chap. 970, Laws of 1867.
2. Required to invest in securities named in charter, except an available fund of not exceeding $100,000, or not exceeding one-third of the total amount of deposits, which may be kept on deposit on interest or otherwise, in such available form as the trustees may direct. Chap. 970, Laws of 1867.

Provisions concerning deposits in bank: Lawful to deposit in any legally organized bank in the city of New York.

Largest amount authorized to receive from one depositor, $5,000.

Regulations or restrictions concerning rate of interest to be paid to depositors: Such that depositors shall receive a ratable proportion of profits.

Surplus authorized: None.

Prohibition concerning rec'ing pay for services, or borrowing funds:

1. The trustees of said corporation shall not, as such, directly or indirectly receive any pay or emolument for their services. Section 3, chapter 370, Laws of 1851.
2. No president, vice-president, trustee, officer or servant of said corporation shall directly or indirectly borrow the funds of said corporation or its deposits, or in any manner use the same, or any part thereof, except to pay necessary current expenses under the direction of said board of trustees. Chapter 970, Laws of 1867.

Provisions of the charter of The Western Savings Bank of Buffalo, located at Buffalo; incorporated by chapter 469, Laws of 1851; charter not amended.

Number of trustees, twenty-one.

Investments authorized:

Bond and mortgage, half value of property, in sums not exceeding $5,000 to any one individual, and not restricted in location.

United States and New York State stocks, and stocks of any city or village authorized by the legislature of this State to be issued.

Real estate, other than under judgment of foreclosure such as may be requisite for the convenient transaction of its business.

Securities on which loans are authorized: None.

Provisions under which right to invest in, or to loan upon, other securities than those named above, may be claimed :

1. Trustees shall not invest in other securities than those named in the charter, in opposition to the vote of any trustee. Section 6 of charter.
2. Required to invest in securities named in charter, except an available fund of not exceeding $50,000, or not exceeding one-third of the total amount of deposits, which

may be kept on deposit, on interest or otherwise, in such available form as the trustees may direct. Section 6 of charter.

Provisions concerning deposits in bank: None except as above.

Largest amount authorized to receive from one depositor, $5,000.

Regulations or restrictions concerning rate of interest to be paid to depositors: Such that depositors shall receive a ratable proportion of profits.

Surplus authorized: Twenty-five thousand dollars.

Prohibition concerning receiving pay for services, or borrowing funds:

1. The trustees of said corporation shall not, as such, directly or indirectly receive any pay or emolument for their services. Section 3 of charter.
2. No president, vice-president, trustee, officer or servant of said corporation, shall, directly or indirectly, borrow the funds of said corporation or its deposits, or in any manner use the same, or any part thereof, except to pay necessary expenses under the direction of said board of trustees. Section 6 of charter.

Provisions of the charter of The Newburgh Savings Bank, located at Newburgh; incorporated by chap. 252, Laws of 1852; charter amended by chap. 150, Laws of 1859, and chap. 567, Laws of 1865.

Number of trustees, twenty-two.

Investments authorized:

Bond and mortgage, half value of property, in sums not exceeding $5,000 to one individual, and located within this State.

United States and New York State stocks, stocks of the States of Ohio and Pennsylvania, and stocks of any city or village authorized by the Legislature of this State to be issued.

Real estate, other than under judgment or foreclosure, such as may be requisite for the convenient transaction of its business.

Securities on which loans are authorized: None.

Provisions under which right to invest in, or to loan upon, other securities than those named above, may be claimed:

1. Trustees shall not invest in other securities than those named in the charter, without the consent of a majority of all the trustees at a regular meeting. Chap. 150, Laws of 1859.

2. Required to invest in securities named in charter, except an available fund of not exceeding one-third of the whole amount of deposits, which may be kept on deposit, on interest or otherwise, in such available form as the trustees may direct. Chap. 150, Laws of 1859.

Provisions concerning deposits in bank: None, except as above.

Largest amount authorized to receive from one depositor, $2,000.

Regulations or restrictions concerning rate of interest to be paid to depositors: Such that depositors shall receive a ratable proportion of the profits.

Surplus authorized, fifteen per cent of the deposits.

Prohibition concerning rec'ing pay for services or borrowing funds:

1. The trustees of said corporation shall not, as such, directly or indirectly, receive any pay or emolument for their services. Sec. 3, chap. 252, Laws of 1852.
2. No president, vice-president, trustee, officer or servant of said corporation shall, directly or indirectly, borrow the funds of said corporation or its deposits, or in any manner use the same or any part thereof, except to pay necessary expenses, under the direction of said board of trustees. Sec. 6, chap. 252, Laws of 1852.

Provisions of the charter of The Mechanics' and Traders' Savings Institution, located in New York; incorporated by chapter 368, Laws of 1852; charter amended by chapter 134, Laws of 1857.

Number of trustees: By original charter, sixty-three; by amendment, thirty.

Investments authorized:

Bond and mortgage, half value of property, and located in the cities of New York, Brooklyn or Williamsburgh.

United States and New York State stocks, and stocks of any city authorized by the Legislature of this State to be issued.

Real estate, other than under judgment or foreclosure, such as may be requisite for the convenient transaction of its business.

Securities on which loans are authorized: None.

Provisions under which right to invest in, or to loan upon, other securities than those named above, may be claimed: Required to invest in securities named in charter, except an available fund of not exceeding $100,000, or not exceeding one-third of the total amount of deposits which may be kept on deposit, on interest or otherwise, in such available form as the trustees may direct.* Section 6, chapter 368, Laws of 1852.

Provisions concerning deposits in bank : None except as above.

Largest amount authorized to receive from one depositor, $5,000.

Regulations or restrictions concerning rate of interest to be paid to depositors : Such that depositors shall receive a ratable proportion of profits.

Surplus authorized : None.

Prohibition concerning receiving pay for services or borrowing funds:

1. The trustees of said corporation shall not, as such, directly or indirectly receive any pay or emolument for their services. Section 3, chapter 368, Laws of 1852.
2. No president, vice-president, trustee, officer or servant of said corporation shall directly or indirectly borrow the funds of said corporation or its deposits, or in any manner use the same, or any part thereof, except to pay necessary expenses under the direction of said board of trustees. Section 6, chapter 368, Laws of 1852.

Provisions of the charter of the Metropolitan Savings Bank (formerly Mariner's), located in New York; incorporated by chap. 371, Laws of 1852; charter amended by chap. 33, Laws of 1854; chap. 517, Laws of 1857; chap. 595, Laws of 1865; and chap. 407, Laws of 1866.

Number of trustees, twenty-three.

Investments authorized :

Bond and mortgage, half value of property, and by amendment, chap. 407, Laws of 1866, to be located in the county of New York, or counties adjoining in this State.

United States and New York State stocks, and stocks of any city authorized by the Legislature to be issued.

Real estate, other than under judgment or foreclosure ; such as may be requisite for the convenient transaction of its business.

Securities on which loans are authorized : None.

Provisions under which right to invest in, or to loan upon, other securities than those named above, may be claimed :

*But not to exceed $10,000 to be deposited unless interest shall be paid thereon.

1. Trustees shall not invest in other securities than those named in the charter, in opposition to the vote of any trustee. Sec. 6, chap. 371, Laws of 1852.
2. Required to invest in securities named in charter, except an available fund of not exceeding $100,000, or not exceeding one-third of the total amount of deposits, which may be kept on deposit, on interest, or otherwise, in such available form as the trustees may direct. Sec. 6, chap. 371, Laws of 1852.

Provisions concerning deposits in bank: None, except as above.

Largest amount authorized to receive from one depositor, $5,000.

Regulations or restrictions concerning rate of interest to be paid to depositors: Such that depositors shall receive a ratable proportion of profits.

Surplus authorized: Ten per cent of deposits.

Prohibition concerning receiving pay for services or borrowing funds:

1. The trustees of said corporation shall not, as such, directly or indirectly, receive any pay or emolument for their services. Sec. 3, chap. 371, Laws of 1852.
2. No president, vice-president, trustee, officer, or servant of said corporation shall, directly or indirectly, borrow the funds of said corporation or its deposits, or in any manner use the same, or any part thereof, except to pay necessary expenses under the direction of said board of trustees. Sec. 6, chap. 371, Laws of 1852.

Provisions of the charter of The Sixpenny Savings Bank of the city of New York, located in New York; incorporated by chapter 328, Laws of 1853; charter amended by chapter 72, Laws of 1855.

Number of trustees, thirty-nine.

Investments authorized:

Bond and mortgage, half value of property, not limited in location.

United States and New York State stocks, and stocks of any city authorized by the Legislature of this State to be issued.

Real estate, other than under judgment or foreclosure, such as may be requisite for the convenient transaction of its business.

Securities on which loans are authorized: Same as for investment.

Provisions under which right to invest in or to loan upon, other securities than those named above, may be claimed: Required to invest in securities named in charter, except an available fund of not exceeding $50,000, which may be kept on deposit, on interest or otherwise, in such available form as the trustees may direct. Section 6, chapter 328, Laws of 1853.

Provisions concerning deposits in bank: None except as above.

Largest amount authorized to receive from one depositor. No limit.

Regulations or restrictions concerning rate of interest to be paid to depositors: Such that depositors shall receive a ratable proportion of profits.

Surplus authorized: Twenty-five thousand dollars.

Prohibition concerning receiving pay for services or borrowing funds:

1. The trustees of said corporation shall not, as such, directly or indirectly receive any payment or emolument for their services. Section 3, chapter 328, Laws of 1853.
2. No president, vice-president, trustee, officer or servant of said corporation, shall directly or indirectly borrow the funds of said corporation or its deposits, or in any manner use the same, or any part thereof, except to pay necessary expenses under the direction of said board of trustees. Section 6, chapter 328, Laws of 1853.

Provisions of the charter of the Westchester County Savings Bank, located at Tarrytown; incorporated by chap. 591, Laws of 1853; charter not amended.

Number of trustees, twenty-three.

Investments authorized:

Bond and mortgage, half value of property, in sums not exceeding $5,000 to any one individual on the same piece of property, and not restricted in location.

United States and New York State stocks, and stocks of any city authorized by the Legislature of this State to be issued.

Real estate, other than under judgment or foreclosure, such as may be requisite for the convenient transaction of its business.

Securities on which loans are authorized: None.

Provisions under which right to invest in, or loan upon, other securities than those named above, may be claimed:

1. Trustees shall not invest in other securities than those named in the charter, in opposition to the vote of three trustees. Section 6 of charter.
2. Required to invest in securities named in charter, except an available fund of not exceeding one-third of total amount of deposits, which may be kept on deposit, on interest, or otherwise, in such available form as the trustees may direct. Section 6 of charter.

Provisions concerning deposits in bank: None except as above.

Largest amount authorized to receive from one depositor, $5,000.

Regulations or restrictions concerning rate of interest to be paid to depositors: Such that depositors shall receive a ratable proportion of profits.

Surplus authorized: None.

Prohibition concerning receiving pay for services, or borrowing funds:

1. The trustees of said corporation shall not, as such, directly or indirectly, receive any pay or emolument for their services. Section 3 of charter.
2. No president, vice-president, trustee, officer or servant of said corporation shall, directly or indirectly, borrow the funds of said corporation or its deposits, or in any manner use the same, or any part thereof, except to pay necessary current expenses under the direction of said board of trustees. Section 6 of charter.

Provisions of the charter of The Sing Sing Savings Bank, located at Sing Sing; incorporated by chapter 55, Laws of 1854; charter amended by chapter 100, Laws of 1859, and chapter 62, Laws of 1864.

Number of trustees, twelve.

Investments authorized:

Bond and mortgage, half value of property, exclusive of buildings, and not limited in location.

United States and New York State stocks, and stocks of any city or county authorized by the Legislature of this State to be issued.

Real estate, other than under judgment or foreclosure, such as may be requisite for the convenient transaction of its business.

Securities on which loans are authorized: Same as for investment.

Provisions under which right to invest in or to loan upon, other securities than those named above, may be claimed:

1. Trustees shall not invest in other securities than those named in the charter, in opposition to the vote of any three trustees. Section 6, chapter 55, Laws of 1854.
2. Required to invest in securities named in charter, except an available fund of not exceeding $40,000, which may be kept on deposit, on interest or otherwise, in such available form as the trustees may direct. Section 6, chapter 55, Laws of 1854.

Provisions concerning deposits in bank: None except as above.

Largest amount authorized to receive from one depositor, $3,000.

Regulations or restrictions concerning rate of interest to be paid to depositors: Such that depositors shall receive a ratable proportion of profits.

Surplus authorized: None.

Prohibition concerning receiving pay for services, or borrowing funds:

1. The trustees of said corporation shall not, directly or indirectly, receive any pay or emolument for their services. Section 3, chapter 55, Laws of 1854.
2. No president, vice-president, trustee, officer or servant of said corporation shall, directly or indirectly, borrow the funds cf said corporation, or its deposits, or in any manner use the same or any part thereof, except to pay necessary current expenses under the direction of said board of trustees. Section 6, chapter 55, Laws of 1854.

Provisions of the charter of the Erie County Savings Bank, located at Buffalo; incorporated by chapter 187, Laws of 1854; charter amended by chapter 99, Laws of 1857, and chapter 195, Laws of 1863.

Number of trustees, twenty.

Investments authorized:

Bond and mortgage, half value of property, exclusive of buildings, and not restricted in location.*

United States and New York State stocks, and stocks of the city of Buffalo or county of Erie.

* Special loan on real estate to Young Men's Association, of the city of Buffalo, authorized by chapter 195, Laws of 1863.

Real estate, other than under judgment or foreclosure, such as may be requisite for the convenient transaction of its business.

Securities on which loans are authorized: United States and New York State stocks.

Provisions under which right to invest in, or to loan upon, other securities than those named above, may be claimed: Required to invest in securities named in charter, except an available fund of not exceeding twenty-five per cent. of the deposits, which may be kept on deposit, on interest, or otherwise, in such available form as the trustees may direct. Section 6, chapter 187, Laws of 1854.

Provisions concerning deposits in bank: None, except as above.

Largest amount authorized to receive from one depositor, $5,000.

Regulations or restrictions concerning rate of interest to be paid to depositors: Such that depositors shall receive a ratable proportion of profits.

Surplus authorized: Twenty-five thousand dollars.

Prohibition concerning receiving pay for services, or borrowing funds:

1. The trustees of said corporation shall not, directly or indirectly, receive any payment or emolument for their services. Section 3, chapter 187, Laws of 1854.
2. No president, vice-president, trustee, officer or servant of said corporation shall, directly or indirectly, borrow the funds of said corporation or its deposits, or in any manner use the same or any part thereof, except to pay necessary expenses under the direction of the said board of trustees. Section 6, chapter 187, Laws of 1854.

Provisions of the charter of The Yonkers Savings Bank, located at Yonkers; incorporated by chapter 214, Laws of 1854; charter not amended.

Number of trustees, forty-one.

Investments authorized:

Bond and mortgage, half value of property, exclusive of buildings, in sums not exceeding $5,000 to any one individual on the same piece of property, and not restricted in location.

United States and New York State stocks.

Real estate, other than under judgment or foreclosure, such as may be requisite for the convenient transaction of its business.

Securities on which loans are authorized: None.

Provisions under which right to invest in, or to loan upon, other securities than those named above, may be claimed:

1. Trustees shall not invest in other securities than those named in the charter, in opposition to the vote of any three trustees. Section 6 of charter.
2. Required to invest in securities named in charter, except an available fund of not exceeding $50,000, which may be kept on deposit, on interest or otherwise, in such available form as the trustees may direct. Section 6 of charter.

Provisions concerning deposits in banks: None, except as above.

Largest amount authorized to receive from one depositor, $5,000.

Regulations or restrictions concerning rate of interest to be paid to depositors: Such that depositors shall receive a ratable proportion of profits.

Surplus authorized: Twenty-five thousand dollars.

Prohibition concerning receiving pay for services, or borrowing funds:

1. The trustees of said corporation shall not, directly or indirectly, receive any pay or emolument for their services. Section 3 of charter.
2. No president, vice-president, trustee, officer or servant of said corporation shall, directly or indirectly, borrow the funds of said corporation or its deposits, or in any manner use the same, or any part thereof, except to pay necessary current expenses under the direction of said board of trustees. Section 6 of charter.

Provisions of the charter of The Third Avenue Savings Bank, (formerly Bloomingdale), located in New York; incorporated by chapter 390, Laws of 1854; charter amended by chapter 17, Laws of 1859, chapter 269, Laws of 1865, and chapter 783, Laws of 1867.

Number of trustees, twenty-two.

Investments authorized:

Bond and mortgage, half value of property, and not limited in location.

United States and New York State stocks.

Real estate, other than under judgment, or foreclosure, such as may be requisite for the convenient transaction of its business.

Securities upon which loans are authorized: Any stocks authorized for investment by the laws of this State applicable to savings banks.*

Provisions under which right to invest in or to loan upon, other securities than those named above, may be claimed.

1. Trustees shall not invest in other securities than those named in the charter, in opposition to the vote of any three trustees. Section 6, chapter 390, Laws of 1854.
2. Trustees in their discretion may keep an available fund of not exceeding one-third of the total amounts of deposits, which may be kept on deposit, or interest or otherwise, in such available form as the trustees may, from time to time, direct. Section 3, chapter 783, Laws of 1867.

Provisions concerning deposits in bank: None except as above.

Largest amount authorized to receive from one depositor, $5,000.

Regulations or restrictions concerning rate of interest to be paid to depositors: Such that depositors shall receive a ratable proportion of profits.

Surplus authorized: Fifteen per cent of the amount of deposits.

Prohibition concerning receiving pay for services, or borrowing funds:

1. The trustees of said corporation shall not directly or indirectly receive any pay or emolument for their services. Section 3, chapter 390, Laws of 1854.†
2. No president, vice-president, or trustee, officer or servant of said corporation shall directly or indirectly borrow the funds of said corporation or its deposits, or in any manner use the same, or any part thereof, except to pay necessary current expenses under the direction of said board of trustees. Section 6, chapter 390, Laws of 1854.

---

*Loans on stocks of United States or State, city or county of New York, must have a margin of ten per cent upon the cash market value. Loans upon any other stocks must have a margin of twenty-five per cent. Section 2, chapter 783, Laws of 1867.

† See section five, 783, Laws of 1867.

Provisions of the charter of the New York Savings Bank, (formerly Rose Hill,) located in New York; incorporated by chapter 394, Laws of 1854; charter amended by chapter 260, Laws of 1857, chapter 289, Laws of 1862, and chapter 463, Laws of 1865.

Number of trustees; seventeen.

Investments authorized:

Bond and mortgage, half value of property, and not restricted in location.

United States and New York State stocks, and stocks of any city or county authorized by the Legislature of this State to be issued.

Real estate, other than under judgment or foreclosure, such as may be requisite for the convenient transaction of its business.

Securities on which loans are authorized: None.

Provisions under which right to invest in, or to loan upon, other securities than those named above, may be claimed:

1. Trustees shall not invest in other securities than those named in the charter, in opposition to the vote of any three trustees. Section 6, chapter 394, Laws of 1854.
2. Required to invest in securities named in charter, except an available fund of not exceeding one-fifth of the total amount of deposits, which may be kept on deposit, on interest or otherwise, in such available form as the trustees may direct. Section 6 of charter, amended by section 1, chapter 463, Laws of 1865.

Provisions concerning deposits in bank: None except as above.

Largest amount authorized to receive from one depositor, $5,000.

Regulations or restrictions concerning rate of interest to be paid to depositors: Such that depositors shall receive a ratable proportion of profits.

Surplus authorized: Fifteen per cent. of deposits.

Prohibition concerning receiving pay for services, or borrowing fund:

1. The trustees of said corporation shall not, directly or indirectly, receive any pay or emolument for their services. Section 3, chapter 394, Laws of 1854.
2. No president, vice president, or trustee, officer or servant of said corporation shall directly or indirectly borrow

the funds of said corporation or its deposits, or in any manner use the same, or any part thereof, except to pay necessary current expenses under the direction of said board of trustees. Section 6, chapter 394, Laws of 1854.

Provisions of the charter of The Onondaga County Savings Bank, located at Syracuse; incorporated by chapter 259, Laws of 1855; charter amended by chapter 109, Laws of 1856; chapter 353, Laws of 1860; chapter 21, Laws of 1863, and chapter 467, Laws of 1865.

Number of trustees, seventeen.

Investments authorized:

Bond and mortgage, half value of property, located in the county of Onondaga, or any county adjoining.

United States and New York State stocks, and stocks of any city or county in this State, authorized by the Legislature to be issued.

Real estate, other than under judgment or foreclosure, such as may be requisite for the convenient transaction of its business.

Securities on which loans are authorized: Same as for investment.

Provisions under which right to invest in, or to loan upon, other securities than those named above, may be claimed: Required to invest in securities named in charter, except an available fund of not exceeding one-third of the total amount of deposits, which may be kept on deposit, on interest or otherwise, or in such available form as the trustees may direct. Section 6 of charter, as amended by chapter 467, Laws of 1865.

Provisions concerning deposits in bank: None except as above.

Largest amount authorized to receive from one depositor, $5,000.

Regulations or restrictions concerning rate of interest to be paid to depositors: Such that depositors shall receive a ratable proportion of profits, and rates of interest in the future may be reduced on giving three months' notice.

Surplus authorized: Ten per cent of deposits.

Prohibition concerning receiving pay for services, or borrowing funds:

1. The trustees of said corporation shall not, directly or indirectly receive any pay or emolument for their services. Section 3, chapter 259, Laws of 1855.

2. No president, vice-president, trustee, officer or servant of said corporation shall, directly or indirectly, borrow the funds of said corporation or its deposits, or in any manner use the same, or any part thereof, except to pay necessary expenses under the direction of the said board of trustees. Section 6, chapter 259, Laws of 1855.

Provisions of the charter of the Mechanics' and Farmers' Savings Bank of Albany, located at Albany; incorporated by chapter 379, Laws of 1855; charter not amended.

Number of trustees, eleven.

Investments authorized:

Bond and mortgage, one-third value of property, unincumbered and productive, and located in the city of Albany, or on unincumbered real estate in any part of the State out of the city, of double the value of the sum loaned, exclusive of buildings.

United States and New York State stocks, stocks of any State in the Union, and stocks of any city in this State, or the stock of any of the banks in the cities of Albany or Troy. Section 6 of charter.

Real estate, other than under judgment or foreclosure, such as may be requisite for the convenient transaction of its business.

Securities on which loans are authorized: New York and United States stocks, and stocks of any city authorized by the Legislature of this State to be issued.

Provisions under which right to invest in, or to loan upon, other securities than those named above, may be claimed: Required to invest in securities named in charter, except an available fund of not exceeding $100,000, which may be kept on deposit, on interest or otherwise, in such available form as the trustees may direct. Section 13 of charter.

Provisions concerning deposits in bank: None, except as above, or in the form of loans to the banks in Albany or Troy, as provided by charter of Albany Savings Bank.

Largest amount authorized to receive from one depositor: Bank may refuse to receive more than $500.

Regulations or restrictions concerning rate of interest to be paid to depositors: None.

Surplus authorized: None.

Prohibition concerning receiving pay for services or borrowing funds:

The trustees of said corporation shall not receive any pay or emolument for their services. Section 3 of charter.

Provisions of the charter of The State Savings Bank of Troy, located at Troy; incorporated by chapter 197, Laws of 1856; charter not amended.

Number of trustees, fifteen.

Investments authorized:

Bond and mortgage, half value of property, and located in "either of the cities of this State."

United States and New York State stocks, and stocks of the cities of Troy or Albany.

Real estate, other than under judgment or foreclosure, such as may be requisite for the convenient transactions of its business.

Securities on which loans are authorized: Same as for investment.

Provisions under which right to invest in, or to loan upon, other securities than those named above, may be claimed: Required to invest in securities named in charter, except an available fund of not exceeding $100,000, which may be kept in deposit, on interest or otherwise, in such available form as the trustees may direct. Section 13 of charter.

Provisions concerning deposits in bank: None, except as above.

Largest amount authorized to receive from one depositor, $5,000.

Regulations or restrictions concerning rate of interest to be paid to depositors: Such that depositors shall receive a ratable proportion of profits.

Surplus authorized: None.

Prohibition concerning receiving pay for services, or borrowing funds:

1. The trustees of said corporation shall not receive any pay or emolument for their services. Section 3 of charter.
2. No president, vice-president, trustee, officer or servant of said corporation shall, directly or indirectly, borrow the funds of said corporation or its deposits, or in any manner use the same, or any part thereof, except to pay necessary expenses under the direction of the said board of trustees. Section 6 of charter.

Provisions of the charter of The Albany Exchange Savings Bank, located at Albany; incorporated by chapter 202, Laws of 1856; charter not amended.

Number of trustees, twenty.

Investments authorized:

Bond and mortgage, half value of property, and located in this State.

United States and New York State stocks, and stocks of any city authorized by the Legislature of this State to be issued.

Real estate, other than under judgment or foreclosure, such as may be requisite for the convenient transaction of its business.

Securities on which loans are authorized: Same as for investment.

Provisions under which right to invest in, or to loan upon, other securities than those named above, may be claimed: Required to invest in securities named in charter, except an available fund of not exceeding $100,000, which may be kept on deposit, on interest, or otherwise, in such available form as the trustees may direct. Section 12 of charter.

Provisions concerning deposits in bank: None except as above.

Largest amount authorized to receive from one depositor, $5,000.

Regulations or restrictions concerning rate of interest to be paid to depositors: Such that depositors shall receive a ratable proportion of profits.

Surplus authorized: None.

Prohibition concerning receiving pay for services, or borrowing funds:

1. The trustees of said corporation shall not receive any pay or emolument for their services. Section 3 of charter.
2. No president, vice-president, trustee, officer or servant of said corporation shall, directly or indirectly, borrow the funds of said corporation or its deposits, or in any manner use the same or any part thereof, except to pay necessary expenses under the direction of the said board of trustees. Section 6 of charter.

Provisions of the charter of the Fishkill Savings Institute, located at Fishkill; incorporated by chapter 52, Laws of 1857; charter not amended.

Number of trustees, twenty-seven.

Investments authorized:

Bond and mortgage, half value of property, exclusive of buildings, in sums not exceeding $5,000, and located in this State.

United States and New York State stocks, stocks of the cities of Poughkeepsie or New York, or of the county of Dutchess.

Real estate, other than under judgment or foreclosure, such as may be requisite for the convenient transaction of its business.

Securities on which loans are authorized: Same as for investment.

Provisions under which right to invest in, or to loan upon, other securities than those named above, may be claimed: Required to invest in securities named in charter, except an available fund of not exceeding $30,000, which may be kept on deposit, on interest, or otherwise, in such available form as the trustees may direct. Section 6 of charter.

Provisions concerning deposits in bank: None, except as above.

Largest amount authorized to receive from one depositor, $5,000.

Regulations or restrictions concerning rate of interest to be paid to depositors: Such that depositors shall receive a ratable proportion of profits.

Surplus authorized: None.

Prohibition concerning receiving pay for services, or borrowing funds:

1. The trustees of said corporation shall not as such, directly or indirectly, receive any payment or emolument for their services. Section 3 of charter.
2. No president, vice-president, trustee, officer or servant of said corporation shall, directly or indirectly, borrow the funds of said corporation or its deposits, or in any manner use the same or any part thereof, except to pay necessary expenses under the direction of said board of trustees. Section 6 of charter.

Provisions of the charter of The Mutual Savings Bank of Troy, located at Troy; incorporated by chapter 561, Laws of 1857; charter amended by chapter 105, Laws of 1860.

Number of trustees, nine.

Investments authorized:

Bond and mortgage, half value of property, exclusive of buildings, in sums not exceeding $5,000, and located in this State.

United States and New York State stocks, and stocks of the cities of Troy or Albany.

Real estate, other than under judgment or foreclosure, such as may be requisite for the convenient transaction of its business.

Securities on which loans are authorized: Same as for investment.

Provisions under which right to invest in, or to loan upon, other securities than those named above, may be claimed: Required to invest in securities named in charter, except an available fund of not exceeding $100,000, which may be kept on deposit, on interest or otherwise, in such available form as the trustees may direct. Section 13 of charter, as amended by chapter 105, Laws of 1860.

Provisions concerning deposits in banks: None, except as above.

Largest amount authorized to receive from one depositor, $2,500.

Regulations or restrictions concerning rate of interest to be paid to depositors: Left to the discretion of trustees.

Surplus authorized: None.

Prohibition concerning receiving pay for services, or borrowing funds:

1. The trustees of said corporation shall not, directly or indirectly, receive any pay or emolument for their services. Section 3 of charter.
2. No president, vice-president, trustee, officer or servant of said corporation shall, directly or indirectly, borrow the funds of said corporation or its deposits, or in any manner use the same, or any part thereof, except to pay necessary expenses under the direction of the said board of trustees. Section 7 of charter.

Provisions of the charter of the Central Savings Bank of Troy, located at Troy; incorporated by chapter 598, Laws of 1857; charter not amended.

Number of trustees, fifteen.

Investments authorized:

Bond and mortgage, half value of property, exclusive of buildings, in sums not exceeding $5,000, and located in this State.

United States and New York State stocks, and stocks of the cities of Troy or Albany.

Real estate, other than under judgment or foreclosure, such as may be requisite for the convenient transaction of its business.

Securities on which loans are authorized: Same as for investment.

Provisions under which right to invest in, or to loan upon, other securities as those named above, may be claimed: Required to invest in securities named in charter, except an available fund not exceeding $50,000, which may be kept on deposit, on interest, or otherwise, in such available form as the trustees may direct. Section 13 of charter.

Provisions concerning deposits in bank: None except as above.

Largest amount authorized to receive from one depositor, $2,500.

Regulations or restrictions concerning rate of interest to be paid to depositors: Left to the discretion of the trustees.

Surplus authorized: None.

Prohibition concerning receiving pay for services, or borrowing funds:

1. The trustees of said corporation shall not, directly or indirectly, receive any pay or emolument for their services. Section 3 of charter.
2. No president, vice-president, trustee, officer or servant of said corporation shall, directly or indirectly, borrow the funds of said corporation or its deposits, or in any manner use the same or any part thereof, except to pay necessary expenses under the direction of said board of trustees. Section 7 of charter.

Provisions of the charter of The Manufacturer's Savings Bank of Troy, located at Troy; incorporated by chapter 600, Laws of 1857; charter amended by chapter 106, Laws of 1860.

Number of trustees, thirteen.

Investments authorized :

Bond and mortgage, half value of property, exclusive of buildings, in sums not exceeding $5,000, and located in this State.

United States and New York state stocks, and stocks of the cities of Troy or Albany.

Real estate, other than under judgment or foreclosure, such as may be requisite for the convenient transaction of its business.

Securities on which loans are authorized: Same as for investment.

Provisions under which right to invest in, or to loan upon, other securities than those named above, may be claimed : Required to invest in securities named in the charter, except an available fund of not exceeding $100,000, which may be kept on deposit, on interest or otherwise, in such available form as the trustees may direct. Section 13 of charter, as amended by chapter 106, Laws of 1860.

Provisions concerning deposits in bank : None except as above.

Largest amount authorized to receive from one depositor, $2,500.

Regulations or restrictions concerning rate of interest to be paid to depositors : Left to the discretion of the trustees.

Surplus authorized : None.

Prohibition concerning receiving pay for services, or borrowing funds :

1. The trustees of said corporation shall not directly nor indirectly receive any pay or emolument for their services. Section 3 of charter.
2. No president, vice-president, trustee, officer or servant of said corporation shall, directly or indirectly, borrow the funds of said corporation or its deposits, or in any manner use the same or any part thereof, except to pay necessary expenses under the direction of said board of trustees. Section 7 of charter.

Provisions of the charter of the Chenango Valley Savings Bank, located at Binghamton; incorporated by chapter 616, Laws of 1857; revived and re-enacted by chapter 477, Laws of 1857.

Number of trustees, eighteen.

Investments authorized:

Bond and mortgage, half value of property, exclusive of buildings, in sums not exceeding $3,000, and located in this State.

United States and New York State stocks, and stocks of the county of Broome, or of the town or village of Binghamton.

Real estate, other than under judgment or foreclosure, such as may be requisite for the convenient transaction of its business.

Securities on which loans are authorized: Same as for investment.

Provisions under which right to invest in, or to loan upon, other securities than those named above, may be claimed: Required to invest in securities named in charter, except an available fund of not exceeding $25,000, which may be kept on deposit, on interest or otherwise, in such available form as the trustees may direct. Section 6. chapter 616, Laws of 1857.

Provisions concerning deposits in bank: None except as above.

Largest amount authorized to receive from one depositor, $3,000.

Regulations or restrictions concerning rate of interest to be paid to depositors: Such that depositors shall receive a ratable proportion of profits.

Surplus authorized: None.

Prohibition concerning receiving pay for services, or borrowing funds:

1. The trustees of said corporation shall not, as such, directly or indirectly, receive any payment or emolument for their services. Section 3, of charter.
2. No president, vice-president, trustee, officer or servant of said corporation shall, directly or indirectly, borrow the funds of said corporation or its deposits, or in any manner use the same, or any part thereof, except to pay necessary expenses under the direction of said board of trustees. Section 6 of charter.

Provisions of the charter of The Southold Savings Bank, located at Southold; incorporated by chapter 118, Laws of 1858; charter amended by chapter 331, Laws of 1860, and chapter 277, Laws of 1863.

Number of trustees, twenty-one.

Investments authorized:

Bond and mortgage, half value of property, exclusive of buildings, in sums not exceeding $10,000, and located in this State.

United States and New York State stocks, stocks of the cities of New York and Brooklyn, of the counties of Suffolk, Queens and Kings, or of the town of Southold.

Real estate, other than under judgment or foreclosure, such as may be requisite for the convenient transaction of its business.

Securities on which loans are authorized: Same as for investment.

Provisions under which right to invest in, or to loan upon, other securities than those named above, may be claimed: Required to invest in securities named in charter, except an available fund of not exceeding $25,000, which may be kept on deposit, on interest or otherwise, in such available form as the trustees may direct. Section 6, chapter 118, Laws of 1858.

Provisions concerning deposits in bank: None except as above.

Largest amount authorized to receive from one depositor, $5,000.

Regulations or restrictions concerning rate of interest to be paid to depositors: Such that depositors shall receive a ratable proportion of profits.

Surplus authorized: None.

Prohibition concerning receiving pay for services, or borrowing funds:

1. The trustees of said corporation shall not, as such, directly or indirectly, receive any pay or emolument for their services. Section 3, chapter 118, Laws of 1858.
2. No president vice-president, trustee, officer or servant of said corporation shall, directly or indirectly, borrow the funds of said corporation or its deposits, or in any manner use the same or any part thereof, except to pay necessary expenses under the direction of said board of trustees. Section 6, chapter 118, Laws of 1858.

Provisions of the charter of The Emigrant Savings Bank of Buffalo, located at Buffalo; incorporated by chapter 344, Laws of 1858; charter not amended.

Number of trustees, sixteen.

Investments authorized:

Bond and mortgage, half value of property, exclusive of buildings, in sums not exceeding $5,000 to any one individual, and not limited in location.

United States and New York State stocks, and stocks of any city authorized by the Legislature of this State to be issued.

Real estate, other than under judgment or foreclosure, such as may be requisite for the convenient transaction of its business.

Securities on which loans are authorized: Same as for investment.

Provisions under which right to invest in, or to loan upon, other securities than those named above, may be claimed: Required to invest in securities named in charter, except an available fund of not exceeding $100,000, but not to exceed one-third the aggregate amount of deposits which may be kept on deposit, on interest or otherwise, in such available form as the trustees may direct.

Section 14 of charter.

Provisions concerning deposits in bank: None except as above.

Largest amount authorized to receive from one depositor, $5,000.

Regulations or restrictions concerning rate of interest to be paid to depositors: Such that depositors shall receive a ratable proportion of profits.

Surplus authorized: None.

Prohibition concerning receiving pay for services, or borrowing funds:

1. The trustees of said corporation shall not receive any pay or emolument for their services. Section 3 of charter.
2. No president, vice-president, trustee, officer or servant of said corporation shall, directly or indirectly, borrow the funds of said corporation or its deposits, or in any manner use the same, or any part thereof, except to pay necessary current expenses under the direction of said board of trustees. Section 6 of charter.

Section 13 of charter applies to this corporation the provisions of section 13 of the charter of the Albany City Savings Institution, incorporated in 1850, and of the general act in relation to savings banks, passed in 1857.

Provisions of the charter of the Oswego City Savings Bank, located at Oswego; incorporated by chapter 28, Laws of 1859; charter amended by chapter 403, Laws of 1866.

Number of trustees, eleven.

Investments authorized:

Bond and mortgage, half value of property, in sums not exceeding $5,000, and located in the county of Oswego.

United States and New York State stocks, and stocks of the city and county of Oswego.

Real estate other than under judgment or foreclosure, such as may be requisite for the convenient transaction of its business.

Securities on which loans are authorized: Same as for investment.

Provisions under which right to invest in, or to loan upon, other securities than those named above, may be claimed: Required to invest in securities named in charter, except an available fund of not exceeding ten per cent. of the whole amount of deposits which may be kept on deposit, on interest or otherwise, in such available form as the trustees may direct. Chapter 403, Laws of 1866, amending section 6 of charter.

Provisions concerning deposits in bank: None except as above.

Largest amount authorized to receive from one depositor, $1,000.

Regulations or restrictions concerning rate of interest to be paid to depositors: Snch that depositors shall receive a ratable proportion of profits.

Surplus authorized: None.

Prohibition concerning rece'ing pay for services or borrowing funds:

1. The trustees of said corporation shall not, as such, directly or indirectly, receive any pay or emolument for their services. Section 3, chapter 28, Laws of 1859.
2. No president, vice-president, trustee, officer or servant of said corporation shall directly or indirectly borrow the funds of said corporation or its deposits, or in any manner use the same or any part thereof, except to pay necessary expenses and outlays under the direction of the said board of trustees. Section 6, chapter 28, Laws of 1859.

Provisions of the Jefferson County Savings Bank, located at Watertown; incorporated by chapter 135; Laws of 1859; charter amended by chapter 147, Laws of 1865.

Number of trustees: Twenty-two by original charter, with authority to reduce the same to 12 by the occurrence of vacancies.

Investments authorized:

Bond and mortgage, half value of property, in sums not exceeding $5,000 to any one individual, and located in the counties of Jefferson, Oswego, St. Lawrence and Lewis, the counties adjoining the same.

United States and New York State stocks, and stocks of the county of Jefferson.

Real estate, other than under judgment or foreclosure, such as may be requisite for the transaction of its business, but not exceeding $50,000 in value.

Securities on which loans are authorized: Same as for investment.

Provisions under which right to invest in, or to loan upon, other securities than those named above, may be claimed: Required to invest in securities named in charter, except an available fund of not exceeding one-third of the deposits, which may be kept on deposit, on interest or otherwise, in such available form as the trustees may direct. Section 12, chapter 135, Laws of 1859.

Provisions concerning deposits in banks: None, except as above.

Largest amount authorized to receive from one depositor, $3,000.

Regulations or restrictions concerning rate of interest to be paid to depositors: Such that depositors shall receive a ratable proportion of profits.

Surplus authorized: None.

Prohibition concerning receiving pay for services, or borrowing funds:

1. The trustees of said corporation shall not receive any pay or emolument for their services. Section 3, chapter 135, Laws of 1859.
2. No president, vice-president, trustee, officer or servant of said corporation shall, directly or indirectly, borrow the funds of said corporation or its deposits, or in any manner use the same, or any part thereof, except to pay the necessary expenses under the direction of the said board of trustees. Section 6, chapter 135, Laws of 1859.

Provisions of the charter of The German Savings Bank in the city of New York, located in New York; incorporated by chapter 210, Laws of 1859; charter amended by chapter 167, Laws of 1864, and chapter 82, Laws of 1865.

Number of trustees, twenty-five.

Investments authorized:

Bond and mortgage, half value of property, and not limited in location.

United States and New York State stocks, and stocks of any city in this State.

Real estate, other than under judgment or foreclosure, such as may be requisite for the convenient transaction of its business.

Securities on which loans are authorized: None.

Provisions under which right to invest in, or to loan upon, other securities than those named above, may be claimed:

1. Trustees shall not invest in other securities than those named in the charter, in opposition to the vote of three trustees. Section 6, chapter 210, Laws of 1859.
2. Required to invest in securities named in charter, except an available fund of not exceeding one-third of the amount of deposits, which may be kept on deposit, on interest or otherwise, in such available form as the trustees may direct, provided no loan shall be made to a greater amount than three-fourths the cash value of the security given. Section 1, chapter 82, Laws of 1865, amending section 6 of charter.

Provisions concerning deposits in banks: None except as above.

Largest amount authorized to receive from one depositor, $5,000.

Regulations or restrictions concerning rate of interest to be paid to depositors: Such that depositors of $500 and under shall receive one per cent more than depositors of over $500.

Surplus authorized: Ten per cent of deposits.

Prohibition concerning rec'ing pay for services or borrowing funds:

1. The trustees of said corporation shall not, directly or indirectly, receive any pay or emolument for their services. Section 3, chapter 210, Laws of 1859.
2. No president, vice-president, trustee, officer or servant of said corporation shall, directly or indirectly, borrow the funds of said corporation or its deposits, or in any manner use the same or any part thereof, except to pay necessary current expenses, under the direction of said board of trustees. Section 6, chapter 210, Laws of 1859.

Provisions of the charter of the Union Dime Savings Institution, located in New York; incorporated by chapter 247, Laws of 1859; charter amended by chapter 406, Laws of 1866.

Number of trustees, thirty-four.

Investments authorized:

Bond and mortgage, half value of property, located in the county of New York, or counties adjoining in this State.

United States and New York State stocks, and stocks of any city or county authorized by the Legislature of this State to be issued.

Real estate, other than under judgment or foreclosure, such as may be requisite for the convenient transaction of its business.

Securities on which loans are authorized: None.

Provisions under which right to invest in, or to loan upon, other securities than those named above, may be claimed:

1. Trustees shall not invest in other securities than those named in the charter, in opposition to the vote of three trustees. Section 6 of charter, amended by chapter 406, Laws of 1866.
2. Required to invest in securities named in charter, except an available fund of not exceeding one-third of the total amount of deposits, which may be kept on deposit in any of the banks of the city of New York, or on interest or otherwise, in such available form as the trustees may direct. See sec. 6 of charter, amended by chapter 406, Laws of 1866.

Provisions concerning deposits in banks: None except as above.

Largest amount authorized to receive from one depositor, $5,000.

Regulations or restrictions concerning rate of interest to be paid to depositors: Such that depositors shall receive a ratable proportion of profits.

Surplus authorized: Ten per cent of deposits.

Prohibition concerning receiving pay for services, or borrowing funds:

1. The trustees of said corporation shall not, as such, directly or indirectly, receive any pay or emolument for their services. Section 3, chapter 247, Laws of 1859.

2. No president, vice-president, trustee, officer or servant of said corporation shall, directly or indirectly, borrow the funds of said corporation or its deposits, or in any manner use the same, or any part thereof, except to pay necessary current expenses, under the direction of the said board of trustees. Sec. 6, chap. 247, Laws of 1859.

Provisions of the charter of The Dime Savings Bank of Brooklyn, located at Brooklyn; incorporated by chapter 248, Laws of 1859; charter amended by chapter 90, Laws of 1864.

Number of trustees, thirty-one.

Investments authorized:

Bond and mortgage, half value of property, located in the county of Kings, or any adjoining county.

United States and New York State stocks, and stocks of any city in this State, or of the county of Kings.

Real estate, other than under judgment or foreclosure, such as may be requisite for the convenient transaction of its business.

Securities on which loans are authorized: None.

Provisions under which right to invest in, or to loan upon, other securities than those named above, may be claimed; Required to invest in securities named in charter, except an available fund of not exceeding one-third the total amount of deposits, which may be kept on deposit, on interest, or otherwise, or in such available form as the trustees may direct. Section 6, chapter 248, Laws of 1859.

Provisions concerning deposits in bank: None, except as above.

Largest amount authorized to receive from one depositor, $3,000.

Regulations or restrictions concerning rate of interest to be paid to depositors: Lawful to allow depositors of $500 or upwards one per cent. less than is allowed to others.

Surplus authorized: Ten per cent. of deposits.

Prohibition concerning receiving pay for services or borrowing funds:

1. The trustees of said corporation shall not as such, directly or indirectly, receive any payment or emolument for their services. Section 3, chapter 248, Laws of 1859.
2. No president, vice-president, trustee, officer or servant of said corporation shall, directly or indirectly, borrow the

funds of said corporation or its deposits, or in any manner use the same, or any part thereof, except to pay necessary expenses under the direction of said board of trustees. Section 7, chapter 248, Laws of 1859.

Provisions of the charter of The Queens County Savings Bank, located at Flushing; incorporated by chapter 342, Laws of 1859; charter amended by chapter 71, Laws of 1861, and chapter 121, Laws of 1866.

Number of trustees: By original charter, 40; by amendment, reduced to 24.

Investments authorized:

Bond and mortgage, half value of property, in sums not exceeding $5,000 to one individual, firm or association, and located in the counties of Queens and Kings.

United States and New York State stocks, and stocks of any city in this State.

Real estate other than under judgment or foreclosure, such as may be requisite for the convenient transaction of its business.

Securities on which loans are authorized: Same as for investment, but not exceeding 90 per cent of cash value of such securities.

Provisions under which right to invest in, or to loan upon, other securities than those named above, may be claimed: None.

Provisions concerning deposits in bank: Lawful to keep on deposit in bank not exceeding 20 per cent of deposits made with said corporation, nor exceeding the sum of $50,000 in any one bank.

Largest amount authorized to receive from one depositor, $3,000.

Regulations or restrictions concerning rate of interest to be paid to depositors: Such that interest on sums of five hundred dollars or more, shall be at least one per cent less than is allowed on smaller sums.

Surplus authorized: None.

Prohibition concerning receiving pay for services, or borrowing funds: The trustees of said corporation shall not, directly or indirectly, receive any payment or emolument for their services. Nor shall any trustee, officer or agent of said corporation, directly or indirectly, borrow the funds of said corporation, or in any manner use the same, except to pay necessary current expenses under the direction of the board of trustees. Section 6, chapter 342, Laws of 1859.

Provisions of the charter of the Peekskill Savings Bank, located at Peekskill; incorporated by chapter 432, Laws of 1859; charter amended by chapter 303, Laws of 1860, and chapter 359, Laws of 1864.

Number of trustees, twenty-four.

Investments authorized:

Bond and mortgage, half value of property in sums not exceeding $10,000 to any one individual, and located in the counties of Westchester, Putnam or Rockland.

United States and New York State stocks, and stocks of any city or county authorized by the Legislature of this State to be issued.

Real estate, other than under judgment or foreclosure, such as may be requisite for the convenient transaction of its business.

Securities on which loans are authorized: Same as for investment.

Provisions under which right to invest in, or to loan upon, other securities than those named above, may be claimed: None. See section 6, chapter 432, Laws of 1859.

Provisions concerning deposits in bank: Authorized to keep on deposit available fund of one-third the amount received.

Largest amount authorized to receive from one depositor, $5,000.

Regulations or restrictions concerning rate of interest to be paid to depositors: Such that depositors shall receive a ratable proportion of profits.

Surplus authorized: None.

Prohibition concerning receiving pay for services, or borrowing funds:

1. The trustees of said corporation shall not, as such, directly or indirectly, receive any pay or emolument for their services. Section 3, chapter 432, Laws of 1859.
2. No president, vice-president, trustee, officer or servant of said corporation shall, directly or indirectly, borrow the funds of said corporation or its deposits, or in any manner use the same, or any part thereof, except to pay the necessary current expenses under the direction of said board of trustees. Section 6, chapter 432, Laws of 1859.

Provisions of the charter of the Chenango County Savings Bank, located at Norwich; incorporated by chapter 75; Laws of 1860; charter not amended.

Number of trustees, fifteen.

Investments authorized:

Bond and mortgage, half value of property, exclusive of buildings, in sums not exceeding $5,000, and located in the county of Chenango.

United States and New York State stocks, and stocks of any city authorized by the Legislature of this State to be issued.

Real estate, other than under judgement or foreclosure, such as may be requisite for the convenient transaction of its business.

Securities on which loans are authorized: Same as for investment.

Provisions under which right to invest in, or to loan upon, other securities than those named above, may be claimed: Required to invest in securities named in charter, except an available fund of not exceeding $50,000, which may be kept on deposit, on interest or otherwise, in such available form as the trustees may direct. Section 6 of charter.*

Provisions concerning deposits in bank: None except as above.

Largest amount authorized to receive from one depositor, $5,000.

Regulations or restrictions concerning rate of interest to be paid to depositors: Such that depositors shall receive a ratable proportion of profits.

Surplus authorized: None.

Prohibition concerning receiving pay for services, or borrowing funds:

1. The trustees of said corporation shall not, as such, directly or indirectly, receive any pay or emolument for their services. Section 3 of charter.
2. No president, vice-president, trustee, officer or servant of said corporation shall, directly or indirectly, borrow the funds of said corporation or its deposits, or in any manner use the same or any part thereof, except to pay necessary current expenses and outlays under the direction of said board of trustees. Section 6 of charter.

*But prohibited from loaning moneys upon notes, bills of exchange, drafts or any other personal securities whatever.

Provisions of the charter of The Citizens' Savings Bank, located in New York; incorporated by chapter 166, Laws of 1860; charter amended by chapter 625, Laws of 1864, and chapter 454, Laws of 1866.

Number of trustees, thirty.

Investments authorized:

Bond and mortgage, half value of property, not limited in location.

United States and New York State stocks, and stocks of any city authorized by the Legislature of this State to be issued.

Real estate, other than under judgment or foreclosure, such as may be requisite for the convenient transaction of its business.

Securities on which loans are authorized: None.

Provisions under which right to invest in, or to loan upon, other securities than those named above, may be claimed:

1. Trustees shall not invest in other securities than those named in the charter, in opposition to the vote of any three trustees. Section 6, chapter 166, Laws of 1860.
2. Required to invest in securities named in charter, except an available fund of not exceeding one-third total amount of deposits, which may be kept on deposit, on interest or otherwise, in such available form as the trustees may direct. Section 6, chapter 166, Laws of 1860.

Provisions concerning deposits in bank: Temporary deposits authorized in any State or National Bank, or incorporated Trust Company, in the city of New York.

Largest amount authorized to receive from one depositor, $5,000.

Regulations or restrictions concerning rate of interest to be paid to depositors: To be uniform, and such that depositors shall receive a ratable proportion of profits.

Surplus authorized: Ten per cent of deposits.

Prohibition concerning rec'ing pay for services or borrowing funds:

1. The trustees of said corporation shall not, directly or indirectly, receive any pay or emolument for their services. Section 3, chapter 166, Laws of 1860.
2. No president, vice-president, trustee, officer or servant of said corporation shall, directly or indirectly, borrow the funds of said corporation or its deposits, or in any manner use the same, or any part thereof, except to pay necessary current expenses under the direction of said board of trustees. Section 6, chapter 166, Laws of 1860.

Provisions of the charter of the Kings County Savings Institution, located at Williamsburgh; incorporated by chapter 214, Laws of 1860; charter amended by chapter 193, Laws of 1863.

Number of trustees, sixteen.

Investments authorized:

Bond and mortgage, half value of property, in sums not exceeding $20,000, and not limited in location.

United States and New York State stocks, and stocks of any city authorized by the Legislature of this State to be issued.

Real estate, other than under judgment or foreclosure, such as may be requisite for the convenient transaction of its business.

Securities on which loans are authorized: None.

Provisions under which right to invest in, or to loan upon, other securities than those named above may be claimed:

1. Trustees shall not invest in other securities than those named in the charter, in opposition to the vote of any three trustees. Section 6, chapter 214, Laws of 1860.
2. Required to invest in securities named in charter, except an available fund of not exceeding one-third of the total amount of deposits which may be kept on depost, on interest or otherwise, in such available form as the trustees may direct. Section 6, chapter 214, Laws of 1860.

Provisions concerning deposits in bank: None except as above.

Largest amount authorized to receive from one depositor, $5,000.

Regulations or restrictions concerning rate of interest to be paid to depositors: Such that depositors shall receive a ratable proportion of profits.

Surplus authorized: None.

Prohibition concerning receiving pay for services, or borrowing funds:

1. The trustees of said corporation shall not, as such, directly or indirectly, receive any pay or emolument for their services. Section 3, chapter 214, Laws of 1860.
2. No president, vice-president, trustee, officer or servant of said corporation shall, directly or indirectly, borrow the funds of said corporation, or its deposits, or in any manner use the same or any part thereof, except to pay necessary current expenses, under the direction of said board of trustees. Section 6, chapter 214, Laws of 1860.

Provisions of the charter of the Atlantic Savings Bank, located in New York; incorporated by chapter 280, Laws of 1860; charter amended by chapter 504, Laws of 1864, and chapter 408, Laws of 1866.

Number of trustees, thirty-four.

Investments authorized:

Bond and mortgage, half value of property, in sums not exceeding $20,000 to any one individual, and not restricted in location.

United States and New York State stocks, and stocks of any city authorized by the Legislature of this State to be issued.

Real estate, other than under judgment or foreclosure, such as may be requisite for the convenient transaction of its business.

Securities on which loans are authorized: None.

Provisions under which right to invest in, or to loan upon, other securities than those named above, may be claimed : Required to invest in securities named in charter, except an available fund of not exceeding one-third the total amount of deposits, which may be kept on deposit, on interest or otherwise, in such available form as the trustees may direct. Section 6, chapter 280, Laws of 1860; amended by section 1, chapter 408, Laws of 1866.*

Provisions concerning deposits in bank: Lawful to make temporary deposits in any State or National bank in the city of New York.

Largest amount authorized to receive from one depositor, $5,000.

Regulations or restrictions concerning rate of interest to be paid to depositors : Intended to be uniform, and to consist of all profits after making reserve for surplus.

Surplus authorized: Ten per cent of deposits.

Prohibition concerning receiving pay for services or borrowing funds :

1. The trustees of said corporation shall not, as such, directly or indirectly, receive any pay or emolument for their services. Section 3, chapter 280, Laws of 1860.
2. No president, vice-president, trustee, officer or servant of said corporation shall, directly or indirectly, borrow the funds of said corporation or its deposits, or in any manner use the same or any part thereof, except to pay necessary current expenses under the direction of said board of trustees. Section 6, chapter 280, Laws of 1860.

* Same section prohibits investing in any other securities than those mentioned in this section.

Provisions of the charter of the Sag Harbor Savings Bank, located at Sag Harbor; incorporated by chapter 312, Laws of 1860; charter not amended.

Number of trustees, thirty.

Investments authorized:

Bond and mortgage, half value of property in sums not exceeding $5,000 to any one individual, firm or association, and located in this State.

United States and New York State stocks, and stocks of any city in this State or of the counties of Suffolk, Queens and Kings.

Real estate, other than under judgment or foreclosure, such as may be requisite for the transaction of its business.

Securities on which loans are authorized: Same as for investment.

Provisions under which right to invest in, or to loan upon, other securities than those named above, may be claimed: Required to invest in securities named in charter, except an available fund of not exceeding one-third of the amount of deposits, which may be kept on deposit, on interest or otherwise, in such available form as the trustees may direct. Section 14 of charter.

Provisions concerning deposits in bank: None except as above.

Largest amount authorized to receive from one depositor, $3,000.

Regulations or restrictions concerning rate of interest to be paid to depositors: Such that depositors shall receive a ratable proportion of profits.

Surplus authorized: None.

Prohibition concerning receiving pay for services or borrowing funds:

1. The trustees of said corporation shall not, as such, receive any pay or emolument for their services. Section 4 of charter.

2. No president, vice-president, trustee, officer or servant of said corporation shall, directly or indirectly, borrow the funds of said corporation or its deposits, or in any manner use the same or any part thereof, except to pay the necessary expenses under the direction of said board of trustees. Section 7 of charter.

Provisions of the charter of the Rhinebeck Savings Bank, located at Rhinebeck; incorporated by chapter 336, Laws of 1860; charter not amended.

Number of trustees, twenty.

Investments authorized:

Bond and mortgage, half value of property, exclusive of buildings, in sums not exceeding $5,000, and located in the county of Dutchess.

United States and New York State stocks, and stocks of any city authorized by the Legislature of this state to be issued.

Real estate, other than under judgment or foreclosure, such as may be requisite for the convenient transaction of its business.

Securities on which loans are authorized: Same as for investment.

Provisions under which right to invest in, or to loan upon, other securities than those named above, may be claimed: Required to invest in securities named in charter, except an available fund of not exceeding one-third of the whole amount of deposits which may be kept on deposit, on interest or otherwise, in such available form as the trustees may direct. Sec. 6 of charter.*

Provisions concerning deposits in bank: None except as above.

Largest amount authorized to receive from one depositor, $1,000.

Regulations or restrictions concerning rate of interest to be paid to depositors: Such that depositors shall receive a ratable proportion of profits.

Surplus authorized: None.

Prohibition concerning receiving pay for services, or borrowing funds:

1. The trustees of said corporation shall not, as such, directly or indirectly receive any pay or emolument for their services. Section 3 of charter.
2. No president, vice-president, trustee, officer or servant of said corporation shall directly or indirectly borrow the funds of said corporation or its deposits, or in any manner use the same or any part thereof, except to pay necessary current expenses and outlays, under the direction of said board of trustees. Section 6 of charter.

* But prohibited from loaning any moneys upon notes, bills of exchange, drafts, or any other personal securities whatever.

Provisions of the charter of The Franklin Savings Bank, in the city of New York, located in New York; incorporated by chapter 409, Laws of 1860; charter amended by chapter 698, Laws of 1867.

Number of trustees: By original charter 33; by amendment reduced to 25, as vacancies occur.

Investments authorized:

Bond and mortgage, half value of property, in sums not exceeding $50,000, and not limited in location.

United States and New York State stocks, and stocks of any city in this State, or in such other manner as is authorized by the laws of this State, applicable to savings institutions.

Real estate, other than under judgment or foreclosure, such as may be requisite for the convenient transaction of its business.

Securities on which loans are authorized: Same as for investment.

Provisions under which right to invest in, or to loan upon, other securities than those named above may be claimed:

1. Trustees shall not invest in other securities than those named in the charter, in opposition to the vote of three trustees. Section 6, chapter 409, Laws of 1860.
2. Required to invest in securities named in charter, except an available fund of not exceeding one-third of the whole amount of deposits, which may be kept on deposit, on interest or otherwise, in such available form as the trustees may direct. Section 6, chapter 409, Laws of 1860. Provided, however, that no loan shall be made upon United States, New York State or city stocks, for a greater amount than ninety per cent of market value, nor upon other stocks for a greater amount than seventy-five per cent of their market value.

Provisions concerning deposits in bank: None except as above.

Largest amount authorized to receive from one depositor: No limit. See section 6 of charter, amended by chapter 698, Laws of 1867.

Regulations or restrictions concerning rate of interest to be paid to depositors: Such that on all deposits of $1,000 and under, the rate shall be the same, and may be one per cent higher than upon deposits exceeding that sum.

Surplus authorized: Fifteen per cent of deposits.

Prohibition concerning receiving pay for services, or borrowing funds:

1. The trustees of said corporation shall not, directly or indirectly, receive any pay or emolument for their services. Section 3, chapter 409, Laws of 1860.
2. No president, vice-president, trustee, officer or servant of said corporation shall, directly or indirectly, borrow the funds of said corporation or its deposits, or in any manner use the same or any part thereof, except to pay necessary current expenses under the direction of the board of trustees, and such compensation to the officers of said bank as the board may deem proper. Section 3, chapter 698, Laws of 1867.

Provisions of the charter of the East Brooklyn Savings Bank, located in Brooklyn; incorporated by chapter 496, Laws of 1860; charter not amended.

Number of trustees, seventeen.

Investments authorized:

Bond and mortgage, half value of property, in sums not exceeding $10,000, and located in the county of Kings.

United States and New York State stocks, and stocks of the city of Brooklyn or county of Kings.

Real estate, other than under judgment or foreclosure, such as may be requisite for the convenient transaction of its business.

Securities on which loans are authorized: same as for investment.

Provisions under which right to invest in, or to loan upon, other securities than those named above, may be claimed: Required to invest in securities named in charter, except an available fund of not exceeding $50,000, which may be kept on deposit, on interest, or otherwise, in such available form as the trustees may elect. Section 6 of charter.*

Provisions concerning deposits in bank: None except as above.

Largest amount authorized to receive from one depositor, $10,000.

*But prohibiting from loaning any moneys upon notes, bills of exchange, drafts, or any other personal securities whatever.

Regulations or restrictions concerning rate of interest to be paid to depositors : Such that depositors shall receive a ratable proportion of profits.

Surplus authorized : None.

Prohibition concerning receiving pay for services or borrowing funds :

1. The trustees of said corporation shall not as such directly or indirectly receive any payment or emolument for their services. Section 3 of charter.
2. No president, vice-president, trustee, officer or servant of said corporation shall directly or indirectly borrow the funds of said corporation or its deposits, or in any manner use the same, or any part thereof, except to pay necessary expenses and outlays under the direction of the said board of trustees. Section 6 of charter.

Provisions of the charter of the Harlem Savings Bank, located at Harlem, in New York; incorporated by chapter 175, Laws of 1863; charter amended by chapter 808, Laws of 1866.

Number of trustees, twenty-eight.

Investments authorized :

Bond and mortgage, half value of property, in sums not exceeding $20,000, and located in the county of New York, or counties adjoining, within this State.

United States and New York State stocks, and stocks of the city of New York, or of the county of Westchester.

Real estate other than under judgment or foreclosure, such as may be requisite for the convenient transaction of its business.

Securities on which loans are authorised : Same as for investment.

Provisions under which right to invest in, or to loan upon, other securities than those named above, may be claimed : Required to invest in securities named in charter, except an available fund of not exceeding $50,000, which may be kept on deposit, on interest or otherwise, in such available form as the trustees may direct. Section 6, chapter 175, Laws of 1863.

Provisions concerning deposits in bank : Not exceeding $25,000 to be deposited in any one bank.

Largest amount authorized to receive from one depositor, $2,000.

Regulations or restrictions concerning rate of interest to be paid to depositors: Such that depositors shall receive a ratable proportion of profits.

Surplus authorized: None.

Prohibition concerning receiving pay for services, or borrowing funds:

1. The trustees of said corporation shall not. directly or indirectly, receive any payment or emolument for their services. Section 3, chapter 175, Laws of 1863.
2. No president, vice-president, trustee, officer or servant of said corporation shall, directly or indirectly, borrow the funds of said corporation or its deposits, or in any manner use the same or any part thereof, except to pay necessary expenses under the direction of the said board of trustees. Section 6, chapter 175, Laws of 1863.

Provisions of the charter of The Emigrant Savings Bank of Brooklyn, located at Brooklyn; incorporated by chapter 233, Laws of 1863; charter amended by chapter 630, Laws of 1865.

Number of trustees, twenty-eight.

Investments authorized:

Bond and mortgage, half value of property, in sums not exceeding $10,000 to any one individual, and not restricted in location.

United States and New York State stocks, and stocks of any city authorized by the Legislature of this State to be issued.

Real estate, other than under judgment or foreclosure, such as may be requisite for the convenient transaction of its business.

Securities on which loans are authorized: Same as for investment.

Provisions under which right to invest in, or to loan upon, other securities than those named above, may be claimed: Required to invest in securities named in charter, except an available fund of not exceeding twenty per cent. of their deposits, which may be kept on deposit, on interest or otherwise, in such available form as the trustees may direct; but such available sum shall at no time exceed one-third of the aggregate amount of said deposits. Section 15, chapter 233, Laws of 1863.

Provisions concerning deposits in bank: None except as above.

Largest amount authorized to receive from one depositor, $2,000.

Regulations or restrictions concerning rate of interest to be paid to depositors: Such that depositors shall receive a ratable proportion of profits.

Surplus authorized: Ten per cent on the amount of deposits.

Prohibition concerning receiving pay for services or borrowing funds: The trustees of said corporation shall not receive any pay or emolument for their services. Section 3, chap. 233, Laws of 1863.

Provisions of the charter of the Market Savings Bank, located in New York, incorporated by chapter 498, Laws of 1863; charter amended by chapter 505, Laws of 1864, and chapter 497, Laws of 1867.

Number of trustees, thirty-seven.

Investments authorized:

Bond and mortgage, half value of property, and not restricted in location.

United States and New York State stocks, stocks of any other State in the Union, and stocks of any city, county or town in this State, authorized by the Legislature to be issued.

Real estate, other than under judgment or foreclosure, such as may be requisite for the convenient transaction of its business.

Securities on which loans are authorized: Same as for investment, but subject to conditions imposed by section 1, chapter 257, Laws of 1853.

Provisions under which right to invest in, or to loan upon, other securities than those named above, may be claimed: Required to invest in securities named in charter, except an available fund in the discretion of the trustees, which may be kept on deposit, on interest or otherwise, in such available form as the trustees may direct. Section 2, chapter 497, Laws of 1867, amending section 6, of charter.

Provisions concerning deposits in bank: None except as above.

Largest amount authorized to receive from one depositor: No limit.

Regulations or restrictions concerning rate of interest to be paid to depositors: Lawful to classify depositors and fix rate of interest to be paid to each class.

Surplus authorized: Fifteen per cent of deposits.

Prohibition concerning receiving pay for services, or borrowing funds:

1. The trustees of said corporation, shall not as such, directly or indirectly, receive any pay or emolument for their services. Section 3, chapter 498, Laws of 1863.
2. No president, vice-president, trustee, officer or servant of said corporation shall, directly or indirectly, borrow the funds of said corporation or its deposits, or in any manner use the same or any part thereof, except to pay necessary current expenses under the direction of said board of trustees. Section 2, chap. 497, Laws of 1867.

Provisions of the charter of the People's Savings Bank located in New York; Incorporated by chapter 504, Laws of 1863; charter amended by chapter 429, Laws of 1867.

Number of trustees, thirty-two.

Investments authorized:

Bond and mortgage, half value of property, in sums not exceeding 10,000, to any one individual, and not restricted in location.

United States and New York State stocks, and stocks of any city authorized by the Legislature of this State to be issued

Real estate, other than under judgment or foreclosure, such as may be requisite for the convenient transaction of its business.

Securities on which loans are authorized: None.

Provisions under which right to invest in, or to loan upon, other securities than those named above, may be claimed:

1. Trustees shall not invest in other securities than those named in the charter, in opposition to the vote of any three trustees. Section 6, chapter 504, laws of 1863.
2. Required to invest in securities named in charter, except an available fund of not exceeding one-third of the total amount of deposits which may be kept on deposit, on interest or otherwise, in such available form as the trustees may direct. Section 6, chapter 504, Laws of 1863.

Provisions concerning deposits in bank: Lawful to make temporary deposits in any national or State banks or incorporated trust company in the city of New York.

Largest amount authorized to receive from one depositor, $2,000.

Regulations or restrictions concerning rate of interest to be paid to depositors: Such that depositors shall receive a ratable proportion of profits.

Surplus authorized: Five per cent on the amount of deposits.

Prohibition concerning receiving pay for services, or borrowing funds:

1. The trustees of said corporation shall not, as such, directly or indirectly, receive any pay or emolument for their services. Section 3, chapter 504, Laws of 1863.
2. No president, vice-president, trustee, officer or servant of said corporation shall, directly or indirectly, borrow the funds of said corporation or its deposits, or in any manner use the same or any part thereof, except to pay necessary current expenses under the direction of said board of trustees. Section 6, chapter 504, Laws of 1863.

Provisions of the charter of the Mutual Savings Bank of Auburn, located at Auburn; incorporated by chapter 212, Laws of 1864; charter not amended.

Number of trustees, seventeen.

Investments authorized:

Bond and mortgage, half value of property, exclusive of buildings, in sums not exceeding 5,000 to any one individual, and not limited in location.

United States and New York State stocks, and stocks of any city or county authorized by the Legislature of this State to be issued.

Real estate, other than under judgment or foreclosure, such as may be requisite for the convenient transaction of its business.

Securities on which loans are authorized: Noue.

Provisions under which right to invest in, or to loan upon, other securities than those named above, may be claimed:

1. Trustees shall not invest in other securities than those named in the charter, in opposition to the vote of any trustee. Section 9 of charter.

2. Required to invest in securities named in charter, except an available fund of not exceeding one-fourth of the total amount of deposits, which may be kept on deposit, on interest or otherwise, in such available form as the trustees may direct. Section 9 of charter.

Provisions concerning deposits in bank: None, except as above.

Largest amount authorized to receive from one depositor: No limit.

Regulations or restrictions concerning rate of interest to be paid to depositors: Such that depositors shall receive a ratable proportion of profits.

Surplus authorized: None.

Prohibition concerning receiving pay for services, or borrowing funds:

1. The trustees of said corporation shall not, as such, directly or indirectly, receive any pay or emolument for their services. Section 4 of charter.
2. No president, vice-president, trustee, officer or servant of said corporation shall, directly or indirectly, borrow the funds of said corporation or its depositors, or in any manner use the same or any part thereof, except to pay necessary current expenses under the direction of the said board of trustees. Section 7 of charter.

Provisions of the charter of the Dime Savings Bank of Williamsburgh, located at Williamsburgh; incorporated by chapter 239, Laws of 1864; charter not amended.

Number of trustees authorized: Twenty-three.

Investments authorized:

Bond and mortgage, half value of property, in sums not exceeding $10,000 to any one individual, and located in Kings county.

United States and New York State stocks, and stocks of any city authorized by the Legislature of this State to be issued.

Real estate, other than under judgment or foreclosure, such as may be requisite for the transaction of its business.

Securities on which loans are authorized: None.

Provisions under which right to invest in, or to loan upon, other securities than those named above, may be claimed:

1. Trustees shall not invest in other securities than those named in the charter, in opposition to the vote of any three trustees. Section 6 of charter.
2. Required to invest in securities named in charter, except an available fund of not exceeding one-third of the total amount of deposits which may be kept on deposit, on interest or otherwise, in such available form as the trustees may direct. Section 6 of charter.

Provisions concerning deposits in bank: Temporary deposits may may be made in any State bank in the city of Brooklyn.

Largest amount authorized to receive from one depositor, $5,000.

Regulations or restrictions concerning rate of interest to be paid to depositors: such that depositors shall receive a ratable proportion of profits.

Surplus authorized: None.

Prohibition concerning receiving pay for services, or borrowing funds:

1. The trustees of said corporation shall not, as such, directly or indirectly receive any pay or emolument for their services. Section 3 of charter.
2. No president, vice-president, trustee, officer or servant of said corporation shall, directly or indirectly, borrow the funds of said corporation or its deposits, or in any manner use the same, or any part thereof, except to pay necessary current expenses under the direction of said board of trustees. Section 6 of charter.

Provisions of the charter of the Port Chester Savings Bank, located at Port Chester; incorporated by chapter 119, Laws of 1865; charter amended by chapter 473, Laws of 1867.

Number of trustees, sixteen.

Investments authorized:

Bond and mortgage, half value of property, in sums not exceeding $5,000 to any one individual on the same piece of property, and not limited in location.

United States and New York State stocks, stocks any of city or county in this State, and of the town of Rye, in the county of Westchester.

Real estate, other than under judgment or foreclosure, such as may be requisite for the transaction of its business.

Securities on which loans are authorized: Same as for investment.

Provisions under which right to invest in, or to loan upon, other securities than those named above, may be claimed: Required to invest in securities named in charter, except an available fund of not exceeding one-fourth the total amount of deposits, which may be kept on deposit, on interest, or otherwise, in such available form as the trustees may direct. Section 6, chapter 119, Laws of 1865.

Provisions concerning deposits in bank: Lawful to make temporary deposits in any State or National bank in the county of Westchester.

Largest amount authorized to receive from one depositor, $5,000.

Regulations or restrictions concerning rate of interest to be paid to depositors: Such that depositors shall receive a ratable proportion of profits.

Surplus authorized: None.

Prohibition concerning receiving pay for services or borrowing funds:

1. The trustees of said corporation shall not, directly or indirectly, receive any pay or emolument for their services. Section 3, chapter 119, Laws of 1865.
2. No president, vice-president, trustee, officer or other servant of said corporation shall, directly or indirectly, borrow the funds of said corporation or its deposits, or in any manner use the same, or any part thereof, except to pay necessary current expenses, under the direction of said board of trustees. Section 6, chapter 119, Laws of 1865.

Provisions of the charter of the National Savings Bank of Utica, located at Utica; incorporated by chapter 162, Laws of 1865; charter not amended.

Number of trustees, twenty-nine.

Investments authorized:

Bond and mortgage, half value of property, and not restricted in location.

United States and New York State stocks, and stocks of any city, county or town, authorized by the Legislature of this State to be issued.

Real estate, other than under judgment or foreclosure, such as may be requisite for the convenient transaction of its business.

Securities on which loans are authorized: None.

Provisions under which right to invest in, or to loan upon, other securities than those named above, may be claimed:

1. Trustees shall not invest in other securities than those named in the charter, in opposition to the vote of any trustee. Section 9 of charter.
2. Required to invest in securities named in charter, except an available fund of not exceeding one-third the total amount of deposits, which may be kept in deposit, on interest or otherwise, in such available form as the trustees may direct. Section 9 of charter.

Provisions concerning deposits in bank: None except as above.

Largest amount authorized to receive from one depositor: No limit.

Regulations or restrictions concerning rate of interest to be paid to depositors: Such that depositors of sums not over five hundred dollars shall receive a ratable proportion of profits.

Surplus authorized: None.

Prohibition concerning receiving pay for services, or borrowing funds:

1. The trustees of said corporation shall not, directly or indirectly, receive any pay or emolument for their services. Section 4 of charter.
2. No president, vice-president, trustee, officer or servant of said corporation shall, directly or indirectly, borrow the funds of said corporation or its depositors, or in any manner use the same or any part thereof, except to pay the necessary current expenses, under the direction of the said board of trustees. Section 7 of charter.

Provisions of the charter of The Long Island Savings Bank of Brooklyn, located at Brooklyn; incorporated by chap. 449, Laws of 1865; charter not amended.

Number of trustees, twenty.

Investments authorized:

Bond and mortgage, half value of property, located in the county of Kings.

United States and New York State stocks, and stocks of any city of this State, or of the county of Kings.

Real estate, other than under judgment or foreclosure, such as may be requisite for the convenient transaction of its business.

Securities on which loans are authorized: None.

Provisions under which right to invest in, or to loan upon, other securities than those named above, may be claimed: Required to invest in securities named in charter, except an available fund of not exceeding one-fifth the total amount of deposits, which may be kept on deposit, on interest or otherwise, or in such available form as the trustees may direct. Section 6 of charter.

Provisions concerning deposits in bank: None, except as above.

Largest amount authorized to receive from one depositor, $5,000.

Regulations or restrictions concerning rate of interest to be paid to depositors: Lawful to allow depositors of $500, or upwards, one per cent less than the amount allowed others.

Surplus authorized: Twenty-five thousand dollars.

Prohibition concerning receiving pay for services or borrowing funds:

1. The trustees of said corporation shall not, directly or indirectly, receive any pay or emolument for their services. Section 3 of charter.
2. No president, vice-president, trustee, officer or servant of said corporation shall, directly or indirectly, borrow the funds of said corporation, or its deposits, or in any manner use the same or any part thereof, except to pay necessary expenses under the direction of said board of trustees. Section 7 of charter.

Provisions of the charter of the New Rochelle Savings Bank, located at New Rochelle; incorporated by chapter 566, Laws of 1865; charter amended by by chapter 245, Laws of 1867.

Number of trustees, thirteen.

Investments authorized:

Bond and mortgage, half value of property, in sums not exceeding $5,000 to any one individual on the same piece of property, and not restricted in location.

United States and New York State stocks, and stocks of any city or county of this State.

Real estate, other than under judgment or foreclosure, such as may be requisite for the transaction of its business.

Securities on which loans are authorized: Same as for investment.

Provisions under which right to invest in, or to loan upon, other securities than those named above, may be claimed: Required to invest in securities named in charter, except an available fund of not exceeding one-fourth the total amount of deposits, which may be kept on deposit, on interest or otherwise, in such available form as the trustees may direct. Section 6, chapter 566, Laws of 1865.

Provisions concerning deposits in bank: Lawful to deposit in any State or National bank in the counties of Westchester and New York.

Largest amount authorized to receive from one depositor, $5,000.

Regulations or restrictions concerning rate of interest to be paid to depositors: Such that depositors shall receive a ratable proportion of profits.

Surplus authorized: None.

Prohibition concerning receiving pay for services or borrowing funds:

1. The trustees of said corporation shall not directly or indirectly receive any pay or emolument for their services. Section 3, chapter 566, Laws of 1865.
2. No president, vice-president, trustee, officer or servant of said corporation shall directly or indirectly borrow the funds of said corporation or its deposits, or in any manner use the same, or any part thereof, except to pay necessary current expenses under the direction of said board of trustees. Section 6, chapter 566, Laws of 1865.

Provisions of the charter of the Oneida Savings Bank; located at Oneida; incorporated by chapter 53, Laws of 1866; charter not amended.

Number of trustees, seventeen.

Investments authorized:

Bond and mortgage, half value of property, exclusive of buildings, in sums not exceeding $10,000 to any one individual, and located in the county of Madison or adjoining counties.

United States and New York State stocks, and stocks of any city or county authorized by the legislature of this State to be issued.

Real estate, other than under judgment or foreclosure, such as may be requisite for the convenient transaction of its business.

Securities on which loans are authorized: Same as for investment.

Provisions under which right to invest in, or to loan upon, other securities than those named above, may be claimed: Required to invest in securities named in charter, except an available fund of not exceeding one-third the total amount of deposits, which may be kept on deposit, on interest or otherwise, in such available form as the trustees may direct. Section 6 of charter.*

Provisions concerning deposits in bank: Lawful to make temporary deposits in any State or National bank in this State.

Largest amount authorized to receive from one depositor: No limit.

Regulations or restrictions concerning rate of interest to be paid to depositors: Left to the discretion of the trustees.

Surplus authorized: Ten per cent of deposits.

Prohibition concerning receiving pay for services, or borrowing funds:

1. The trustees of said corporation shall not, as such, directly or indirectly receive any pay or emolument for their services. Section 3 of charter.
2. No president, vice-president, trustee, officer or servant of said corporation shall, directly or indirectly, borrow the funds of said corporation or its deposits, or in any manner use the same or any part thereof, except to pay necessary current expenses under the direction of said board of trustees. Section 6 of charter.

Provisions of the charter of The Mechanics' Savings Bank of Fishkill, on the Hudson, located at Fishkill-on-Hudson; incorporated by chapter 103, Laws of 1866; charter not amended.

Number of trustees, twenty-five.

Investments authorized:

Bond and mortgage, half value of property, in sums not exceeding $5,000, to any one individual on the same piece of property, and located in the county of Dutchess or counties adjoining.

United States and New York State stocks, and stocks of any city or county of this State.

Real estate, other than under judgment or foreclosure, such as shall be requisite for the transaction of its business.

Securities on which loans are authorized: None.

* By same section prohibited from investing any moneys in other securities than those named above.

Provisions under which right to invest in, or to loan upon, other securities than those named above, may be claimed : Required to invest in securities named in charter, except an available fund of not exceeding one-fifth of the total amount of deposits, which may be kept on deposit, on interest or otherwise, or in such available form as the trustees may direct. Section 6 of charter.

Provisions concerning deposits in bank : None except as above.

Largest amount authorized to receive from one depositor, $5,000.

Regulations or restrictions concerning rate of interest to be paid to depositors : Left to the discretion of trustees.

Surplus authorized : Ten per cent. of deposits.

Prohibition concerning receiving pay for services, or borrowing funds :

1. The trustees of said corporation shall not, directly or indirectly, receive any pay or emolument for their services. Section 3 of charter.
2. No president, vice-president, trustee, officer or other servant of said corporation shall, directly or indirectly, borrow the funds of said corporation or its deposits, or in any manner use the same or any part thereof, except to pay the necessary current expenses under the direction of the said board of trustees. Section 6 of charter.

Provisions of the charter of The People's Savings Bank of the town of Yonkers, located at Yonkers; incorporated by chapter 405, Laws of 1866; charter not amended.

Number of trustees, twenty-one.

Investments authorized :

Bond and mortgage, half value of property, in sums not exceeding $5,000, to any one individual on the same piece of property, and located in the county of Westchester, or the counties adjoining, in this State.

United States and New York State stocks, and stocks of the county of Westchester, or of any town in the county of Westchester authorized by the Legislature to be issued.

Real estate, other than under judgment or foreclosure, such as may be requisite for the convenient transaction of its business.

Securities on which loans are authorized : Same as for investment.

Provisions under which right to invest in, or to loan upon, other securities than those named above, may be claimed: Trustees shall not invest in other securities than those named in the charter, in opposition to the vote of any three trustees. Section 6 of charter.

Provisions concerning deposits in bank: Lawful to keep available fund of not exceeding $25,000 on deposit in any of the incorporated banks in the village of Yonkers or elsewhere.

Largest amount authorized to receive from one depositor, $5,000.

Regulations or restrictions concerning rate of interest to be paid to depositors: Such that depositors shall receive a ratable proportion of profits.

Surplus authorized: Twenty-five thousand dollars.

Prohibition concerning receiving pay for services or borrowing funds:

1. The trustees of said corporation shall not, directly or indirectly, receive any pay or emolument for their services as such, or otherwise, from said corporation. Section 3 of charter.
2. No president, vice-president, trustee, officer or servant of said corporation shall, directly or indirectly, borrow the funds of said corporation or its deposits, or in any manner use the same, or any part thereof, except to pay necessary current expenses under the direction of said board of trustees. Section 6 of charter.

Provisions of the charter of The Up-Town Savings Bank in the city of New York; located in New York; incorporated by chapter 435, Laws of 1866; charter not amended.

Number of trustees, twenty-two.

Investments authorized:

Bond and mortgage, half value of property, located in the city of New York or counties adjoining.

United States and New York State stocks, and stocks of any city in this State.

Real estate, other than under judgment or foreclosure, such as may be requisite for the convenient transaction of its business.

Securities on which loans are authorized: None.

Provisions under which right to invest in, or to loan upon, other securities than those named above, may be claimed: Required to invest in securities named in charter, except an available fund of not exceeding one-third the whole amount of deposits which may be kept on deposit, on interest or otherwise, in such available form as the trustees may direct. Section 6 of charter.*

Provisions concerning deposits in bank: None except as above.

Largest amount authorized to receive from one depositor, $5,000.

Regulations or restrictions concerning rate of interest to be paid to depositors: Such that depositors of $1,000 and under, shall receive one per cent. greater interest than is allowed to others.

Surplus authorized: Ten per cent. of deposits.

Prohibition concerning receiving pay for services, or borrowing funds:

1. The trustees of said corporation shall not, directly or indirectly, receive any pay or emolument for their services. Section 3 of charter.
2. No president, vice-president, or trustee, officer or servant of said corporation shall, directly or indirectly, borrow the funds of said corporation or its deposits, or in any manner use the same or any part thereof, except to pay necessary current expenses, under the direction of said board of trustees. Section 6 of charter.

Provisions of the charter of the Cortland Savings Bank, located at Cortland village; incorporated by chapter 557, Laws of 1866; charter not amended.

Number of trustees, twenty.

Investments authorized:

Bond and mortgage, half value of property, in sums not exceeding $5,000 to any one individual on the same piece of property, and located in the county of Cortland, or any adjoining county.

United States and New York State stocks, and stocks of the county of Cortland, or of any town in said county.

Real estate, other than under judgment or foreclosure, such as may be requisite for the convenient transaction of its business.

* Provided, however, that no loan shall be made under this section upon any stocks or security whatever to a greater amount than three-fourths the actual cash value of such stocks or security at the time of making such loan. Same section.

Securities on which loans are authorized: None.

Provisions under which right to invest in, or to loan upon, other securities than those named above, may be claimed: None.

Provisions concerning deposits in bank: Lawful to keep $25,000 as an available fund on deposit in any of the incorporated banks in the village of Cortland.

Largest amount authorized to receive from one depositor, $5,000.

Regulations or restrictions concerning rate of interest to be paid to depositors: Such that depositors shall receive a ratable proportion of profits.

Surplus authorized: Twenty-five thousand dollars.

Prohibition concerning receiving pay for services, or borrowing funds:

1. The trustees of said corporation, shall not, directly or indirectly, receive any pay or emolument for their services as such, or otherways, from the corporation. Section 3, of charter.
2. No president, vice-president, trustee, officer or servant of said corporation, shall directly or indirectly, borrow the funds of said corporation or its deposits, or in any manner use the same or any part thereof, except to pay necessary current expenses under the direction of said board of trustees. Section 6 of charter.

Provisions of the charter of the Skaneateles Savings Bank, located at Skaneateles; incorporated by chapter 600, Laws of 1866; charter not amended.

Number of trustees, fifteen.

Investments authorized:

Bond and mortgage, half value of property, exclusive of buildings, and located in the county of Onondaga or counties adjoining.

United States and New York State stocks, and stocks of any city, county or town, authorized by the Legislature of this State to be issued.

Real estate, other than under judgment or foreclosure, such as may be requisite for the convenient transaction of its business.

Securities on which loans are authorized; None.

Provisions under which right to invest in, or to loan upon, other securities than those named above, may be claimed: Required to invest in securities named in charter, except an available fund of not exceeding one-third of the total amount of deposits, which may be kept on deposit, on interest, or otherwise, in such available form as the trustees may direct. Section 9 of charter.*

Provisions concerning deposits in bank: None, except as above.

Largest amount authorized to receive from one depositor, $5,000.

Regulations or restrictions concerning rate of interest to be paid to depositors: Such that depositors shall receive a ratable proportion of profits.

Surplus authorized: Ten per cent. of deposits.

Prohibition concerning receiving pay for services, or borrowing funds:

1. The trustees of said corporation shall not, directly or indirectly, receive any pay or emolument for their services as such or otherwise, from said corporation. Section 4 of charter.
2. No president, vice-president, trustee, officer or servant of said corporation shall, directly or indirectly, borrow the funds of said corporation or its deposits, or in any manner use the same, or any part thereof, except to pay the necessary current expenses, under the direction of the said board of trustees. Section 7 of charter.

Provisions of the charter of the Chautauqua County Savings Bank, located at Fredonia; incorporated by chapter 660, Laws of 1866; charter not amended.

Number of trustees, nine.

Investments authorized:

Bond and mortgage, half value of property, exclusive of buildings, in sums not exceeding $5,000 to any one individual, and located in Chautauqua county, or adjoining counties in this State.

United States and New York State stocks, and stocks of any city, county or town of this State, authorized by law.

Real estate, other than under judgment or foreclosure, such as may be necessary in the convenient transaction of its business.

* First clause of same section provides that "no moneys deposited with said corporation shall be invested, except in the securities or stocks mentioned in this act."

Securities on which loans are authorized: Same as for investment.

Provisions under which right to invest in, or to loan upon, other securities than those named above, may be claimed: Required to invest in securities named in charter, except an available fund of not exceeding one-third of the total amount of deposits, which may be kept on deposit on interest or otherwise, in such available form as the trustees may direct. Section 6 of charter.

Provisions concerning deposits in bank: Lawful to make temporary deposits in any State or National bank.

Largest amount authorized to receive from one depositor, $5,000.

Regulations or restrictions concerning rate of interest to be paid to depositors: Such that depositors shall receive a ratable proportion of profits.

Surplus authorized: Ten per cent of deposits.

Prohibition concerning receiving pay for services, or borrowing funds:

1. The trustees of said corporation shall not, directly or indirectly, receive any pay or emolument for their services done and rendered as such trustees, or otherwise, from said corporation. Section 3 of charter.
2. No president, vice-president, trustee, officer or servant of said corporation shall, directly or indirectly, borrow the funds of said corporation or its deposits, or in any manner use the same, or any part thereof, except to pay necessary current expenses, under the direction of the board of trustees. Section 6 of charter.

Provisions of the charter of The German Savings Bank of Brooklyn, located at Williamsburgh; incorporated by chapter 714, Laws of 1866; charter amended by chapter 776, Laws of 1867.

Number of trustees, twenty-one.

Investments authorized:

Bond and mortgage, half value of property, located in the county of Kings and any adjoining county.

United States and New York State stocks, and stocks of any city of this State, or of the county of Kings.

Real estate, other than under judgment or foreclosure, such as may be requisite for the convenient transaction of its business.

Securities on which loans are authorized: None.

Provisions under which right to invest in, or to loan upon, other securities than those named above, may be claimed: Required to invest in securities named in charter, except an available fund of not exceeding one-third of total amount of deposits, which may be kept on deposit, on interest or otherwise, or in such available form as the trustees may direct. Section 6, chap. 714, Laws of 1866.

Provisions concerning deposits in bank: None except as above.

Largest amount authorized to receive from one depositor, $5,000.

Regulations or restrictions concerning rate of interest to be paid to depositors: Not to exceed seven per cent., and lawful to allow depositors of $1,000 or upwards one per cent. less interest than is allowed to others.

Surplus authorized: Ten per cent of deposits.

Prohibition concerning receiving pay for services, or borrowing funds;

1. The trustees of said corporation shall not, directly or indirectly, receive any payment or emolument for their services. Section 3, chapter 714, Laws of 1866.

2. No president, vice-president, trustee, officer or servant of said corporation shall, directly or indirectly, borrow the funds of said corporation or its deposits, or in any manner use the same, or any part thereof, except to pay necessary expenses, under the direction of said board of trustees. Section 6, chapter 714, Laws of 1866.

Provisions of the charter of The Jamaica Savings Bank, located at Jamaica; incorporated by chapter 717, Laws of 1866; charter not amended.

Number of trustees, nineteen.

Investments authorized.

Bond and mortgage, half value of property, exclusive of buildings, in sums not exceeding $5,000, and located in this State.

United States and New York State stocks, and stocks of the city of New York, or of any county or town in this State, authorized to be issued.

Real estate, other than under judgment or foreclosure, such as may be requisite for the convenient transaction of its business.

Securities on which loans are authorized: Same as for investment.

Provisions under which right to invest in, or to loan upon, other securities than those named above, may be claimed: Required to invest in securities named in charter, except an available fund of not exceeding twenty-five per cent of all deposits, which may be kept on deposit, at interest or otherwise, in such available form as the trustees may direct. Section 6 of charter.

Provisions concerning deposits in bank: Not exceeding $20,000 to be deposited in any one bank.

Largest amount authorized to receive from one depositor, $2,000.

Regulations or restrictions concerning rate of interest to be paid to depositors: Such that depositors shall receive a ratable proportion of profits.

Surplus authorized: Ten per cent of deposits.

Prohibition concerning receiving pay for services or borrowing funds:

1. The trustees of said corporation shall not, directly or indirectly receive any pay or emolument for their services as trustees or otherwise. Section 3 of charter.
2. No president, vice-president, trustee, officer or servant of said corporation shall, directly or indirectly, borrow the funds of said corporation or its deposits, or in any manner use the same, or any part thereof, except to pay necessary expenses under the direction of said board of trustees. Section 6, of charter.

Provisions of the charter of the North River Savings Bank located in New York; incorporated by chapter 739, Laws of 1866; charter not amended.

Number of trustees, twenty-eight.

Investments authorized:

Bond and mortgage, half value of property located in the city of New York or the counties adjoining.

United States and New York State stocks, and stocks of any city, county or town, authorized by the Legislature of this State to be issued.

Real estate, other than under judgment or foreclosure, such as may be requisite for the convenient transaction of its business.

Securities on which loans are authorized: Stocks of the United States and of the State or city of New York.*

Provisions under which right to invest in, or to loan upon, other securities than those named above, may be claimed: None.

Provisions concerning deposits in bank: Temporary deposits authorized in any State or National bank, or any incorporated trust company in the city of New York.

Largest amount authorized to receive from one depositor, $5,000.

Regulations or restrictions concerning rate of interest to be paid to depositors: Such that depositors shall receive a ratable proportion of profits.

Surplus authorized: Ten per cent of deposits.

Prohibition concerning receiving pay for services or borrowing funds:

1. The trustees of said corporation shall not, directly or indirectly, receive any pay or emolument for their services as trustees or otherwise. Section 3 of charter.
2. No president, vice-president, trustee, officer or servant of said corporation shall borrow, directly or indirectly, the funds of said corporation, or its deposits, or in any manner use the same, or any part thereof, except to pay necessary current expenses, under the direction of said board of trustees. Section 6 of charter.

Provisions of the charter of The Hope Savings Bank, located at Albany; incorporated by chapter 842, Laws of 1866; charter not amended.

Number of trustees, thirteen.

Investments authorized:

Bond and mortgage, half value of property, exclusive of buildings, and located in the county of Albany and counties adjoining.

United States and New York State stocks, and stocks of any city or county in this State.

Real estate, other than under judgment or foreclosure, not exceeding an annual value of five thousand dollars.

Securities on which loans are authorized: None.

Provisions under which right to invest in, or to loan upon, other securities than those named above, may be claimed: None.

* Such loans to be on call, or not to exceed ten days' notice nor more than ninety per cent. of the market value of the securities, and with the amount on hand or on deposit in bank, not to exceed one-third the deposits received. Section 6 of charter.

Provisions concerning deposits in bank : None.

Largest amount authorized to receive from one depositor : No limit.

Regulations or restrictions concerning rate of interest to be paid to depositors : Sums less than $2,000 shall receive one per cent more interest than is paid depositors of larger sums.

Surplus authorized : Ten per cent of deposits.

Prohibition concerning receiving pay for services, or borrowing funds :

1. The trustees or managers of said institution shall not, directly or indirectly, receive any pay or emolument for their services. Section 1 of charter.
2. No president, vice-president, trustee, manager, accountant or other officer shall, directly or indirectly, borrow or use the funds of the corporation except to pay the necessary and current expenses. Section 2 of charter.

Provisions of the charter of The Orleans Savings Bank, located at Albion ; incorporated by chapter 190, Laws of 1867.

Number of trustees, twenty-one.

Investments authorized :

Bond and mortgage, two-thirds value of property, in sums not exceeding $5,000 to any one individual on the same piece of property, and located in the county of Orleans, and in adjoining counties in the State.

United States and New York State stocks, and stocks of the county of Orleans, and of adjoining counties in this State.

Real estate, other than under judgment or foreclosure, such as may be requisite for the convenient transaction of its business.

Securities on which loans are authorized : Same as for investment.

Provisions under which right to invest in, or to loan upon, other securities than those named above, may be claimed : Trustees shall not invest in other securities than those named in the charter, in opposition to the vote of any three trustees. Section 6 of charter.

Provisions concerning deposits in bank : Lawful to keep available fund, not exceeding $25,000, on deposit with any bank or banker in the county of Orleans.

Largest amount authorized to receive from one depositor, $5,000.

Regulations or restrictions concerning rate of interest to be paid to depositors: Such that depositors shall receive a ratable proportion of profits.

Surplus authorized: Twenty-five thousand dollars.

Prohibition concerning receiving pay for services, or borrowing funds: The trustees of said corporation shall not directly or indirectly receive any pay or emolument for their services or otherwise from said corporation. Section 3 of charter.

Provisions of the charter of the Mechanics' Savings Bank of Rochester, located at Rochester; incorporated by chapter 411, Laws of 1867.

Number of trustees, twenty-one.

Investments authorized:

Bond and mortgage, half value of property, exclusive of buildings, in sums not exceeding $10,000 to any one individual, and not limited in location.

United States and New York State stocks, and stocks of any city in this State, or of the county of Monroe.

Real estate, other than under judgment or foreclosure, such as may be requisite for the convenient transaction of its business.

Securities on which loans are authorized: None.

Provisions under which right to invest in, or to loan upon, other securities than those named above, may be claimed:

1. Trustees shall not invest in other securities than those named in the charter, in opposition to the vote of any trustees. Section 6 of charter.
2. Required to invest in securities named in charter, except an available fund of not exceeding one-third of the total amount of deposits, which may be kept on deposit, on interest, or otherwise, or in such available form as the trustees may direct. Section 6 of charter.

Provisions concerning deposits in bank: None, except as above.

Largest amount authorized to receive from one depositor, $5,000.

Regulations or restrictions concerning rate of interest to be paid to depositors: Such that depositors shall receive a ratable proportion of profits.

Surplus authorized: None.

Prohibition concerning receiving pay for services or borrowing funds:

2. The trustees of said corporation shall not, directly or indirectly, receive any payment or emolument for their services. Section 3 of charter.
2. No president, vice-president, trustee, officer or servant of said corporation shall, directly oa indirectly, borrow the funds of said corporation, or its deposits, or in any manner use the same, or any part thereof, except to pay necessary expenses under the direction of said board of trustees. Section 6 of charter.

Provisions of the charter of the Binghamton Savings Bank, located at Binghamton; incorporated by chapter 423, Laws of 1867.

Number of trustees, thirteen.

Investments authorized:

Bond and mortgage, half value of property, located in the county of Broome, or adjoining counties in this State.

United States and New York State stocks, and stocks of any city, county or village in this State.

Real estate, other than under judgment or foreclosure, such as may be requisite for the convenient transaction of its business.

Securities on which loans are authorized: None.

Provisions under which right to invest in, or to loan upon, other securities than those named above, may be claimed: Required to invest in securities named in charter, except an available fund of not exceeding one-third the total amount of deposits, which may be kept on deposit, on interest or otherwise, or in such available form as the trustees may direct. Section 6 of charter.

Provisions concerning deposits in bank: None, except as above.

Largest amount authorized to reecive from one depositor, $5,000.

Regulations or restrictions concerning rate of interest to be paid to depositors: Such that depositors shall receive a ratable proportion of profits.

Surplus authorized: Ten per cent of deposits.

Prohibit'n concerning receiving pay for services or borrowing funds:

1. The trustees of said corporation shall not directly or indirectly receive any pay or emolument for their services. Section 3 of charter.

2. No president, vice-president, trustee, officer or servant of said corporation shall, directly or indirectly, borrow the funds of said corporation or its deposits, or in any manner use the same, or any part thereof, except to pay necessary expenses, under the direction of said board of trustees. Section 6 of charter.

Provisions of the charter of the Germania Savings Bank, Kings county; located at Brooklyn; incorporated by chapter 466, Laws of 1867.

Number of trustees, thirty-one.

Investments authorized:

Bond and mortgage, half value of property, located in the county of Kings or counties adjoining.

United States and New York State stocks, and stocks of any city or county in this State.

Real estate, other than under judgment or foreclosure, such as may be requisite for the convenient transaction of the business.

Securities on which loans are authorized: None.

Provisions under which right to invest in, or to loan upon, other securities than those named above, may be claimed: Required to invest in securities named in charter, except an available fund of not exceeding one-third the whole amount of deposits, which may be kept on deposit, on interest or otherwise, in such available form as the trustees may direct. Section 6 of charter.*

Provisions concerning deposits in bank: None, except as above.

Largest amount authorized to receive from one depositor, $5,000.

Regulations or restrictions concerning rate of interest to be paid to depositors: Left to discretion of trustees.

Surplus authorized: Ten per cent of deposits.

Prohibition concerning receiving pay for services, or borrowing funds:

1. The trustees of said corporation shall not, directly or indirectly receive any pay or emolument for their services. Section 3, of charter.

2. No president, vice-president, trustee, officer or servant

* Provided, however, that no loan shall be made under this section upon any stock or security whatever, to a greater amount than three-fourths of the actual cash value of such stocks or security at the time of making such loan. And same section provides that no moneys shall be invested except in the securities or stocks mentioned in said section.

of said corporation shall, directly or indirectly, borrow the funds of said corporation or its deposits, or in any manner use the same, or any part thereof, except to pay necessary current expenses under the direction of said board of trustees. Section 6 of charter.

Provisions of the charter of The Central Park Savings Bank, located in New York; incorporated by chapter 467, Laws of 1867.

Number of trustees, thirteen.

Investments authorized:

Bond and mortgage, half value of property, located in the city of New York, or counties adjacent thereto.

United States and New York State stocks, and stocks of any city or county in this State issued in pursuance of law.

Real estate, other than under judgment or foreclosure, such as may be requisite for the convenient transaction of its business.

Securities on which loans are authorized: None.

Provisions under which right to invest in, or to loan upon, other securities than those named above, may be claimed: Required to invest in securities named in charter, except an available fund of not exceeding one-third of the whole amount of deposits, which may be kept on deposit, on interest, or otherwise, in such available form as the trustees may direct. Section 6 of charter.*

Provisions concerning deposits in bank: None, except as above.

Largest amount authorized to receive from one depositor, $5,000.

Regulations or restrictions concerning rate of interest to be paid to depositors: Left to discretion of trustees.

Surplus authorized: Ten per cent of deposits.

Prohibition concerning receiving pay for services, or borrowing funds:

1. The trustee of said corporation shall not, directly or indirectly, receive any pay or emolument for their services. Section 3 of charter.

*Provided, however, that no loan shall be made under this section upon any stocks or security, whatever, to a greater amount than three-fourths of the *equal* (?) cash value of such stock or security at the time of making such loan. But same section provides that no money shall be invested except in the securities or stocks mentioned in said section.

2. No president, vice-president, trustee, officer or servant of said corporation shall, directly or indirectly, borrow the funds of said corporation, or its deposits, or in any manner use the same, or any part thereof, except to pay necessary current expenses under the direction of said board of trustees. Section 6 of charter.

Provisions of the charter of the National Savings Institution, located in New York; incorporated by chapter 472, Laws of 1867.

Number of trustees, twenty-one.

Investments authorized :

Bond and mortgage, half value of property, and not restricted in location.

United States and New York State stocks, and stocks of any city authorized by the Legislature of this State to be issued.

Real estate, other than under judgment or foreclosure, such as may be requisite for the convenient transaction of its business.

Securities on which loans are authorized : None.

Provisions under which right to invest in, or to loan upon, other securities than those named above, may be claimed :

1. Trustees shall not invest in other securities than those named in the charter, in opposition to the vote of any three trustees. Section 6 of charter.
2. Required to invest in securities named in charter, except an available fund of not exceeding one-third the total amount of deposits, which may be kept on deposit, on interest, or otherwise, in such available form as the trustees may direct. But no moneys not on deposit in bank or trust company shall be invested except as provided for in this act. Section 6 of charter.

Provisions concerning deposits in bank : Temporary deposits may be made in any State or National Bank, or in any incorporated trust company in the city of New York.

Largest amount authorized to receive from one depositor, $5,000.

Regulations or restrictions concerning rate of interest to be paid to depositors : One per cent more shall be paid on sums less than $1,000, than is paid on sums of more than $1,000.

Surplus authorized: Ten per cent of deposits.

Prohibition concerning receiving pay for services, or borrowing funds:

1. The trustees of said corporation shall not, directly or indirectly, receive any payment or emolument for their services. Section 3 of charter.
2. No president, vice-president, trustee, officer or servant of said corporation shall, directly or indirectly, borrow the funds of said corporation or its deposits, or in any manner use the same, or any part thereof, except to pay necessary current expenses under the direction of said board of trustees. Section 6 of charter.

Provisions of the charter of The Saratoga Savings Bank, located at Saratoga Springs; incorporated by chapter 626, Laws of 1867.

Number of trustees, nine.

Investments authorized:

Bond and mortgage, half value of property, exclusive of buildings, in sums not exceeding $5,000 to any one individual, firm or association, and located in the county of Saratoga, or an adjoining county.

United States and New York State stocks, and stocks of any city, county or village authorized by the Legislature of this State to be issued.

Real estate other than under judgment or foreclosure, such as may be requisite in the convenient transaction of its business.

Securities on which loans are authorized: Same as for investment.

Provisions under which right to invest in, or to loan upon, other securities than those named above, may be claimed: Required to invest in securities named in charter, except an available fund of not exceeding $5,000, and twenty-five per cent of the deposits which may be kept on temporary deposit, on interest or otherwise, in such available form as the trustees may direct. Section 5 of charter.

Provisions concerning deposits in bank: No sum exceeding $25,000 shall be deposited in any one bank.

Largest amount authorized to receive from one depositor: No limit.

Regulations or restrictions concerning rate of interest to be paid to depositors: Left to the discretion of the trustees.

Surplus authorized : None.

Prohibition concerning receiving pay for services, or borrowing funds: The trustees of said corporation, as such, shall not directly or indirectly, receive any pay or emolument for their services, nor shall any trustee, officer or agent of said corporation, directly or indirectly borrow the funds of said corporation, or in any way use the same, except to pay necessary current expenses under the direction of the board of trustees. Section 2 of charter.

Provisions of the charter of the Carthage Savings Bank, located at Carthage; incorporated by chapter 701, Laws of 1867.

Number of trustees, sixteen.

Investments authorized:

Bond and mortgage, half value of property, located in this State.

United States and New York State stocks, and stocks of any counties of this State, issued in pursuance of law.

Real estate other than under judgment or foreclosure, such as may be requisite for the convenient transaction of business.

Securities on which loans are authorized : Bonds (!) See sec. 7 of charter.

Provisions under which right to invest in, or to loan upon other securities than those named above, may be claimed: Required to invest in securities named in charter, except an available fund of not exceeding one-fifth of the total amount of deposits which may be kept on deposit, on interest or otherwise, in such available form as the trustees may direct. Section 7 of charter.

Provisions concerning deposits in bank : None except as above.

Largest amount authorized to receive from one depositor: $5,000.

Regulations or restrictions concerning rate of interest to be paid to depositors: Left to the discretion of trustees.

Surplus authorized: Ten per cent of the deposits.

Prohibition concerning receiving pay for services, or borrowing funds :

1. The trustees of said corporation shall not directly or indirectly, receive any pay or emolument for their services. Section 4 of charter.

2. No president, vice-president, trustee, officer or servant of said corporation shall directly or indirectly borrow the funds of said corporation or its deposits; nor shall such president, vice-president, trustee, officer or servant of said corporation use any of the funds of said corporation, or any of its deposits, except to pay necessary expenses under the direction of said board of trustees. Section 8 of charter.

Provisions of the charter of The National Savings Bank of Buffalo, located at Buffalo; incorporated by chapter 777, Laws of 1867.

Number of trustees, twenty-eight.

Investments authorized:

Bond and mortgage, half value of property, not limited in location.

United States and New York State stocks, stocks of any State, and stocks of any city or county authorized by the Legislature of this State to be issued.

Real estate, other than under judgment or foreclosure, such as may be requisite for its immediate accommodation in the transaction of its business.

Securities on which loans are authorized: None, unless subdivision two and last clause of subdivision three of section five, and first clause of second sentence in section nine, may be construed as authority to make loans.

Provisions under which right to invest in, or to loan upon, other securities than those named above, may be claimed: Required to invest in securities named in the charter, except an available fund of not exceeding one-third of the total amount of deposits, which may be kept on deposit, at interest or otherwise, in such available form as the trustees may direct. Section 9 of charter.

Provisions concerning deposits in bank: None, except as above.

Largest amount authorized to receive from one depositor: No limit.

Regulations or restrictions concerning rate of interest to be paid to depositors: To be one per cent greater on sums not exceeding $1,000 than on larger sums.

Surplus authorized: None.

Prohibition concerning receiving pay for services, or borrowing funds:

1. The trustees or managers of the said corporation shall not directly or indirectly receive any compensation for their services. Section 4 of charter.
2. No president, vice-president, or other officer or servant of said corporation shall, directly or indirectly, borrow the funds of said corporation or its depositors, or in any manner use the same, or any part thereof, except to pay the necessary current expenses of said corporation, under the direction of its trustees. Section 7 of charter.

GENERAL LAWS RELATING TO SAVINGS BANKS.

CHAP. 262.

AN ACT RELATIVE TO UNCLAIMED BANK DIVIDENDS AND DEPOSITS.

Passed May 9, 1835.

The People of the State of New York, represented in Senate and Assembly, do enact as follows:

§ 1. Each of the banks in this State, on or before the first day of September next, and annually thereafter, shall cause to be published for six successive weeks in one public newspaper printed in the county in which such bank may be located, and in the State paper, a true and accurate statement, verified by the oath of the cashier or presiding officer, of all the deposites made in said bank, and of all the dividends declared upon its stock, which at the date of such statement shall have remained unclaimed by any person authorized to receive them for two years then next preceding.

§ 2. Such statement shall set forth the time such deposite was made, its amount, the name and the residence, if known, of the person making it, the name of the person in whose favor the dividend may have been declared, the time it was declared, its amount, and upon what number of shares of the stock of said bank.

§ 3. Each of the savings banks shall, within the same time above stated, and annually thereafter, cause to be published in the same manner and for the same period of time, a like statement, verified by the oath of the president or other presiding officer, of the names of all persons who have made deposites in such bank, and have not, within two years next preceding the date of said statement, either drawn out any part of the money so deposited, or of the interest accruing upon it.

§ 4. Such statement shall contain the name of the depositor and his residence and occupation, if known, the time the deposit was made and its amount, together with the sum due for interest.

§ 5. In all cases the expenses of advertising shall be deducted from its sums unclaimed, in proportion to the amount of each respectively.

§ 6. It shall be the duty of the presiding officer of each of the said banks, and savings banks, to report the same statement as above required to be published, at each session of the Legislature, within ten days after its commencement.

§ 7. This act shall take effect immediately.

CHAP. 347.

AN ACT IN RELATION TO SAVINGS BANKS.

Passed May 6, 1839.

The People of the State of New York, represented in Senate and Assembly, do enact as follows:

§ 1. The report and publication of the statement of unclaimed dividends and deposites, and of the names residence and occupation of the depositors required to be made by the several savings banks in this State by an act passed May 9th, 1835, shall only be in relation to such dividends and deposites, no part of which, or the interest accruing thereon, shall have been claimed or drawn out within three years next preceeding the date of such statement; and such statement shall also be made annually to the Comptroller of this State on or before the first day of January in each year.

§ 2. [Inapplicable; virtually repealed.]

§ 3. The board of trustees of the said savings banks are hereby authorized to accumulate gradually and hold invested in like securities, as authorized by the act incorporating said banks, a surplus fund not exceeding ten per cent. on the amount of deposites, in said banks respectively, to the end that in case of a reduction in the market price of the securities or public stocks, held or to be held by the said banks, or any of them, below the par value thereof any loss to the depositors by reason of such reduction may be prevented or made good to them by means of said surplus fund.

§ 4. The fourteenth and sixteenth sections of the act to incorporate the Bowery Savings Bank, passed May 1, 1834, are hereby repealed.

CHAP. 478.

AN ACT IN RELATION TO DEPOSITS BY BANKS FOR SAVINGS.

Passed December 15th, 1847.

The People of the State of New York, represented in Senate and Assembly, do enact as follows:

§ 1. It shall be lawful for the trustees of banks for savings, who are authorized to make temporary deposites in any of the incorporated banks, to make such deposites with any of the associations which are now or may hereafter be formed under the general banking law.

§ 2. This act shall take effect immediately.

CHAP. 437.

AN ACT TO AMEND AN ACT RELATIVE TO UNCLAIMED BANK DIVIDENDS AND DEPOSITS, PASSED MAY 9TH, 1835, AND FOR OTHER PURPOSES.

Passed April 11th, 1849.

The People of the State of New York, represented in Senate and Assembly, do enact as follows:

§ 1. Every company or association, now or hereafter incorporated or organized, or doing business under any general or special law of this State, on or before the first day of September next, and annually thereafter, shall cause to be published, for six successive weeks, in one public newspaper printed in the county in which such company or ascociation may be located, and in the State paper, a true and accurate statement, verified by the oath of the cashier, treasurer, or presiding officer, of all deposits made with said company or association, and of all dividends and interests declared and payable upon any of the stock, bonds or other evidence of indebtedness of said company or association, which, at the date of such statement, shall have remained unclaimed by any person or persons authorized to receive the same for two years then next preceding.

§ 2. Such statement shall set forth the time that every such deposit was made, its amount, the name and the residence, if known, of the person making it, the name of the person in whose favor the dividend or interest may have been declared, its amount and upon what number of shares and on what amount of stock, bonds, or other evidence of indebtedness of any such company or association.

§ 3. The term "association" shall include every individual doing business alone, under any general or special law of this State.

CHAP. 91.

AN ACT FOR THE PROTECTION OF SAVINGS BANKS AND INSTITUTIONS RECEIVING DEPOSITS FROM MARRIED WOMEN.

Passed March 25, 1850.

The People of the State of New York, represented in Senate and Assembly, do enact as follows:

§ 1. When any deposit shall be made in any savings bank or institution, by any female, being or hereafter becoming a married woman, in her own name, it shall be lawful for the trustees or officers of such bank or institution to pay such depositor such sum or sums as may be due such female, and the receipt or acquittance of such depositor shall be a sufficient legal discharge to the said corporation therefor.

§ 2. If any trustee of any savings bank or institution shall fail to attend the regular meetings of the board of trustees thereof, or to perform the duties devolving on him as a member of said board for the term of six successive months, without excuse satisfactory to the board, he may be removed from the office as such trustee at the pleasure of the board.

§ 3. This act shall take effect immediately.

CHAP. 257.

AN ACT RELATIVE TO SAVINGS BANKS OR INSTITUTIONS FOR SAVINGS IN THE CITY AND COUNTY OF NEW YORK AND COUNTY OF KINGS.

Passed April 15th, 1853.

The People of the State of New York, represented in Senate and Assembly, do enact as follows:

§ 1. It shall be lawful for the several savings banks or institutions for savings in the city and county of New York and county of Kings, now chartered or which may be hereafter chartered, in addition to the powers granted by their respective acts of incorporation to loan the moneys which they have received or shall hereafter receive on deposit, or the accumulations thereof, or purchase of any stock or securities for the redemption or payment of which the faith of any State in the Union shall be pledged, or in the public debt or stock of any incorporated city, county or town in this State which shall have been authorized by the Legislature of this State to issue such stock; provided that the cash value of such stock or securities shall, at the time of making such investments, be at or above its par value; and such loans, so made, shall not exceed in amount ninety per cent of the par value of such stock or securities. Should the stock or securities above mentioned depreciate in value, so that the amount loaned thereon shall exceed ninety per cent of its par value, it shall be the duty of the directors or trustees of any savings bank or institution for savings to require the immediate payment of any loan made by them thereon, or additional security therefor, so that at all times the amount so loaned shall be at least ten per cent less than the par value of such stock or securities.

§ 2. It shall be lawful for any such savings banks or institutions for savings to make temporary deposits in any bank or banking association, to an amount equal to ten per cent of the actual cash capital stock paid in of such bank or banking associations, and to receive interest thereon at such rates, not exceeding that allowed by law, as may be agreed upon; provided that all the deposits in any one bank or banking association shall not exceed in amount twenty per cent of all the deposits belonging to such savings bank or institution for savings, and that no contract or agreement in relation to said deposits shall be for a longer period than one year.

§ 3. It shall not be lawful for any of such savings banks or institions for savings to make any loans to any bank or banking association, exceeding the limits above prescribed, unless such savings bank or institution for savings shall require and receive of such bank, for all sums so deposited exceeding the limits above prescribed, such securities therefor, and equal in amount, as the Comptroller or Superintendent of the Banking Department is now lawfully authorized to receive in exchange for bills or notes for circulation; nor shall it be lawful for any trustee of a savings bank or institution for savings to be a trustee of more than one savings bank or institution for savings at the same time; nor shall the trustees of any savings bank or institution for savings hereafter to be incorporated be directors at the same time in any bank or banking association wherein any part of the moneys of said savings bank or institution for savings shall be deposited.

§ 4. All the assets of any bank or banking association, now or hereafter to be created, that shall become insolvent, shall, after providing for the payment of its circulating notes, be applied by the directors thereof, in the first place, to the payment of any deficiency that may arise on the sales of the securities aforesaid, and thereafter of any sum or sums of money deposited with such bank or banking association by any savings bank or institutions for savings, within the range of twenty per cent, as provided in the second section of this act.

§ 5. No such savings bank or institution for savings hereafter to be incorporated, shall receive from any individual depositor a larger sum than one thousand dollars; and the rate of interest on all deposits of five hundred dollars and under, shall be one per cent per annum greater than shall be allowed on any sum exceeding five hundred dollars. [As amended by section 1, Laws of 1867, chapter 32, page 64.]

§ 6. The provisions of this act shall apply to all savings banks or institutions for savings in said counties, which savings banks or institutions for savings are hereby prohibited from loaning the moneys deposited with them, or any part thereof, upon notes, bills of exchange, drafts or any other personal securities whatever.

§ 7. All acts and parts of acts inconsistent with this act, are hereby repealed.

§ 8. This act shall take effect immediately.

CHAP. 492.

AN ACT TO AMEND AN ACT ENTITLED "AN ACT RELATIVE TO SAVINGS BANKS OR INSTITUTIONS FOR SAVINGS IN THE CITY AND COUNTY OF NEW YORK AND THE COUNTY OF KINGS," PASSED APRIL 15, 1853.

Passed June 30, 1853.

The People of the State of New York, represented in Senate and Assembly, do enact as follows:

§ 1. So much of section third of the act hereby amended as prohibits any person from being, at the same time, a trustee or director in more than one savings bank or institution for savings, shall not be so construed as to prevent any person from acting as an ex-officio trustee or director of any one or more savings banks or institutions for savings, when so required during a membership in any other incorporation under any law of this State passed prior to the date of this act; and nothing in said act shall prevent the savings banks in the county of Kings from loaning their funds on, or investing said funds in bonds of said county of Kings.

§ 2. This act shall take effect immediately.

CHAP. 72.

AN ACT TO AUTHORIZE SAVINGS BANKS OR INSTITUTIONS FOR SAVINGS TO DEPOSIT SURPLUS FUNDS IN TRUST COMPANIES,

Passed March 21, 1854.

The People of the State of New York, represented in Senate and Assembly, do enact as follows:

§ 1. It shall be lawful for any savings bank or institution for savings, to make temporary deposits in any trust company incorporated under the laws of this State, and authorized by the Supreme Court to receive and hold trust funds, and subject to examination by said court.

§ 2. This act shall take effect immediately.

CHAP. 336.

AN ACT TO REGULATE THE DISTRIBUTION OF THE ASSETS OF SAVINGS BANKS OR INSTITUTIONS FOR SAVINGS, BY RECEIVERS THEREOF.

Passed April 12, 1855, three-fifths being present.

The people of the State of New York, represented in Senate and Assembly, do enact as follows:

§ 1. The receiver or receivers of any savings bank or institution for savings, now or hereafter appointed in pursuance of section forty-one of article two of title four of chapter eight of the third part of the Revised Statutes, shall, after having complied with all the provisions of said title, from the section aforesaid to and including section seventy-eight of said title, distribute the residue of the moneys in their hands among all the creditors of said savings bank or institution for savings, whose debt shall have been ascertained from an examination of the books of account which shall have been kept by such savings bank or institution for savings, or otherwise, in the order prescribed by section seventy-nine of said title, whether such creditors shall then have exhibited their claims or not.

§ 2. This act shall take effect immediately.

CHAP. 136.

AN ACT IN RELATION TO SAVINGS BANKS.

Passed March 20, 1857; three-fifths being present.

The People of the State of New York, represented in Senate and Assembly, do enact as follows:

§ 1. The several savings banks or institutions for savings now incorporated, or which may hereafter be incorporated, shall, on or before the twenty-fifth day of January, and on or before the twenty-fifth day of July in each year, make a report in writing to the Superintendent of the Bank Department, of the condition of such savings bank or institutions for savings, on the first days of January and July; which report shall be verified by the oath of the two principal officers thereof; and shall state therein the total amount due to depositors; the total amount of assets of every kind; the principal sum of each and every bond and mortgage, with the estimated value of the property on which it is based; the amount invested in stock, designating each particular kind of stock, and the estimated market value of the same; the amount loaned upon the security of stock, with a description of all stocks so held; the amount, if any, loaned on personal securities; the amount vested in real estate; the amount of cash on hand, or on deposit in bank, with the names of the banks where deposited, and the amount placed in each; and the amount loaned or deposited in any other manner than herein described. The report of January in each year, shall, in addition, also state the number of open accounts; the amount deposited, and the amount withdrawn; also, the amount of interest received, and the amount placed to the credit of depositors during the year preceding the date of such report. Any willful false swearing in respect to such reports, shall be deemed perjury, and subject to the punishments prescribed by law for that offence. And if any savings bank or institution for savings, shall fail to furnish to the Superintendent of the Banking Department, its report at the times herein stated, it shall forfeit the sum of one hundred dollars per day for every day such report shall be so delayed; and the said Superintendent may maintain an action in his name of office to recover such penalty, and when collected the same shall be paid into the treasury of the State.

§ 2. It shall be the duty of the Superintendent of the Bank Department, on or before the twentieth day of February in each year, to communicate to the Legislature a statement of the condition of every savings bank and institution for savings from which reports have been received for the preceding year; and to suggest any amendments in the laws relative to savings banks or institutions for savings, which in his judgment may be necessary or proper to increase the security of depositors.

§ 3. Whenever any savings bank or institution for savings shall fail to make a report in compliance with this act, or whenever the Superintendent of the Banking Department shall have reason to believe that any savings bank or institution for savings is loaning or investing money in violation of its charter or of law, or conducting business in an unsafe manner, it shall be his duty, either in person, or by one or more competent persons by him appointed to examine their affairs; and whenever it shall appear to the Superintendent, from such examination, that any savings bank or institution for savings has been guilty of a violation of its charter or of law, he shall communicate the fact to the Attorney-General, whose duty it shall then become to institute such proceedings against said savings bank or institution for savings, as are now authorized in the case of insolvent corporations. The expense of any such examinations shall be paid by the savings bank or institution for savings so examined, in such amount as the Superintendent of the Banking Department shall certify to be just and reasonable.

§ 4. No savings bank shall hereafter be required to make an annual report to the Legislature, any provisions in their charter to the contrary notwithstanding.

§ 5. The Superintendent of the Banking Department is hereby authorized to employ from time to time so many clerks as may be necessary to discharge the duties hereby imposed; the salary of said clerks shall be paid to them monthly, on his certificate, and upon the warrant of the Comptroller, out of the treasury; and it shall be the duty of the said superintendent, in his annual report to the Legislature, to state the names of the clerks so employed, and the compensation allowed to them severally.

§ 6. Each savings bank or institution for savings, shall pay five dollars towards defraying the expenses incurred in the performance of the duty hereby imposed, and the residue of such expenses shall be paid by them in proportion to the amount of deposits held by them severally, and the sums thus contributed shall be paid into the treasury of the State; but when the deposits of any such savings bank or institution for savings are less than five hundred dollars, it shall be exempt from such contribution. If any savings bank or institution for savings shall, after due notice, refuse or neglect to pay its proper share of charges so allotted, then the said Superintendent may maintain an action against such savings bank or institution for savings, for the recovery of such charges. [As amended by sec. 1, chap. 32, Laws of 1867—vol. 1, page 64.]

CHAP. 132.

AN ACT TO RESTRAIN BANKS, BANKING INSTITUTIONS AND INDIVIDUAL BANKERS FROM ASSUMING THE TITLE OF SAVINGS BANKS OR RECEIVING DEPOSITS AS SUCH.

Passed April 9th, 1858.

The People of the State of New York, represented in Senate and Assembly, do enact as follows:

§ 1. It shall not be lawful for any bank, banking association or individual banker, authorized to issue circulating notes, by the laws of this State, established in any city or village where a chartered savings bank is located and transacting business, to advertise or put forth a sign as a savings bank, or in any way to solicit or receive deposits as a savings bank, and any bank, banking association or individual banker, which shall offend against these provisions, shall forfeit and pay for every such offence the sum of one hundred dollars for every day such offence shall be continued, to be sued for and recovered in the name of the people of this State, by the district attorneys of the several counties in any court having cognizance thereof, for the use of the poor, chargeable to said county in which such offence shall be committed.

§ 2. This act shall take effect on the first day of May next.

CHAP. 136.

AN ACT IN RELATION TO SAVINGS BANKS IN THE CITY OF BUFFALO, AND TO AMEND AN ACT ENTITLED "AN ACT RELATIVE TO SAVINGS BANKS OR INSTITUTIONS FOR SAVINGS IN THE CITY AND COUNTY OF NEW YORK AND THE COUNTY OF KINGS," PASSED APRIL 15, 1853.

Passed April 10th, 1858.

The People of the State of New York, represented in Senate and Assembly, do enact as follows:

§ 1. The temporary deposits which any savings bank or institution for savings in the city and county of New York and the county of Kings, is authorized to make, by the second section of chapter two hundred and fifty-seven of the laws of eighteen hundred and fifty-three, shall not exceed in amount twenty per cent of all the deposits belonging to any such bank or institution for savings; nor shall the deposits of any such bank or institution for savings in any bank of issue, exceed in the aggregate, at one time, the sum of one hundred thousand dollars.

§ 2. It shall be lawful for the trustees of such savings banks or institutions for savings, to pay to their respective presidents such compensation for their services as shall in the opinion of the said trustees be reasonable. But no person shall be elected or remain such president whose professional or other engagements shall prevent his regular and faithful attendance to the duties of his office.

§ 3. All acts or parts of acts in relation to savings banks or institutions for savings, inconsistent with this act, are hereby repealed.

§ 4. The second section of this act shall apply to savings banks in the city of Buffalo.

§ 5. This act shall take effect immediately.

CHAP. 315.

AN ACT TO AMEND AN ACT IN RELATION TO SAVINGS BANKS.

Passed April 29, 1863.

The People of the State of New York, represented in Senate and Assembly, do enact as follows:

§ 1. It shall be lawful for the trustees of savings banks and institutions for savings to loan the funds of such banks and institutions on the bonds of counties and cities of this State, authorized to be issued by the Legislature: provided, that by the terms of the act authorizing such issue, provision be made for the payment of such bonds by tax for that purpose.

§ 2. This act shall take effect immediately.

CHAP. 113.

AN ACT TO AUTHORIZE SAVINGS BANKS AND SAVINGS INSTITUTIONS OF THIS STATE TO MAKE LOANS TO COUNTIES ON THEIR BONDS.

Passed April 2, 1864.

The People of the State of New York, represented in Senate and Assembly, do enact as follows:

§ 1. It shall be lawful for the different savings banks and savings institutions in this State to make loans to the counties of this State, to be secured by the bonds of such counties issued in pursuance of law.

§ 2. This act shall take effect immediately.

CHAP. 214.

AN ACT RELATING TO DEPOSITS BY SAVINGS BANKS.

Passed March 25, 1865.

The People of the State of New York, represented in Senate and Assembly, do enact as follows:

§ 1. It shall be lawful for the trustees of banks for savings, who are authorized to make temporary deposits in any of the incorporated banks, or in the associations which now are or hereafter may be formed under the general banking law, to make such deposits with any of the banks called national banks, which now are or hereafter may be organized according to the laws of the United States, or of this State, or of both.

§ 2. This act shall take effect immediately.

CHAP. 761, LAWS OF 1866.

Section 7, (the only section applicable to savings banks) of chap. 761, Laws of 1866, entitled "An act authorizing the taxation of stockholders of banks and the surplus funds of savings banks," passed April 23, 1866, is as follows:

§ 7. The privileges and franchises granted by the Legislature of this State to savings banks or institutions for savings, are hereby declared to be personal property, and liable to taxation as such in the town or ward where they are located, to an amount not exceeding the gross sum of their surplus earned, and in the possession of said banks or institutions, and the officers of such institutions or banks may be examined on oath by assessors, as to the amount of such surplus; and the property of such banks and institutions shall be liable to seizure and sale for the payment of all taxes assessed upon them for said privileges and franchises.

CHAP. 32.

AN ACT TO AMEND CHAPTER ONE HUNDRED AND THIRTY-SIX, LAWS OF EIGHTEEN HUNDRED AND FIFTY-SEVEN, AND CHAPTER TWO HUNDRED AND FIFTY-SEVEN OF THE LAWS OF EIGHTEEN HUNDRED AND FIFTY-THREE, IN RELATION TO SAVINGS BANKS.

Passed February 13, 1867.

The People of the State of New York, represented in Senate and Assembly, do enact as follows:

§ 1. Amends section 6, chap. 136, Laws of 1857; see page 346.

§ 2. Upon the organization of any savings bank or institution for savings, it shall be the duty of the secretary, or some officer thereof, before receiving any deposits, to transmit to the Superintendent of the Banking Department a list of the officers of such savings bank or institution for savings, with their post office address and the location of such savings banks or institution for savings.

§ 3. Amends section 5, chapter 257, Laws of 1853, see page 343.

CHAP. 761.

AN ACT TO AMEND CHAPTER SEVEN HUNDRED AND SIXTY-ONE OF THE LAWS OF EIGHTEEN HUNDRED AND SIXTY-SIX, IN RELATION TO THE TAXATION OF THE SURPLUS FUNDS OF SAVINGS BANKS.

Passed May 9, 1867.

The People of the State of New York, represented in Senate and Assembly, do enact as follows:

§ 1. Section seven of chapter seven hundred and sixty-one of the laws of eighteen hundred and sixty-six, is hereby amended so as to read as follows, namely:

§ 1.* The privileges and franchises granted by the legislature of this State to savings banks or institutions for savings, are hereby declared to be personal property, and liable to taxation as such, in a town or ward where they are located, to an amount not exceeding the gross sum of their surplus earned (after deducting the amount of such surplus invested in United States securities), and the officers of such banks or institutions may be examined on oath by assessors, as to the amount of such surplus and securities; and the property of such banks and institutions shall be liable to seizure and sale for the payment of all taxes assessed upon them for said privileges and franchises.

§ 2. This act shall take effect immediately.

[This law is not to be found in the index to the Laws of 1867.]

---

*So in original.

NOTE.—The acts of 1835, 1839 and 1849, in so far as they relate to savings banks, are superseded by the act of 1857.

GENERAL ACT

IN RELATION TO

SAVINGS BANKS,

PREPARED AND SUBMITTED PURSUANT TO JOINT RESOLUTION

OF THE

SENATE AND ASSEMBLY.

AN ACT

To provide for the organization of Savings Banks, for their more thorough supervision, and for a more safe and efficient administration of their affairs.

The People of the State of New York, represented in Senate and Assembly, do enact as follows:

ARTICLE I.

OF INCORPORATION.

SECTION 1. Any number of persons, not less than seven, nor more than twenty-one, residents of this State, may associate themselves together for the purpose of organizing a savings bank in the county in which they reside, in accordance with the provisions of this act.

SECTION 2. Such persons, under their hands and seals, shall execute a certificate in which shall be set forth—

First: The name assumed to distinguish such association and to be used in its dealings, which shall be in no material respect similar to the name of any other savings bank, organized and doing business in the same or in an adjoining county.

Second: The place where its business is to be transacted, designating the particular city, village or town, and, if in any city, the ward in such city.

Third: The name, residence, (if in any city, the street and number,) occupation, and post-office address of each member of such association.

Fourth: A declaration that each member of such association will accept the responsibilities and faithfully discharge the duties of a trustee in such institution, when authorized according to the provisions of this act.

SECTION 3. Such certificate shall be executed in duplicate, and be duly acknowledged before an officer of this State, authorized to take the acknowledgment of conveyances of real estate for record, and shall, within sixty days after such acknowledgment, be filed, one copy in the office of the county clerk of the county wherein such savings bank is proposed to be located, and one copy in the office of the Superintendent of the Banking Department of this State.

SECTION 4. A notice of intention to organize such savings bank shall be published at least once a week for four weeks previous to filing the certificate of association, as provided in the last preceding section, in at least one newspaper published in the city, village or town where such savings bank is proposed to be located; or, if there be no newspaper published in such village or town, then in some newspaper published in such county; which notice shall specify the names of the proposed corporators, the name of the proposed savings bank, and the location of the same, as set forth in the certificate of association; and, if there is any savings bank organized and doing business in such county, a copy of such notice shall be also be sent to each such savings bank so organized and doing business, at least fifteen days before the filing of such certificate of association, as provided for in the last preceding section.

SECTION 5. Upon the receipt of any such certificate of association at the office of the Superintendent of the Banking Department, if the same is in due form and duly executed according to the provisions of sections two and three of this act, and is accompanied by evidence satisfactory to the Superintendent of the proper publication, and service in good faith of the notice required in the last preceding section, he shall forthwith endorse the same over his official signature, "Filed for examination," with the date of such endorsement.

SECTION 6. If such certificate shall not be in form and substance as required by section two of this act, or shall not be duly and properly acknowledged, as required by section three of this act, or shall not be accompanied by evidence, satisfactory to the Superintendent, of the publication and service in good faith, according to the intent and purpose of this act, of the notice required by section four of this act, the Superintendent shall refuse to file such certificate until the same shall be amended in such form as he shall direct, or until satisfactory evidence of the publication and service of such notice shall be furnished to him.

SECTION 7. It shall be the duty of the Superintendent of the Banking Department, and he shall have power, in regard to any certificate of association, so filed by him as hereinbefore provided, to ascertain from the best sources of information at his command:

1 Whether greater convenience of access to a savings bank will be afforded to any considerable number of depositors by opening a savings bank at the place designated in such certificate.

2. Whether the density of the population, in the neighborhood designated for such savings bank, and in the surrounding country, affords a reasonable promise of adequate support to the enterprise.

3. Whether the responsibility, character and general fitness for the discharge of the duties appertaining to such trust, of the persons named in such certificate, are such as to command the confidence of the community in which such savings bank is proposed to be located, in an institution organized and conducted under such auspices.

SECTION 8. If the Superintendent shall be satisfied from his knowledge, or from information gained, concerning the several points named in the last preceding section, that the organization of a savings bank, as proposed in such certificate, will be a public benefit, he shall, within sixty days after the same has been filed by him for examination, issue, under his hand and official seal, a certificate of authorization to the persons named in such certificate, or to them or to a portion of them, together with such other persons, not exceeding twenty-one in all, as a majority of those named in such certificate of association, shall, in writing approve, which certificate so issued by him, shall AUTHORIZE the persons named therein to open an office for the deposit of savings, as designated in the certificate of association, subject to the provisions of this act; *Provided, however*, that no person shall be named in such certificate of authorization, who shall not have duly made and acknowledged the declaration prescribed in subdivision four of section two of this act.

SECTION 9. The Superintendent shall transmit such certificate of authorization to the county clerk of the county in which the savings bank, so authorized, is to be located, who shall file the same and attach it to the certificate of association, previously filed by him, relating to the organization of such savings bank; and he shall also file a duplicate copy of such certificate in his own office.

SECTION 10. If the Superintendent shall not be satisfied that the establishment of a savings bank, as proposed in any certificate of association filed by him, is expedient and desirable, he shall, within sixty days after the filing of such certificate by him, give notice to the county clerk of the county in which such savings bank is proposed to be located, that he refuses to issue a certificate of authorization for such savings bank, which notice shall forthwith be filed by the county clerk with the certificate of association of such savings bank.

SECTION 11. Within three months after the filing of the notice, as provided in the last preceding section, the persons named in the certificate of association to which such notice relates, or a majority of them, may appeal from the refusal of the Superintendent to issue such certificate of authorization, to a board, to be composed of the Comptroller, Secretary of State, Attorney General, State Treasurer, and Superintendent of the Banking Department, who are hereby made and constituted, for such purpose, a SAVINGS BANK BOARD OF APPEAL.

SECTION 12. Such board shall convene upon notice by the Comptroller, (who is hereby constituted the president of such board,) at such times as may be practicable, or shall be found necessary, in order to hear and determine the appeals brought before it. A majority of the board shall be a quorum, and it shall require a majority of the whole board to reverse any decision of the Superintendent in refusing to issue a certificate of authorization of a savings bank.

SECTION 13. Whenever the decision of the Superintendent, in refusing to issue any certificate of authorization, shall be reversed by the Savings Banks Board of Appeal, such board shall have power, and it shall be their duty, to execute such certificate of authorization under their hands and the seals of their respective offices; and the hands and seals of a majority of such board shall be requisite to the validity of such certificate; and the same shall be transmitted to the county clerk of the county in which the savings bank, authorized thereby, is to be located, to be filed by him, as provided by section nine of this act, and a duplicate copy shall also be filed in the office of the Superintendent of the Banking Department.

SECTION 14. Upon the filing of any certificate of authorization of a savings bank, as hereinbefore provided, the persons named therein, and their successors, shall thereupon and thereby be duly and lawfully constituted a body corporate and politic, with power to sue and be sued in any of the courts of this State, and shall be vested with all the powers and charged with all the liabilities conferred and imposed by this act.

SECTION 15. Before any savings bank, so incorporated, shall be authorized to receive deposits, they shall transmit to the Superintendent of the Banking Department the name, residence and post-office address of each of the officers of such savings bank, and the place where its business is to be carried on, designating the same by street and number, when practicable.

SECTION 16. Any savings bank, so incorporated, that shall not organize and commence business within one year after the certificate of authorization of the same has been filed, as hereinbefore provided, shall forfeit its rights and privileges as a corporation under this act; but the Superintendent of the Banking Department may, for satisfactory cause to him shown, extend the term within which such organization may be effected and such business commenced, but not for a longer period than one year; and the order, so extending such term, shall be under his hand and seal, and shall be transmitted to the county clerk of the county in which such savings bank is to be located, who shall file the same, together with the certificate of association and the certificate of authorization of such savings bank.

SECTION 17. It shall be lawful for the Superintendent to receive from the corporators of any savings bank authorized by him pursuant to the provisions of this act, a deposit of not less than $25,000, nor exceeding $100,000, in such public stocks or municipal securities as are by this act authorized for investment by savings banks, but bearing interest at not less than six per cent per annum, as a guarantee capital for the payment of expenses or of losses incurred by such savings bank, to be held by the Superintendent in trust for such savings bank; and the interest from such securities shall be applied, first, to the payment of any expenses incurred by such savings bank, which the gains or profits thereof are insufficient to pay, after declaring and crediting therefrom to depositors, dividends of not less than four per cent per annum upon their deposits, besides reserving not less than one-half per cent per annum upon such deposits from such gains or profits for account of the surplus fund authorized and required by this act, until the same shall equal fifteen per cent, and second to the payment of any losses sustained in the exercise of the discretion conferred by section 38 of this act. Any balance of interest from such deposit of guarantee capital may be distributed by such savings bank to the subscribers thereto, or otherwise, as the rules and regulations of the corporation shall authorize or direct.

SECTION 18. Whenever the surplus fund of any savings bank, having a guarantee capital as authorized in the last preceding section, shall be not less than ten per cent upon its deposits, and the annual gains and profits from the investments of its deposits, after paying expenses, shall enable the trustees to pay dividends to depositors, of not less than five per cent upon all deposits of not exceeding $5,000, besides reserving one-half per cent per annum for account of the surplus fund, until the same shall be equal to fifteen per cent upon its deposits; it shall be lawful to pay to the subscribers or owners of the guarantee capital, from the residue of any gains or profits of the said savings bank, a dividend of not exceeding one per cent per annum, in addition to the interest received from the securities in which such guarantee capital is invested, as provided in the last preceding section.

SECTION 19. The Superintendent of the Banking Department, shall have power in his discretion to exchange the securities held by him as a guarantee capital as hereinbefore provided, for other securities authorized to be held by him for such purpose, when authorized so to do by a majority of the trustees of such savings bank, and upon the order of the president, countersigned by the secretary or treasurer of such savings bank. And it shall be his duty, in regard to such deposit of guarantee capital, to see that the income derived therefrom is faithfully applied to the purposes named in section 17 of this act; and upon the redemption of any of the securities held by him on account of such deposit, to require the deposit of other securities in their place, or if such deposit is not made within three months, after the redemption of such securities. he shall be authorized himself to invest the proceeds from the redemption of such matured securities, in other securities authorized to be held by him for such purpose.

SECTION 20. Whenever the surplus of any savings bank, having a guarantee capital as hereinbefore provided, shall be not less than fifteen per cent upon its deposits, it shall be lawful for the Superintendent to surrender such guarantee capital deposited with him, upon a vote of its shareholders owning a majority of the shares in such guarantee capital, directing the same to be withdrawn, and to whom the same shall be surrendered.

ARTICLE II.

OF ORGANIZATION AND CORPORATE POWERS.

SECTION 21. The persons named in the certificate of authorization, issued pursuant to the provisions of this act, shall be the first trustees of such corporation, and shall have the entire management and control of all the affairs of the corporation, subject to the provisions of this act.

SECTION 22. Vacancies occurring in the office of trustee of any savings bank shall be filled by the board of trustees by ballot, and a majority of the legal number of trustees shall be necessary to a choice. In case of failure to fill any vacancy for six months after the same shall occur, upon the application in writing of any two trustees, the mayor of the city, the president of the village, or the supervisor of the town in which such savings bank shall be located, may appoint some proper and discreet person to fill such vacancy, until the same shall be filled by an election as herein provided.

SECTION 23. The trustees of any savings bank shall elect from their number a president, and one or more vice-presidents, and may also choose from their number or otherwise, such other officers as they may deem expedient, and the term for which any officer shall be elected shall not exceed one year, but shall continue until another is elected in his place.

SECTION 24. The board of trustees of any savings bank shall have power, from time to time, to make such by-laws, rules and regulations as they may think proper, for the election of officers, for prescribing their respective powers and duties, and the manner of discharging the same; for the appointment and duties of committees, and generally for transacting, managing and directing the affairs of the corporation; provided, such by-laws, rules and regulations are not repugnant to, nor inconsistent with the provisions of this act, to the Constitution and laws of this State, or of the United States; and a copy of the same shall be transmitted to the Superintendent of the Bank Department, who shall also be notified of any amendment or change therein.

SECTION 25. A quorum of the board of trustees of any savings bank shall not be less than five, of whom the president or a vice-president shall be one; but it shall be lawful for the trustees in their by-laws to provide for a larger quorum, and where such quorum shall be nine trustees or more, it may be composed without the attendance of the president or a vice-president; but where the number of such trustees is fifteen or more, the quorum shall not be less than seven, with the president or a vice-president in attendance.

SECTION 26. It shall be lawful for the trustees of any savings bank, by a resolution to be incorporated in their by-laws, to reduce the number of the trustees as provided in their charter or certificate of authorization, to a number not less than the minimum prescribed by this act, and thereafter, as vacancies occur, the same shall not be filled until the number is reduced to such minimum, or to such other number as the board in such resolution shall designate; and a copy of such resolution shall be transmitted to the Superintendent of the Banking Department, for his information.

SECTION 27. Regular meetings of the board of trustees of any savings bank shall be held as often as once in two months, and they may prescribe in their by-laws for more frequent regular meetings, and for the calling of special meetings.

SECTION 28. Upon the removal of a trustee of any savings bank from the county in which such savings bank is located, or upon his becoming a trustee, officer, clerk or employee in any other savings bank, or upon his borrowing directly or indirectly any of the funds of the savings bank of which he is trustee, or becoming a surety or guarantor for any money borrowed of or loan made by such savings bank, or upon his failure to attend the regular meetings of the board, or to perform any of the duties devolved upon him as such trustee, for six successive months, without having been previously excused by the board for such failure, the office of such trustee shall thereupon immediately become vacant; but the trustee vacating his office by failure to attend meetings or to discharge his duties, may, in the discretion of the board, be eligible to a re-election.

SECTION 29. The trustees of any savings bank shall have power to require, from the officers and agents of the corporation, such security for their fidelity and the faithful performance of their duties, as they shall deem necessary, and to fix the salaries of such officers and agents, subject to the provisions of this act.

SECTION 30. No trustee of any savings bank shall, directly or indirectly, receive for his services or otherwise, any pay or emolument, except as hereinafter provided; and no trustee, officer or servant of any savings bank shall, directly or indirectly, for himself, or as the partner or agent of others, borrow any of the funds of such savings bank or its deposits, or in any manner use the same, except to pay necessary expenses, or to make investments, or to deposit for safety, as directed by the board of trustees; nor shall any trustee, officer or servant of any savings bank be an indorser or surety for loans to others, nor in any manner be an obligor for moneys borrowed of or loaned by such savings bank.

ARTICLE III.

OF DEPOSITS AND DEPOSITORS.

SECTION 31. It shall be lawful for any savings bank to receive on deposit any sum or sums of money that may be offered for that purpose by any person or persons, or by any religious or charitable corporations or societies, and to invest the same, and declare, credit and pay dividends thereon, as hereinafter authorized and provided, and not otherwise.

SECTION 32. The sums so deposited, shall be repaid to each depositor or his legal or authorized representatives, when required by him or by them, but at such times, and with such dividends from profits, and under such regulations as the board of trustees may prescribe, not inconsistent with the provisions of this act, which regulations shall be put and kept up in some public and conspicuous place in the room where the business of the savings bank shall be transacted, and shall not be altered so as to affect any deposits which shall have been made previous to such alteration until after notice to the persons making the deposits so to be affected:

Provided, however, that in order to prevent loss to the depositors by an enforced sale of considerable amounts of securities below their par value, it shall be lawful for the trustees, in their discretion to require a notice of five days before the withdrawal of any part of any deposit of more than $10 and not exceeding $100, of ten days for any part of any deposit of more than $100 and not exceeding $500, of twenty days for any part of any deposit of more than $500 and not exceeding $1,000, and of thirty days for any part of any deposit of more than $1,000, and not exceeding $5,000 ; and

Provided further, That any deposit exceeding the sum of $5,000, in the name of any one individual, or the aggregate of any deposits in the name of one individual, whether in trust or otherwise, exceeding $5,000, shall always be subject to at least ninety days' notice, before withdrawal of the same, and to such further notice as the trustees in their by-laws may provide for and require.

SECTION 33. Whenever any deposit shall be made in any savings bank by any person being an alien, or minor, or a female being or thereafter becoming a married woman, the same shall be held for the exclusive right and benefit of such depositor, and free from the control or lien of all persons whatsoever except creditors ; and shall be repaid, together with the dividends thereon, to the person making the deposit, and the receipt or acquittance of such alien, minor or female, shall be a valid and sufficient release and dischaige for such deposit to the corporation.

SECTION 34. In all actions in any court of this State against any savings bank by a husband to recover for moneys deposited by his wife in her own name, or as her own money, the wife may be examined and testify as a witness in like manner as if she were an unmarried woman. And in all actions against any savings bank to recover for moneys in deposit therewith, if there be any person or persons, whether husband or wife or otherwise, claiming the same fund, who are not parties to the action, the court in which such action is pending, shall, on the petition of such savings bank, and upon five days' notice to the plaintiff and such claimants, make an order amending the proceedings in said action, by making such claimants parties defendant thereto ; and the said court shall thereupon proceed to hear and determine the rights and interests of the several parties to said action, in and to said funds. The said funds or deposits, which are the subject of the said action, shall remain with such savings bank, upon the same interest as other deposits of like amount, to the credit of the action until final judgment therein, and the same shall be paid by such savings bank, in accordance with the provisions of said final judgment.

The question of costs in the actions referred to in this section shall, in all cases, be in the discretion of the court; but the amount, when allowed, shall be the same as in other actions of a similar character.

ARTICLE IV.

OF INVESTMENTS.

SECTION 35. It shall be lawful for the trustees of any savings bank to invest the moneys deposited therein only as follows, to wit:

1st. In the stocks or bonds or interest bearing treasury notes of the United States.

2d. In the stocks or bonds or evidences of debt, bearing interest, of this State.

3d. In the stocks or bonds of any county, city, village or town in this State, issued pursuant to the authority of any law of this State.

4th. In the stocks or bonds of any State in the Union, that has for three years previous to such investment being made, regularly paid the interest on its legal bonded debt, in lawful money of the United States.

5th. In bonds and mortgages on improved, productive real estate, situate in this State, worth at least twice the amount loaned thereon; but not to exceed forty per cent of the whole amount of deposits shall be so loaned or invested.

6th. In real estate subject to the provisions of sections 47, 48 and 49 of this act.

SECTION 36. It shall be lawful for the trustees of any savings bank, while awaiting opportunity for the judicious investment of the funds deposited with them, to loan the moneys so deposited upon the security of the stocks mentioned in subdivisions one, two, three and four of the last preceding section; provided that not exceeding ninety per cent of the cash market value of such securities shall be loaned thereon; and the discretion hereby conferred shall always be subject to the inspection and control of the Superintendent of the Banking Department.

SECTION 37. Should the stock of securities on which loans are made, pursuant to the provisions of the last preceding section, deprecate in value after making any loan thereon, it shall be the duty of the trustees to require the immediate repayment of such loan made by them thereon, or additional security therefor, so that the amount so loaned shall at no time exceed ninety per cent of the market value of such securities; and no loan shall be so made, without a stipulation from the borrower, that the same shall be subject to the conditions of repayment, or of additional security required by this section.

SECTION 38. It shall be lawful for the trustees of any savings bank to keep in reserve, to meet current payments, an available fund of not exceeding twenty per cent of the total amount of deposits in such savings bank, which they may keep on hand, on deposit, as hereinafter provided, with or without interest, or loaned on call on the securities authorized for investment in subdivisions 1, 2, 3 and 4, of section 35, or on other good and marketable corporate securities, the interest or dividends upon which have been regularly paid during not less than two years previous to any loan being made thereon; *Provided*, that no loan shall be made on any securities other than those authorized for investment, for an amount exceeding three-fourths of the par value, or of the market value when less than par, of such securities; and *provided further*, that the trustees shall be personally liable for any loss, beyond an amount equal to fifty per cent of the surplus held by the institution at the time of such loss, sustained through loaning moneys upon any other securities than those named in subdivisions 1, 2, 3 and 4, of section 35, of this act; and the discretion hereby conferred, shall always be subject to the inspection and control of the Superintendent of the Banking Department.

SECTION 39. It shall not be lawful for the trustees of any savings bank to loan the moneys deposited with them, or any part thereof, upon notes, bills of exchange, drafts or any other personal securities whatever, except in the case of the personal bond given as collateral to secure a loan made upon a mortgage of real estate, as provided in the next succeeding section.

SECTION 40. In all cases of loans upon real estate, a sufficient bond or other personal security shall be required of the borrower, and all the expenses of searches, examinations and certificates of title or appraisals of value, and of drawing, perfecting and recording papers, shall be paid by such borrower.

SECTION 41. Where loans are made upon real estate situated outside of the limits of any city or incorporated village, the estimated or appraised value of the premises shall be made exclusive of the buildings thereon.

SECTION 42. Whenever buildings are included in the valuation of any real estate upon which a loan shall be made by any savings bank, they shall be insured by the mortgagor for at least two-thirds their value, in such company of this State as the trustees shall direct, and the policy of insurance shall be duly assigned to the corporation making the loan ; and it shall be lawful for such corporation to renew such policy of insurance, in the same or in any other company of this State as they may elect, from year to year, or for a longer or shorter term, in case the mortgagor shall neglect to do so, and may charge the same to him. And all the necessary charges and expenses paid by any such corporation for such renewal or renewals, shall be paid by such mortgagor to the said corporation, and shall be a lien upon the property so mortgaged until paid.

SECTION 43. No loan shall be made upon the security of real estate situate outside of the limits of any county in which the savings bank making such loan is located, or of a county adjoining, without a certificate of the value of such premises from the supervisor of the town, the president of the village, or the mayor of the city in which such premises are situated.

SECTION 44. It shall require a vote of a majority of all the trustees of a savings bank to authorize any loan upon the security of real estate, or loans upon any other securities than those authorized for investment by subdivisions 1, 2, 3 and 4 of section 35 of this act.

SECTION 45. It shall be lawful for the trustees of any savings bank to keep the available fund, hereinbefore provided for, or any part thereof, on deposit in any bank or banking association organized under any law or laws of this State, or of the United States, or in any trust company incorporated by the laws of this State, with interest, at such a rate, not exceeding seven per cent, as may be agreed upon; but the sum so kept on deposit, in any one bank or trust company, shall not exceed ten per cent of the capital of such bank or trust company, and shall not exceed five per cent of the whole amount of deposits in such savings bank.

SECTION 46. The banks or trust companies in which the deposits from the available fund shall be kept, shall be designated by a vote of a majority of the trustees, exclusive of any who are at the time directors of any bank of discount, or trustees of any trust company, in which the deposits of such saving bank are authorized, by the provisions of the last preceding section, to be kept; *Provided*, however, that where a majority of such trustees are now directors of any such bank, or trustees of any such trust company, such depositories may be designated by the vote of a majority of such trustees, approved by the Superintendent of the Banking Department; and *provided further*, that as vacancies occur in the office of trustee in such savings bank, the same shall be filled from others than directors of any bank, or trustees of any trust company, until these shall not exceed one-third of the whole number of trustees in such savings bank; and in no savings bank, hereafter to be organized, shall the number of trustees, who are directors of any bank, or trustees of any trust company, in this State, exceed one third of the whole number of such trustees, and where they now exceed that proportion, vacancies occurring shall be filled from others than such directors or trustees.

SECTION 47. It shall be lawful for the trustees of any savings bank to purchase, hold and convey real estate as follows:

1. A lot and banking house requisite for the transaction of its business, and for an income from such portions of the same as are not required for its own use.

2. Such as shall have been mortgaged to it in good faith for money loaned.

3. Such as shall have been purchased at sales upon judgments or decrees obtained or rendered for money loaned.

SECTION 48. No banking house shall be erected or purchased by any savings bank, until the estimated cost of the same, and of the income that may be derived therefrom, shall be submitted to and approved by the Superintendent of the Banking Department; nor shall such banking house and lot, when erected or purchased, be sold and conveyed without the consent and approval of the said Superintendent.

SECTION 49. All such real estate as is described in the second and third subdivisions of section 47 of this act, shall be sold by the corporation holding the same, within five years after the same shall be vested in such corporation by purchase or otherwise; but the Superintendent of the Banking Department may, in his discretion, upon the application of any savings bank, extend the time within which such sale shall be effected, but not for a longer period than one year.

SECTION 50. It shall be unlawful for any savings bank, directly or indirectly, to deal or trade in real estate, in any other case or for any other purpose than authorized in section 47 of this act, or to deal or trade in any goods, wares, merchandise or commodities whatever, except as authorized by the terms of this act, and except such personal property as may be necessary in the transaction of its business.

ARTICLE V.

OF SURPLUS.

SECTION 51. It shall be the duty of the trustees of any savings bank, to reserve and to set aside, from the gross amount of gains or profits of the institution, not less than one-half of one per cent per annum on the deposits with such institution, to be held and invested as provided for in this act, as a surplus fund to meet any contingency in its business, until such surplus shall be equal to ten per cent upon the amount of such deposits; and it shall be lawful to accumulate such surplus until the same shall equal fifteen per cent upon the whole amount of deposits so held.

SECTION 52. In determing the per cent of surplus held by any savings bank, its interest-paying, stock investments shall be estimated at their par value; its bonds and mortgages on which there are no arrears of interest for a longer period than three months shall be estimated at their face, and its real estate at its cost. Concerning such stock investments and such bonds and mortgages as are in arrears of interest for three months or more, and concerning any and all other investments or assets of whatever nature, the Superintendent of the Banking Department shall fix the valuation, or the basis of the valuation of the same, from the best information he can obtain concerning their present condition and future prospects, and he may change such valuation or basis of valuation, from time to time, according to the known or ascertained facts concerning them.

ARTICLE VI.

OF DIVIDENDS.

SECTION 53. All savings banks shall make up their accounts semi-annually, to the first days of January and July, in each year; and all dividends or profits shall be divided, credited or paid to the depositors, on or before the thirtieth days of January and July, respectively, in each year.

SECTION 54. It shall be unlawful for the trustees of any savings bank, or for any officers or agents thereof, to declare or pay any dividends, except from profits actually earned during the period for which such dividend is made, after deducting therefrom the necessary expenses incurred in transacting the business of the corporation, and not less than one-half of one per cent upon the deposits with the institution at the time of making such dividend, for account of the surplus fund as provided in section fifty-one of this act; but it shall be lawful for the trustees of any savings bank, to advance from their private means the amount necessary to pay the current expenses of such savings bank, under a stipulation with the Superintendent of the Banking Department, that the same shall be without interest, and shall be repaid only when the same can be done without reducing the surplus of such savings bank below two per cent upon the deposits with the institution. And upon entering into such stipulation, with such sureties for its faithful performance as the Superintendent shall approve, it shall be lawful to declare the dividend from profits, without deducting expenses therefrom.

SECTION 55. It shall be unlawful for the trustees of any savings bank to declare or allow dividends on any deposit for a longer period than the same has been deposited, except that deposits made not later than the fifth day of January and July, in each year, may have dividends declared upon them the same as though deposited on the first day of either of those months, respectively.

SECTION 56. No dividend shall be declared upon any deposit exceeding the sum of $5,000 or upon any or all of several deposits standing in the name of any one depositor, in trust or otherwise, whose aggregate shall exceed the sum of $5,000, unless the same shall have been on deposit for at least six months prior to such dividend being declared thereon.

SECTION 57. It shall be lawful for the trustees of any savings bank to discriminate in the dividends declared by them, between the deposits of $1,000 and under, and the deposits of more than $1,000; and between those deposits that have remained undiminished for one year and upwards, and those that have had some portion withdrawn within one year preceding such dividend, in such manner that deposits of the smaller amount, or remaining undiminished the longer time, shall receive a larger *pro rata* dividend than the others.

SECTION 58. It shall be the duty of the trustees of any savings bank, after deducting the necessary expenses and the reserve for the surplus fund, as required by section 54 of this act, (but such reserve not to exceed the rate of one per cent per annum upon the deposits), to divide, as nearly as may be practicable, all the remaining profits, ratable among the depositors, within the discretion conferred in the last preceding section ; but such regular dividends shall in no case exceed seven per cent per annum.

SECTION 59. Any residue of profits remaining undivided after compliance with the provisions of the last preceding section, shall as often as once in three years be divided among those depositors whose accounts have not been diminished during the period of one or more years prior to such dividend, in such manner as the trustees shall direct.

SECTION 60. After the organization of any savings bank hereafter incorporated, and before any dividend shall be declared, it shall be the duty of the trustees of such savings bank to notify the Superintendent of the Banking Department that they are prepared to declare the first dividend to depositors, and shall state the rate per cent which they propose to declare. Thereupon the Superintendent in person, or by one or more competent persons by him appointed, shall examine the affairs of such savings bank, and from such examination shall certify what rate per cent of dividend such savings bank is able and shall be authorized to pay, and the trustees shall thereupon declare and credit the dividend so authorized.

ARTICLE VII.

OF REMOVAL OF TRUSTEES.

SECTION 61. The Superintendent of the Banking Department may, at any time, by an order under his hand and seal, for due cause to be set forth in such order, suspend any trustee from his office; and upon the application of two-thirds of the trustees of any savings bank, setting forth good and satisfactory reasons for such action, in regard to any trustee, it shall be his duty to issue such order.

SECTION 62. Upon issuing any such order, a copy shall be transmitted to the savings bank of which the person so suspended is a trustee, and such order shall be entered in full upon the minutes of such savings bank, and notice thereof be given to such trustee, to whom, upon application, such original order shall be delivered.

SECTION 63. The Superintendent of the Banking Department shall also transmit a duplicate copy of such order to a justice of the supreme court of the judicial district within which such savings bank is located, by whom, after proper notice to such trustee, affording him an opportunity to be heard in his defence, such order may be vacated or confirmed, and the confirmation of such order shall be equivalent to an order for the removal of such trustee from office.

ARTICLE IX.

OF THE DISSOLUTION OF SAVINGS BANK CORPORATIONS.

SECTION 64. Whenever the trustees of any savings bank shall, by a vote of three-fourths of their number, resolve that it is expedient to discontinue the business and operations of such savings bank, they shall transmit a copy of such resolution to the Superintendent of the Banking Department, with the names of the trustees voting upon such resolution in the affirmative or negative, the names of those present and not voting, and the names of those absent at the time of such vote being taken.

SECTION 65. Upon receiving a copy of such resolution, it shall be the duty of the said Superintendent, himself, or by one or more competent persons by him appointed, to examine the affairs of such savings bank and to prepare a full and accurate statement of its condition, as regards its resources and liabilities.

SECTION 66. Upon the completion of such examination, it shall be the duty of the Superintendent to advertise for four weeks, in one or more papers in the county where such savings bank is located, for proposals to assume the charge and control of such savings bank, at the place where the same has been transacting business, or elsewhere in the same county ; and such notice shall contain a general statement of the condition of such savings bank.

SECTION 67. Whenever, within sixty days after the first publication of the notice required in the last preceding section, seven or more persons, whom the Superintendent shall approve, shall agree to assume the charge and control of such savings bank, and to continue its business in the city, town or village where the business of such savings bank has been transacted, it shall be lawful for the Superintendent, and it shall be his duty, to take possession of all the assets, books, papers, records, accounts and property of whatsoever nature, belonging to such savings bank, and to transfer and deliver the same to the persons so agreeing to assume and carry on its business; and thereupon the Superintendent shall issue to such persons his certificate, under his hand and seal of office, which certificate shall be filed in the office of the county clerk of the county in which such savings bank is located, and a duplicate copy shall also be filed in the Bank Department, and shall declare the persons named therein duly incorporated as the legal successors of the late trustees of the savings bank so transferred.

SECTION 68. Upon the execution of such certificate of incorporation, pursuant to the provisions of the last preceding section, the persons named therein shall be, and thereby become a body corporate and politic under the name and title of the savings bank whose assets have been so transferred, and shall have, by act of law, and without any other or further transfer or conveyance, full possession, right, title and ownership in and to all the real and personal estate of such savings bank, with power to hold and convey the same, subject to the uses for which such savings bank was instituted, and to the provisions and requirements of this act.

SECTION 69. If proposals satisfactory to the Superintendent shall not be received from seven or more persons, as provided in section sixty-seven of this act; or if it shall appear to the Superintendent inexpedient to continue the business of such savings bank as an independent organization in the city, village or town where its business has been transacted, it shall be lawful for him to consider and accept of the proposal of any savings bank in the same county to assume the assets and liabilities of such savings bank.

SECTION 70. Upon accepting the proposal of any savings bank in the same county to assume the assets and liabilities of such dissolving savings bank, the Superintendent shall take possession of the assets of such dissolving savings bank, as provided in section sixty-seven of this act, and shall transfer and deliver the same to the savings bank from which such proposal has been accepted; and the deed or instrument of conveyance executed by the Superintendent of the Banking Department under his hand, and seal of office, or of the savings bank in whose name the same are held, shall be a good, valid and sufficient conveyance for any real estate requiring to be transferred or sold and disposed of and conveyed under these provisions, or for the transfer of any stocks or bonds, or of any mortgages requiring to be transferred or assigned, and such conveyances of real estate, or assignments of mortgages, shall be entitled, without other or further proof than the hand and official seal of the Superintendent of the Banking Department, to be recorded in any county in this State, where the lands so conveyed or mortgaged, or any part thereof, shall lie.

SECTION 71. Upon the completion of such transfer and delivery, the Superintendent of the Banking Department shall file in the office of the county clerk of the county where the savings bank whose assets have been so transferred was located, and also in his own office, his certificate declaring the incorporation of such savings bank to be terminated, and thereupon such savings bank shall be dissolved, and its corporate existence shall cease and determine; and the savings bank to which such transfer of assets has been made, shall thereafter be deemed and taken to be solely responsible to the depositors of the savings bank so dissolved, for the full amount due by it to all of its depositors; and the assets so transferred to it shall be and constitute a part of its aggregate assets, and the liabilities so assumed by it shall be and constitute a part of its aggregate liabilities, and it shall not be required to keep any separate account, or to make any separate statement of the assets or liabilities so acquired or assumed.

SECTION 72. If no proposal satisfactory to the Superintendent shall, within sixty days after the publication of the notice required in section sixty-six of this act, be received by him from any seven or more persons nor from any savings bank agreeing to assume the assets and liabilities of such closing savings bank, the said Superintendent shall take possession of all the assets, books, papers, records and accounts and property, of whatsoever nature belonging to such savings bank, and shall convert such assets into money as fast as practicable, and shall proceed to pay off and discharge its liabilities in the following order:

First. The expenses of the examination, and the liquidation of the affairs of such savings bank.

Second. All other lawful indebtedness of such savings bank, except for deposits and dividends.

Third. The remaining assets *pro rata* among its depositors.

And he shall, upon taking possession of such assets, file in the office of the county clerk of the county where the savings bank was located, and in his own office, the certificate of dissolution required in the last preceding section, and such savings bank shall thereupon be dissolved as in said last preceding section provided.

SECTION. 73. Upon taking possession of the assets, as provided in the last preceding section, the Superintendent shall give notice once a week for four weeks, in some newspaper published in the city, village or town where the savings bank was located, or in some newspaper in the county, to all depositors or other creditors, to present their claims at some place in such city, village or town, to be named in such notice, for payment; and at the expiration of one year from the publication of such notice, all claims other than of depositors, shall cease to be valid against the assets remaining in his hands, and he shall then publish a list of all the depositors of one dollar and upwards appearing upon the books of such savings bank who have not called for or received their *pro rata* distribution, with the amount of their deposits respectively, and the amount awarded to them by the *pro rata* distribution of the assets, which list shall be published once a week for six weeks in one or more newspapers published in the city, village, town or county in which such savings bank was located, and shall state where in such city, village or town, payment of the same will be made.

SECTION 74. At the expiration of one year after the publication of the list and notice, as provided in the last preceding section, any assets remaining unconverted shall be converted into money by the Superintendent of the Bank Department, and such moneys remaining uncalled for shall be by him paid into the treasury of the State.

SECTION 75. It shall be lawful for the Superintendent to employ some competent and trustworthy person, residing in the city, village or town where such dissolved savings bank was located, as his agent to receive the money derived from the conversion of the assets, and to pay the depositors and other creditors, as hereinbefore provided.

SECTION 76. Whenever, upon any examination by the Superintendent, of any savings bank, as hereinafter provided, he shall find that its business is conducted in an illegal or in an unsafe manner, or that its income is not sufficient to pay expenses and at least four per cent dividends per annum to depositors, together with a reserve of one-half per cent per annum upon deposits for surplus, he may make any order in the premises, concerning the conduct of the business of such savings bank, which he shall deem necessary to improve its condition and to protect its depositors from loss; and it shall be the duty of the savings bank receiving such order, forthwith to obey the same; and, if any savings bank receiving such order, shall neglect or refuse to obey the same it shall be lawful for the Superintendent to proceed, in regard to such savings bank, in the manner provided in sections sixty-six to and including section seventy-five of this act.

ARTICLE X.

OF REPORTS AND SUPERVISION.

SECTION 77. Every savings bank shall, on or before the first day of February, in each year, make a report in writing to the Superintendent of the Banking Department, in such a form as he shall prescribe, of its condition on the first day of January preceding, after the dividend up to that day shall have been allowed and credited to the accounts of the depositors.

SECTION 78. Such report shall state the total amount of assets of every kind, the amount loaned on bond and mortgage, and the rate of interest, the cost, par value, estimated market value, and rate of interest of all stock investments designating each particular kind of stock; any stock investments, the interest on which is in arrears for three months or upwards, with a particular account of the same; also, any bonds and mortgages, the interest on which is in arrears for three months or upwards; the amount loaned upon the security of stock and to whom loaned, with a description of all the stocks held as security for such loans, and the rate of interest received on said loans, and separately any loans on which the interest is not regularly paid; the amount invested in real estate, its cost, estimated market value, and the yearly income derived from the same; the amount of cash on hand or on deposit in banks or trust companies, with the names of the banks or trust companies, where deposited, the amount in each, and the rate of interest received on such deposit; and the highest amount so had on deposit in any bank or trust company during the year, and the name of such bank or trust company, also the highest amount at any one time on deposit in all banks or trust companies, and the average monthly balances so had on deposit in all banks and trust companies; and any other item of assets or resources owned or possessed by such savings bank on that day.

SECTION 79. Such report shall also state all the liabilities of the savings bank making the same, on the said first day of January, the amount due depositors including the dividend credited to them for that day—stating such dividend as a separate item—and any other debts against or claims upon such savings bank, which may become a charge upon its assets. Such report shall also state the number of open accounts on said first day of January, the amount deposited and the amount withdrawn during the previous year, the whole amount of interest earned, and the amount of dividends credited to depositors for the year preceding the date of such report, the number of new accounts opened and the number of accounts closed during the year, and any other facts or information which the Superintendent of the Banking Department shall require, and in such form as he shall prescribe.

SECTION 80. Such report shall be verified by the oath of the two principal officers of the institution, and the statement of assets shall be verified by the oath of one or more of the trustees who examined the same, pursuant to the requirements of section 92 of this act; and any willful false swearing in regard to such reports, or in regard to any reports made to the Superintendent of the Banking Department pursuant to the provisions of this act, shall be deemed perjury, and be subject to the prosecutions and punishments prescribed by law for that offence.

SECTION 81. Each savings bank shall, on or before the first day of August next, make a full and detailed report to the Superintendent of the Banking Department, of its condition on the first day of July preceeding, in form and manner as required by section 78 of this act, and by so much of section 79 as requires a statement of its liabilities; which report shall be in such form as the Superintendent of the Banking Department shall prescribe; and in addition to what is above required, shall state the principal sum of each and every bond and mortgage held by such savings bank, the town or city and the county in which the mortgaged premises are situate, and the rate of interest of each such bond and mortgage, and any other facts that may more clearly reveal its true condition on the first of July then preceding, and that the Superintendent shall require; and such report shall be verified in the manner required in the last preceding section; and this report shall also state the name, residence and occupation of each trustee of such savings bank on the first day of July then preceding.

SECTION 82. Each savings bank shall, on or before the fifth day of August next, and on or before the fifth day of each and every month thereafter, transmit to the Superintendent of the Banking Department a full statement, in such form as the Superintendent shall prescribe, of all its transactions during the calendar month preceding the date of such report, which statement shall set forth the cash received, and from what sources, the cash paid, and for what purposes, the changes in investments of stocks, by redemption, sale or purchase; and of bonds and mortgages by payment, wholly or in part, by foreclosure, or by additional loans; in loans upon stock securities, by repayment or by new loans; and the profit or loss incident to such changes; and any other facts that the Superintendent shall require for his information, concerning the operations, workings and interior processes of each and every savings bank in the State. Such monthly statement to be verified by the oath of the cashier, accountant, treasurer or equivalent officer of the institution.

SECTION 83. After the report required by section eighty-one to be made for the first day of July next, the annual reports thereafter to be made for the first day of January in each year, as required by sections seventy-eight and seventy-nine of this act, shall state, concerning mortgages, only such as have been paid wholly or in part, and how much has been so paid since the date of the last report, or have been foreclosed, or such new bonds and mortgages as have been taken for investment since the date of such last report.

And no savings bank shall hereafter be required to make any annual or other report to the Legislature, nor to the mayor and commonalty of any city, nor to the board of supervisors of any county, nor to any other authority whatsoever, except as in this act provided—any provisions in the charter of any savings bank to the contrary notwithstanding; nor shall they be subject to the inspection or supervision of any local officer or authority, nor to any interference from any such local officer or authority, in matters pertaining to their business or dealings.

SECTION 84. After the name and residence of the trustees of each savings bank shall have been reported to the Superintendent of the Banking Department, as required by section eighty-one of this act, it shall be the duty of the secretary of any savings bank to give notice at once to the Superintendent of the occurrence of any vacancy, and of the manner in which the same was occasioned; and also of the filling of the same, when it occurs, and the name, residence and occupation of such new trustee.

SECTION 85. If any savings bank shall fail to furnish to the Superintendent of the Banking Department any report or statement required by this act, at the time so required, it shall forfeit the sum of one hundred dollars per day for every day such report or statement shall be so delayed or withheld; and the said Superintendent may maintain an action in his name of office to recover such penalty, and when collected, the same shall be paid into the treasury of the State, and be applied to the expenses of the Bank Department.

SECTION 86. It shall be the duty of the Superintendent of the Banking Department, on or before the first day of March in each year, to communicate to the Legislature a statement of the condition of every savings bank from which a report has been received for the preceding year, and to suggest any amendments to the laws relating to savings banks which, in his judgment, may be expedient or necessary, to increase the security of depositors, or impart greater efficiency to the administration of the affairs of savings banks.

SECTION 87. It shall be the duty of the Superintendent of the Banking Department, as often as once in two years, himself, or by one or more competent persons to be by him appointed, to visit and thoroughly examine the condition, working and affairs generally of each and every savings bank organized and doing business in this State, and he shall certify to the result of such examination, upon the records of each savings bank so examined; and to this end the books, papers, records and assets of every savings bank, shall at all times during the hours of business, be open for inspection and examination by the Superintendent or such other persons as he may designate as his agents for that purpose; and such examination shall always be made without previous notice of the same being given.

SECTION 88. It shall be the duty of the Superintendent of the Banking Department, and he shall have power

To require of each savings bank strict conformity to the provisions of this act, or any laws in force in relation to savings banks.

To supervise the exercise of the discretion vested in trustees of savings banks by law, and see that the same is not abused to the injury or insecurity of depositors.

To supervise and direct the change of investments by savings banks, so as to conform to the provisions of this act, in such manner as not to embarrass their operations, render their condition insecure, or expose them to sacrifice and loss upon their securities.

To examine, estimate, and certify to the surplus fund of any savings bank upon the basis prescribed in section fifty-two of this act, whenever under the provisions of this act such estimate shall be necessary.

And generally to exercise vigilant inspection over the affairs of savings banks, counsel and advise with the trustees, and officers thereof, and in all suitable ways promote their efficiency, security and welfare.

SECTION 89. The Superintendent of the Banking Department is hereby authorized to employ, from time to time, so many clerks as may be necessary to discharge the duties hereby imposed, and the salaries of such clerks shall be paid to them monthly, on his certificate, and upon the warrant of the Comptroller, out of the treasury; and it shall be the duty of the Superintendent, in his annual report to the Legislature, to state the names of the clerks so employed, and the compensation allowed to them severally.

SECTION 90. Each savings bank organized and doing business in this State shall pay five dollars towards defraying the expenses incurred by the Superintendent of the Banking Department in the performance of the duties imposed upon him by this act, and the residue of such expenses shall be paid by them, in proportion to the amount of deposits held by them severally, and the sums thus contributed shall be paid into the treasury of the State; but when the deposits of any savings bank are less than five thousand dollars, it shall be exempt from such contribution; and the expense of any special service done for or rendered to any savings bank, in examining its affairs or otherwise, shall be paid by the savings bank for which such service is done, in such sums as the Superintendent of the Banking Department shall certify to be just and reasonable.

SECTION 91. If any savings bank shall, after due notice, refuse or neglect to pay its proper share of charges so alloted, or such sum as the Superintendent shall certify to be just and reasonable, for any special service rendered on its behalf, then the said Superintendent may maintain an action in his name of office against such savings bank, for the recovery of such charges, or sums so certified.

ARTICLE XI.

MISCELLANEOUS PROVISIONS.

SECTION 92. It shall be the duty of the trustees of every savings bank, by a committee of not less than three of such trustees, on or about the first day of January in each year, to thoroughly examine the books, vouchers and assets of such savings bank, and its affairs generally, and the statement or schedule of assets reported to the Superintendent of the Banking Department for the first of January in each year, shall be based upon such examination, and shall be verified by the oath of the trustee making such examination; but nothing herein contained shall be construed as prohibiting the trustees of any savings bank from requiring such examinations, at such other times as they shall prescribe.

SECTION 93. It shall be lawful to pay trustees of a savings bank, acting as officers of the same, whose duties require and receive their regular and faithful attendance at the institution, such compensation as in the opinion of a majority of the board of trustees shall be just and reasonable; but such majority shall be composed exclusive of any trustees to whom such compensation shall be voted, and the vote fixing or altering the compensation of any officer, who is also a trustee, shall be transmitted to the Superintendent of the Banking Department, with the yeas and nays upon such vote, for his information.

SECTION 94. It shall be lawful for any savings bank that has accumulated a surplus of not less than five per cent upon its deposits, to pay trustees who render special personal service, (beyond the ordinary duty of attending meetings and serving upon committees other than of examination), such compensation as may be determined upon by the board of trustees, and approved by the Superintendent of the Banking Department. The trustee or trustees for whom compensation for such special service is voted, shall have no voice in the decision of such question. But no such compensation shall be voted by any savings bank to any trustee, until the Superintendent of the Banking Department has made or caused to be made an examination of the affairs of such savings bank, and certified to its possession of the requisite surplus; and if such surplus shall thereafter become impaired, so as to be less than five per cent of its deposits, such compensation to trustees shall cease, until such surplus is again restored to five per cent.

SECTION 95. Whenever any savings bank has accumulated a surplus equal to fifteen per cent of its total amount of deposits, it shall be lawful, with the approval of the Superintendent of the Bank Department, to award and pay to such trustees as have attended every regular meeting of the trustees during the year, a gratuity of not exceeding three dollars for each meeting so attended, as a reward for faithful service.

SECTION 96. All certificates or other evidences of deposit, made in pursuance of the regulations of any savings bank, shall be as binding upon the corporation, issuing the same, as if made under its common seal.

SECTION 97. The misnomer of any savings bank, in any deed, gift, grant, contract, conveyance, or other instrument, shall not vitiate or impair the same, if the corporation be sufficiently described therein to ascertain the intention of the parties.

SECTION 98. It shall not be lawful for any bank, banking association, or individual, or private banker, to advertise or put forth a sign as a savings bank, or in any way to solicit or receive deposits as a savings bank; and any bank, banking association, or individual, or private banker, that shall offend against the provisions of this section shall forfeit and pay for every such offense the sum of one hundred dollars for every day such offense shall be continued; and the Superintendent of the Banking Department may maintain an action in his name of office for the recovery of such penalties, and when collected the same shall be paid into the treasury of the State.

SECTION 99. All the assets of any bank or banking association now or hereafter to be created that shall become insolvent shall, after providing for the payment of its circulating notes, be applied by the directors, assignee, or receiver thereof, in the first place to the payment of any sum or sums of money deposited with such bank or banking association by any savings bank, but not exceeding the amount authorized to be so deposited by section forty-five of this act, and the provisions of this section shall also extend and apply to trust companies authorized to receive deposits of savings banks under the provisions of this act.

SECTION 100. The term savings bank as used in this act, shall include and be construed to mean and apply to all banks or institutions for savings, or savings banks or savings institutions, by whatever name known, in this State; and the provisions, regulations, prohibitions and directions of this act, shall also include and apply to every savings bank or institution for savings, that now is or may hereafter be incorporated in this State, and to their trustees, officers, servants and agents; and their respective charters are hereby so amended as to conform to this act: Except that the provisions of section one to section 21, both inclusive, shall only apply to savings banks hereafter to be incorporated ; and the provisions of the charter of the Institution for the Savings of Merchants' Clerks, relative to the election or appointment of trustees therein, and the amendment to said charter by chapter 550 of the Laws of 1867, shall not be affected by the provisions of this act; and all provisions of law, respecting the power and authority of the supreme court over trustees, officers and servants of these corporations, are continued, and shall remain in full force and effect.

SECTION 101. All acts or parts of acts inconsistent with this act, in so far as they conflict with the same, except as excepted in the last preceding section, are hereby repealed.

SECTION 102. This act is hereby declared to be a public act, and shall be construed favorably for every beneficial purpose therein contained.

SECTION 103. This act shall take effect immediately.

EXPLANATORY COMMENTS ON THE FOREGOING ACT.

SECTION 1.

Some question may arise as to whether the just minimum and maximum of corporators is reached in this section. That they should be residents of the county, and hence have a *home interest* in the institution, seems every way desirable.

SECTION 2.

Provides for such information as will give assurance concerning the character and fitness of the corporators, and prevent the evils considered in this appendix, pages 189, 190, 194. The idea is derived from the free banking law.

SECTION 3.

Requires no comment.

SECTION 4.

Is designed to make public the fact of the incorporation of a savings bank, and the auspices under which it is instituted, so that any objections to either may be communicated to the Superintendent.

SECTION 5.

Provides for a necessary formality.

SECTION 6.

Affords a means of enforcing the requirements of section two.

SECTION 7.

Imposes a duty of inspection on the Superintendent, which gives effect to the provisions of section four, by authorizing and, indeed, requiring him to hear and consider any objections that may be made to the incorporation of any savings bank.

SECTION 8

Makes essential a due AUTHORIZATION by the certificate of the Superintendent, before *incorporation* shall be effected. It also provides for a change in the corporators proposed in the certificate of association, by leaving out any against whom valid objections may be urged, or by including others who may give character to the corporation; but the power to make such changes is to be exercised concurrently by the Superintendent and a majority of the proposed corporators.

SECTION 9

A formality requiring no comment.

SECTION 10

Invests the Superintendent with discretion to refuse his sanction to the incorporation of a savings bank. Without such discretion vested *somewhere*, a general act of incorporation might lead to abuses.

SECTIONS 11, 12, 13

Explain themselves. They are introduced to meet an anticipated objection, that the large discretion vested in the Superintendent, to refuse to authorize the incorporation of a savings bank, might be abused or exercised arbitrarily. For myself I have no apprehension that it would be so, but to remove any objection to the "Act" on that ground the sections are introduced. If they should be stricken out by the Legislature, the harmony or consistency of the "Act" would not thereby be in the least impaired.

SECTION 14

Is the usual incorporating clause in savings bank charters.

SECTION 15

Is derived from section 2, chapter 32, Laws of 1867.

SECTION 16

Is a modification of the general statute concerning forfeiture from *non user*. It is to prevent the incorporation of a savings bank by parties, for the purpose only of keeping others from becoming so incorporated.

Sections 17, 18, 19, 20.

These are introduced to meet a possible and suggested contingency. I can see no objection to allowing a guarantee capital in the manner provided. I have intended to guard the privilege from abuse by stringent provisions, too stringent to incite investments of capital very generally in such enterprizes. The only way that more than seven per cent can be realized from it is by depositing seven per cent stocks with the Superintendent. Then, when the surplus has reached ten per cent, they *may*, under favorable conditions, receive besides the interest on their stocks, one per cent more from the profits of the savings bank. But prior to that, they are liable to pay expenses and losses. The provisions are not essential to the completeness of the "Act," but may have an independent value of their own.

Section 21

Is the common declaratory provision in all charters of savings banks.

Section 22.

It would seem that more than the majority of a quorum ought to be required to pass upon so important a question as the admission of new trustees. So, too, indifference or perversity ought not to be permitted to leave vacancies unfilled, and the interests of the institution thus to fall into the hands of a select few. Hence the provision of the last clause of the section. I apprehend its chief use will be to prevent vacancies from lapsing, except in the manner provided in section 26.

Section 23

Is a common provision in savings bank charters, except the last clause, which limits the term to one year. This latter provision seems desirable in order to hold officers always subject to the control of the board of trustees.

Section 24

Embraces provisions also common to all charters, except the requirement to transmit a copy of by-laws to the Superintendent. The propriety of this cannot be questioned.

Section 25.

I have endeavored to adapt the provisions relating to a quorum to the present requirements of charters and the practices of savings banks, and at the same time in harmony with the provisions of this act.

Section 26.

Savings banks frequently find themselves embarrassed by the provisions of their charter in regard to the number of their trustees, which can only be changed by legislative amendment. This section relieves them from this embarrassment, and at the same time does not interfere with the constituency of any savings bank now working satisfactorily.

Section 27.

The only doubt in my mind concerning the propriety of this provision is whether regular meetings ought not to be required monthly. I leave the question with the Legislature.

Section 28.

A portion of this section is derived from a report on savings banks made by Elliott F. Shepard and William H. Thomson, Examiners appointed by Hon. H. H. Van Dyck, under a resolution of the Legislature of 1863. I have made use of their recommendations elsewhere in the foregoing "Act," as will be found as we proceed. Other portions are derived from existing provisions of law. I believe good results will follow from making the occurrence of a vacancy for neglect of duty absolute, and not contingent upon the action of the board. A feeling of delicacy commonly restrains trustees from giving effect to the provision in its present form. As here proposed, this difficulty is overcome, and at the same time ample opportunity is given for discrimination where this is desirable.

Section 29.

This contains a provision common in savings bank charters.

Section 30.

The same may be said of this, except that the provisions recommended meet, by the letter of the law, conditions which the spirit of existing law fails fully to provide for. These conditions and the practices under them are fully considered on pages 143, 144 of the Report, which furnish all the commentary needed concerning this section.

SECTION 31

Is the common provision of charters, except in the admission of deposits from religious or charitable corporations. I can see no good reason why such, as well as the savings banks, should not have the benefit which would accrue to both from the connection here authorized.

SECTION 32.

The first part of this section is substantially a transcript from existing charters.

The first proviso gives the sanction of *law* to provisions common in the by-laws of savings banks. As the purpose is to prevent a too rapid run upon savings banks in time of panic, the notice required is properly graded by the amount of the deposit. The policy of such provision is considered in the report, under the head of PANICS, on page 76.

The second proviso is an enforcement of the policy concerning large deposits, discussed in the Report under the title DEPOSITS, on pages 116, 117.

SECTION 33

Is a provision substantially as found in the charters of savings banks, though in some of the older charters, it is more restricted than in the form here given.

SECTION 34

Is a perfect transcript of section 4, chapter 783, of the Laws of 1867, and the object and occasion of it will be found fully set forth on pages 186 and 187 of this appendix.

SECTION 35

Has its full exemplification in the discussion of the question of INVESTMENTS, pages 37 to 58 of the report. The extent to which the general subject is there considered renders any comment upon the section, here, unnecessary.

Section 36.

This is a modified form of the first part of section 1, chapter 257, Laws of 1853, concerning loans. That, however, allowed to trustees the wide discretion of substituting loans altogether for investments. I would make it a provision for temporary and exceptional conditions, and, as such, subject it to supervisory control in order that it may not become a fixed policy of any savings bank to *loan* and *not to invest* its moneys. The discussion of an "available fund," on pages 61 and 62 of the Report, has some thoughts pertinent to the subject.

Section 37

Is substantially the last part of section 1, chapter 257, Laws of 1853, with a condition to be exacted from the borrower designed to give it practical effect.

Section 38.

The discussion of the subject of CALL LOANS, pages 68 to 74 of the Report, affords ample commentary upon this section. It may be observed that I have excluded *mortgage assignments* from the securities on which loans may be made. This is for the reason that the care and circumspection which is generally exercised in making loans upon real estate to be secured by bond and mortgage, or in the purchase absolutely of such securities, in the matter of searches for title, and in attending to having it recorded, are almost certain to be relaxed when a mortgage is taken merely as collateral for a temporary loan.

Section 39

Is a provision in many charter, and it seems to me that no question of its propriety or importance can arise.

Section 40.

This provision is common to most charters, and is, doubtless, observed in practice by all savings banks.

Section 41.

I have some doubt in my own mind concerning the necessity for this provision.

SECTION 42

Is a transcript in nearly the exact language of section 1, chapter 331, Laws of 1860, amending the charter of the Southold Savings Bank. The provision seems to me to be eminently a salutary one to extend to all these institutions.

SECTION 43

Has its commentary on page 50 of the Report, and all the sections that relate to investments in bond and mortgage will find the theory of their provisions discussed in the Report, under the title BONDS AND MORTGAGES, pages 48 to 52.

SECTION 44.

As more judgment and discretion must be exercised in passing upon the security or value of a bond and mortgage, or of those stocks which are not *authorized* but are *permitted* as a collateral for loans from the available fund, it is deemed proper to require more than a majority of a mere quorum to sanction such investments or securities. Concerning bonds and mortgages some of the charters are more rigid than this section in their requirements, some, indeed, requiring a unanimous vote to approve them; but I believe the requirements of this section, with the further restrictions elsewhere found, will be a sufficient protection.

SECTION 45

Has its provisions fully discussed on pages 66 to 68 of the Report, and an illustration of their importance will also be found in the Report on pages 107 to 109.

SECTION 46

Meets the requirements of the discussion on pages 97 to 109 of the Report.

The provisos of the section are awkward and cumbrous, but are indispensable to avoid the disorganization of some savings banks if the "Act" should become a law. On the whole, though not so easy to express clearly, I believe the provisions will effect the same object as the existing one prohibiting directors of banks from being trustees, and at the same time it overcomes the objections to which that would be liable if it were made general.

SECTIONS 47, 48, 49.

The question of REAL ESTATE INVESTMENTS for savings banks, provided for in these sections, is fully considered in the Report, pages 52 to 57.

The provisions hereof are substantially the same as in all charters relating to savings banks, except that the erection or purchase of a banking house for income, as well as for use, is here expressly authorized. Section 48, however, is designed to keep a check upon the power thus conferred.

Section 49 is a common provision in existing laws, except so far as relates to the discretionary power vested in the Superintendent to extend the time.

SECTION 50

Is copied from existing laws, and its propriety is too obvious to require comment.

SECTION 51

Makes imperative what in existing law is permissive only. Under the title, SURPLUS AS AN ELEMENT OF SAFETY, pages 58 to 60, the occasion for the provision is considered.

SECTION 52.

That some uniform basis for the valuation of assets, and hence of the surplus of savings banks, is essential to any intelligible estimate or comparison of their real condition, must be apparent without argument, and that such estimate should be authoritative, if any effect is to be given to provisions of this Act in which the per cent of surplus enters as a condition, is equally apparent.

Whether the basis assumed in this section is the most fair, just and equitable that could be instituted, is the question to be determined. I believe it to be so for reasons set forth on pages 168 to 170 of the Report. But as it has been fixed in my own mind, without consultation generally with trustees of savings banks, any sugtions which they may offer upon the subject for the consideration of the Legislature, will be entitled to and should receive careful attention.

The power vested in the Superintendent to change the valuation of securities is essential, that justice may be promoted, in the case of the improvement in the condition of securities that are in arrears of interest, giving promise of the payment of arrears and of future accruing interest regularly.

SECTION 53.

The reason for desiring uniformity in the periods for crediting dividends is stated on pages 125 and 126 of the report. Very nearly all savings banks now declare dividends in conformity with this section. I cannot think the inconvenience of change for the few who have adopted other periods, will nearly counterbalance the benefits to be derived from uniformity.

SECTION 54.

The principal designed to be enforced in practice by the prohibitions of this section are exemplified under the title DIVIDENDS, on page 125, and under the title SURPLUS AS AN ELEMENT OF SAFETY, pages 58 to 60 of the Report. The last clause finds apt illustration of its propriety in the REMARKS concerning the Franklin Savings Bank, on page 61 of this appendix.

SECTION 55.

The too common practice prohibited by this section, is fully illustrated on pages 127 and 128 of the Report.

SECTION 56.

The object of this section is to discourage transient deposits in large sums, which are a source of weakness rather than strength to a savings bank. If a degree of permanence can be given to them, by such provisions as that of this section, they may be a source of profit, and hence should not be imperatively excluded. It is enough to place them under such restrictions as will prevent their being an injury rather than a benefit to the institution receiving them. Further suggestions upon the principles involved will be found on page 117, and elsewhere in the Report.

SECTION 57.

The principle of uniformity in the rate of dividends, and of diversity by allowing a higher rate to the smaller depositors, is discussed at length on pages 118 to 123 of the Report. The conclusion there reached, of leaving the question to the discretion of trustees, is embodied in this section, except, that instead of the limit of classification being $500, as in the act of 1853, it is placed at $1,000.

I regard undisturbed deposits as being entitled to equally favorable recognition with small deposits, and have therefore given authority for such recognition. Perhaps, however, the provision in section fifty-nine confining extra dividends so this class is sufficient. I presume it would be found so in the practical experience and action of savings banks, but would prefer, that besides, trustees should have the option granted by this section.

Section 58

Is substantially the same as is found in nearly all charters, except as modified by the requirement concerning surplus, and the limitation of ordinary dividends to seven per cent. This limitation, however, can have very little practical importance.

Section 59.

The comments on section fifty-seven, state the purpose of this section with sufficient fullness, if indeed the section does not. The value to a savings bank, of long term deposits, as contrasted with those for a short term, is obvious, and that discrimination should be made in favor of those deposits that earn the most, seems to me equally clear.

Section 60.

This section is designed to ensure to every savings bank a fair and safe start upon its career. It secures, at the outset, a compliance with the provisions of the previous sections relating to dividends. The necessity for the examination required will be apparent, when it is considered that the first dividend of a savings bank may be, and probably will be made before its first annual report, by which its condition would be disclosed.

Sections 61, 62, 63—Article VII.

I do not apprehend that the provisions of this article will, often, if they should ever, become operative. But that such a power should be held in reserve, somewhere, seems every way desirable. Such power is now vested in the supreme court. I have thought that the inception of its exercise would be better delegated to some officer more likely than the court to be familiar with the conditions demanding its exercise. As his action is subject to review, there is little danger that his power would be abused; and, at the same time, the court has jurisdiction of the institution of proceedings on its own motion, the same as now. See section 100.

SECTIONS 64 TO 75—ARTICLE VIII.*

The importance, not to say the necessity, of the provisions of these sections, will find ample illustration in the Report, under the title THE ELMIRA SAVINGS BANK, pages 114, 115. The object aimed at is, first, to avoid the necessity of closing a savings bank, so long as worthy and responsible parties can be found willing to take charge of it; and, second, if closing becomes necessary, to do this, with the least possible expense, and in such manner as to ensure to depositors the full benefit of any surplus that may have been accumulated.

The provisions in the last clause of section seventy, relative to the sufficiency of the official hand of the Superintendent to any conveyance, is an application of similar provisions in existing law in regard to transfers of stocks and mortgages held by him for banks of issue.

For the idea of transferring the business and affairs of a closing institution to another, willing to accept the trust, I am indebted to the report referred to in the comments on section 28.

SECTION 76.

The sections last considered relate to the voluntary closing of a savings bank. This section vests the same powers in the Superintendent with reference to closing a savings bank, whose affairs or workings are such as to render it unsafe to continue business. But, before the expedient of closing can be resorted to, the trustees must have an opportunity of correcting their own errors, by such change of policy, within the requirements of law, as the Superintendent may direct. I can conceive of no abuse likely to result from the exercise of the authority here vested. It seems to me preferable as a mode of securing obedience to the law, and generally prudent and careful management on part of trustees, to any system of fines and penalties. I suppose that, in the nature

* Numbered IX in the Act by error.

of things, any abuse of his power by the Superintendent would be subject to the control of and to correction by the Supreme Court, though, if there is any doubt of this, such control might be provided for.

SECTION 77

Is a general requirement concerning reports in regard to which subsequent sections particularize.

The time is extended beyond that in the present law, for the reason that as more detailed information is called for, more time for its preparation should be allowed.

SECTIONS 78, 79, 80.

These are derived chiefly from section 1, chapter 136, Laws of 1857, with such additional requirements as are suggested generally in the Report under the title REPORTS OF SAVINGS BANKS, page 146.

The requirement that the statement of assets shall be verified from a p rsonal examination, finds its justification in the remarks upon pages 28 to 31 of the report.

SECTION 81

Is introduced to afford a starting point from which, in connection with the monthly reports required in the next succeeding section, the annual reports required by the preceding sections of this article, may be compared and their accuracy verified. It is a preparation necessary to give value to the first annual report required by this Act.

The names of the trustees are required to be reported, for reasons sufficiently apparent from the experience of THE SIXPENNY SAVINGS BANK OF THE CITY OF ROCHESTER, as detailed on pages 112 to 114 of the Report.

SECTION 82.

The requirements of this section being wholly new, should be carefully considered. I desire them to be submitted to the test of a rigorous examination, believing that the more thoroughly they are considered, in connection with the suggestion and illustrations in the Report, pages 146 to 157, and in this appendix, page 173 and table C, which follows, the more earnestly will they be approved.

If the suggestion should arise that monthly reports are too frequent, and that quarterly reports would suffice, I will only say that it occurred to me that monthly reports would be made more easily by the institutions than quarterly. It would divide the labor of compiling the statements from their books, more evenly through the year.

The question of the labor involved in making such reports, either monthly or quarterly, is of no importance compared with the benefits derived from the information thus afforded, of the working operations of savings banks.

But with annual instead of semi-annual reports of the condition of each institution, and from these the schedule of mortgages omitted, I believe the labor involved would very little, if it should at all, exceed that now required.

Section 83.

The first clause is a practical application of the remarks on page 168 of the Report, and designed to relieve savings banks from a perfectly useless labor.

The last clause also exempts some savings banks from requirements of their charters which have no value, in view of the careful supervision provided for by the foregoing Act. See also opinions of Buffalo Savings bank, pages 192, 193 of this appendix.

At the time the savings banks, whose charters require a report to some local authority, were incorporated, there was no general supervision of their affairs, and hence the requirement to report to local authority was the only means by which their condition or affairs could be made public. But since the law of 1857, requiring reports from all these institutions to the Superintendent, there has been no occasion for enforcing the provisions of such charters, though they have, I presume, been generally complied with.

Section 84

Follows out the purpose which has its inception in the last clause of sections 81, which purpose is illustrated on pages 112 to 114, as before cited.

Section 85

Is the last clause of section 1, chapter 136, Laws of 1857.

Section 86

Is substantially section 2, of chapter 136, Laws of 1857, except that the time in which the Superintendent is required to report is extended to correspond with the extension of the time in which savings banks are required to report to him. A few days, more or less, at that period in the session of the Legislature, is of little or no account, for with a report prepared and submitted on the twentieth of February, it is impossible for the public printer to have it printed for the use of members under two or three weeks, and this brings it too late for the Legislature to act upon any of its suggestions at that session.

Section 87

Makes imperative what in the present law is only permissive. It also removes from an examination the odium that attaches to it under the present provisions of law, by which it can only be made upon the assumption of illegal practices, or unsafe conduct of business.

My experience has been, that savings banks, as a rule, court rather than shun official examination.

The certificate of the Superintendent as to their solvency and general prosperous condition on a given day, would be a valuable testimonial, and further would afford a substantial basis of confidence on part of the public in dealing with these institutions, whenever such confidence was deserved. My opinion as to the solvency and general responsibility of a savings bank was solicited by a depositor in the course of my visitations. Though my own personal examination had necessarily been superficial, that, in connection with its report, enabled me to give him ample assurance that his deposit was abundantly secured. If it were generally known that these official examinations were made, depositors would rely upon them with great confidence, and with a feeling of security that would have its effect in time of general panic or distrust.

Section 88

The first clause enforces a duty too obviously necessary to require comment.

The second clause imposes as a duty the exercise of the power conferred by the last clause of sections 36 and 38 respectively.

The importance of the provisions of the third clause will be apparant after very slight consideration. As this act imposes certain restrictions (as concerning investments) not found in the present law, some means must be devised whereby savings banks whose investments are not in conformity with this act, may adapt themselves easily and safely to its requirements. Take for instance one which has sixty per cent of its investments in bond and mortgage. It would be most unwise and imprudent to require an immediate substitution of other securities for this excess. Under this clause the Superintendent might find it expedient to direct simply, that no more should be invested in that way until it could be done without exceeding the proportion authorized by this act.

The necessity of the fourth clause is apparent from a consideration of previous provisions of the Act.

The propriety of the fifth clause needs no enforcement.

Sections 89, 90, 91

Are all compiled with such slight modification of language as was necessary to their arrangement with a different context, and in separate sections, from section 3 and 5, of chapter 136, Laws of 1857, and section 1 of chapter 32, Laws of 1867; except that the limit of exemption, from contributing to the expenses, is here placed at $5,000, instead of $500. It might, with propriety, have been placed much higher, as a savings bank with no more than $5,000 cannot long continue to do business.

Section 92

Makes obligatory a practice very general among savings banks, but of such importance as to seem to be worthy of recognition by law. It affords also a better basis than " information and belief" for the verification of reported assets. The policy upon which the requirement is founded is discussed in the Report, pages 28 to 31,

Section 93.

The principle recognized in this section is discussed in the Report, pages 136 to 141, and if the conclusions reached there and embodied in this section are *wrong*, any further comment, either brief or extended, would not make them *right*. They are, therefore, respectfully submitted.

SECTION 94

Finds its appropriate comment in the Report on pages 141, 142, as well as on the pages cited in reference to the last preceding section. Let it stand or fall, as the considerations there urged are found conclusive or otherwise.

SECTION 95

Has enough said for it on pages 142 and 143 of the report.

SECTION 96, 97

Are common provisions found in most savings bank charters, and the propriety of which is obvious.

SECTION 98

Is derived from section 1, chapter 132, Laws of 1858, and its propriety is discussed on pages 99 and 100 of the report. The suggestions there made concerning prohibiting banks of discount from paying interest on individual deposits are not given effect in this Act, for the reason that it would be of little use to impose such restriction upon the few banks subject to State authority, while the much greater number of National banks are left free to their own devices in this respect. In regard to advertising as savings banks, there is but one way in which State and National banks can be put upon an equality by State law, and that is by having the prohibition apply to publishers of newspapers as well as to the banks. There is in its results to publishers no difference, whether the prohibition be applied to them, or to those who would, but for such prohibition, be paying customers. But I leave the question, with this suggestion, to the Legislature.

SECTION 99

Is section 4, of chapter 257, Laws of 1853, extended so as to embrace trust companies that receive deposits from savings banks.

SECTTON 100,

Perhaps, explains itself sufficiently. To avoid the constant repetition of the term "institution for savings," it was deemed desirable to remove all doubt as to the effect of this Act, by the provisions of the first clause in this section.

The exception made in favor of the institution for the Savings of Merchants' clerks, is in deference to the peculiar and unusual provisions of its charter, concerning the election of trustees, for which see sections 3, 4 and 5, chapter 324, Laws of 1848. The amendment, also excepted, authorizes the accumulation of a surplus equal to twenty per cent of its deposits, which, if it be an error, and I am not prepared to affirm that it is, is in the *right direction*, and I should be loth to interfere with the privilege thus accorded.

SECTION 101

Requires no comment.

SECTION 102

Is a provision in many charters and may be unnecessary, but I think could do no harm.

SECTION 103

Has the not inconsiderable merit of being the *last!*

COMMENTS GENERALLY.

I have aimed in the foregoing act, with what success is for you and the Legislature to decide:

First. To render uniform and consistent the provisions of law relative to savings banks.

Second. To embrace such provisions as would more surely promote the security of depositors and the general prosperity of these institutions.

Third. To arrange the topics in such order, under titled articles, as would make reference to them convenient, and preserve the subject matter generally free from confusion and repetition.

Fourth. To the same end, to make the different sections brief and comprehensive.

Though the act is more extended than I supposed It would be, it is yet much shorter than the general laws relating to any other considerable public interest, as for instance, insurance and banking.

That I have thought of everything which such an Act should embrace is *hardly* possible; that I may have included some objectionable provision is *very* possible.

I have endeavored, however, to put it in such form, and to present it with such comments and references as would best conform to the spirit and purpose of the resolution directing it, and as would render your labor, and that of the Legislature in considering its provisions, the least burdensome possible. In the hope that this effort has not been wholly in vain, it is submitted.

INDEX TO REPORT.

INDEX TO APPENDIX.

A.

B.

C.

D.

E.

N.

O.

T.

NOTE.—On page 80, of the Report, a suggestion is made, that the new savings bank in Rochester will be fortunate, if in two years its deposits equal the surplus of the two older institutions, which was 330,119. The report from this new savings bank, the Mechanics', of Rochester, for 1st January, since received, shows deposits on that day equal to $521,681. They have thus, in six months, exceeded my estimate of their business in two years. It is with pleasure that I thus correct my prediction. It still remains to be seen how far the prosperity of the other institutions has been affected by this remarkable success.

www.ingramcontent.com/pod-product-compliance
Lightning Source LLC
LaVergne TN
LVHW021226110826
845150LV00002B/258

* 9 7 8 1 4 2 5 5 6 3 8 8 2 *